BY JELANI COBB

Three or More Is a Riot: Notes on How We Got Here: 2012–2025

The Substance of Hope: Barack Obama and the Paradox of Progress

To the Break of Dawn: A Freestyle on the Hip Hop Aesthetic

The Devil & Dave Chappelle and Other Essays

THREE
OR MORE
IS A RIOT

THREE
OR MORE
IS A RIOT

Notes on How We Got Here: 2012–2025

JELANI COBB

ONE WORLD
NEW YORK

One World
An imprint of Random House
A division of Penguin Random House LLC
1745 Broadway, New York, NY 10019
oneworldlit.com
penguinrandomhouse.com

All the essays in this work were originally published in *The New Yorker,* some in different form, except for "Lincoln Died for Our Sins" (*Washington Monthly,* January 22, 2013) and "Black Lives Cost," which is previously unpublished.

Grateful acknowledgment is made to The Estate of Amiri Baraka c/o The Chris Calhoun Agency for permission to reprint excerpts from poems by Amiri Baraka. Reprinted by permission of The Estate of Amiri Baraka c/o The Chris Calhoun Agency.

Hardcover ISBN 978-0-593-97820-7
Ebook ISBN 978-0-593-97821-4

Printed in the United States of America on acid-free paper

1st Printing

First Edition

BOOK TEAM: Production editor: Luke Epplin • Managing editor: Rebecca Berlant • Production manager: Nathalie Mairena • Proofreaders: Melissa Churchill, Michael Burke, Jane Hardick, Nicole Ramirez

Book design by Caroline Cunningham

The authorized representative in the EU for product safety and compliance is Penguin Random House Ireland, Morrison Chambers, 32 Nassau Street, Dublin D02 YH68, Ireland. https://eu-contact.penguin.ie.

For August Ash: Boy, wonder

CONTENTS

II   WINTER IN AMERICA

III HISTORY LESSENS

A NOTE ON PROPER NOUNS
AND PROPER NEGROES

In the summer of 2020, amid the reverberations of George Floyd's brutal death at the hands of a white Minneapolis police officer, a demand was issued for a new, grammatical form of reparations. Up to that point, the first letter in the word "black" was lowercased, including in instances when it referred to people of African descent. The demand, in that moment, was that the letter "B" should be uppercase as a gesture of respect toward the putatively "Black" community. There was a rough symmetry here: A century earlier the scholar and sage W. E. B. Du Bois had initiated a campaign to pressure publications to capitalize the first letter of the word "negro," recognizing the lowercase as a metaphor for the broader societal diminution of a race of people. "The use of a small letter for the name of twelve million Americans and two hundred million human beings," he noted, served as "a personal insult." *The New York Times,* after rejecting Du Bois's entreaty in 1926, acceded in 1930. Ninety years later a number of publications, including *The New Yorker,* adopted the house style of capitalizing the letter "B" when referring to black people. History repeats, et cetera. Yet the symmetry should not be mistaken for similarity.

In Du Bois's time, the work of dismantling the mythology of race had scarcely gotten under way. The pioneering anthropologist

Franz Boas had already highlighted the contradictions and outright untruths of the idea that humanity could be neatly divided into distinct typologies, but for men of Du Bois's era—people who were literally known as "race men"—the battle was not primarily to dispatch the categories of race but to dispute the idea that those categories were arranged hierarchically. Du Bois sought to grammatically place Negroes on par with Anglo-Saxons, Teutons, and Asiatics— a term that has fallen all the way out of the language but was nonetheless laureled with an uppercase A when it was in use. By the summer of 2020 we knew—or should have known—better. The idea of race as a biological fixture has been thoroughly discredited. To the extent that race remains salient, it is as a marker for particular social histories and the identities forged by that history. The people whom Du Bois successfully helped promote from negro to Negro had, amid the revolution of consciousness in the 1960s, self-designated as "black." The change was a bit of reclamation that, retrospectively, seems less revolutionary than it must have felt at the time. The polarizing pan-Africanist Marcus Garvey was an early adopter, coining the phrase "Black is beautiful" in the post-WWI era of Harlem radicalism. He meant to destigmatize the word "black," which had heretofore been seen as a term of derision among people of African descent. By the late 1960s, an entire "Black Power" movement had reversed this situation—"black" was the affirming designation and "Negro" was the pejorative one. In etymological terms, we had simply shifted from a word with Romantic origins, "negro," to a Germanic word, "black," that carried an identical meaning. True enough, the term "negro," likely applied by Portuguese-speaking slavers in the sixteenth century, had been corrupted into the radioactive and anglicized *nigger,* and since "black" had no such parallel, the change represented a kind of lateral progress.

This brings us back to the matter of case. By 2020, the reference to the community of Africa-descended people in the United States as "black" held different implications than the word "negro" had a hundred years earlier. It reflected the accurate designation of racial categories as improper nouns. The uppercase designation of *Afri-*

can American reflected the full, equal humanity of this group in relation to their ethnic counterparts. So the well-intentioned, rhetorically satisfying language demands of that tumultuous summer represented a step backward. It unwittingly mirrored the demands of resurgent white nationalists for the capitalization of the letter "W" in reference to white people—demands made because they believe in both the categories of race and the aged, invalid hierarchies attached to them. One must be careful when they find themselves in agreement with their most intractable enemies. It is for this reason that the people who traversed the Middle Passage, suffered the travails of slavery, and became the active agents of American democracy are referenced in this book as "black," not "Black." Our existence as a community need not be premised on the canards of charlatans seeking to justify murder and slavery. The bonds of shared history and culture will suffice. In short, black people exist; Black people need not.

INTRODUCTION

The news trickling up from Florida appeared, at first glance, to be missing key facts: an unarmed seventeen-year-old fatally shot in a gated suburb by a self-appointed neighborhood watchman who had stalked and harassed the teenager for several blocks before initiating the conflict that culminated in his death—yet police had declined to make any arrests. From the vantage point of the newsroom, the first story is almost never the full story. You hear stray wisps of information, almost always the most inflammatory strands of a much bigger, more complicated set of circumstances. Reporting, more often than not, is the work of turning bold-print allegations into finer-print news. Yet, as a growing number of media—local, regional, and eventually national—turned their attention to the events of February 26, 2012, the story remained stubbornly consistent: the seventeen-year-old was a black boy named Trayvon Martin, who'd been walking home from a nearby store where he'd purchased Skittles and an Arizona iced tea, when George Zimmerman, a white Hispanic man who'd been driving around the neighborhood, began following him. Against the advice of the police dispatcher he was talking to, Zimmerman, who was twenty-eight, pursued and confronted Martin before killing him with what forensic examiners later categorized as a single, intermediate-range gunshot from a firearm between one and eighteen inches from Martin's chest. Upon reviewing these facts, the Sanford Police Department determined that Zimmerman's actions were consistent with Florida's "Stand Your Ground" self-defense laws and it declined to make an arrest in the incident.

The Martin case—the nightmare specter of a lynching screaming across the void of history—ruined the mood of a nation that had, just a few years earlier, elected its first black president and, in a dizzying moment of self-congratulation, began to ponder on editorial pages whether the nation was now "post-racial." What, then, to do with the dead black boy on the suburban street? In that moment, there was no way to know what the reverberations of Martin's death—and Zimmerman's subsequent 2013 acquittal after sustained pressure eventually forced Florida authorities to charge him with second-degree murder—would yield. But it wasn't hard to know that it would mean *something,* and that it might carry that meaning for a very long time.

Not long before that night, I'd been invited to contribute to the newly launched website NewYorker.com, the legacy magazine's foray into the emerging digital landscape. During one of our early conversations, Amy Davidson Sorkin wondered if there was something to be written about the neighborhood watch incident in Florida and I agreed to look into it. A few days later I wrote my first Comment for *The New Yorker.* In a piece titled "Trayvon Martin and the Parameters of Hope," I wrote about the contradictions Martin's death brought to the surface, most prominently the fact that it had occurred during Barack Obama's presidency. In time, Martin's death and his killer's acquittal would become a lens through which many of the events of the next decade would be clarified. In Oakland, California, a thirty-three-year-old labor activist and organizer reeling from news of Zimmerman's 2013 acquittal wrote a long Facebook post that concluded with the words "Our lives matter"—the formative expression of the idea "Black Lives Matter." In South Carolina, a scrawny white teenager binged white supremacist disinformation in the aftermath of Martin's death, and the kernel of contempt it planted in him germinated until three years later he massacred nine black congregants at the Emanuel AME Church in Charleston. The 2014 deaths of Michael Brown in Ferguson, Missouri, Eric Garner in Staten Island, and Tamir Rice in Cleveland; the death of Freddie Gray in Baltimore the following year; of Breonna Taylor in Louisville, Kentucky, in 2020; and of George Floyd in Minneapolis, Minnesota, that same year were, to varying degrees, made more legible by the brief life and tragic end of Trayvon Martin. The poet Elizabeth Alexander has referred to the young people who came of age in the aftermath of these events as "the Trayvon Generation," such was the formative weight of that moment. Nick Thompson, then the editor of *The New Yorker*'s digital side, recognized this early on and encouraged me to pursue that thread. This collection is, in some respects, a document of that thread, which took me from New York to Charleston, to Baltimore, Minneapolis, and beyond. Martin's death became a point of incitement but equally important, it formed a sensibility that underlies much of what is collected here. We lived (and I frequently wrote) with the understanding that Trayvon had lived, that he was no longer among the living and the cruelly redundant reasons why that was the case.

The title, *Three or More Is a Riot,* is a reference to the frequent criminal code definition holding that a riot is the concerted unlawful actions of "three or more" people. When I came across that definition in the course of covering these stories, it recalled the South Carolina code that, in the aftermath of the great Stono slave rebellion of 1739, defined a slave revolt as the mere presence of more than two Negroes without the company of a white man. The earliest pieces in this collection were published during the Obama presidency at a moment when the contours of the backlash to his mere existence were just becoming visible. These resurgent, open tides of white nationalism and belligerence culminated in the election of Donald Trump as president of the United States in 2016, a harrowing development that imperiled not only the fragile and partial progress achieved by the civil rights movement of the 1950s and

1960s, but American democracy itself. The most recent pieces were filed in an election year that already saw the reemergence of the themes of race, rage, and enfeebled democracy that had been so prominent in the previous two races. In curating this collection, I've pulled together pieces that shed light on the places, events, and personalities that are important to understanding how we navigated a besieged decade.

All writing is autobiographical, some just more transparently so. Many years ago, I used to have a habit of using the Washington, D.C., metro's transfer tickets as bookmarks. They were convenient since I invariably read during my commutes to work and my classes at Howard University, and the fact that the tickets were time-stamped meant that, in the distant future, I could revisit a book and know the month, year, and hour at which I had last encountered it. Writing for publication works in the opposite way: the words themselves are timestamped and you have to work backward to remember who and where you were at the time they were composed. The fifty-nine pieces included here were filed from various datelines—Charleston, Pittsburgh, San Francisco, London, Ferguson, Washington, D.C., Minneapolis, and others—and written on planes, in cars, on airport floors, in the dusty storage room of a venue where a gala was being hosted, and, occasionally, at my desk at home. They represent an inadvertent diary of my reactions, reporting, and commentary on our besieged moments. Perhaps more important, they pull together chronology and relationships between seemingly disparate events that, in retrospect, were very much connected.

As a young, aspiring writer, I was drawn to the essay as a form and I began mainlining collections from a variety of its practitioners. I first encountered *The Price of the Ticket,* James Baldwin's collected essays, as a broke twenty-something and hid the last copy in a different section of the bookstore until I could scrounge up enough money to purchase it a few days later. I consumed collections by Joan Didion, Jimmy Breslin, George Orwell, Ralph Ellison, Susan Sontag, Greg Tate, and Stanley Crouch. I dabbled in some E. B. White and, for a moment, fixated on the seemingly inexhaustible stream of work being produced by Christopher Hitchens. I happened across a copy of Pete Hamill's collection *Piecework* shortly after it was published in 1996 and the first sentence I read, the opening sentence of his masterful essay "The Lost City"— "Once there was another city here, and now it is gone"—immediately turned me into an acolyte. Two years later I ran into Hamill at the Borders bookstore on the ground floor of the old World Trade Center. I introduced myself and the two of us fell into an extended conversation about our particular literary interests, the history of New York City, the quirks of the essay as a genre, and what it meant to be a writer in his generation and, comparatively, in mine. "The question," he asked me, "is what does it mean to be a young black man living in New York City at this particular moment in its history?" Two years after that, the World Trade Center had been obliterated and both the city and the nation that housed it embarked upon a volatile new chapter in their existence. Writers, if they've been at it long enough, know that grand events are often conveyed most cleanly through their smallest moments. Watching the chaotic collapse of the Twin Towers, I recalled that small moment with Hamill and the fact that we'd spent twenty minutes talking about New York City history in a place that would very shortly come to define a great deal of it.

On some level, the question Hamill asked me lies at the center of this collection: What does it mean to be a (not-so-young) black man living in this specific moment of American history? What turning point is poised to take place on the ground we're standing upon in the not too distant future? This collection is my serial attempt to sort through some of those questions, in the hope that a random sentence may catch the attention of some other aspiring writer with a furtive ambition to produce something worthy of being hidden on another bookshelf until it can be purchased. My late friend Stanley Crouch would close his personal correspondence (and his book introductions) with the words "Victory Is Assured." The "victory" I've hoped for and worked toward is a world in which our chances at dignity and equality are a given and no longer fluctuate like the stock market and where our lives are no longer imperiled by the new guises of ancient bigotries. I believe that victory is in no way certain, a perspective that is confirmed by revisiting the work collected therein. But I hope that this collection conveys one other point—that it's damn sure worth fighting for.

Manhattan, 2024

I

THE PARAMETERS OF HOPE

Eras have a way of defining themselves. We navigate the random scroll of life and world affairs until we happen upon those singular occurrences that seem to put everything else into the proper context, highlighting the patterns in what had previously seemed to be arbitrary events. It's easier to see these patterns in retrospect, which is part of what makes history indispensable to understanding current events. Sifting through the work I produced between 2012 and 2016, I saw the relationships between various topics, and certainly my impressions of them, begin to emerge. Even the obituary columns I wrote in those years—for Ruby Dee, Amiri Baraka, Nelson Mandela, and David Carr—added to this perception, if only because each of that disparate lot had, at some point, seemed to be a fixture in the world that was. Their transitions marked, among other things, the point at which that landscape was irrevocably altered, and we were left to ponder the questions confronting us sans their unique insights. If the first four years of Barack Obama's presidency had been defined by idealistic aspirations and the heady afterglow of achieving a racial landmark, the second term required us to come to terms—in realistic sobriety—with what it actually meant for a black man to be president of the United States. We'd moved from the dawn of a new day to the harsh daylight of high noon, and the growing fissures in American society were becoming more visible. The period coincided with other developments, like the emergence of social media as a force in human communications. The naïve early perspective looked at the Obama campaign's shrewd use of Facebook in the 2008 election and the 2011 Arab Spring uprisings and saw a force for democratizing the world. By the second term, though, we had begun to recognize that the picture was far more complex than we might've suspected. Were these new platforms better suited to demagoguery than democracy?

I spent much of these years on the road, exploring our new American landscape with all its contradictions. The era was seeking to define itself and I wanted to be out there to witness it.

TRAYVON MARTIN AND THE PARAMETERS OF HOPE

March 21, 2012

Were the elements of the Trayvon Martin story—the plaintive cry for help punctuated by a gunshot; the image of Martin, seventeen and looking young for his age, in a football jersey; the iced tea and Skittles he carried—not so indelible, the events would seem like something from a Tom Wolfe novel: in a presidential election year, an unarmed black teen is shot by a Hispanic man in a county the *African American* president narrowly lost, in a state that accounts for twenty-nine electoral votes, resulting in demands that the attorney general (also black) open an investigation. The miasma of racism in this storyline is compounded by a police department's refusal to make an arrest, gun laws that confuse jurisprudence with football and suggest that a good offense is now the equivalent of self-defense, and wild rumors of a black militia preparing to occupy the town and take the shooter into custody. That Al Sharpton will be covering a planned rally rather than leading it is perhaps an irony too far even for Wolfe. More than that, the case, like similar ones, highlights the complicated matter of expectations and a black presidency. Call it the parameters of hope.

In August 2008, at the point in his presidential campaign where his political support had nearly morphed into messianic fervor, Barack Obama delivered a speech in St. Petersburg, Florida, touting his economic stimulus plan. That Obama was heckled during the speech was surprising enough; that he was heckled by a group of black protesters holding a sign that read "What about the Black community, Obama?" seemed, at first glance, to verge upon the surreal. Or maybe not; four months earlier, black activists had grumbled when he released a tepid statement calling for calm after a jury acquitted three New York Police Department detectives who fatally shot Sean Bell (unarmed, black, male) on the eve of his wedding. Yet earlier in his campaign, Jesse Jackson had criticized Obama for refusing to comment upon or participate in rallies surrounding the Jena Six—young men (black) who were arrested and initially charged with attempted murder after a fight in school. That banner in Florida pointed to a mild but noteworthy backlash against Obama's effort to remain above the racial fray. Its question, particularly as it pertains to cases involving young men and law enforcement, was subsumed by the vast significance of the 2008 election but has bobbed to the surface with semi-regularity during his presidency. It is present again in the case of Trayvon Martin, a seventeen-year-old shot dead in Florida.

During the 2008 campaign season Barack Obama made a habit of substituting cynicism for racism in his rhetoric. Suspicions that the country would never elect a black president weren't racist, he would imply; they were *cynical*. His opponents' worst slanderings of his background, religion, and patriotism were not race-baiting; they were cynical attempts to mislead the public. Yet incidents like the Bell shooting inspired a kind of split-screen effect, with one side featuring the meteoric ascent of a black presidential candidate and the other replaying a wretched but familiar scene of excessive police force directed at a black male victim. Thus there was a tincture of cynicism infecting even the most triumphal moment in the nation's recent history.

If his historic levels of support with black voters in 2008 offered, in response to persistent questions from the press, a declarative statement—*Barack Obama is black enough*—subsequent events slyly turned it interrogative: Barack Obama: Is black *enough*? Amid the collective self-congratulation that surrounded the election, separate police shootings of unarmed black men in New Orleans, Texas, and Oakland during the same month as Obama's inauguration were scarcely noticed. In the most widely discussed of the incidents, Oscar Grant was shot while lying face down in an Oakland BART station by a police officer who claimed to have accidentally pulled his gun when he was reaching for his Taser.

The election of a black president and appointment of a black attorney general could not realistically remedy decades of complex relations between African American men and law enforcement. The parameters of hope had already become vividly apparent in October of last year, when the state of Georgia executed Troy Davis despite serious questions about his guilt. Some quarters of black (and white) America demanded, or at least hoped for, some type of presidential intervention—even though, under the law, there was no clear route into a state case for Obama.

In this context, the shooting death of Trayvon Martin (black, male, seventeen, unarmed save for a packet of candy and a bottle of iced tea) did not so much raise questions as it confirmed suspicions: that we remain stratified or at best striated by race, that "innocent" is a relative term, that black male lives can end under capricious circumstances, and that justice is in the eye of the beholder—ideas that are as cynical as they are applicable. At this juncture, events in Sanford, Florida, suggest the benefit of the doubt in the shooting of a black teenager extends even to unauthorized, untrained, weapon-toting private citizens who pursue unarmed pedestrians.

That the Justice Department announced a probe and a grand jury has been convened is likely a result of the outrage seething across multiple social media platforms, television, and traditional corporeal protesting. Yet the failure of the Sanford Police Department to make an arrest nearly a month after Martin's death, and the fact that, if it weren't for half a million petition signatures and national outrage, this shooting would have gone un-investigated, has already confirmed yet another assumption: our worst problem is not cynicism; it's the frequency with which that cynicism proves accurate.

RODNEY KING, 1965–2012

June 19, 2012

The old adage holds that history occurs twice—first as tragedy, then as farce—but if anything is to be learned from the tragic tale of Rodney King, it's that history's encores are often just as brutal as its débuts. King, who died Sunday at age forty-seven, was inducted, unwitting and unwilling, into a fraternity of men whose experiences seem like a series of historical paraphrases. There's John Weerd Smith, the Newark cabdriver whose arrest sparked the 1967 riots in that city; Marquette Frye, whose 1965 DUI arrest in Watts ignited days of chaos and fire. In 1964, fifteen-year-old James Powell was shot and killed by an NYPD officer in Harlem—word of his death was just so much kindling to an already tense city, and riots broke out in Manhattan and Brooklyn. During the Second World War, the police shooting of Robert Bandy, a soldier, inaugurated the 1943 Harlem riot. And there are more. That roll call explains why the disbelief that swaths of America felt when viewing the videotape of Rodney King's beating was scarce in black America, why so many African Americans saw it through eyes jaundiced by similar experience—a civic violation as lived cliché.

King later recalled that, during the beating, he thought of slaves being beaten in the old South. Not everyone needed to reach that far into history to find an analogy. In 1992, I was a college senior living in Washington, D.C. The images of King being struck more than fifty times by four police officers resonated with my own experience, recalled my own sharp memories of my fourteen-year-old self being stopped on my way home from a baseball game in Queens, shoved against a mailbox and searched because, the cop said, I fit the description of a mugger. I was wearing a mud-caked gray-and-orange uniform with the words "Laurelton Little League" emblazoned on the front. The policing of urban communities is full of complexities, but there is a social constant here: the combustible resentment that comes with the feeling that you're more likely to be brutalized or killed by people whom your taxes pay to protect you than by the people they're paid to protect you from. The blue line is thinner and more frayed in some places than others.

King's experience wasn't novel, nor is it unusual for police to be exonerated in excessive-force trials. Yet the verdict in the trial of Officers Stacey Koon, Theodore Briseno, Laurence Powell, and Timothy Wind stripped away the bit of idealism about the judicial system that remained in places like South Central Los Angeles. In a single volatile moment, people confronted two irreconcilable truths: George Holliday's grainy footage meant that no longer could reports of LAPD behavior be dismissed as hyperbole from the race-hustle crowd, and that even video evidence of a man being beaten wasn't enough to prove police brutality. And for the next three days, a fiery scene from America's urban history replayed itself yet again.

The video also ensured that, unlike Smith, Frye, Powell, and Bandy, Rodney King's name would remain permanently tethered to the bedlam that reigned in Los Angeles for a time in the spring of 1992. It remade a common man as a vector of history. The role never really fit him. In later years his pupils appeared to be permanently dilated by the glare of public attention. And in a country that demands its heroes pure, King remained a troubled soul—his blood-alcohol content was twice the legal limit on the night he was beaten by the LAPD, and the next couple decades of his life were dotted with more arrests and flailing attempts at sobriety. At this remove, after all that, it's possible to forget the smaller details of how he rose to his occasion: the way his voice quavered when he made his plaintive request that we all get along, the stooped posture that suggested he was physically burdened by the ruin being done across his native city in his name.

King's later foray into reality television looked at first like a strange twist in an already convoluted plot, but on a deeper level it seems like the logical extension of his experiences. For a genre that consistently conflates trauma with drama, where the public beatings are metaphorical but no less ubiquitous, King was, yet again, an unwitting trailblazer. If you've lived through something out of an episode of *Caught on Camera,* showing up on *Celebrity Rehab with Dr. Drew* no longer seems like such a stretch.

King was changed by what transpired on March 3, 1991, and we'd like to believe we have been also, though precisely how is hard to pinpoint. The three levels of bureaucratic self-defense are to deny a problem exists; admit that it exists but say it's confined to a few rogue individuals; or admit to systemic troubles, create a commission, and then claim that reforms have completely eliminated the problem. After the Los Angeles riots, the LAPD went directly to level three. In the wake of the Christopher Commission's findings, the department took steps to diversify its ranks. The removal of Police Chief Daryl Gates and the subsequent appointment of Willie Williams, the first black police chief in LA history, was directly related to King's beating. But in 2009, television viewers saw grainy footage of another black man lying prone at the feet of a California police officer, this time in Oakland. The man, Oscar Grant, had been shot and killed. Earlier this year, the New York Civil Liberties Union released a report pointing out that in 2011 the NYPD conducted nearly 686,000 stop-and-frisks, with blacks and Latinos accounting for more than 86 percent of those targeted by police. A little leaguer has a vastly higher chance of being thrown against a mailbox and searched in New York City than when I was growing up there.

BARACK X

October 7, 2012

1.

It's mid-March in Harlem and the streets are an improvised urban bazaar. Young men hawk umbrellas, vintage vinyl, and knit caps. The aromas of curry and fried plantains waft out from the Caribbean spot, and just ahead of me is a teenager so slight that I scarcely notice him at first. There's a perfectly calibrated swagger in his stride. He's swaddled in an oversized black leather jacket, his jeans cinched five inches below the waist, his footwear immaculate. I've nearly passed him before I notice something that makes me pause for a second and then snap a picture with my cellphone: stitched onto the back of the jacket, in dimensions broader than his back, is the seal of the president of the United States. He is standing on Malcolm X Boulevard, and a generation ago that jacket would've been emblazoned with a defiant "X" in homage to a man who defined radical black dissent. There are a dozen questions I could ask him—whether there are metal detectors in his school or when was the last time he was frisked by the NYPD, whether he sees his future as an amorphous blob of curtailed possibilities or if he has real plans. But I don't have to ask how the most revered symbol of the American establishment came to adorn his jacket.

In the halcyon days after Barack Obama's inauguration, newspapers ran stories marveling at an Obama effect that seemed to lift black students beyond the achievement gap. Some openly hoped that his election would inspire increased numbers of black law school applicants, the way that *CSI* spawned a generation of forensic science majors. In a poll taken just after the 2009 inauguration, some 70 percent of respondents said that they expected his tenure to bring an improvement in race relations. Obama himself played to this dynamic early on, saying that in a crowded field of talented Democratic contenders the rationale for his campaign was that his election would tell every child in this country that anything was possible. And for a brief moment, it seemed that might actually be true.

Nearly four years later, the fickle-hearted arbiters of cool have migrated onward, finding new cultural pastures to stake out. There are no A-list rappers crafting themes in Obama's honor, no catchy call-and-response phrases on par with "Fired up and ready to go." Yet here on Lenox Avenue is an Obama testimony in clashing motifs that underscores the complexity of the president's current undertaking. A handful of men have been elected president and then become a symbol for an era, but very few beyond the current occupant of 1600 Pennsylvania Avenue have made the opposite transition. And it is for this reason that 2012 seems like so much anticlimax: a symbol ran for president four years ago; today a man is seeking to hold on to that position.

Prior to 2008, the distinctions between a black leader and a leader who is black were largely semantic. There had been black leaders of largely white enterprises—Richard Parsons, Condi Rice, Ken Chenault—but they were seen as inspired anomalies, envoys dispatched to the broadened frontiers of possibility. In the days leading up to the 2008 election, it was common to hear African Americans ask whether white America was "ready" for a black president. I tended to wonder if *black* America was. To the extent that the public thinks of our presidents, it tends toward a kind of cultural shorthand. We think of Teddy Roosevelt as a trustbuster despite the fact that Taft moved more aggressively against the nascent corporate order than he did. JFK's reputation as a civil rights stalwart is all but immunized against his record of foot-dragging on racial matters. Beyond wonks and history grad students, there aren't many Americans who hedge Reagan's standing as an avatar of small government with his multiple tax increases. We tend toward a glossy, forgiving view of historic presidencies. For African Americans in particular, however, Obama presented a dilemma—he is both a figure of history, a representative of a centuries-long struggle to have our humanity recognized, and a contemporary elected official sent to Washington to address specific problems and policies. It is a balancing act that few of us were prepared for, nor ever thought we would need to be.

At a casual glance it seems contradictory that African American unemployment remains double white unemployment but that the president retains a 90 percent approval rate among black people. But that fails to recognize many of us who remember that blacks were disproportionately unemployed under Bush, Clinton, Bush, and Reagan. The black community understood better than anyone else how intractable this problem was. Obama would not be measured by whether he fixed the problem; he would be measured by how credibly and diligently he attempted to.

In black America—where people have been voting for presidential candidates who didn't share their racial background since even before the Fifteenth Amendment—the 2008 election wasn't seen as the star-spangled "Kumbaya" it was billed as elsewhere. White rejoicing at Obama's racial landmark seemed tone-deaf, unduly self-congratulatory. White voters had simply done something black voters had been doing for at least the previous 134 years. For this reason and others like it, there was a tendency among blacks to see Obama as an extension of black achievement—but not necessarily a barometer of changing white attitudes. The hyperbolic talk of a post-racial society suggested that white voters, or at least a highly visible segment of them, tended to see the election in precisely the opposite terms.

2.

The more onerous aspects of Jim Crow conspired to obscure a reality key to understanding Barack Obama's complicated relationship to black America: simply put, the colored section was far more democratic than the ostensibly free segments of America because virtually *any* tincture of black ancestry was sufficient to gain admission. The boundaries of whiteness required vigilant policing and scrutiny, but black people were far more catholic in our self-perception.

In response, America conjured a usable mythology, one in which the products of interracial unions were uniformly doomed to suffer disproportionate woe. Fiction, folklore, and films like *Imitation of Life* cinched the concept of the tragic mulatto in American popular imagination. But the concept didn't square with our own lived experience. There was nothing tragic about the trajectories of Frederick Douglass, Booker T. Washington, Mordecai Wyatt Johnson, or any other biracial black person—aside from the burden of racial inequality they shouldered along with anyone else of African descent. The activist Walter White used his nearly white skin as a kind of camouflage that allowed him to investigate lynchings for the NAACP in the 1920s. Obama understood this history well enough to stand nearly outside of it. In 2008, Barack Obama authored a new archetype—a biracial man who was not so much tragic as ironic. Unlike the maligned mulattoes of old, Obama wasn't passing for white—he was passing for mixed. For those with an eye to this history, it was a masterful performance, a riff as adroit as anything conjured by Dizzy Gillespie or Sonny Rollins.

Early on, observers noted Obama's Ebonics lapses when speaking to black audiences and saw in them a sly attempt to pander to African American voters. But they had it precisely backward: to black audiences, his ability to speak in pulpit inflections one moment and concave Midwestern tones the next made him seem *more* black, not less. We saw him as no different than any African American lawyer who speaks black English at home and another, entirely more formal language, in his professional environment.

Not surprisingly, this has translated into confusion over who the president of the United States is. A 2010 Pew poll showed that 53 percent of whites see the president as biracial while only a quarter see him as black. At the same time, 55 percent of African Americans see Obama as black while a third see him as mixed race. What the poll failed to ask, however, was whether African Americans see those two categories as mutually exclusive. Slavery, coercion, and the randomness of social exchange conspired to ensure that virtually all of black America is biracial in some regard. Walter White had blond hair, fair skin, and blue eyes—yet was black enough to serve as the NAACP's chief executive for twenty-four years. What was known but left unsaid is that Obama was at least as black as any of the other forty million of us and biracial in the same sense that Douglass, Washington, and White were.

This is not a simple equation: Obama received more white support than John Kerry or Al Gore, both of whom have *two* white parents. Yet there was a notable *hmph* of dissatisfaction, in 2010, when Obama noted that he identified as black on the census. What it meant was that a quorum of white voters were not going to let *Dreams from My Father*, the South Side of Chicago, and Obama's own census form prevent them from debiting some aspect of identity and remaking him as *meta* black.

A sharp politician looking to maximize his surface area with voters would see no upside in further clarifying this state of affairs. As the actor Vin Diesel found some years back, the guiding principle was that as long as people were intrigued about where you fit in the racial taxonomy, they'd remain fundamentally intrigued by you. In an undertaking as vast and unwieldy as the United States, any president is required to simultaneously be many things—ideologically, socially, politically—but not until November 4, 2008, was any of them required to be many things racially.

The received wisdom holds that Obama has been reluctant to deal explicitly with race for fear of igniting the ire of his white detractors. But this is only part of the equation—the ground is nearly as fraught for his dealings with his white supporters, particularly those who took him as validation for the counterfeit belief that we were beyond the racial dramas of old. By the time of the 2008 election Obama had become a sort of racial O-negative, a fragile position he could maintain only so long as circumstance cooperated. (Circumstance, as Skip Gates, Shirley Sherrod, and especially Trayvon Martin could attest, chose not to.) All this meant that black America knew that, contrary to the *New York Times* headline following the 2008 election, "the racial barrier" had not fallen with Obama's election; it had become a selectively permeable membrane, though that in itself was reason enough to do the Electric Slide in the streets.

The post-racial myth is the logical outgrowth of an older mythology that the black struggle for freedom was anchored in a moral crusade to redeem America at large. The truth of the matter is that Martin Luther King, Jr., was more of a backroom operator than that. The idea of redemption stemmed from a moral sales pitch proffered by King, a transaction in which whites would confront the awful contours of American history and be granted exemption from its implications. Black people had a more tangible yield in mind: removing the dusty boot of Jim Crow from our necks. If fashioning spiritual redemption as a form of higher patriotism was enough to end abominations like the waterlogged obscenity that was Emmett Till's body, then so be it. But the deeper truth is that black people were more concerned with saving our own necks than saving America's soul.

For this reason, white claims to have "marched with Dr. King" eventually became an unintentional punch line, a disclaimer for whatever racially obtuse commentary followed that preface. The joke, however, was on us. Few could conceive that, forty years after King's death, the nation would elect a black president—an event deeply rooted in the civil rights ethos, a bolder redemption, a stronger immunization against the claims of history. And, as with the claims to have marched with Dr. King, the very fact of Obama's election has been a disclaimer against the racism that came after it.

3.

I pointed out earlier that a majority of people polled felt that race relations would improve under Obama, but a more honest statement would be that there is no such thing as "race relations." There is only the relative presence or absence of racism and beyond that the fuzzy euphemisms that are just a notch better than inflammatory code words ("welfare," "crime") in our stilted racial dialogue. Good race relations meant that hundreds of thousands of diverse Americans could huddle together against the arctic cold on the National Mall to celebrate the inauguration of Barack Obama. Racism, however, meant that those black celebrants would disproportionately face police brutality, foreclosure, health disparities, and unemployment after the festivities were over.

The faulty gospel of good race relations means that, in his dealings with black America, Obama has to abide by the old guideline of ethics: avoid not only a conflict of interest but the *appearance* of a conflict of interest. And by all appearances Obama's administration overlearned this lesson. It was a backhanded compliment that the same polls show that 57 percent of whites think that he has paid "about enough" attention to black issues.

The net result of this awkward act is that Obama's presidency appears like a type of infidelity: married to America at large but conducting an affair with black people. As such, he speaks to us most often in veiled dispatches and surreptitious winks. Our most intimate recognition occurs behind closed doors.

It is this theme that his black critics seized upon even before he'd won the election. In 2008, at the point where enthusiasm for Obama had nearly morphed into messianic fervor, a group of black protesters at a Florida rally hoisted a banner that asked "What about the Black community, Obama?" At first glance the visual was jarring, discordant. It seemed like a question for which the answer could be presumed—certainly by that segment of America that viewed his election as an antidote for the previous three centuries of racial history. But the banner was a response in very specific terms to Obama's tepid remarks on the acquittal of the police officers who had gunned down Sean Bell, an unarmed black man, on the eve of his wedding. It spoke to a broader suspicion that a candidate, even a black one, who would scarcely talk about black concerns (until his pastor's radioactive sermons gave him no choice), could not be trusted to address those same concerns when elected.

In the days before he lost his perspective amid a froth of personal animus toward Obama, Cornel West made this point repeatedly. Following Obama's speech at the Democratic National Convention, which coincided with the forty-fifth anniversary of the "I Have a Dream" speech, West lit into Obama for referring to Dr. King only obliquely as a "young preacher from Georgia."

Fredrick Harris, a professor of political science at Columbia University, has argued that Obama's allergy to race is so severe as to invalidate the idea that we've seen a black presidency:

> Obama's defenders have repeatedly said he must be a president for all Americans, not just African Americans, and Obama himself has made similar statements. But this argument is disingenuous. When other important constituencies ask the president to support their policy initiatives—say, Jewish groups on Middle East matters, or the LGBT community on "don't ask, don't tell" and marriage equality, or women's groups on reproductive rights—can you imagine him responding that he can't address their particular interests because, as president, he has to be concerned with all people? So on racial inequality, why do black voters have to take a back seat? . . .
>
> When a reporter for BET asked the president in 2009, during the debate over the stimulus bill, if he would do something to specifically address high unemployment among blacks and Latinos, Obama responded that "every step we are taking is designed to help all people" and reiterated that "my general approach is that if the economy is strong, that will lift all boats." But what of those who have no boats to begin with?

If these criticisms haven't put a dent in Obama's approval ratings, it's not because black people disagreed—it's because they ultimately place the blame for this state of affairs elsewhere. We, too, witnessed a nation ripped at its seams in 2009: when a president tried to provide citizens with affordable healthcare, we saw Glenn Beck achieve a demagogic cachet that made Father Coughlin look like a Henry Wallace liberal. We remember circumstances of the first-generation black mayors of major cities and the ways in which they inherited declining tax revenues, evaporating industrial bases, and white flight but were nonetheless given all the blame for the misery of the urban black poor. It also has to be understood that African American perspectives on Obama have been filtered, first and foremost, through an abiding concern for his safety. During the 2008 primaries, I encountered black voters who spoke of voting against Obama because they didn't believe a black man could be elected president and live through his entire term.

At every turn at which black people might have evaluated him more harshly on his political choices, Obama's most irrational foes forced African Americans to consider him as a proxy for our own contused personal experiences. To be clear, 80 percent of blacks feel that Obama has paid about enough attention to black concerns— that's 23 percentage points *more* than whites who feel this way. But "about enough" doesn't really mean about enough; it means we understand that he's paid as much attention as he could while performing the racial high-wire act required of a black man leading a nation populated by two hundred million whites. The question was not whether he'd paid enough attention to our concerns; it was whether you would prefer circumstances in which he could reasonably pay more.

Nothing better defined the precise nature of his circumstances than that triumphal moment of birtherism, in which a sitting president was forced to prove his own citizenship. Viewed through the lens of black history, that moment appeared as Dred Scott remixed, the means by which a president is racially profiled. That humiliation resounded with every black person who's ever felt that their qualifications were questioned despite years of education, hard work, and sacrifice. It made perfect sense that Donald Trump would follow up the question of Obama's citizenship with one casting doubts on his academic performance at Columbia. He was trafficking in the greatest hits of white entitlement. For black people, the implications of this were clear: if the most powerful man in the world could be played like that because he's black, what hope was there for the rest of us?

Cornel West himself unintentionally made the most cogent defense of Obama when he criticized the 2008 race speech. After rightfully citing it for the false evenhandedness with which it treated racial conflict, West offered that it was the best speech that could be given "in a racially immature society." There is a thematic bond that connects a broad swath of our contemporary politics, a bratty truculence that gives context to the rebranded nativism of birthers, to Representative Joe Wilson's Tourette's-like outburst during a State of the Union address, to Beck's fevered dissociative ramblings, and the Muslim-socialist-fascist axis imagined by the unhinged. That immaturity found its most honest expression in a 2011 poll in which 11 percent of white respondents said they felt that *they* are now the primary victims of racism. It is not hard to imagine that some future historian will refer to the Obama era, or at least the first four years of it, as the Age of Tantrums. Twenty years ago, in the midst of the culture wars, establishment critics assailed multiculturalism as an assault on the fabric of common citizenship. How ironic that it would be a black man—who rose to prominence in 2006 by asserting that "there is not a black America and a white America and Latino America, an Asian America; there's the United States of America"—whose presidency would ignite the balkanization they warned of.

There is an obvious downside to this familiarity with the obstacles implicit within a black presidency. Obama at times tends toward insouciance regarding black voters, who, epidermal affiliations aside, nonetheless represent roughly a quarter of his electorate and the single largest and most reliable voting block in the Democratic Party. That casual arrogance was on display when he warned the Congressional Black Caucus (already wavering in their support for him) to "stop complaining," during a speech in 2011. There are moments where even amid the racial minefield his presidency inhabits, he appears to have been let off easy; black America has set-tled for a brother who feels our pain, rather than evaluated how effectively he's alleviated it. Yet even this frustration yields layers of complexity.

It's also worth noting that, despite the gossamer-thin margin separating them in this election, the Romney campaign did not, until relatively late in the game, resort to the kinds of coded racial appeals that were a cornerstone of presidential politics. And when it did, the campaign's loose talk about Obama undoing welfare re-form and its head nod at birtherism seemed half-hearted and des-perate, not an integral part of the strategy. Indeed, Romney's most inflammatory statement—his reference to a parasitic 47 percent of the population—suggested bigoted attitudes that ran along class lines, not epidermal ones. It's possible that Romney, perhaps in-spired by his father's example, has no stomach for such racial mea-sures. Or that the blowback would alienate more voters than those tactics would win over. It's also possible that the Southern Strategy wouldn't fly today because it would ruin our national high. We like ourselves now in the way the blissfully un-self-aware people often do. Even slick, encrypted racism might inspire a kind of historical reflux, remind us of the terrible limbic appeal of bigotry, and put us collectively in a bad headspace. Things have changed, just not the things that many of us suspected on Election Day.

Malcolm X occupied a similar crossroads in American history, a point at which a vast chunk of history had fallen away and a new vista of possibilities emerged. His criticism of integration inspired a view of him as the antithesis of the movement associated with King. A more subtle reading of him suggested that he was a herald who saw more starkly than many the unpaved places in the road ahead. The demise of segregation was as stunning to his generation as the election of Barack Obama was to this one. The troubles and com-plexities that would follow both those events were seemingly cloaked by momentous victories—encrypted, as it were, by the tides of change.

The Obama presidency has thus far validated both our hopes and our fears and given dueling legitimacy to optimism and cynicism simultaneously. It has pitted the audacity of hope against the recalcitrance of memory. If his election validated the ideals of King, what has happened since then lends credence to Malcolm X. What remains clear is that whether it's a function of defiance or affirmation, Obama has already been inducted into a narrative black America tells itself, one in which we are the central characters and we are the primary deed-holders to our own triumphs. Whether or not he is reelected is secondary to this concern. The more enduring question is whether black people will maintain a broader faith in America because a black man has been elected president, or despite it.

POSTSCRIPT TO "BARACK X"

Presidential terms are allotted the same number of years as the typical high school enrollment. The stakes for the latter are generally much lower—at least in world-historical terms—but the two undertakings do share particular similarities: they provide a crucial context for our lives while they're happening, even as their personal significance begins a rapid decline the moment they conclude. The two terms Barack Obama spent in the White House—high school and college, to continue the analogy—were freighted with a significance we may never again witness in our lifetimes. Obama, the first black president, represented the culmination of a centuries-long struggle for equality. At the same time, his presidency became a curious barometer of the persistence of those same inequalities. The febrile Republican stonewalling, the outraged declarations of the Tea Party movement, the hallucinatory yet widely believed canards about healthcare death panels and secret Muslim religious affiliation—all of it reflected the allergic reaction that a swath of the nation developed in response to the mere reality of a black man elected to the (heretofore) White House. It's easy to see in retrospect that these dynamics were, along with an ancient and resurgent xenophobia, core elements coalescing into what eventually became Trumpism.

That movement has subsequently become many things, most of them destructive, but it owes its existence to the resentments swirling around the lanky, light-skinned, half-Kenyan, half-Kansan forty-fourth president of the United States.

I didn't see all of that yet. That kind of racial and political forecasting was impossible at the time that this piece was written. Clarity would come later. The shrapnel flying around Obama made it difficult for black observers and critics to parse the fair critiques of his presidency from those who naïvely treated him like any other president, difficult to understand the reason for the gap between what Obama did and what was actually possible for him to have done in the context he operated in. On some level, this is a question that vexes the assessment of any presidency, but in Obama's case the political strictures he encountered—as I noted here—paralleled the very same restrictions that his core constituency had experienced and hoped he might transcend. In short, that stricture can be called race. This piece, written at the midpoint of his presidency, was equidistant from both the idealism of 2008 and the despair of 2016. That complex, tragic positioning has ensured at least one thing: Obama's presidency did not lose resonance like maudlin memories of high school. It is, nearly a decade after he left office, still, in many ways, the thing we are talking about when we are talking about other things.

TARANTINO UNCHAINED

January 2, 2013

In early 2010, not long after the release of Quentin Tarantino's Second World War revenge epic, *Inglourious Basterds,* I began teaching a course on American history at Moscow State University. When a Russian friend asked me what I thought of the film, I told him I loved the way the director created an alternate history in order to make a larger point about the universal nature of heroism. My friend and, as I later learned, lots of other Russians took issue with the film for precisely that reason. "Is this," he asked, "how Americans really perceive World War II?" In Russia, where the annual May 9 celebrations of the German surrender dwarf those of the Fourth of July in this country, the sacrifices that were crucial to defeating Hitler are a point of huge national pride. The history department at the university features a marble monument to hundreds of university students who died defending the country. Because many Russians feel that the world—and particularly the United States—has never properly recognized the scale of their losses, they tend to see *Inglourious Basterds* not as a revenge fantasy but as an attempt to further whitewash their role in Hitler's demise. The alternate history in *Inglourious Basterds* failed there because the actual history had yet to be reconciled. The movie's lines between fantasy and the actual myopic perspectives on history were so hazy that the audience wasn't asked to suspend disbelief; they were asked to suspend conscience. With *Django Unchained,* Tarantino's tale of a vengeful ex-slave, what happened in Russia is happening here.

The theme of revenge permeates Tarantino's work. If the violence in his films seems gratuitous, it's also deployed as a kind of spiritual redemption. And if this dynamic is applicable anywhere in American history, it's on a slave plantation. Frederick Douglass, in his slave narrative, traced his freedom not to the moment when he escaped to the North but the moment in which he first struck an overseer who attempted to whip him. Quentin Tarantino is the only filmmaker who could pack theaters with multiracial audiences eager to see a black hero murder a dizzying array of white slaveholders and overseers. (And, in all fairness, it's not likely that a black director would've gotten a budget to even attempt such a thing.)

The most recent Hollywood attempt to grapple with slavery was Steven Spielberg's *Lincoln,* a biopic that presents the final four months of the president's life and his attempts to shepherd the Thirteenth Amendment through Congress. Lincoln as he appears in the film is a man fully formed and possessed of a vast wellspring of indignation about slavery. But he also appears as the moral vector of his age in ways that don't square with history. In focusing so directly on Lincoln's efforts, Spielberg's film slights abolitionists, radical Republicans, and, crucially, the African Americans—slave and free—who pushed Lincoln to the positions he eventually adopted.

From its opening scene, *Django* inverts this scenario. Here is the spaghetti Western about an ex-slave turned bounty hunter who takes the bloody business of emancipation into his own hands. This is not Tarantino's best film, but it is probably his most clever. He plays fast and loose with history here, but there are risks implicit in doing this with a film about slavery that aren't nearly as significant in toying with the history of the West. The history of the West is settled in ways that are not the case for the history of the American South and slavery. The film's premise alone was enough to spark controversy. Spike Lee—a longtime critic of Tarantino—took the unwieldy position that he refused to see the film but knew that it would be disrespectful to his ancestors.

There are moments where this convex history works brilliantly, like when Tarantino depicts the KKK a decade prior to its actual formation in order to thoroughly ridicule its members' (literally) veiled racism. But, as my Russian friend pointed out about *Inglourious Basterds, Django Unchained* makes it apparent that not even an entertaining alternate history can erase our actual conceptions of the past.

In *Django,* the director creates an audacious black hero who shoots white slavers with impunity and lives to tell about it. In the Harlem theater where I saw the film, the largely black audience cheered each time an overseer met his end. There is a noble undertaking at the heart of all this gunplay. Django, played brilliantly by Jamie Foxx, and King Schultz, his white bounty hunter mentor—played by an equally adroit Christoph Waltz—are on a mission to rescue Hildi (Kerry Washington), the enslaved woman Django loves. The trade-off for an audience indulging in that emotionally powerful and rarely depicted brand of black heroism is overlooking aspects of the film that were at least as troubling as the other parts were affirming.

Primary among these concerns is the frequency with which Tarantino deploys the n-word. If ever there were an instance in which the term was historically fitting, it would seem that a Western set against the backdrop of slavery—a Southern—would be it. Yet the term appears with such numb frequency that *Django* manages to raise the epithet to the level of a pronoun. (I wonder whether the word "nigger" is spoken in the film more frequently than the word "he" or "she.") Had the word appeared any more often, it would have required billing as a co-star. At some point, it becomes difficult not to wonder how much of this is about the film and how much is about the filmmaker. Given the prominence of the word in *Pulp Fiction* and *Jackie Brown*—neither of which remotely touch on slavery—its usage in *Django* starts to seem like racial ventriloquism, a kind of camouflage that allows Tarantino to use the word without recrimination.

This is just the first path in the labyrinth of racial concerns that *Django* constructs. Here, as in *Lincoln,* black people—with the exception of the protagonist and his love interest—are ciphers passively awaiting freedom. Django's behavior is so unrepentantly badass as to make him an enigma to both whites and blacks who encounter him. For his part, Django never deigns to offer a civil word to any other slave, save his love interest. In a climactic scene, Django informs his happily enslaved nemesis that he is the one n-word in ten thousand audacious enough to kill anyone standing in the way of freedom.

Is this how Americans actually perceive slavery? More often than not, the answer to that question is answered in the affirmative. It is precisely because of the extant mythology of black subservience that these scenes pack such a cathartic payload. The film's defenders are quick to point out that *Django* is not about history. But that's almost like arguing that fiction is not reality—it isn't, but the entire appeal of the former is its capacity to shed light on how we understand the latter. In my sixteen years of teaching African American history, one sadly common theme has been the number of black students who shy away from courses dealing with slavery out of shame that slaves never fought back.

It seems almost pedantic to point out that slavery was nothing like this. The slaveholding class existed in a state of constant paranoia about slave rebellions, escapes, and a litany of more subtle attempts to undermine the institution. Nearly two hundred thousand black men, most of them former slaves, enlisted in the Union Army in order to accomplish en masse precisely what Django attempts to do alone: risk death in order to free those whom they loved. Tarantino's attempt to craft a hero who stands apart from the other men—black and white—of his time is not a riff on history; it's a riff on the mythology we've mistaken for history. Were the film aware of that distinction, *Django* would be far less troubling—but it would also be far less resonant. The alternate history is found not in the story of a vengeful ex-slave but in the idea that he could be the only one.

Django's true nemesis is not the slaveholder who subjects Hildi to cruel punishments but Stephen, the house slave devoutly allied with the slaveholder. The central conflict is not between an ex-slave and a slaver but between two archetypes—the militant and the sell-out. But in creating Stephen, Tarantino necessarily trafficked in the stereotypes he was ostensibly responding to. Samuel L. Jackson plays Stephen's overblown insouciance and anachronistic mf-bombs to great comedic effect. There are moments, however, when ironies cancel each other out, and we're left with a stark truth—at its most basic, this is an instance in which a white director holds an obsequious black slave up for ridicule. The use of this character as a comic foil seems essentially disrespectful to the history of slavery. Oppression, almost by definition, is a set of circumstances that bring out the worst in most people. A response to slavery—even a cowardly, dishonorable one like what we witness with Stephen—highlights the depravity of the institution. We've come a long way racially, but not so far that laughing at that character shouldn't be deeply disturbing.

On the 150th anniversary of the Emancipation Proclamation, it's worth recalling that slavery was made unsustainable largely through the efforts of those who were enslaved. The record is replete with enslaved blacks—even so-called house slaves—who poisoned slaveholders, destroyed crops, "accidentally" burned down buildings, and ran away in such large numbers that their lost labor crippled the Confederate economy. The primary sin of *Django Unchained* is not the desire to create an alternative history. It's in the idea that an enslaved black man willing to kill in order to protect those he loves could constitute one.

LINCOLN DIED FOR OUR SINS

January 22, 2013

The opening scene of Steven Spielberg's cinemythic portrait of the sixteenth president features President Abraham Lincoln seated on a stage, half cloaked in darkness, and observing the Union forces he is sending into battle. It's an apt metaphor for the man himself—both visible and obscure, inside the tempest yet somehow above the fray. *Lincoln* was released in early November, just in time to shape our discussions of January 1, 2013, the 150th anniversary of the Emancipation Proclamation. Yet with its themes of redemption and sacrifice, Spielberg's film could seem less suited for an anniversary celebration than an annual one. Here is a vision of a lone man, tested by betrayal, besieged by enemies whom he regards without malice, a man who is killed for his convictions only to be resurrected as a moral exemplar. Spielberg's *Lincoln* is perhaps less fitted to January 1 than it is to the holiday that precedes it by a week.

In fairness, this narrative of Lincoln's Civil War, equal parts cavalry and Calvary, did not originate with Spielberg. The legend of the Great Emancipator began even as Lincoln lay dying in a boardinghouse across from Ford's Theatre that night in April 1865. (In the same way that JFK's mythic standing as a civil rights stalwart was born at Dealey Plaza in November 1963.) In the wake of his assassination, Lincoln the controversial and beleaguered president was remade into Lincoln the Savior, an American Christ figure who carried the nation's sins. Pulling off this transformation, this historical alchemy, has required that we as a nation redact the messier parts of Lincoln's story in favor of an untainted, morally unconflicted commander in chief who was untouched by the biases of the day and unyielding in his opposition to slavery. We have little use for tainted Christs. Through Lincoln the Union was "saved" in more than one sense of the word.

History is malleable. There is always the temptation to remake the past in the contours that are most comforting to us. In a nation tasked with reconciling its democratic ideals with the reality of slavery, Lincoln has become a Rorschach test of sorts. What we see when we look at him says as much about ourselves as it does about him. And what we see, or choose to see, most often is a figure of unimpeachable moral standing who allows Americans to gaze at ourselves in the mirror of history and smile. If the half-life for this kind of unblemished heroism is limited—we've grown more cynical across the board—it has remained resonant enough for our politicians today to profit from their association with it. The signal achievement of Spielberg's *Lincoln* is the renovation of that vision of Lincoln, a makeover for a nation that had elected its first black president to a *second* term just three days before the film hit theaters.

In 2007 Barack Obama announced his presidential candidacy in Springfield, Illinois, deliberately conjuring comparisons to that other lanky lawyer who spent time in the state legislature there. There is no shortage of politicians claiming an affinity with Lincoln— George W. Bush saw himself as a Lincolnesque figure when he was prosecuting the war on terror—but rarely have the parallels been as apparent as they are with Obama. The candidate played up that angle, visiting the Lincoln Memorial just before his inauguration, carrying a well-thumbed copy of *Team of Rivals* on the campaign trail, slipping sly riffs on Lincoln's second inaugural address into his own first one, and taking the oath of office on the Lincoln Bible.

Beyond the obvious, though, lies a deeper theme between Obama and Lincoln: the identities of both men are inextricably bound to questions of both disunity and progress in this country. It's worth recalling that Obama's rise to prominence was a product of his 2004 speech to the Democratic National Convention, in which he offered a compelling, if Photoshopped, vision of a United States where there are no red states or blue states, where neither race nor religion nor ideology can undermine national unity. Obama walked onto that stage an obscure state legislator; he left it a virtual avatar of American reconciliation, the most obvious brand of which was racial. Implicit within his subsequent campaign, particularly after the flash point of controversy over Jeremiah Wright's sermons, was the possibility of amnesty for the past. Nowhere was this more apparent than in Obama's "More Perfect Union" speech in Philadelphia in March 2008. Delivered at a time when the campaign was virtually hemorrhaging hope, the speech was a deft manipulation of the very human aspiration to break with the messy past, to be reborn in an untainted present.

In the wake of the release of Spielberg's *Lincoln*, it was common to see pundits remark with amazement on the enduring public fascination with the sixteenth president. The biopic grossed $84 million by the beginning of December—a grand haul for a historical drama with no special effects and an ending we've known since grade school. But viewed from another angle, the question becomes not why we are still intrigued by Lincoln but how we could not be. His life contains epic themes: genius, war, personal loss, a narrative arc in which a barely schooled young man goes on to produce some of the most elegant prose in the American canon and play a role in ending the wretchedness of slavery. The capacity of his life to inspire and intrigue is rivaled only by its capacity to exonerate. It is this last element that takes center stage in Spielberg's film. The director's artistic choice to focus on the last four months of the president's life is simultaneously a choice to focus on his finest hour and to not focus on the troubled, torturous path he traveled to get there. There is no Frederick Douglass here goading the president toward the more humanitarian position, no whites rioting at the prospect of being drafted to fight for Negro freedom.

On the 150th anniversary of the Emancipation Proclamation, we see unwitting testimony to our ongoing racial quagmire in the reductive ways we discuss the author of that document and the reasons for slavery's end. We speak volumes about our impasses in the glib, self-congratulatory way we discuss the election of the president most ostensibly tied to Lincoln's legacy.

It's important to note that Spielberg's film about the death of slavery all but ignores the Proclamation. That choice allowed the director—and his audience—to avoid both Lincoln's support for the mass colonization of free blacks and also the fact that the now hallowed Proclamation left nearly a million slaves in chains. It also made unnecessary any discussion of the uncomfortable truth that the Proclamation was devised in part as a war measure to ensure the loyalties of border states and deprive the Confederacy of its labor force, while leaving open the question of the South getting those very slaves back, should they return to the Union.

Instead, Spielberg's *Lincoln* centers on the comparatively clean moral lines surrounding the Thirteenth Amendment. But like a great deal of the popular ideas about Lincoln, the film confuses the president's strategic ideas with his moral ones, and in so doing shifts the landscape toward redemption. At issue here are not just Lincoln's actions, but the context for those actions and the motives behind them. The film highlights that Lincoln, in fighting for a constitutional amendment, freed four million enslaved blacks, as well as untold generations yet to be born. The film does not highlight that, by 1865, Lincoln would have known very well that permanently ending slavery would also deprive the readmitted Southern states of the labor force that had allowed it to nearly tear the country in half. The amendment was no less strategically motivated than the Proclamation had been. Arguing that the end of the war gave Lincoln leeway to strike the blow against slavery he'd patiently waited for overlooks the fact that Congress had attempted to pass the amendment in the previous session—when the outcome of the war was far less certain. After the amendment passed, Lincoln referred to it as a "king's cure for all the evils," but in his annual address given months earlier, in December 1864, he spoke of it as a prerogative of preserving the nation:

> *In a great national crisis like ours, unanimity of action among those seeking a common end is very desirable, almost indispensable. And yet no approach to such unanimity is attainable unless some deference shall be paid to the will of the majority simply because it is the will of the majority.* In this case the common end is the maintenance of the Union, and among the means to secure the end such will, through the election, is more clearly declared in favor of such Constitutional amendment. (*Emphasis added.*)

The strategic and moral benefits of Lincoln's actions are not mutually exclusive, but the need for a redemption figure makes us behave as if they are. The fact that black freedom occurred because a particular set of national interests aligned with ending slavery doesn't diminish the moral importance of it. Indeed, the moral high ground here is that Lincoln, unlike millions of Americans in both the South and the North, was able to recognize that slavery was not more important than the Union itself. This seems somehow insufficient to the definition of heroism today, but it shouldn't. The byproduct of our modern, mythical Lincoln is that he allows us to shift our gaze to one American who ended slavery rather than the millions who perpetuated and defended it. By lionizing Lincoln, we are able to concentrate on the death of an evil institution rather than its ongoing legacy. The paradox is that Lincoln's death enabled later generations to impatiently wonder when black people would cease fixating on slavery and just get over it.

When Obama cast himself in the mold of Lincoln in 2007, he could not have known how deeply he would find himself mired in the metaphor. As a recent Pew study revealed, our country is more divided along partisan lines today than at any point since they've been conducting studies. Basic demographic divisions—gender, race, ethnicity, religion, and class—do not predict differences in values more than they have in the past. Men and women, whites, blacks, and Hispanics, the highly religious and the less religious, and those with more and less education differ in many respects, but those differences have not grown in recent years, and for the most part they pale in comparison to the overwhelming partisan divide we see today. This is only partly because of the growth of cable news programs offering relentless blue-versus-red commentary and à la carte current events. It's also because party identity has become a stand-in for all the other distinctions the study explained.

That chasm is the stepchild of the sectionalism of Lincoln's era. Today, we are another House Divided, though the lines are now drawn more haphazardly. And this is where Obama and Lincoln part ways. In future feature films about the current era, it won't be the details of the president's life that will be redacted, but the details of our own. More specifically, it will be the details of those Americans who greeted Obama's reelection with secession petitions; those who reacted to the 2008 election by organizing themselves and parading racially inflammatory banners in the nation's capital; those who sought solace from demagogues and billionaire conspiracy theorists who demanded that a sitting president prove his own citizenship.

The heralded "Age of Obama" began with a sugar high of postracialism, but four years later the number of whites subscribing to explicitly racist ideas about blacks had *increased,* not diminished. The vision of a black person executing the duties of the nation's highest office was supposed to become mundane; we were supposed to take his identity for granted. Somewhere there was a little-voiced hope among black people that his simple existence as president would be a daily brief for our collective humanity, that we would be taken to be every bit as ordinary as the man occupying the Oval Office. At points in the last four years, it seemed as if we could live in a poetic moment, as if our founding documents could be taken at face value. But the numbers tell us it's not true. Many Americans have reacted to the promise of the Obama era as a threat, as a harbinger of the devaluing currency of whiteness. The problem is not that these people want to take their country back; it's that they were loath to share it in the first place. The recalcitrant racism of the Obama era will be as vexing to the story of American virtue as Lincoln's racial failings were to those of his era. Lincoln was not as flawless as we've been told, and we are not as virtuous as we've begun to tell ourselves.

To be clear, though, something in the nation has changed. At no point prior to 2008 could a presidential aspiration have been so effectively yoked to this yearning for a clear racial conscience. But beneath the high-blown, premature rhetoric of post-racialism lies the less inspirational fact that those changes were as much about math as they were about morality. Depending on your perspective, either we have reached a point of racial maturity that facilitated the election of an African American president or we've reached a point where a supermajority of black voters, a large majority of Latino and Asian ones, and a minority of white people are capable of winning a presidential election. Again, these ideas need not be mutually exclusive, but the need for clean lines and easy redemption makes us behave as if they are.

Lincoln's apotheosis inspired self-congratulation among whites and a backlash of doubt and outright disdain among blacks. Among many African Americans, a justifiable skepticism of Lincoln as the original Friend of the Negro has morphed into a broader dismissal of him altogether. But however conservative and incrementalist his policies seemed to them, and to many of us today, they were still far too radical for John Wilkes Booth and the millions who sympathized with him. Lincoln's death is further evidence that men who are ahead of their times have a tendency to die at the hands of men who are behind them. It is also proof that the simple sentiment that the Union was more important than slavery was, in its own right, radical. However far Lincoln was from advocating racial equality, his second inaugural address stands as a monument of national conscience:

Fondly do we hope, fervently do we pray, that this mighty scourge of war may speedily pass away. Yet, if God wills that it continue until all the wealth piled by the bond-men's two hundred and fifty years of unrequited toil shall be sunk, and until every drop of blood drawn with the lash, shall be paid by another drawn with the sword, as was said three thousand years ago, so still it must be said "the judgments of the Lord, are true and righteous altogether."

Indeed, the real problem is not that the nation has so consistently sought balm for its racial wounds, and drafted Lincoln—and Obama—for those purposes; it's the belief that we could be absolved from the past so cheaply. No Lincoln, not even an unfailingly moral one who was killed in service of a righteous cause, could serve as an antidote for ills that persisted, and continue to persist, for a century and a half after his demise. We find ourselves now in circumstances where actual elements of racial progress are jeopardized precisely because we've smugly accepted the idea of ourselves as racially progressive.

The Thirteenth Amendment states that "[n]either slavery nor involuntary servitude, except as a punishment for crime whereof the party shall have been duly convicted, shall exist within the United States, or any place subject to their jurisdiction." We are a nation in which a black president holds office while more than half a million duly convicted black men populate the prisons, and county and municipal jails hold hundreds of thousands more. The symbolic ideal of post-racialism masks a Supreme Court that may undermine affirmative action in higher education and the preclearance clause of the Voting Rights Act. Our most recent election saw both unprecedented black turnout and efforts at black voter suppression that resound with echoes of bad history. Black unemployment, even among the college-educated, remains vastly higher than it is for whites. (Among the more hideous hypocrisies of the recent election was Mitt Romney's cynical appeals to black Americans, pointing out that blacks have suffered disproportionately in the Obama economy. The black president, we were to believe, is now also responsible for racism in the labor market.)

Obama himself was wise to these contrasts as far back as 2008, when he gave the speech in Philadelphia that saved his political career.

Words on a parchment would not be enough to deliver slaves from bondage, or provide men and women of every color and creed their full rights and obligations as citizens of the United States. What would be needed were Americans in successive generations who were willing to do their part—through protests and struggle, on the streets and in the courts, through a civil war and civil disobedience and always at great risk—to narrow that gap between the promise of our ideals and the reality of their time.

The election of an African American president is a watershed in our history. But the takeaway is that what we do during these moments is somehow smaller than what we do between them, that our heroes are no better than we are, nor do they need to be. Harriet Tubman is often cited as saying she could have freed more blacks if only she'd been able to convince them they were slaves. In our own era, the only impediment to realizing the creed of "We Shall Overcome" is the narcotic belief that we already have.

POSTSCRIPT TO "LINCOLN DIED FOR OUR SINS"

I missed a key point in this piece. Steven Spielberg's *Lincoln* is really meant to highlight the ways in which even the loftiest of democratic objectives are subject to the sausage-making of the political process. Tony Kushner's script is ostensibly concerned with the dimensions of Lincoln's greatness. Rather than finding it in Lincoln's grand vision and dignified reserve, Kushner identifies it in his capacity for navigating the gutters of early American politics. His Lincoln is akin to Lyndon B. Johnson, another president whose ability to persuade, trade, intimidate, or outright bully friend and foe alike was key to the passage of landmark legislation that moved the nation closer to equality. That said, the Lincoln hagiography that I challenge in this piece is prominent enough to get in the way of Kushner's bigger point. He made a statement about us misunderstanding Lincoln's greatness; I challenged the need for Lincoln to be thought of as great in the first place.

Americans are, it has often been noted, generally less invested in questions of history than their counterparts around the world. There's an idea common among armchair historians that one strength of this nation, with its comparatively short two and a half centuries of existence, is its willingness to shrug off history. Where Europe is perceived as hidebound in tradition, with social stations rusted in place by aged habits and ideas, social mobility in the United States was enabled by this very lack of tradition. One side effect of this liberation, however, has been the nation's relative nonchalance about its own past. Lincoln is the glaring exception. There have been more books written about Lincoln than any other American. The country's investment in the sixteenth president is partly a product of the extraordinary circumstances of his life, his preternatural political abilities, the unequaled stakes of the time in which he governed, and the dramatic circumstances of his death. But part of that investment is also about the ideas I highlighted in this essay. Lincoln represents a kind of redemptive escape valve, a salve for Americans who can scarcely countenance that this nation's origins are entangled in the profound exploitation of the Africans kidnapped and dragged to these shores. Lincoln's grappling with the moral questions bound up in the nation's racial history make him an example that many contemporary white Americans cast as an ideal. Had I been born two hundred years ago, the white thinking goes, I would've been like Lincoln, not those cruel slaveholders. Black people indulge a parallel countermyth. Ashamed of the abject servility and humiliation imposed upon our ancestors by the regime of slavery, we at times imagine that, had we been born two hundred years earlier, we would have been more like Nat Turner than Uncle Tom.

The fact is that history is too often skewed toward the exceptions. We recognize Lincoln and Turner because they were atypical in their times. Had we been born two centuries ago, most of us—black or white—would have found ways to accommodate the moral contradictions of our time in order for us and those we loved to live as safely as possible. Even when those contradictions were abominable. We know this because of the ways in which we so often accommodate similar contradictions in our own times. Perhaps, in this hypothetical past, we would have sought to retain our integrity through small acts of defiance—an important tradition in its own right. But few of us would have been Lincoln or Turner—and that is precisely the point.

Lincoln's harshest black critics (the historian and journalist Lerone Bennett comes to mind) have often centered their criticism on his more backward racial ideas—his willingness to voice support for white supremacy in his campaign rhetoric, his tenuousness on matters of emancipation, his support for the idea of colonizing the emancipated black population. Part of this critique is less about Lincoln himself than it is about his most fervent supporters, who frame freedom as something bestowed upon the enslaved by the so-called Great Emancipator. By knocking Lincoln off his pedestal, they undercut the inane idea that the formerly enslaved owed him anything at all, even a thank-you, for his self-interested decision to end a practice that the nation should never have begun in the first place. For what it matters, not even Lincoln saw emancipation as an act of pure beneficence. He spoke of the enlistment of black soldiers in the Union cause as a transaction, one in which two self-interested parties—one seeking to preserve the nation and one seeking an end to bondage—struck a deal that, if successful, would achieve both ends. Kushner had this point about Lincoln the political operator right.

Against the sprawl of history, Lincoln's backwardness takes on smaller dimensions than the fact that he was a white man publicly grappling with these questions in the first place. He did so under duress, but he groped his way toward the light nonetheless. It is worth noting that among Lincoln's final public pronouncements was the magisterial second inaugural address, as subtle and stern a parsing of American morality as has ever been produced here. If there need be a case for Lincoln's greatness, it rests in the distance between the uncompromising language of that address and the contradictory, confused rhetoric that preceded it at other points in Lincoln's public career. His hand had been forced by history and the imperatives of politics. But no other philosopher of American life could have composed that address with a gun—figuratively or literally—pointed at their heads.

THE SEGREGATIONIST'S DAUGHTER

February 7, 2013

Among the lessons to be gleaned from the life of Essie Mae Washington-Williams is that truth need not be stranger than fiction; there are points where the two become nearly indistinguishable. Washington-Williams, who died this week at age eighty-seven, came to the public's attention a decade ago, when she announced that she was the daughter of the late Senator Strom Thurmond. A media crush and a memoir followed, most playing up the seemingly obvious irony of a black woman fathered by the most recognizable segregationist in twentieth-century politics. Yet only in the most benign of readings could his behavior be understood as contradictory. For all his rhetoric about preserving racial purity, interracial sex was not contrary to Thurmond's goals as a segregationist; on some level, it was entirely the point. His daughter's tale stirred public controversy but its themes had been enshrined, if ignored, in the history, fiction, and lore of American racial history.

James Baldwin once remarked that segregationists weren't truly driven by the cliché concern of preventing black men from marrying their daughters. Rather, he said, "You don't want us to marry your *wives'* daughters—we've been marrying *your* daughters since the days of slavery." This is a truth that is forgotten among whites and rarely spoken among blacks. Revelations of the type Washing-

Williams made in 2003 were shocking only to those privileged enough to not have this knowledge inflicted upon them personally or etched into their lineage and shaded—literally—into their family history.

In 2003, when the hazy borders between current events and reality TV were still intact, we processed the Washington-Williams story as a political scandal, albeit a posthumous one. But in truth this was an affair of an altogether different genus than the family-values pol caught in a brothel or the homophobic pastor found to be conducting a same-sex affair. Hypocrisy may be the price we pay for having our biases catered to in public, but Thurmond's actions weren't so much hypocritical as they were surreptitious: not uncommon, just unspoken.

The historian Darlene Clark Hine has written that a key if seldom-discussed factor in the Great Migration was the desire of black women to escape the sexual exploitation implicit in domestic work—a concern that had also driven enslaved women to run away.

> [In] Black women's migration across time, from the flights of runaway slaves in the antebellum period to the great migrations of the first half of the twentieth century . . . the most compelling motive for running, fleeing, migrating was a desire to retain or claim some control and ownership of their own sexual beings and the children they bore.

In the midst of Essie Washington-Williams's unburdening, it seemed callous to reflect upon the ways in which her story pointed to the sexual vulnerability of women domestic workers, how her mother's story was something closer to a rule than an exception.

Nor was it difficult to see in her story strains of Thomas Jefferson and Sally Hemings. The broad contours are similar: a powerful white political figure; an illicit sexual relationship with a black woman of vastly subordinate status; offspring who are, at best, tacitly acknowledged. The most substantial similarity lies in the response to these revelations: shock among white observers, little more than a raised eyebrow among many black ones. These stories were not about the failings of individual imperfect men but parables for an entire set of experiences.

And as with the tale of Hemings and Jefferson, the initial shock gave way to a version improbably tinged in sepia and set to harp strings. Washington-Williams's book, *Dear Senator: A Memoir by the Daughter of Strom Thurmond* (her mother is unmentioned in the title), implies that she owes her birth to a forbidden love between her parents. She was born to the twenty-two-year-old white scion of a powerful South Carolina family and a sixteen-year-old black domestic worker (likely just fifteen when she became pregnant). The question, of course, was not whether the women in these stories consented to these relationships but whether they could reasonably have chosen not to.

Following a meeting when Washington-Williams herself was sixteen, Thurmond assumed financial responsibility for his daughter. He appeared in her life as a remote figure, dispensing resources and the occasional oblique acknowledgment of his paternity over the next six decades, during which time he ran for president on the 1948 Dixiecrat ticket, frequently denounced racial intermixture, and, most memorably, filibustered the 1964 Civil Rights Act to prevent its passage by the Senate. His largesse may have betrayed a genuine attachment to his daughter, but Thurmond was a political operator. He also knew his money helped secure his secret at a point when it might have immolated his political standing.

Within certain blinkered quarters during that era, children of Washington-Williams's parentage were thought doomed to live tragic lives. Washington married Julius Williams, a black civil rights attorney who detested Thurmond so fervently that she initially kept her relationship to the senator secret from him. She earned a college degree, moved to Los Angeles, had children, and enjoyed a long career as an educator. The act of reconciling the failings of one's parents is rarely simple. Yet Washington-Williams's magnanimity toward Thurmond, even after six decades of silence, was striking, if not unsettling.

Her father was not an ambient racist, carried along by the provincial thinking of his times; he was dynamically racist, a man who helped shape and amplify those currents. That he had a black daughter doesn't simply complicate his legacy; it further damns it. In ways that run contrary to any parental creed, he worked to make the world a worse place for his child and her children. He was unable to extrapolate the humanity he saw in the teenage Essie Washington to a whole population who looked like her and shared her experiences. For her part, Washington-Williams seemed to have offered him amnesty on the most charitable of terms. If the story she told was meant to humanize her father, it tended, intentionally or not, to further elide her mother, of whom she spoke little, at least in public, and who died at the age of thirty-eight. Carrie Butler remains in the penumbra of history: obscured, but certainly not alone.

BOSTON AND THE PROBLEM WITH COLLECTIVE GUILT

April 20, 2013

Among the index of absurdities that defined this week were a terrorist act for which no one stepped forward to claim responsibility and a day in which no one seemed willing to take responsibility for the alleged terrorists themselves. Long before the nightmarish saga ended with Dzhokhar Tsarnaev in custody, Chechen government officials had rushed to point out that he and his brother had not lived in their country for many years, and that any impetus for them to behave as "bad guys" was rooted in poor parenting and American soil. Two uncles and an aunt distanced themselves from the boys in ways ranging from oblique to prosecutorial. Their estranged uncle, Ruslan Tsarni, denounced them in the most American of vernacular, using the one term perfect for cutting across ideological, ethnic, and social lines: "losers." If international terrorism seemed too grandiose a motive for his wayward kin, he neatly dispatched them as something lesser—haters who were unable to "settle themselves" in a new country and therefore struck out at those who had.

There was another, more troubling note. His nephews, Tsarni said, had brought shame upon the family and upon all Chechens. Collective guilt is an idea with fading resonance in this country—a good thing, in balance, however one feels about the reasons. Our bitter partisanship, for example, ensures that even our worst civic acts can be attributed to a convenient "they," not a shame-inducing "we." And though we think of ourselves as a nation of immigrants, many Americans are removed enough from identity-based communities to recoil at the idea that they'd be held accountable for someone else's crimes. But recent immigrants know that, even in a country founded upon the premise of individual rights, there is no guarantee that a person will be treated as an individual. This isn't solely a dynamic about immigration. For those with long enough memories, the ambiguous description of a "dark-skinned male" suspect brought to mind the 1989 Charles Stuart case—itself a case study in collective suspicion and guilt in the city of Boston. Stuart, a white store manager, fatally shot his pregnant wife and placed the blame on an imaginary black assailant. This week, there was not—as there was then—a massive arrest campaign in which race was the only criterion, but there was an immediate reliance upon old suspicions based on religion and ethnicity.

Friday was not the first time I'd heard this sentiment uttered in response to an act of terrorism—nor even the first time I'd heard it said about a Chechen. I was teaching American history in Moscow in 2010 when the subways there were bombed. Even a foreign observer like me could tell that Chechens occupied a precipitous place in the city. They did much of the essential manual labor but were also subject to a kind of casual disregard. Once, when I stopped to admire floral arrangements at a street kiosk, a Russian friend advised me, "These are done by Chechens and they know nothing of beauty." When I saw a group of young men mock-fighting on a subway platform, someone remarked that Chechens could be expected to behave in such ways. Those sentiments were amplified in the days after the Moscow bombing—in which two rural women were placed in explosive vests, put on subways, and then detonated by remote control—and I heard tales of Muslims refusing to come out in public for fear of retribution. In the wake of decades of struggle with Russia, there was a sense among Chechens in the city that blame for the bombings would be placed collectively upon their shoulders.

The circumstances in Moscow and Boston are very different. Russians and Chechens fought two bitter wars and share a history of hostility that dates back to the Tsarist times. And in the United States, few of us think of Chechens as a distinct group, if we think of them at all. According to the most recent available data, only 596 people identified themselves as being of North Caucasus origins on the 2000 census. But a casual glance at the front page of the *New York Post*—not to mention the immediate presumption of guilt directed at a Saudi national, himself a victim of the blast— confirms the bleak logic of Ruslan Tsarni's thinking. There's a pragmatic understanding that, even if you don't feel guilty for the actions of random individuals with whom you happen to share pigment or faith or language, there are surely outsiders who will assign it to you nonetheless.

Perhaps we have little concept of Chechens, but we've developed quite a defined concept of Muslims in the past eleven years. One reaction to being asked to think, for the first time, about who Chechens are seems to have been to answer "Muslims" and leave it at that, perhaps with variations like "jihadis" or "Islamic extremists." In the dizzy aftermath of September 11, Vladimir Putin even said as much, cozying up to George W. Bush and informing him that his Chechen problem was akin to our al-Qaeda concerns. Viewed through this lens, the actions attributed to the Tsarnaev brothers carry even more weight. A nation that knew next to nothing about Chechens last week might now view them in terms akin to those of a man who prosecuted two brutal wars against them. Every step in the sequence points at something that's broken. Two bombs went off this week. No one stepped forward to claim responsibility. Ruslan Tsarni worried that his nephews—one deceased, the other in custody—brought shame upon all Chechens. And it's all Muslims who have reason to fear that they'll bear the brunt of it.

THE MANY BATTLES OF HARRY BELAFONTE

November 11, 2013

Two days before his landslide victory in the mayoral election, Bill de Blasio received an endorsement that placed him in the company of John F. Kennedy, Eugene McCarthy, and Hugo Chávez. Before a packed sanctuary at the First Corinthian Baptist Church, in Harlem, Harry Belafonte—eighty-seven years old and using a cane, but possessed of undiminished elegance—spoke for fifteen minutes on behalf of the candidate. His endorsement, a bit of extemporized eloquence, detoured into a denunciation of the Koch brothers as contemporary Klansmen, "men of evil" who must be stopped. The proximity of Belafonte's remarks to Election Day spared de Blasio a Jeremiah Wright–level debacle, but he did issue an apology. (That a Belafonte endorsement would require an apology to offended parties from its intended beneficiary is an entirely predictable turn of events.)

We've become accustomed to the inflammatory pronouncements of late-stage celebrity males—Charlton Heston, Bill Cosby, Clint Eastwood—though their evolution into conservatives, curmudgeons, or cranks is usually explained as a function of age. Belafonte offers a variation on the theme: the senior celeb who grows more radical with time. His excoriation of George W. Bush as "the greatest terrorist in the world" was later revised, but only, Belafonte said, because he hadn't met all the other terrorists. Last summer, he criticized Jay-Z and Beyoncé for their meager social justice efforts and sparked, among other things, a cross-generational Twitter fight within black America. During the 2008 election, his criticism of Barack Obama was so lacerating that the senator asked him, "When are you going to cut me some slack?" Belafonte replied, "What makes you think that's not what I've been doing?"

Belafonte's embrace of Chávez led, indirectly, to his being disinvited from the funeral of his close friend Coretta Scott King by her children, whom he is currently suing. The King children are a litigious lot, and the three siblings have engaged in a good deal of semi-public feuding, but the clash with Belafonte, however foreseeable, is a disturbing one. Their zealous stewardship of their father's legacy has always skewed toward protecting its monetary value, while Belafonte very much sees himself as a keeper of the movement's insubordinate idealism. As a young man, Belafonte befriended Martin Luther King, Jr., and invested, quite literally, in the movement he led. The present legal battle concerns the ownership of several documents that belonged to Belafonte, including handwritten notes for a speech King was planning to deliver in Memphis, which were in his pocket on the day he was assassinated. Belafonte put the items up for auction in 2008, intending to donate the proceeds to an anti-gang-violence charity; the King children successfully blocked the auction, and he is now suing to establish his ownership of the materials.

Belafonte, who considered King one of his best friends, never reconciled himself to King's posthumous transition from symbol to brand. In his 2011 memoir, he wrote of the King Center for Nonviolent Social Change:

Nobel laureates are welcomed; younger, more cutting-edge scholars are not vigorously pursued. Now, under the leadership of Martin's children, it is basically a crypt with a reflecting pool, selling trinkets and memorabilia and books to tourists and students.

Belafonte's indignation is only partly fueled by loyalty to his martyred friend. He's also a man whose largesse underwrote a great deal of the work undertaken by King's Southern Christian Leadership Conference. He purchased the life insurance policy that was Coretta Scott King's sole source of income following her husband's assassination, and personally supported the family in the wake of the death. In 1955, Belafonte promised King that he would help the movement in any way he could; thirteen years later, he was helping King's widow pick out the suit he'd be buried in, and sitting next to her at the funeral service. Thirty-eight years later, King's children were withdrawing his invitation to their mother's funeral, presumably to avoid offending one of the other guests, George W. Bush.

There may be an inverse principle that works in history, in which the measure of one's significance can be determined by the status of one's nemeses. By that scale, Belafonte is indispensable. No minor figure manages to alienate the president of the United States, a pair of politically powerful billionaire siblings, the country's reigning entertainment power couple, and the scions of the most revered American activist of the twentieth century. Those are just the beefs Belafonte has ignited in his eighties.

The line running through all these episodes is that, while it may be a curse to live in interesting times, it's more painful to live in ironic ones. Belafonte's central conflict is not with any of these individuals but, rather, with the ethos that produced them. A younger Belafonte almost certainly imagined that, as he grew older, his once audacious political beliefs would increasingly be seen as moderate— the impossible demands of one generation becoming the overlooked entitlements of the next. Instead, history looks to have flowed in the opposite direction, and he now finds himself worried that the causes for which he sacrificed yielded fragile gains, whose imperiled state is all the more difficult to realize after the election of a black president. Belafonte now occupies a bitterly ironic position, an octogenarian radical whose politics are well to the left of many people half his age.

Belafonte's relationship with Chávez soured when he concluded that the regime was using his efforts to create trade opportunities between poor Venezuelan farmers and low-income communities in America as a cynical ploy to embarrass the United States. If nothing else, Belafonte has consistently chosen principle over pragmatism—which suggests that his endorsement is an ambivalent blessing for a politician. De Blasio is still enjoying the crush of elated attention that comes with an overwhelming victory, but, sooner or later, he will start to make the difficult decisions that come with the mayoralty. De Blasio may yet retain his blessing, but one thing is certain: Belafonte will not hesitate to let him know when it's been lost.

MANDELA AND THE POLITICS OF FORGIVENESS

December 6, 2013

In 1966, Senator Robert F. Kennedy delivered a speech at the University of Cape Town. He began by stating that he was there to talk about a country settled by the Dutch, which fought a bloody war of independence, and had then become an international pariah for its treatment of black people. He allowed a tense moment to pass and then added, "I'm here tonight to talk about the United States of America." To an extent greater than most Americans recognize, but which Nelson Mandela understood implicitly, the United States and South Africa are products of kindred histories: both founded by settlers, both emerged from wars to overthrow British colonialism, both forged national identities on their respective frontiers. Before the election of Barack Obama allowed this country, albeit briefly, to indulge the idea of post-racialism, Mandela was revered here as a proxy for the American past. His capacity to emerge from twenty-seven years in prison without bitterness broadcast the hope that this country's own racial trespasses might be forgiven.

If the American reverence for Mandela is at least partly self-interested, the country has not just wandered into someone else's story. Prior to becoming prime minister of South Africa, Jan Smuts had studied the issues of race and federalism at the heart of the

American Civil War in hopes of avoiding the same outcome. Years later, the architecture of apartheid was explicitly modeled on America's Jim Crow system of segregation. Decades before Reagan rejected sanctions against the regime or Dick Cheney denounced Mandela as a terrorist, this country had planted its feet firmly on the wrong side of South African history. When Mandela declined to press charges for the past, it was not just white South Africans he was absolving.

The twentieth century produced a tiny number of figures—King, Gandhi—who changed world history through the weight of their moral example, and an equally small number of heads of state—Wałęsa, Havel—whose emergence was as intimately tied to a collective realization of freedom. But only Nelson Mandela's name would appear on both lists. In the tide of remembrances that began Thursday, Mandela has invariably been compared to Martin Luther King, Jr. President Obama borrowed King's language about the moral arc of the universe bending toward justice in his homage to Mandela. Yet it's one thing to make forgiveness an element of a humanitarian movement; it's quite another to enact it as public policy. King sagely and sincerely presented racial reconciliation as a function of Christian love; Mandela knew that beyond his own spiritual inclinations racial reconciliation was an imperative of national survival.

Mandela's release from prison and the collapse of apartheid were direct consequences of the demise of the Soviet Union; the South African regime could no longer rely upon its anti-communism as a counterbalance to its miserable human rights record. Like the civil rights movement in the United States, the racial struggles in South Africa were intertwined with the efforts of that country's communists to build radical cross-racial coalitions. (It is not coincidental that, beyond their common faith in forgiveness, King and Mandela both saw their efforts dismissed as part of a left-wing conspiracy.) King's activism was informed by the organizing insights of former communists like Bayard Rustin and Stanley Levison. Mandela's formative relationship was with Joe Slovo, of the South African Communist Party, which had been an enemy of apartheid for decades. (Slovo's wife, Ruth First, was killed in 1982 when the South African police sent her a letter bomb.) On the other side, the collapse of the USSR—long a supporter of independence movements on the African continent—halved the political options of any emerging black-led government that would take root in South Africa. The irony of the negotiations between former South African president F. W. de Klerk and Mandela, his successor, is that, despite their vastly differing histories, they arrived at the bargaining table for precisely the same reason: the end of the Cold War left them with few other options.

It's also worth thinking about Mandela as simply the most successful of his generation of anticolonial radicals, many of whose names are scarcely known in this country. Those peers of his who are known—Castro and Arafat, for instance—are widely reviled. King has become the default comparison for Mandela, but for a large swath of his life the more apt American parallel was the late-life Malcolm X. His advocacy of armed struggle against the apartheid government was not an isolated foray into radicalism; it was consistent with the tactics of his cohort. The forces that pushed the African National Congress toward violent engagement were akin to the forces that inspired the Muslim Brotherhood in Egypt.

Mandela's twenty-seven years in prison condemned the South African regime in a way few could have predicted at the time of his sentencing. But it also allowed him to view the trajectory of other anticolonial movements from the sidelines. When he was sworn in as president, he had the perspective of three decades of postcolonial history, much of it validating the idea that reconciliation held more promise than the decidedly less charitable route that states like Zimbabwe took. No figure could garner Mandela's moral standing by simply pantomiming forgiveness out of necessity. He believed in the redemptive power of forgiveness. But he also recognized that it was the only route that lay between civil war and the mass exodus of the moneyed, educated class of white people who were integral to the economy.

Contrary to the broad narratives about his tenure, that move was not universally lauded in South Africa or abroad. Despite its overlapping relationship with South Africa's Communist Party, the ANC commonly found itself outflanked by more radical black organizations. After apartheid was dismantled, those elements viewed Mandela's emphasis on reconciliation as placating whites at the expense of the black South Africans who remained exiled at the economic periphery. In the United States, it was not uncommon to hear his allies in African American political circles—some of whom had spent decades fighting for his freedom—grumble that the "new" Mandela was too cozy with corporations that had shown little concern for human rights issues during apartheid. But it was difficult to hear the strain of discontent given the decibel of the applause.

It's entirely reasonable that the first black president of the United States began his public career agitating on behalf of the man who became the first black president of South Africa. It's also consistent that Barack Obama emerged as a presidential contender on the strength of the Mandela-esque speech he delivered to the 2004 Democratic National Convention, in which he opined that there was no black America or white America, simply the United States of America. Such sentiment was no truer in post-apartheid South Africa than it was in the United States that night, but it does suggest the political potency of redemption. Mandela has been praised in this country largely for the moral principles he calls to mind. A good part of that adoration, though, is owed to the moral felonies he allowed this country to forget.

It was Mandela's good fortune that his moment inverted the demands commonly placed upon a politician's shoulders. His country needed him to publicly and explicitly act on his firmest convictions, not bend them on the altar of expediency. Mandela emerged at that rare point in history where idealism and pragmatism were practically indistinguishable.

WHAT WE TALK ABOUT WHEN WE TALK ABOUT REPARATIONS

May 29, 2014

A century and a half ago, after the start of the Civil War, the federal government took up the question of reparations for slavery. The matter had been under discussion for years, both in the corridors of power and in the abolitionist movement, but it was only in 1862—with Congress dominated by Republicans after most Democratic members had joined the Confederacy—that it was possible to pass the Compensated Emancipation Act. It was the sole instance in which slavery reparations were authorized—and it compensated *slaveholders* in Washington, D.C., for the cost of emancipating their human chattel. The enslaved—the cornerstone of the South's economy, the collateral that allowed Northern lenders to profit from the cotton trade, the involuntary producers of the raw material around which the textile industry was built—were given nothing but a deeply compromised facsimile of freedom.

Ta-Nehisi Coates's magisterial essay in this month's *Atlantic* has reintroduced the subject of reparations. But it would be a mistake to assume that it ever completely disappeared between that earlier episode, when the federal government disbursed funds to whites to offset the inconvenience of democracy, and our present moment, in which white families earn on average two dollars for every dollar earned by black ones. Coates's sixteen-thousand-word story is a tour through the economic consequences of discrimination, which have compounded, over decades, into a kind of racial windfall for white Americans—so securely possessed that it is all but invisible, and incapable of being revoked by anything short of a massive redistributive program.

During an interview earlier this week with *BuzzFeed*, Shani Hilton asked Coates why he thought the essay had attracted so much attention—it set new records for traffic at *The Atlantic*'s website. Coates basically shrugged, and tossed the question to the audience. ("Because you wrote the hell out of it," came one response.) But it is not a coincidence that this piece has resonated at this particular point in our history. As we near the end of the Obama administration, it has become possible to estimate the yield of the first black presidency—and the dividends are far smaller than many had hoped.

Consider the fact that, when the president unveiled his My Brother's Keeper initiative, designed to help "young men and boys of color facing tough odds reach their full potential," he took pains to explain that its funding would come entirely from private sources. It's not an indictment of Obama to observe that philanthropy, in this context, is effectively the opposite of reparations: it's money given voluntarily for social betterment, not issued as recompense for a wrong. But it does say a great deal about the moment he inhabits, defined in part by the ersatz sincerity of our repeated calls to "move beyond race," even as the president is dogged by ludicrous charges that his healthcare reform was an attempt at stealth reparations.

Even in early 2008, at that heady moment when the thought of a black president became a real possibility, there was a cynical murmur among African Americans that Obama's election—like so many other examples of putative racial progress—would be widely understood as a kind of gift to black people. Jonathan Chait, of *New York*, betrayed that tendency earlier this spring, in the midst of a heated debate with Coates on the subject of black pathology. Chait argued, from on high:

It is hard to explain how the United States has progressed from chattel slavery to emancipation to the end of lynching to the end of legal segregation to electing an African-American president if America has "rarely" been the ally of African-Americans and "often" its nemesis. It is one thing to notice the persistence of racism, quite another to interpret the history of black America as mainly one of continuity rather than mainly one of progress.

This kind of rhetoric is akin to an abusive husband who cites the number of times he stopped beating his wife as a testament to his own high character. The tendency, in selective recollections of history, is to choose the version that looks most like an alibi—and it is for this reason that the conversation Coates has restarted is not really about reparations. It is, more fundamentally, about acknowledging the bastard history that would warrant reparations in the first place.

The unspoken divide between black people and white people—whether over reparations, affirmative action, or the question of paying NCAA athletes—comes down to a question of history. In one version, that history appears as an incremental movement toward equality after a long night of discrimination; in the other, history looks like a balance sheet, and the cumulative debits of sanctioned theft, enforced poverty, and scant opportunity far outweigh the inconsistent credits of goodwill. Few whites recall, for instance, that General William Sherman, during his March to the Sea, issued orders mandating the redistribution of land seized from Confederates, in forty-acre parcels, to newly emancipated black families. But within black America, that fact—and the fact that the orders were revoked following Lincoln's assassination—is common knowledge, recalled with the bitterness of an outstanding debt.

Absent an understanding of this past, it's possible—even entirely reasonable—to conclude that affirmative action represents a full recompense for the social engineering that produced a disproportionately black underclass in the United States. To the extent that the history remains obscured, the narrative looks like a lineage of failed handouts to a feckless and troublesome population, never quite capable of pulling themselves up, and mired in their own self-defeating ways. These deletions in our own history deliver various national oddities, like an overwhelmingly white Tea Party movement that is fixated on government encroachment on liberty and yet has almost no regard for the concerns of African Americans, whose history is defined by the government-sanctioned theft of their freedom.

Congressional Republicans were certainly satisfied with themselves after passing the 1862 Emancipation Act: they had leveraged the power of government to end the scourge of slavery, and achieved it so cleverly that the phantom hope for compensation might entice slaveholding states to remain within the Union. Lincoln's reputation as the greatest American president has much to do with his eloquence, fortitude, and foresight—but a portion of the esteem for him is derived from the fact that his Emancipation Proclamation enabled generations of Americans to focus on that singular act of ending slavery, not the two and a half centuries in which this government and the colonies that preceded it had allowed human bondage to persist. Michele Bachmann's statement that the founders "worked tirelessly" to end slavery was only factually wrong; emotionally, it was a perfect rendering of the past to which most Americans—even those who know otherwise—subscribe out of emotional necessity.

Barack Obama is also a tall and thin attorney who served in the Illinois legislature, but this isn't the only reason he can't escape a comparison with Lincoln. There is, in his two terms, a similar volume of work left undone, despite the apparent racial hallmarks of his presidency. From the vantage point of 2014, history was seemingly lying in wait for Obama from the moment he was sworn in. The pattern established by emancipation—in which black progress was valued chiefly in proportion to its ability to assuage white unease, in which self-congratulation became a national motif—remains with us.

The battles of the civil rights movement were enormously contentious and divisive until they began to achieve victories; at that point, they became a useful means of allowing the country to forget its complicity in the state of affairs that had made the movement necessary in the first place. We know, or ought to know, how this story invariably ends. It's worth recalling that Lincoln, in his initial draft of the Emancipation Proclamation, sought the repatriation of the freed slaves—thus rewarding black people who had helped save the Union with exile, while granting continued residence to the Confederates who had tried to overthrow the government. In 2005, the United States Senate offered an apology for the decades during which it did nothing to halt the tide of lynchings that claimed the lives of nearly 3,400 black people between 1880 and 1920. Yet that apology—which was tied directly to government inaction that facilitated terrorism directed at a subject population—was not accompanied by any order for compensation to the descendants of those victims. Once again, the point was not contrition, merely the appearance of it.

We are discussing reparations at this moment because in two years Barack Obama will leave the White House, having repaired the economic collapse that greeted his inauguration, but with African Americans still unemployed at a rate twice that of whites, and struggling to see how this world differs from the status quo ante. Those who saw Obama's election as redemption for slavery were off by fourteen decades: his election was supposed to expiate sins much closer to the surface, and therefore far more difficult, and far too expensive, to confront.

The point of Coates's essay—and, ultimately, the point of this conversation, despite the political impossibility of enacting reparations—is a broader understanding of black poverty as the product of public policy and private theft facilitated by racism. The belief that blacks have been given too much is made possible by the refusal to countenance how much was actually taken away in the first place.

RUBY DEE, 1922–2014

June 13, 2014

Long before her death this week, at the age of ninety-one, Ruby Dee had come to be something of a load-bearing column in American culture—recognizably essential to that portion of it most closely identified with African Americans, but also upholding something bigger. And there is the sense that her absence, coming in such close conjunction with the death of her peer Maya Angelou, leaves something less wieldy and in need of shoring up. Between 1946 and 2013, Dee appeared in more than a hundred films, plays, and television shows, but her legacy can be only partially understood through her credits. Dee, along with Ossie Davis, her husband of fifty-seven years, was an actor—in both meanings of the word—during the civil rights movement. She was in the generation of artists, few of whom remain among us, whose work served as a brief for the ideal of racial equality, and who formed part of the cultural front of the era.

Dee was born in Ohio but grew up on 137th Street and Seventh Avenue in Harlem, three blocks from where the Schomburg Center for Research in Black Culture now stands. She and her husband (until his death, in 2005) were mainstays of the center; I happened to be there on Thursday afternoon, and, as word of her death made its way through the building, clusters of staff and visitors began sharing memories of their encounters with the couple. It was a fitting venue for such remembrances in more ways than one. Before the Schomburg Center was built, the space housed the American Negro Theatre, a repertory company best known for launching the careers of Sidney Poitier and Harry Belafonte. In 1940, a teenage Ruby Wallace (she took the surname Dee after her first marriage) wandered into the building with the recalcitrant notion that she would pursue a career in the theater. The arts are seldom hailed for their career practicality, but in prewar New York, when blacks were locked out of even many blue-collar professions, it required a particular brand of audacity to embark on something as ephemeral as acting. She'd broached her interest in drama with one of her teachers at Hunter College High School, she remembered, only to be told that she couldn't be cast because that year's production didn't feature any maids. (The same year, Hattie McDaniel won an Oscar for her role as a house servant in *Gone with the Wind*.) Much later, in a memoir she co-wrote with Davis, she recalled her first audition at the American Negro Theatre:

> After I don't remember how long, I came out of the backstage area, which I discovered later, was to become the dressing room. I felt cold. One knee trembled. My throat didn't belong to me. Howard began to read. Although breathing is considered a very natural and ordinary activity, there are times when you can forget how. No matter that I'd read, played the piano and violin and even danced in front of people, the emotional attack was severe . . . As I left they were talking as if I had never been there. I ran into this below-ground alley, mounted the steps, ran up 135th street all the way to 137th and 7th avenue, apartment 52, plunked down on the couch and pretended I hadn't even gone out.

She managed to land the part despite herself. Six years later, she was cast in a play called *Jeb,* opposite a gangly newcomer she thought had "picked out his clothing from a Salvation Army bin with his eyes closed." She went on to marry her castmate in 1948, and she and Davis began a nearly six-decade-long personal and artistic collaboration that earned a degree of public reverence quite distinct from the usual fatuous fondness for celebrity coupledom. By the time many people of my generation first became aware of them, in Spike Lee's 1989 film *Do the Right Thing*, they were spoken of in tandem: Ossie Davis and Ruby Dee, the eight syllables running together in the way we usually reserve for law partnerships or musical duos. The marvel at their marriage was based in part on their mutual admiration, which had not been effaced by the passing of decades, but, particularly among African Americans, their union was also seen as a kind of emblem of possibility against great odds. (Many people now see the Obamas' marriage in a similar way.) At the time of Davis's death, they had shared more than thirty joint credits in theater, television, and film, and had co-hosted a radio program for four years in the seventies. They were also co-emcees at the 1963 March on Washington. Their work as activists brought them into contact with a widening circle of artists and radicals that included Paul Robeson, W. E. B. Du Bois, and Malcolm X, who defied a Nation of Islam prohibition against theater to attend one of their plays. Years later, in the wake of his assassination, the couple stayed up all night revising versions of Malcolm X's eulogy, which Davis delivered at the Faith Temple Church in Harlem.

In 1960, Dee starred opposite Poitier in the original production of Lorraine Hansberry's *A Raisin in the Sun,* which became a major theatrical hit, furthering her increasingly substantial artistic reputation. She worked steadily throughout the decade and was one of a small number of actors who made the transition from civil rights–era fare into the more confrontational work of the Blaxploitation era, in the seventies. In the eighties, she wrote children's books and published *My Last Good Nerve,* a collection of short essays and poems. And she kept appearing in dozens of plays and films. I had the occasion to see Ruby Dee perform, twelve years ago, in a small theatrical production in Atlanta. She was cast as an imperious 1960s-era community leader trying to organize a presidential visit to a blighted Philadelphia neighborhood. She played the character with a cultivated reserve that was at once credible and completely superficial, recalling the contradictions in the lives of a generation raised to believe personal dignity was among the most potent weapons against segregation. I remember being convinced by the performance, but more impressed that she'd embodied a phenomenon that is seldom spoken about. Such humanizing of people who remain invisible in plain view was central to her work, evidence that audacity is sometimes its own best reward.

WHAT I SAW IN FERGUSON

August 14, 2014

Nothing that happened in Ferguson, Missouri, on the fourth night since Michael Brown died at the hands of a police officer there, dispelled the notion that this is a place where law enforcement is capable of gross overreaction. Just after sundown on Wednesday, local and state officers filled West Florissant Avenue, the main thoroughfare, with massive clouds of tear gas. They lobbed flash grenades at protesters who were gathered there to demand answers, and, at times, they just propelled them down the street. That they ordered the crowd to disperse was not noteworthy. That the order was followed by successive waves of gas, hours after the protests ended, became an object lesson in the issues that brought people into the streets in the first place. Two journalists, Wesley Lowery of *The Washington Post* and Ryan Reilly of *The Huffington Post*, and a St. Louis alderman, Antonio French, were arrested. (The journalists were let go without charges; the alderman, as his wife told reporters, was released after being charged with unlawful assembly.) What transpired in the streets appeared to be a kind of municipal version of shock and awe; the first wave of flash grenades and tear gas had played as a prelude to the appearance of an unusually large armored vehicle, carrying a military-style rifle mounted on a tripod. The message of all of this was something beyond the mere maintenance of law and order: it's difficult to imagine how officers, armored with what looked like a mobile military sniper's nest, could quell the anxieties of a community outraged by allegations regarding the excessive use of force. It revealed itself as a raw matter of public intimidation.

Whatever happened to Michael Brown in the moments before he died has become secondary to what the response to his death has revealed. The name of the officer who shot him remains unknown. Even the number of times that Brown was shot has not been disclosed, despite the completion of a preliminary autopsy. Jon Belmar, the St. Louis County chief of police, justified withholding the officer's name by citing a deluge of threats against the department and noting that he has not been charged with a crime. In the same press conference, Belmar released the name of a nineteen-year-old young man who was shot in the head by a police officer during the previous night, who Belmar said brandished a firearm during a protest. The young man remains in critical condition, but, if he survives, he will be charged with felony assault of a police officer. Belmar stated that he saw no reason to doubt the officer's version of the events.

Two days earlier, the police department had pledged to investigate Brown's death while simultaneously stating that the shooting was the result of a struggle in which Brown allegedly went for an officer's weapon. They had, at that point, not interviewed the witnesses who claimed that Michael Brown was shot down while running away or attempting to surrender. Inside of a week, two black teenagers have been shot by police and, in both instances, the bureaucratic default setting has favored law enforcement, fueling a perception that the department is either inept or beholden to a certain nonchalance about the possibility of police brutality.

I watched the events that led up to the eruption of tear gas with Etefia Umana, an activist who is chairman of the board of an organization called Better Family Life, and who lives about fifteen hundred feet from the spot where Brown was shot. Umana explained to me that the durable anger in Ferguson is fueled by the enigma of the officer's identity and the perceived possibility that, should the department fail to bring charges against him, his name may never be known. Umana, who is forty-three years old, has worked on grassroots development projects in the area for the past twenty-six years, but even he has been surprised by the depth of the anger about Brown's death. "There's not a tradition of unrest in St. Louis," he said to me. "Even in the sixties, when the rest of the country was exploding, you didn't have that kind of thing here. And if there was some kind of problem it almost never lasted more than a day." Neither the police nor many of the residents expected the fury to remain undimmed over the past four days. When I spoke to Umana and Malik Ahmed, the CEO of Better Family Life, they acknowledged that the anonymity of the officer may have something to do with the death threats, but said that it also would make it easier for the department to avoid scrutiny until an official narrative has been crafted. "Nobody out here believes that young man actually went for the officer's gun," Ahmed told me.

The people who live in Canfield Green, the apartment complex where Brown was shot while on his way to visit his grandmother, not only witnessed his death but were subjected to an undignified wake: his prone figure sprawled on the street for four hours in the unforgiving August sun, with blood on the asphalt—an indignity in sharp contrast with the quick departure of the officer from the scene. "This was brazen," Umana said to me. "It was done out in the open." Better Family Life arranged for a bus with volunteer social workers and psychologists to be stationed near the spot to help community members cope with the trauma.

The police rejected the idea of a curfew during a press conference on Wednesday afternoon, but suggested that protests should be finished before sundown. Unofficially, people believed that protests would be forcibly shut down after dark. Sporadic looting on Sunday night had left even some of the residents edgy about what might happen if protests went unchecked late into the evening. Wesley Bell, a black law professor who this summer ran unsuccessfully for a county council seat representing Ferguson, told me, "the narrative changed after they began looting," making some people sympathetic to highly aggressive policing. Bell and LaRhonda Williams, who works in Ferguson, didn't believe that the violence was a product of the town's own residents. "The people who are doing this are not even from here," Williams told me. Ahmed took a different view. "The civic leaders and the middle class are pushing this not-in-my-backyard narrative," he said. "This is homegrown. The clock is ticking and the time is late. This situation has been thirty years in the making." Better Family Life's largest program is an annual warrant amnesty that attracts between three and four thousand people who come out for a chance to have arrest warrants suspended and court fees renegotiated. The program is a window into the intertwined economic and law enforcement issues underlying the protests. Fees for minor infractions become their own, escalating, violations. "We have people who have warrants because of traffic tickets and are effectively imprisoned in their homes," he said. "They can't go outside because they'll be arrested. In some cases people actually have jobs but decide the threat of arrest makes it not worth trying to commute outside their neighborhood." (This phenomenon, increasingly common, is one that Sarah Stillman has written about for *The New Yorker*.)

High among the redundancies on display in Ferguson is that Tracy Martin, whose son Trayvon was killed by a neighborhood watch volunteer two years ago, agreed three weeks ago to participate in an annual Peace Fest event scheduled for Sunday. Martin, who is from the area, will be appearing in an atmosphere radically different from the one that was anticipated. Two years ago, national protests raged as people counted the number of days that had lapsed with no arrest in the killing of Trayvon Martin. In a parking lot just outside the neighborhood of the protests in Ferguson, I passed a car with the words "Who shot Mike Brown? 72 hours" painted on the side.

Late in the afternoon on Wednesday, the armored vehicles rolled into place just beyond the charred shell of the QuikTrip gas station that was burned on the first night of protests. Police, some outfitted in riot gear, others in military fatigues, barricaded the streets. At least one of them draped a black bandanna over his face; others covered their badges. Two hundred feet away, a local church group blared gospel music from a sound truck, hoping to quell tensions. Half a dozen students performed a dance routine punctuated by calls for justice in the Brown case. Near the front, a handful of young men jeered the police officers. One woman with an infant in a stroller walked up to the police barricade and screamed her contempt. A few people held signs comparing Ferguson to Gaza.

Umana, who is visually impaired and can't navigate the streets at night, stood just off to the left of the front line. "They're going to set it off out here just as soon as the sun sets," he told me. His seventy-one-year-old mother stood nearby despite his periodic pleas for her to return to their home.

At 8:22 P.M., the police began demanding that the crowd stay twenty-five feet away from them and their vehicles. A voice in the crowd shouted, "Michael Brown was thirty-five feet away when you killed him!" I stood near a cluster of journalists, but less than two hours after Lowery and Reilly had been arrested, nothing suggested that the police there would make distinctions between the people protesting and those who were covering it. Officers demanded that we move farther back, as well. People began chanting, "Hands up—don't shoot!" Ten minutes later, the sound of breaking glass was heard and the police demanded that the crowd disperse. Only seconds after that I saw a half dozen canisters launch into the air and the streets were bathed in the strobe lights of flash grenades.

The crowd scattered into the surrounding subdivisions as a haze of white smoke drifted outward through the neighborhood. Some, choked by the fumes, covered their eyes and coughed by the side of the road. Umana grabbed my arm and we ran into a nearby park. The protest dispersed immediately; still, the streets were tear-gassed for the next two hours.

The area just north of the protest borders a quiet middle-class neighborhood of precisely trimmed lawns and towering oaks, the type of community that, under other circumstances, would be pointed to as evidence of black social mobility. On this night, a thick haze drifted through the area, a chemical fog rolling in. Because the main streets cut a semicircle through the neighborhood and intersect with West Florissant in two places, the cloud on the main street effectively barricaded the entire development. Police stopped anyone but residents from entering, but the tear gas also prevented the people who were already there from getting out. Umana invited me into his home; outside, clusters of protesters and journalists wandered the side streets, hemmed in for hours. One homeowner walked out of his house to find a spent flash grenade on his lawn. An armored truck rolled down the street, a flume of tear gas issuing from the back.

The day began with questions about why a young man was killed just days before he was due to begin college. It ended as a referendum on the militarization of American police forces. There is a feedback loop of recrimination playing in the streets of Ferguson. With the thinnest of rationales, the police here responded to community anger in the self-justifying language of force, under circumstances that call for a more humane tongue.

BETWEEN THE WORLD
AND FERGUSON

August 26, 2014

When I was eighteen, I stumbled across Richard Wright's poem "Between the World and Me." The poem, a retelling of a lynching, shook me, because while the narrator relays the details in the first person, the actual victim of that brutish ritual is another man, unknown to him and unknown to us. The poem is about the way in which history is an animate force, and how we are witnesses to the past, even to that portion of it that transpired before we were born. He writes,

> The dry bones stirred, rattled, lifted, melting themselves
> into my bones.
> The grey ashes formed flesh firm and black, entering into
> my flesh.

Nothing save random fortune separated the fate of the man who died from that of the one telling the story. The journalists Errin Haines and Isabel Wilkerson have both written compellingly about the long shadow of lynching. It is, too often, a deliberately forgotten element of the American past—one that is nonetheless felt everywhere in Ferguson, Missouri, where protests followed the shooting of Michael Brown, who was eighteen years old, by a police officer. One can't make sense of how Brown's community perceived those events without first understanding the way that neglected history has survived among black people—a traumatic memory handed down, a Jim Crow inheritance.

It took sixteen days for Brown's body to be buried, an extended postscript that included three separate autopsies, the emergence of dueling interpretations of his last moments, and the resolution of precisely nothing about how race, media, and policing operate in the United States. A year ago, people gathered in anticipation of a verdict in the trial of George Zimmerman, the man who killed Trayvon Martin. During that case, images of people wearing hoodies, as Martin had when he was shot, proliferated on social media. This month, it has been portraits of people with their hands raised, in recognition of a number of witness accounts that Brown tried to surrender before being shot by police officer Darren Wilson. (Wilson, according to press reports, has told people that Brown was running at him.) The idea, in both instances, is that, like Wright's narrator, any of us could be Martin, Brown, or one of the hundreds of others who have died under questionable circumstances. There is a disturbing sense that this is how we spend our summers now, submerged in outrage, demonstrating, yet again, the hard parameters of public sympathy and the damnable, tiresome burden of racism.

In the days after 9/11, it was common to hear people say that it was the first time Americans had really experienced terrorism on their own soil. Those sentiments were historically wrong, and willfully put aside acts that were organized on a large scale, had a political goal, and were committed with the specific intention of being nightmarishly memorable. The death cult that was lynching furnished this country with such spectacles for a half century. (The tallies vary, but, by some estimates, there were 3,400 lynchings in the decades between the end of Reconstruction and the civil rights era.) We know intuitively, not abstractly, about terrorism's theatrical intent. The sight of Michael Brown, sprawled on Canfield Drive for four hours in the August sun, dead at the hands of an officer who was unnamed for a week, recalled that memory. It had the effect of reminding that crowd of spontaneous mourners of their own refuted humanity. A single death can be understood as a collective threat. The media didn't whip up these concerns among the black population; history did that.

For fifteen days this month, people marched in heat and thunderstorms, amid tear gas, despite the warnings of police styled as a militia, undeterred by the tear gas or the obstinacy of the local bureaucracy. They persisted despite the taint that opportunistic violence and looting imposed upon their efforts.

Linda Chavez wondered on Fox News whether "the 'unarmed teen' mantra" really fit Brown, who was six feet four and nearly three hundred pounds and had been caught on video shoplifting—and, it perhaps bears repeating, was a teen, and was unarmed. Chavez was roundly criticized, but she was really only guilty of saying aloud what many others have thought. Whatever happened or did not happen between Michael Brown and Darren Wilson on a winding side street, in the middle of the afternoon, in a nondescript outpost on the edge of a midsized city—whatever we imagine we know of the teenager—the salient fact is that he did not live long enough to cultivate his own answers.

I spent eight days in Ferguson, and in that time I developed a kind of between-the-world-and-Ferguson view of the events surrounding Brown's death. I was once a linebacker-sized eighteen-year-old, too. What I knew then, what black people have been required to know, is that there are few things more dangerous than the perception that one *is* a danger. I'm embarrassed to recall that my adolescent love of words doubled as a strategy to assuage those fears; it was both a pitiable desire for acceptance and a practical necessity for survival. I know, to this day, the element of inadvertent intimidation that colors the most innocuous interactions, particularly with white people. There are protocols for this. I sometimes let slip that I'm a professor or that I'm scarcely even familiar with the rules of football, minor biographical facts that stand in for a broader, unspoken statement of reassurance: there is no danger here. And the result is civil small talk and feeble smiles and a sense of having compromised. Other times, in an elevator or crossing a darkened parking lot, when I am six feet away but the world remains between us, I remain silent and simply let whatever miasma of stereotype or fear might be there fill the void.

Fuck you, I think. *If I don't get to feel safe here, why should you?*

POSTSCRIPT TO "BETWEEN THE WORLD AND FERGUSON"

Late in the summer of 2014, when the activist Al Sharpton was made aware of the situation unfolding in Ferguson, he purportedly remarked that he would go there "as soon as someone tells me where it is." The events touched upon in this piece transformed Ferguson from a nondescript Missouri suburb known mostly to locals into shorthand for the American crisis of race and policing. Michael Brown's death at the hands of Officer Darren Wilson recalled those holographic paintings that show completely different images to the viewer depending upon where they are standing when they look at it. For a portion of the public, nothing mattered beyond the fact of Brown's size and presumed strength and the fact that he appeared to have engaged in some sort of verbal conflict with the officer who eventually shot him dead. For others, many of them black, the facts of Brown's death could not be separated from the context in which it occurred. Ferguson's historic existence as a "sundown town"—a community that prohibited black people from being there after dark—was part of a long, unbroken racial inheritance, one that explained not only the contemporary problems of brutal policing but the substandard educational and healthcare outcomes there as well. It was notable to me that, when Democratic governor Jay Nixon arrived in Ferguson to talk about the investigation into Brown's death, the residents asked him as many questions about unemployment and education as they did about policing.

In the fall of that year, a grand jury declined to indict Darren Wilson on murder charges. The decision fit into a general pattern of reluctance to indict police officers for the use of force in their official duties, but the news sparked outrage on South Florissant

Road, where demonstrators had gathered in anticipation of the decision. A throng of police in riot gear descended upon the street, protecting the precinct and the adjoining commercial district. West Florissant, on the black side of town, had scarcely any police presence. This had the effect of deflecting the fury of the crowd from the white areas back into the neighborhood where Brown died. I walked down West Florissant, witness to the impotent fury and destruction as bullets whizzed around the street. (At least one driver cruised down the thoroughfare, casually firing shots at shop windows and establishments as he went by.) The local pharmacy and other businesses were set afire. The system, it appeared, had made its point exceedingly clear.

The difference between those who saw Brown's death as a cut-and-dry incident and those who understood it as part of a much bigger complex of problems could be seen in other places. In the aftermath of the riots following Brown's death, Attorney General Eric Holder announced that the Department of Justice's Civil Rights Division would launch a federal investigation. The possibility that the Department of Justice would deliver some form of justice was enough to forestall additional violence in the intervening week. The March 2015 DOJ report, however, largely validated Darren Wilson's claim that Brown had reached into his vehicle and struck him in the moments before the fatal rounds were fired. Moreover, the autopsy findings cast doubt on the contention that Brown's hands had been in the air when he was shot. On its face, it appeared, as then *Washington Post* columnist Jonathan Capehart wrote, that the movement in Ferguson had been based upon a lie. Of equal importance, however, was the second report that Holder's DOJ produced, one that examined the patterns and practices of Ferguson's police department. The findings revealed a department that was shot through with racial bias and pointed to discriminatory enforcement of laws and revenue-driven policing that sought to balance the municipal budget on the backs of drivers and pedestrians on Ferguson's black side of town. Depending upon where you stood when looking at the portrait of Ferguson, either the first or the second of those reports carried more weight. What Ferguson revealed—though we should've already known—is that two seemingly contradictory things can be true at once. We tend to have a hard time with that one.

The other thing that stands out about this piece is the final sentence. I wrote it as a perfect encapsulation of the exhaustion and anger I'd cultivated while writing about stories like this. My editor reached out to me not long after I'd filed it, asking, "Are you sure this is the note you want to end that piece on?" Yes, I said. That is *exactly* the note I want to close on.

THE PATH CLEARED BY AMIRI BARAKA

January 15, 2015

Long before his death last week at the age of seventy-nine, Amiri Baraka attained the status reserved for those Americans whose unruly complexities and contradictions spill beyond the neat categories we prefer for our public figures. Baraka was part trickster and part provocateur, a brilliant juggler of genres, ideas, and identities, whose career spanned nearly six decades. Words like "controversial" and "polarizing" crowded his obituaries, but these terms, while technically accurate, are about as revelatory as calling winter cold. The received wisdom about Baraka in his later years dismissed him as a relic of the sixties, a rage prophet still shouting in an era when the anger had long since dissipated. But to draw this conclusion was to ignore a great deal of evidence to the contrary.

Baraka was foundational for a generation of writers who emerged in his wake, a singular figure whose work laid down the terms of engagement for many, if not most, of us who came to the craft after him. In his poems, plays, essays, criticism, and fiction, he achieved an absolute democracy of language—a poetry forged in the crucible of a collective experience, a musical fusion of history, irony, and art. His artistic forebears, like Paul Laurence Dunbar, Langston Hughes, and Sterling Brown, had combed the black vernacular for literary value. In Baraka's hands, that undertaking pitched in a new direction, equal parts hood and haute. His poetic voice, with its Ebonics conjugations and sly rhythms, was that of the man on the Newark boulevard or the Harlem avenue. If black people can exert a valid claim on American democracy, Baraka seemed to be saying, then there's no reason for their language not to have equally powerful standing in American literature.

Looking back at the expanse of Baraka's works, that black ancestral tradition is the recurring theme. The man riffed on history like jazz. The name he gave to his epic poetic tribute to the saxophonist Arthur Blythe, "In the Tradition," could also serve as a title for his own sprawling oeuvre. From *Blues People,* his influential 1963 history of African American music and culture, to the polemical poem "I Am," written nearly half a century later, Baraka's work excavated the past and laid bare its human consequences, charting the genealogy of history's survivors and their claims on the present.

In Baraka's retelling of history, music served as a primary source. *Blues People* established the idea that the trajectory of black life in America was most reliably recorded in the music that the experience had produced. Those of us who came of age listening to hip-hop and infused its idioms into our own prose were, knowingly or not, traveling the path that Baraka had cleared with the bebop-suffused lyricism of his writing. In fact, the birth of hip-hop, in the 1970s, was itself an outgrowth of the poetic experiments Baraka had helped to pioneer a decade earlier, with the Black Arts Movement. When Los Angeles exploded after the Rodney King verdict in 1992, Ice Cube's songs seemed like the soundtrack to the simmering discontent that spawned the riots. I only later understood that Ice Cube, too, was echoing a tradition, doing for South Central what Baraka's poem "Black People!," written amid the fire and chaos of the 1967 Newark riots, had done for New Jersey. To cast Baraka as a superannuated sixties radical is to miss the point: he understood himself, rightly, as a single link in an ancestral chain that is older than slavery and unbroken by history's detours and convolutions.

I first encountered Baraka on the page, in the spring of 1989. I was a sophomore at Howard University, and I happened upon a copy of his 1964 play *Dutchman,* which I read in a single sitting. I grasped just enough of it to recognize that there was a great deal more to those pages than what I could immediately understand. Soon afterward, I read *Blues People.* Together, those two works suggested the continent of ideas that I would have to grapple with, ideas that I was just becoming aware of, but which Baraka had deeply considered.

I met Baraka in person a few months later. I was part of a group of student activists, which also included Baraka's son Ras, that had shut down the school for nearly a week protesting the appointment of Lee Atwater, at that time the chair of the Republican National Committee, to the university's board of trustees. This was less than a year after Atwater had run George H. W. Bush's presidential campaign, with its infamous Willie Horton ads, and the sentiment among the students who locked themselves inside the administration building was that Atwater could not be trusted with the leadership of a historically black university. Baraka, who had dropped out of Howard in the fifties, alienated by what he saw as a culture of bourgeois racial rectitude, came down from Newark to speak to us. He encouraged our efforts, reminded us that students have always been key to movements for social reform, and connected our protest to broader historical currents and to older struggles for justice— again, to a tradition.

To an almost embarrassing extent, Baraka's voice was a template for my early literary efforts. But I was hardly the only one who tried to mimic him. Baraka already occupied a complicated niche in the world of letters; by the late eighties, his early work had come under considerable critique, much of it well founded. Critics rightly damned the masculinist excesses and ambient homophobia of his brand of sixties black nationalist sexism. In time, Baraka came full circle on these matters, denouncing his missteps, but this, too, was characteristic of the trajectory of his thinking—he didn't so much evolve from his old positions as ricochet into new ones.

In later years, Baraka cast his Beat period of the 1950s as a rejection of the middle-class values of his upbringing and the stale conventions of Negro uplift at Howard, though the luxury of alienation in Greenwich Village was the ultimate expression of that very background. He began to reexamine his idea that art was apolitical after a 1960 trip to Cuba, where he met the poet Nicolás Guillén and attended a massive Fidel Castro rally, but it was not until after the assassination of Malcolm X, five years later, that Baraka fully devoted himself to creating a black nationalist aesthetic. He was the cornerstone of a new movement that both embraced and rejected the themes of the Harlem Renaissance: it adopted the cultural idealism of writers like Langston Hughes and Zora Neale Hurston, but, rather than producing art for white consumption, the Black Arts Movement fixed its attention on a black audience, which was primed for its message by a decade of turmoil. Like the social realist writers of the 1930s, the members of the Black Arts Movement embraced political themes, creating work that they thought was necessary for survival in the racial wilds of the United States.

In *Home*, a collection of Baraka's essays from this period, published in 1966, he wrote:

> The black artist's role in America is to aid in the destruction of America as he knows it. His role is to report and reflect so precisely the nature of the society, and of himself in that society, that other men will be moved by the exactness of his rendering and, if they are black men, grow strong through this moving, having seen their own strength, and weakness; and if they are white men, tremble, curse, and go mad, because they will be drenched with the filth of their evil.

Reading these lines now, in an era defined by a black presidency, I sense an almost comic undertone in the kill-whitey rhetoric. But in the years between the murders of Malcolm X and Martin Luther King, Jr., when this paragraph was written, Baraka's articulation of the zeitgeist made him essential reading. And, even after those tense years, it was Baraka's black critics, rather than his white ones, whose censure hit hardest. By the early nineties, it was not uncommon to hear the Black Arts Movement and its most visible progenitor dismissed for prescribing a straitjacketing black nationalist orthodoxy, one that denied African Americans the democratic acceptance that was ostensibly its goal. Baraka was denied tenure at Rutgers University in 1990, a time when other scholars were being granted tenure for their books about him, evidence of the way the winds were blowing. At this point, Baraka had already migrated to another new approach to art and politics, a Third World Marxism that, in the long drought of the Cold War, delivered diminishing returns in the world of letters.

Just as he had rejected the bohemian irresponsibility of the Beat scene, Baraka eventually condemned as backward an entire catalog of ideas—and their implicit misogyny and homophobia—that had given him national recognition. He discarded ideologies like a man tossing away wrenches that didn't fit the bolt he was desperately trying to loosen. In the later phases of his career, he frequently held forth in the opaque densities of leftism, but he was still capable of producing exquisite images, metaphors that stayed with you as if they were personal memories, like the line, "At the bottom of the Atlantic Ocean there's a railroad made of human bones," or the deft onomatopoeia:

If you ever find
yourself, some where
lost and surrounded
by enemies
who won't let you
speak in your own language
who destroy your statues
& instruments, who ban
your omm bomm ba boom
then you are in trouble
deep trouble
they ban your
own boom ba boom

you in deep deep
trouble

humph!

probably take you several hundred years
to get
out!

For those watching from the sidelines, his was a difficult sojourn to keep track of. My parents, for instance, were great admirers of the Negro writer LeRoi Jones—as he was earlier known—but they never quite made the transition to Amiri Baraka. They were not alone. Each stage of Baraka's life, like a new theatrical production, featured a fresh cast. Some relationships endured, like his decades-long friendship with Allen Ginsberg, whose poem *Howl* had drawn him into the Beat movement, or with Sonia Sanchez, another primary voice from the Black Arts era. But his first marriage, to Hettie Cohen, a Jewish woman he'd met during his Greenwich Village years, was a casualty of his transition into black nationalism. By the eighties, bitter enmities had erupted with some of his closest collaborators. The scholar and activist W. E. B. Du Bois, who, in the course of his ninety-five years, had been, successively, a bourgeois reformist, an apostle of black nationalism, a socialist democrat, and, ultimately, a radical communist, became a central point of reference for Baraka. When I asked him, in an interview fifteen years ago, how he wanted to be remembered, he said, simply, as an artist who relentlessly sought better solutions.

In 2002, Baraka was singed by the controversy over his poem "Somebody Blew Up America," about the nearly three thousand Americans who died on September 11. The poem was assailed as anti-Semitic for a stanza implying Israel had prior knowledge of the attack:

Who knew the World Trade Center was gonna get bombed
Who told 4000 Israeli workers at the Twin Towers

To stay home that day
Why did Sharon stay away?

After the publication of the poem, Baraka gave interviews suggesting that he did genuinely believe that the Israeli and American
governments had had forewarning of the attacks. But the outrage
over these lines obscured the meaning of the poem: it's a conspira-
cist's view of history, placing September 11, and its victims, in the
context of a lineage of inhumanities that includes colonialism, the
Armenian genocide, Irish subjugation, apartheid, the Holocaust,
class exploitation, and enough other cruelties to fill a syllabus on
human rights abuses. Lesser discussed were these lines:

Who killed Huey Newton, Fred Hampton,
Medgar Evers, Mikey Smith, Walter Rodney,
Was it the ones who tried to poison Fidel
Who tried to keep the Vietnamese Oppressed

Who put a price on Lenin's head

Who put the Jews in ovens,
and who helped them do it
Who said "America First"
and ok'd the yellow stars

Who killed Rosa Luxemburg, Liebknecht
Who murdered the Rosenbergs
And all the good people iced,
tortured, assassinated, vanished

The broader point of the poem—that a vast diversity of people
have been done in by the dark hand of malice—was overlooked in
the ensuing controversy. The governor of New Jersey at the time,
James McGreevey, demanded that Baraka apologize and resign
from his position as the state's poet laureate. Baraka refused, and
later he gleefully noted that McGreevey ended up resigning before

he did. (The state legislature eventually abolished the position entirely.)

Baraka was a controversial figure. He was also enigmatic, eccentric, brilliant, and possessed of a fount of indignation at the wrongs of the world as he understood them. To those who shared his reference points, he contained a black-brown diaspora of multitudes. In "In the Tradition," Baraka writes, "Our fingerprints are everywhere on you, America, our fingerprints are everywhere." In ways that were apparent to those who cared to recognize it, his were, too.

DAVID CARR, 1956–2015

February 13, 2015

In the spring of 1996, I walked into the offices of the *Washington City Paper* for what turned out to be the most bizarre job interview of my life. It took place in a darkened office—shades drawn, lights off, just a bit of illumination filtering in from the hallway. I reached for the light switch when I walked in, but a man sitting behind a desk said, "No, leave it off. I used to spend a lot of time in dark crack houses and now I can't deal with overhead light." I remember looking around and thinking I'd been roped into a practical joke, but without missing a beat he told me he'd read my clips and thought I had potential. I was twenty-six years old, and that was my first conversation with David Carr, who had become editor in chief of the weekly paper the year before. A few weeks later, I started as part of the first class of interns he brought on during his tenure.

When Carr arrived at the *City Paper* in 1996, it was widely regarded as a smug outlet that issued condescension and ridicule at the foibles of Marion Barry–era Washington. The fact that few black people worked at the paper furthered the perception that it was a Bantustan of white entitlement braying at the surrounding black majority. This wasn't a unique state of affairs—none of the Washington, D.C., publications, including *The Washington Post,* had levels of diversity commensurate with the city's. Carr went about changing this, not as a part of a liberal uplift mission but out of a sincere commitment to finding writers who could help him tell a full spectrum of Washington stories. During his first year, he hired me alongside Neil Drumming, who is now a television critic at *Salon;* Holly Bass, a performance artist and playwright; and Ta-Nehisi Coates. He gave us all a space to write, learn, and make mistakes. He was never self-congratulatory about this. There was never the sense that he saw us as his prize Negro finds, but he clearly understood the implications of what he'd done, because he saw how few other people were doing it.

Carr, who died last night at the age of fifty-eight, was a journalist from the ink-and-paper era who found a foothold in the digital environment. As a media reporter for *The New York Times* and a central figure in a 2011 documentary about the paper, *Page One,* he became a figure of note, a fittingly meta development for the age. Yet he never stopped being a newsman in the old mold: he didn't develop a brand; he built a reputation. At the *City Paper,* he was the editor every young writer should hope to encounter: as harsh as he was forgiving, accessible, with an outlook that could be described as jaded idealism. He was allergic to euphemism and a believer that journalism was the art of curating minutiae. He also had one of the most valuable attributes a writer can claim—an ability to withhold personal judgment.

Maybe that openness was always part of his disposition, but if you read *The Night of the Gun,* his memoir about his harrowing years as a crack addict in Minnesota, you got the impression that his reluctance to judge others was a product of a hard-won understanding of human fallibility, beginning with his own. That world-weary outward expression was not an affect—if he hadn't seen it all, he'd at least witnessed enough to issue some preliminary findings, and, from that vantage point, had accumulated a good deal of sympathy for others.

What made him more than simply a humbled former user, however, was the fact that he didn't confuse his unwillingness to judge with an absence of standards. During one early editorial meeting at the *City Paper,* Carr walked in, sat down, and matter-of-factly explained that we'd embarrassed ourselves with the previous issue. He pointed to our exact failings and demanded explanations—very specific explanations—for how we planned to avoid embarrassing ourselves in the future. I started at the paper very much afflicted with the insufferable omniscience of many twenty-something writers. I came out of one of Carr's legendarily scalding critiques—of a story in which I'd gotten facts wrong—wanting to pack my byline into a lead-lined case and slip out the back door. But a few days later he was offering helpful suggestions for my next story. With him, this truth was implicit: writing is a craft, none of us is beyond making mistakes, and certainly none of us is above being called on it.

He stood out for other reasons. Unlike the Washington journalists, who all but wore cufflinks inscribed with their IQs, Carr never needed people to think that he was the smartest guy in the room. He could be self-deprecatingly funny. He was substantially bigger then than he was in later years, and he occasionally left the office on his bicycle, calling himself "the fat guy on the bike."

The recognition he achieved at *The New York Times* didn't diminish his capacity for clear-eyed critique of himself or others. When more than a dozen new allegations of sexual assault were launched at Bill Cosby, Carr took himself to task in print for not having paid more attention to the earlier claims in a profile he'd written. Much has been made of the unyielding honesty of his memoir, but few recall that he published that journalistic investigation of his own life at a point when autobiography was increasingly indistinguishable from fiction. His pursuit of veracity not only spoke to his own character but implicitly damned the work that had fallen far short of that standard. I only once saw him refer in print to his success at bringing more diversity to the *Washington City Paper* masthead, and that was in an article in which he cautioned the industry against doing away with internship programs. He wrote:

Unfortunately, creating meaningful internships and funding them seems like a low priority for an industry that is in a knife fight to survive. But if magazines are going to be anything other than gossamer artifacts of declining interest, the people who run them might want to rethink how they employ their interns. Bringing on young people from all kinds of backgrounds is less a moral nicety than a business imperative.

This is classic Carr—the uncommon phrasing "gossamer artifacts of declining interest" used to relay an unsentimental truth. Just a few days ago, he broke with the hosannas that accompanied the news of Jon Stewart's departure from *The Daily Show* to offer his opinion that the show had been fraying around the edges for years. Many shared this thought, but it took David Carr to write it, with none of the hostility or recrimination that so often accompanies unpleasant truths.

After leaving the *City Paper,* I didn't maintain close contact with Carr, but when I'd written myself into a corner or found myself intimidated by an assignment, I frequently fell back upon what I'd learned from him. In one of his more notable generosities back in Washington, he purchased copies of Joseph Mitchell's *Up in the Old Hotel* for the entire staff. He signed mine, "To Jelani, This will show you the way." Not quite. That was a distinction that belonged largely to him.

BLACK LIKE HER

June 15, 2015

On June 7, Elinor Burkett published an op-ed in *The New York Times* expressing what she portrayed as a feminist's reluctant skepticism about aspects of the transgender movement. She argued, in part, that the notion of men simply transitioning into women was equivalent to a white person darkening their skin and professing to be black. The example was meant as a reductio ad absurdum—but, less than a week later, Rachel Dolezal, the president of the Spokane, Washington, chapter of the National Association for the Advancement of Colored People and a professor of Africana studies, was unveiled as a white woman who has for some years presented herself and identified as black. On Monday, Dolezal resigned, in a statement that didn't answer questions about what she referred to as "my personal identity," though it did refer obliquely to "challenging the construct of race." That answer is clearly inadequate; many people have challenged the construct of race without lying about their lives. But there is something more worth discussing here.

The easy presumption about Dolezal, who has two white parents and light skin and eyes—and hair that has ranged from blond to brown, though she has worn it in ways that are culturally associated with black women—is that this is an instance in which someone finally pointed out the obvious: the emperor is naked. But, in truth, Dolezal has been dressed precisely as we all are, in a fictive garb of race whose determinations are as arbitrary as they are damaging. This doesn't mean that Dolezal *wasn't* lying about who she is. It means that she was lying about a lie.

Dolezal's name has been added to a running discussion of racial appropriation. Two weeks ago, Chet Haze, the putative rapper and son of the actor Tom Hanks, took to Instagram with a questionable syllogism. Because hip-hop is, in his view, "not about race," and because he so closely identifies with the genre, he should be allowed to use the word "nigger" (or its variant "nigga") without recrimination. His comments recalled the feeble musings of John Mayer, five years ago, when he lamented to *Playboy* that his level of black cred was high enough, his standing within the race so unimpeachable, that he ought to be able to toss the epithet with the same sort of entitlement as Jay-Z. And last week, *The Washington Post* published a timeline of the career implosion of Iggy Azalea, the white Australian rapper notable for her transparent racial affectations.

Among African Americans, there is a particular contempt, rooted in the understanding that black culture was formed in a crucible of degradation, for what Norman Mailer hailed as the "white Negro." Whatever elements of beauty or cool, whatever truth or marketable lies there are that we associate with blackness, they are ultimately the product of a community's quest to be recognized as human in a society that is only ambivalently willing to see it as such. And it is this root that cannot be assimilated. The white Negroes, whose genealogy stretches backward from Azalea through Elvis and Paul Whiteman, share the luxury of being able to slough off blackness the moment it becomes disadvantageous, cumbersome, or dangerous. It is an identity as impermanent as burnt cork, whose profitability rests upon an unspoken suggestion that the surest evidence of white superiority is the capacity to exceed blacks even at being black. The black suspicion of whites thus steeped in black culture wasn't bigotry; it was a cultural tariff—an abiding sense that, if they knew all that came with the category, they would be far less eager to enlist.

But this is precisely what makes the Dolezal deception complicated. Artists like Eminem and Teena Marie, white people who
were by and large accepted by black people as a legitimate part of
black cultural life, nonetheless had to finesse a kind of epidermal
conflict of interest. Irrespective of their sincerity, a portion of their
profitability lay in their status as atypically white. Dolezal's transra-
cialism was imbued with exactly the opposite undertaking. She
passed as black and set about shouldering the inglorious, frustrating
parts of that identity—the parts that allocate responsibility for what
was once called "uplifting the race." It's an aspect of her story that
at least ought to give her critics—black ones, particularly—a moment of pause.

Dolezal is, like me, a graduate of Howard University, a place
where the constellation of black identities and appearances is so
staggeringly vast as to ridicule the idea that blackness could be, or
ever has been, any one thing. What I took from Howard, besides
that broadened sense of a world I'd presumed to know, was an abiding debt to those who'd fought on its behalf and a responsibility to
do so for those who came afterward. It's easy to deride Dolezal's
dishonesty—to ridicule her hoax as a clever means of sidestepping
the suspicion with which white liberals are commonly greeted—
until we reflect on a photograph of Walter White, the aptly named
man who served as the second black president of the NAACP. Or
one of Louis T. Wright, who served as the national chairman of the
NAACP board during the Great Depression. In the 1920s, amid a
feud with the organization, the black nationalist Marcus Garvey
criticized the NAACP for being an organization whose black and
white members were essentially indistinguishable.

The spectrum of shades and colorings that constitute "black"
identity in the United States, and the equal claim to black identity
that someone who looks like White or Wright (or, for that matter,
Dolezal) can have, is a direct product of bloodlines that attest to
institutionalized rape during and after slavery. Nearly all of us who
identify as African American in this country, apart from some more
recent immigrants, have at least some white ancestry. My own white
great-grandparent is as inconsequential as the color of my palms in

terms of my status as a black person in the United States. My grand-parents had four children: my father and his brother, both almond brown with black hair and dark eyes, and two girls with reddish hair, fair skin, freckles, and gray eyes. All of them were equally black because they were equal heirs to the quirks of chance determining whether their ancestry from Europe or Africa was most apparent. Dolezal's primary offense lies not in the silly proffering of a false biography but in knowing this ugly history and taking advantage of the reasons that she would, at least among black people, be taken at her word regarding her identity.

Race, in this country and under certain circumstances, functions like a faith, in that the simple profession of membership is sufficient. The most—possibly the sole—democratic element of race in this country lies in this ecumenical approach to blackness. We are not in the business of checking membership cards. In this way, Dolezal's claim on black identity is of a different order than the hollow decla-ration of a Hollywood scion or anyone else who opted to be Negro for a season. They can plead ignorance. But Dolezal spent four years at an institution steeped in the delicacies of race. If nothing else, she understands the exact nature of the trust she violated.

Despite the interchangeability of the terms "African American" and "black," this is a community in which ancestry is one, but clearly not the sole or necessarily even the primary, basis for inclusion. Walter White was only fractionally more African than Dolezal, but he was black enough to be accepted as not only a member of that community but one of its leaders. There is also a disquieting notion inherent in this approach to identity—that if anyone can indeed be "black," then we all are, that Morrison and Coltrane and Chisholm and Malcolm are both unhyphenated Americans and indistinct. (And yet, in circumstances where someone named Eric Garner or Walter Scott is looking nervously over his shoulder, they are still vulnerably intelligible.) It putatively means that Chet Haze is as qualified to utter the word "nigga" as anyone for whom dark skin and skewed life chances have given the word connotations Haze would never countenance. It means, most damningly, that black people are not distinctly bound to each other. Yet both of these things—a community rooted in race and a deep-seated skepticism about the very existence of race—coexist.

Rachel Dolezal is not black—by lineage or lifelong experience— yet I find her deceptions less troubling than the vexed criteria being used to exclude her. If blackness is simply a matter of a preponderance of African ancestry, then we should set about the task of excising a great deal of the canon of black history, up to and including the current president. If it is simply a matter of shared experience, we might excommunicate people like Walter White, whose blue eyes were camouflage that could serve both to spare him the direct indignity of racism and enable him to personally investigate and expose lynchings. Dolezal was dishonest about an undertaking rooted in dishonesty, and no matter how absurd her fictional blackness may appear, it is worth recalling that the former lie is far more dangerous than the latter. Our means of defining ourselves are complex and contradictory—and could be nothing other than that. But if the rubric is faulty it remains vital. The great majority of Americans recognize slavery as a figment of history, interred in a receding past. But, for black people, that past remains at the surface—close at hand, indelible, a narrative as legible as skin.

TERRORISM IN CHARLESTON

June 29, 2015

During the second debate of the 2012 presidential campaign, Mitt Romney repeated the frequently leveled Republican charge that it had taken Barack Obama many days to refer to the attack upon the U.S. Embassy in Benghazi as terrorism. Obama disputed that, and the two men argued back and forth until the moderator, Candy Crowley, intervened to say that the president had in fact referred to the incident as an "act of terror" the day after it happened. In the ensuing partisan scrum, conservatives and liberals debated the nuances between an "act of terror" and "terrorism" proper. Beneath this philological fracas lay a truth evident to political speechwriters, eulogists, and news anchors: in times of tragedy, language matters.

The Charleston police were quick to label what happened in the sanctuary of Emanuel African Methodist Episcopal Church last Wednesday night a "hate crime." Many crimes are motivated by hatred, yet we reserve the term "hate crime" for an act motivated by an animus that has been extrapolated beyond any single individual and applied to an entire segment of the populace. The murder of nine black churchgoers during Bible study is an act so heinous as to be immediately recognizable as a hate crime. But it was not simply this. We should, for all the worst reasons, be adept by now at recognizing terrorism when we see it, and what happened in Charleston was nothing less than an act of terror.

Yet the term was missing from early descriptions of the incident. Senator Lindsey Graham of South Carolina, in his initial assessment, said, "I just think he was one of these whacked-out kids. I don't think it's anything broader than that." On Thursday, Governor Nikki Haley posted a statement on Facebook noting that "while we do not yet know all of the details, we do know that we'll never understand what motivates anyone to enter one of our places of worship and take the life of another." As a matter of morality, the actions of Dylann Roof, who confessed to the murders, may be a conundrum, but his motivations are far from inscrutable.

The Patriot Act defines "domestic terrorism" as activities that:

> involve acts dangerous to human life that are a violation of the criminal laws of the United States or of any State; (B) appear to be intended—(i) to intimidate or coerce a civilian population; (ii) to influence the policy of a government by intimidation or coercion; or (iii) to affect the conduct of a government by mass destruction, assassination, or kidnapping; and (C) occur primarily within the territorial jurisdiction of the United States.

At a minimum, the murders were intended to intimidate and coerce the black civilian population of Charleston, and beyond. A friend of Roof's said that he had talked about wanting to start a "race war"—something that Roof also reportedly confessed to investigators. And he apparently based his acts on vintage rationalizations for terrorist violence in American history.

When Tywanza Sanders, a twenty-six-year-old man who was in the church, urged Roof to spare the lives of the congregants, Roof stated that his actions were necessary. "You are raping our women and taking over the country," he reportedly told Sanders, before killing him. A century ago, the film *The Birth of a Nation* exalted the Ku Klux Klan's reign of terror during Reconstruction as the necessary deeds of men committed to defending white women from the sexual menace of newly emancipated black men. American anti-terrorism law has its legislative roots in the Ku Klux Klan Act of 1871, which broadly empowered President Ulysses S. Grant to prosecute Klan members for abrogating federal law regarding black rights. Nine counties in South Carolina were so deeply suffused with Klan influence that they were placed under martial law. The Klan emerged not solely as an expression of concern for women but also in response to the growing political power of blacks in the postbellum South—people who, from the Klan's vantage point, were taking over the country. In *The Prostrate State: South Carolina Under Negro Government,* published in 1873, the journalist James Shepherd Pike described a set of circumstances in which the white population was imperiled by the presence of black elected officials in the state legislature. The practice of lynching—184 lynchings were documented in South Carolina between 1877 and 1947—facilitated the disenfranchisement of blacks and the retention of political power in white hands.

Twenty years ago, when Timothy McVeigh bombed the Alfred P. Murrah Federal Building in Oklahoma City, killing 168 people, the act was quickly understood as terrorism. We tend not to recall, however, that McVeigh was trying to realize the plot of *The Turner Diaries,* an apocalyptic novel that details a white man's war against a federal government under the control of minorities and their white enablers. The FBI web page on the Murrah bombing lists it as "the worst act of homegrown terrorism in the nation's history." That designation overlooks the Tulsa race massacre of 1921, in which a white mob, enraged by a spurious allegation that a black teenager had attempted to assault a young white woman, was deputized and given carte blanche to attack the city's prosperous black district of Greenwood, resulting in as many as three hundred black fatalities. From one perspective, the Murrah bombing was the worst act of domestic terrorism in our history, but, as the descendants of the Greenwood survivors know, it was not even the worst incident in *Oklahoma's* history.

Another word has remained absent from the discussion of the events in Charleston: Obama. The president is an unnamed but implicit factor in the paranoid assertion—attributed to Roof but certainly not limited to him—that blacks are taking over the country. In January 2008, Barack Obama won the South Carolina Democratic primary, largely on the strength of African American votes; a state in the Deep South gave a black candidate a crucial push in his campaign for the White House. The recalcitrant pledges to "take our country back" that began after the inauguration were simply more genteel expressions of the sentiments that Roof articulated.

The fact that Roof appears to have acted without accomplices will inevitably be taken as solace. He will be dismissed as a deranged loner, connected to nothing broader. This is untrue. Even if he acted by himself, he was not alone.

POSTSCRIPT TO "TERRORISM IN CHARLESTON"

It has largely been forgotten in the two decades since Timothy McVeigh detonated a truck bomb outside the Alfred P. Murrah Federal Building in Oklahoma City, killing 168 people, that he did so in the vain hope of igniting a race war as detailed in *The Turner Diaries*, a staple of right-wing samizdat fiction at the time. It has been almost entirely forgotten that "Helter Skelter," the deranged, apocalyptic vision of Charles Manson that inspired the 1969 murder spree conducted by his acolytes, was code for an anticipated race war in which Manson's army hoped to prevail. In that regard, Dylann Roof and his fanatic aspirations toward a racial conflagration were not unique. Roof was notable nonetheless. The murder of nine African American congregants at the Emanuel AME Church in Charleston in June 2015 did not ignite a war between the so-called races. But it is a neat preface to the dark era that has since ensued.

The Federal Bureau of Investigation defines terrorism as "the unlawful use of force or violence against persons or property to intimidate or coerce a government or civilian population in furtherance of political or social objectives." For opaque reasons, the FBI withheld this designation from Roof's crimes even though he undoubtedly targeted a civilian population in furtherance of political objectives—he admitted to committing those murders because black people were, in his words, "taking over the world." The murders were a direct reaction to the fact that the president of the United States was a black man. This blindness is habitual. At the time it occurred, the Oklahoma City bombing was widely spoken of as being the "worst" incident of domestic terrorism in American history, a sentiment that conveniently elided the history of racial pogroms that defined the nineteenth and twentieth centuries in the United States. As noted in the above piece, the 1921 Tulsa massacre claimed the lives of as many as three hundred African Americans in the city's black district of Greenwood. In terms of casualties, McVeigh's bombing was not the worst act of terrorism in the United States; it was not even the worst in the state of Oklahoma.

In Part II of this book, three consecutive pieces grapple with terroristic mass murders in Pittsburgh, New Zealand, and El Paso, all of which were motivated by white supremacism. In the first days of his second term, Donald Trump issued presidential pardons for members of the white nationalist militias who were among those convicted of mounting an insurrection against the U.S. government on January 6, 2021. Roof hoped to serve as inspiration to a cadre of like-minded white people. On some level he did. For all the madness that abetted Roof and his actions, we are still engaged with its consequences—in some respects, we now live in Dylann Roof's country.

LAST BATTLES

July 6 and 13, 2015

In some future footnote or parenthetical aside, it may be observed that, although General Robert E. Lee surrendered in 1865, the Confederacy's final retreat did not occur until a century and a half later. The rearguard movement of Republicans in the aftermath of the slaughter in Emanuel African Methodist Episcopal Church marked the relinquishing of the Confederacy's best-fortified positions: the cultural ones. We have for decades willfully coexisted with a translucent lie about the bloodiest conflict in American history and the moral questions at its center. Amid the calls last week to lower the Confederate battle flag at the South Carolina state capitol, the defenders of the flag averred that it represents "heritage, not hate." The great sleight of hand is the notion that these things were mutually exclusive.

Americans, both in the South and beyond, attach a particular brand of exceptionalism to the region. This is the reason that there is a Southern Historical Association but not a Northern one; a genre known as Southern literature but no Northern corollary; and a concept of Southern politics as something distinct from the national variety. The notion of the Confederate flag as a benign tribute to that exceptionalism rests upon another premise that illustrated, long before our present concerns with climate change and vaccination did, the political usefulness of denial: the idea that the Civil War was not fought over slavery—a claim that would have bewildered those who served in it—allowed Southerners to memorialize the leaders of an armed insurrection without the sticky moral baggage of bondage attached.

That interpretation held that the war was sparked by a conflict over tariffs that penalized Southern agriculture to the benefit of Northern industry. Or, more vaguely, that the war was fought over "states' rights." This evasion proved amazingly effective. Monuments to the valor of the Confederate ideal dot the South like matériel left on a battlefield. But none of these arguments bear scrutiny. Were the Southerners who erected those monuments concerned primarily about the valor of men, there would be many more dedicated to the former slaves who fought for the Union and risked death or, arguably worse, re-enslavement. Were the war mainly about tariffs, we would be left to think that these fugitives fled farms and plantations to join the Union Army because of their abiding belief in trade protectionism. Or that the nearly forty thousand of them who died did so defending their views on federalism. The Confederates themselves did not believe this. Here is the South Carolina convention in 1860, explaining the rationale for secession:

A geographical line has been drawn across the Union, and all the States north of that line have united in the election of a man to the high office of President of the United States, whose opinions and purposes are hostile to slavery. He is to be entrusted with the administration of the common Government, because he has declared that that "Government cannot endure permanently half slave, half free," and that the public mind must rest in the belief that slavery is in the course of ultimate extinction.

This sectional combination for the submersion of the Constitution, has been aided in some of the States by elevating to citizenship, persons who, by the supreme law of the land, are incapable of becoming citizens; and their votes have been used to inaugurate a new policy, hostile to the South, and destructive of its beliefs and safety.

The South is exceptional not primarily because of its literature or its food or its politics but because, as historians have pointed out, it is the only region of the United States that has lived for the majority of its history with the experience of military defeat. Four decades after the U.S. withdrawal from Saigon, Vietnam remains a spectral presence in American foreign policy and military strategy. But when the Vietnam War began, the South had already been familiar with that kind of recrimination and self-doubt for a hundred years. It not only fought tenaciously for the right to own human beings; it did so unsuccessfully. Neither of these facts can be easily accepted, but only one of them can be easily denied. So detached from slavery is the conception of the war that the controversial Memorial Day tradition of sending a presidential wreath to the Confederate Memorial in Arlington National Cemetery, which began with Woodrow Wilson, continued into the present. (President Obama amended the tradition by also sending a wreath to the African American Civil War Memorial in Washington, D.C.)

Such denialism has governed an important portion of our national affairs and distorted our self-image, but it collapsed in the hail of fire in the sanctuary of Emanuel AME Church. As is often the case, tragedy was the burden we shouldered for a moment of square introspection. This is probably why the eulogy that Barack Obama delivered for the Reverend Clementa Pinckney on Friday was sober and self-reflective in a way that we seldom hear. "The flag," the president said, "has always represented more than just ancestral pride. For many, black and white, that flag was a reminder of systemic oppression and racial subjugation. We see that now. Removing the flag from this state's capitol would not be an act of political correctness." He added, in reference to the Confederate soldiers, that "it would simply be an acknowledgment that the cause for which they fought, the cause of slavery, was wrong."

It may seem odd, decades after the civil rights movement, to note that for a sitting president to say that the Confederacy fought for the institution of slavery—and that doing so was a moral wrong—is a radical statement. Yet it is, and shortly after making it the president fell silent. It appeared that perhaps he had lost his way, but then, in a remarkable moment, he began to sing "Amazing Grace," a hymn that is at once a lament, a prayer, and a hope—written by John Newton, a onetime slave trader who became an abolitionist. Immediately after the speech, people began debating whether the song had been part of the prepared text or whether the president sang it out of an impromptu spiritual imperative. In either case, he was likely hoping to see in the national culture precisely the transformation that Newton had experienced in himself, one that facilitated his first truthful accounting of the evil of slavery.

CLASS NOTES

August 31, 2015

Jamaica High School in Queens, New York, was once the largest high school in the United States. For most of its history, it occupied a majestic Georgian Revival building on Gothic Drive, designed in the 1920s by William H. Gompert, who had begun his career at McKim, Mead & White. With east and west wings, granite columns, and an elaborate bell tower, the building looked like a state capitol that had been dropped into the middle of a residential neighborhood; it sat on the crest of a hill so imposing that planners would have been guilty of pretense had it housed anything other than a public institution.

One evening in June of last year, Jamaica students wearing red-and-blue gowns gathered with their families and teachers and with members of the school staff at Antun's, a catering hall in Queens Village, for the senior-class commencement ceremony. Accompanying the festivities was the traditional graduation boilerplate—about life transitions and rising to new challenges—but it carried a particular significance on this occasion, because it was as applicable to the faculty and the staff, some of whom had been at the school for nearly three decades, as it was to the students. After 122 years, Jamaica High School was closing; the class of 2014, which had just twenty-four members, would be the last.

The New York City Department of Education had announced the closure three years earlier, citing persistent violence and a graduation rate of around 50 percent. Accordingly, the department had begun to "co-locate" four newly created "small schools" in the old building. Advocates argue that small schools can best resolve many of the ills associated with urban education, but the reorganization produced a logistical problem. The schools tended to operate like siblings competing for bathroom time. Access to the building's communal spaces was at a premium. Unable to secure the auditorium for a graduating class of two dozen, Jamaica High School found itself, both figuratively and literally, pushed out.

Underscoring the indignities that attended the school's last days was a difficult irony: for much of its time, Jamaica was a gemstone of the city's public education system. In 1981, the schools chancellor, Frank Macchiarola, decided to take on the additional role of an interim high school principal in order to better appreciate the daily demands of school administration. He chose Jamaica, and was roundly criticized for picking such an easy school to lead. Four years later, the U.S. Department of Education named it one of the most outstanding public secondary schools in the nation. Alumni include Stephen Jay Gould, Attorney General John Mitchell, Representative Sheila Jackson Lee, Walter O'Malley, Paul Bowles, and three winners of the Pulitzer Prize: Gunther Schuller, Art Buchwald, and Alan Dugan. Bob Beamon, who set a world record for the long jump in the 1968 Olympics, graduated with the class of '65. The school's closure felt less like the shuttering of a perennial emblem of stagnation than like the erasure of a once great institution that had somehow ceased to be so.

Jamaica had become an institution of the type that has vexed city policymakers and educators: one charged with serving a majority-minority student body, most of whose members qualified as poor, and whose record was defined by chronic underachievement and academic failure. Even so, word of the school's closure angered students and their families, the community, and alumni. I was among them—I graduated with the class of '87—and for me, as for many former students, the school was a figment of recollection, frozen in its academic glory. George Vecsey, the former *New York Times* sports columnist and a member of the class of '56, accused Joel Klein, Mayor Michael Bloomberg's schools chancellor, of "cooking the books" to make schools slated for closure appear worse than they were and compared the Department of Education's closure policies to the nihilism of Pol Pot. Vecsey later apologized for having slighted the suffering of Cambodia, but he held to his contention that Klein ruled by dictatorial fiat. He wrote, in a blog, "The city destroyed a piece of history because of its own failure."

There are two broadly competing narratives about school closure. The one commonly told by teachers, students, and many parents at underperforming schools centers on a lack of financial and material resources, which ensures that the schools will be unable to meet even minimum standards. Strongly connected to this version is a belief that closure functions as a kind of veiled union busting: shutting a school allows reformers to sidestep contracts and remove long-term teachers.

Reformers view closure as a necessary corrective to what they see as bloated bureaucracies, inept teachers, and unaccountable unions. They argue that urban schools are often too large to give students the attention they need. In 2000, the Gates Foundation began funding education reform, with an emphasis on reducing school size. Nine years later, in an annual newsletter, the foundation reported that its efforts had not met with significant success, particularly with schools "that did not take radical steps to change the culture, such as allowing the principal to pick the team of teachers or change the curriculum." The foundation also said that it "had less success trying to change an existing school than helping to create a new school." The reform movement nationwide increasingly saw closure and the creation of new institutions—as opposed to funding and reorganizing existing schools—as the way forward.

Joel Klein, who as chancellor closed seventy-four schools, disputes the notion that institutions like Jamaica failed owing to a lack of resources. Nor does he believe that size is the only issue. "Where there were thriving large schools, we didn't try to replace them," he told me. The real problem was that the schools had "started getting many kids who were low-performing and entering high school a couple of years behind." The solution was to create "a much more intimate and personalized setting for them"—a phrase at odds with the disruption and the discord that often greet the end of a long-established community institution.

Jamaica's demise became part of the litany of resentments voiced by opponents of school closure across the country. Rahm Emanuel's shuttering of nearly fifty schools in Chicago angered black voters and became a major issue in the city's recent mayoral election. In 2010, Adrian Fenty, the mayor of Washington, D.C., was dispatched in an election that was also a referendum on his schools chancellor, Michelle Rhee, who had closed two dozen schools. Yet that reaction raises another confounding question: Why do communities most in need of strong schools oppose shutting down institutions that are failing them? In demanding that a school remain open, are alumni hewing closer to nostalgia than to current reality? Or is the conversation about school closure really a proxy for something more subtle, complex, and intractable?

The impulse to reform public schools in the United States has existed nearly as long as the impulse to build them. The tides of immigrants arriving at the turn of the twentieth century, and the nativist hostilities that greeted them, imbued educators with an assimilationist mission. At midcentury, schools were instilled with Cold War anxiety; the subtext of films like *Blackboard Jungle* and *Rebel Without a Cause* was not only the perils of dissolute youth but also the dangers posed by families and schools that were seen as failing to meet the Soviet challenge. In the civil rights era, American classrooms were called on to propagate racial equality in the broader society. But no mission completely displaced the one that preceded it, so that, by the end of the century, we expected public education to assimilate students, equalize them, and prepare them to compete globally.

The history of Jamaica High School roughly correlates with the evolving demands placed on public education in New York City. The school was founded in 1892 and, five years later, moved into a small building on Hillside Avenue, with an enrollment of eighty students. Rural Queens County was formally incorporated as a borough of the city in 1898. During the next fifteen years, the Queensboro Bridge opened and the Long Island Rail Road's Jamaica station was expanded, becoming the largest in the system. Commuting presented a novel alternative to life in the uncorralled bedlam of Manhattan; Queens was transformed into a kind of suburb within the city, and the population boomed. Schools citywide struggled to keep up with the demands created by both immigration and population redistribution. In *The Great School Wars,* a history of public education in the city, Diane Ravitch writes, "In the early twentieth century the public school was transformed into a vast, underfinanced, bureaucratic social-work agency, expected to take on single-handedly the responsibilities which had formerly been discharged by family, community, and employer. . . . [T]he idea took hold that the public school was uniquely responsible for the Americanization and assimilation of the largest foreign immigration in the nation's history." Jamaica's population reflected the demographic tides in Queens; its classrooms were laboratories for the shaping of better Americans.

In 1925, construction began on the new building, the school's last home, on Gothic Drive. Jamaica took its name from the Jameco, or Yameca, Indians, who once inhabited the area where Kennedy Airport now stands. The name meant "beaver," and the animal, a symbol of industriousness, was chosen as the school mascot. (When I enrolled, students were grumbling that it was time for a new mascot—particularly the cheerleaders, whose sweaters were emblazoned with the word.) The grand structure, completed in 1927, accommodated 3,400 students.

Over the years, the walls of the east wing became an evolving exhibit of the school's history, adorned with photographs of generations of students, faculty, and staff. Those from the first decades showed stern-faced young men in football uniforms; genial, avuncular-looking teachers in suits; and earnest Second World War–era teenagers, many of them from the growing Greek, Italian, and Jewish neighborhoods to the north and west of the school. Though racially homogeneous, the student body drew from a cross section of economic backgrounds. Kids from middle-class Flushing and Kew Gardens sat with students from working-class areas south of the school and others from more affluent enclaves, like Jamaica Estates. By 1950, the No. 7 subway line had attracted families to the formerly sparse expanses of northern Queens, and the school's enrollment grew to 4,600.

Yearbooks from the fifties show only a few dozen Latino and black students. In 1948, the Supreme Court struck down racially restrictive housing covenants, and a handful of African American celebrities, including Jackie Robinson, Count Basie, Ella Fitzgerald, and Roy Campanella, bought homes in the exclusive Addisleigh Park section of Queens. (Fame provided only partial insulation from racial resentment; in 1952, a cross was burned near the homes of Robinson and Campanella.) Still, 85 percent of the new housing developments in the borough were closed to blacks. Today, the name South Jamaica includes any number of mostly black neighborhoods south of Liberty Avenue, but at that time it was a well-defined sliver of real estate between the more middle-class areas of St. Albans and Ozone Park. It was where most of the African American population, including the students enrolled at the high school, lived.

During the 1940s, in a series of landmark tests conducted around the country, the psychologists Kenneth and Mamie Clark demonstrated that black children associated virtue and intelligence with whiteness and had correspondingly internalized racist stereotypes of inferiority. Robert Carter, an attorney with the NAACP Legal Defense Fund, heard of the Clarks' work and brought it to the attention of Thurgood Marshall, who was then the legal fund's director-counsel. Marshall made the Clarks' findings central to the argument for school desegregation in the Supreme Court case of *Brown v. Board of Education*. The decision made Kenneth Clark famous, while largely overlooking his wife's role in structuring the experiment. Clark, who had grown up in Harlem and was a professor at the City College of New York, then turned his attention to the city government, which, he charged, had fostered segregation in the schools.

Arthur Levitt, then the president of the New York City Board of Education, responded that the schools merely reflected residential patterns: children who attended overwhelmingly black schools lived in overwhelmingly black neighborhoods. A Commission on Integration was set up to examine the issue, with Clark as one of the commissioners and Levitt as co-chair, and it issued recommendations, which were never quite translated into policy. (Clark resigned, but continued to push for integration throughout his career.) In 1959, the Board of Education experimented by sending four hundred students from overcrowded black schools in Brooklyn to underattended white schools in the Ridgewood and Glendale sections of Queens. The move was met with rancorous opposition and a brief boycott that anticipated the riotous response to busing in the seventies.

In 1949, John Ward, an African American student whose family had migrated to New York from Virginia after the Second World War, enrolled at the school. Ward's father was a bus mechanic and his mother worked as a domestic; between them, they earned enough to buy a home in Jamaica. Ward recalls the area as a place where Italian Americans, Polish Americans, African Americans, and Jews lived in peaceful proximity. His house was not far from the grocery store that Mario Cuomo's parents owned, and Ward, who played baseball as a boy, remembers the future governor from games in the neighborhood sandlots. The area had not yet entirely shaken its rural roots. "There were still people farming there," Ward told me. "I remember seeing people butcher hogs on Linden Boulevard in the forties and fifties."

Ward wanted to be a teacher, but Woodrow Wilson, the high school that most blacks in the area attended, was a vocational trade school. So he applied to Jamaica, which had acquired a reputation as one of the city's strongest academic high schools. Ward initially found the rigor daunting. "My first semester, I failed about three major classes," he told me. "My father said, 'If you're not going to work at school, you'll have to get a job.' " Ward studied hard and spent an extra semester earning enough academic credits to apply to college. He played baseball well enough to be selected for the All-City team in 1954, his senior year. "I don't really recall there being much racial tension," he said of the school. "The blacks mostly hung out with other black students, but, being an athlete, I interacted with a lot more of the white students." For a few years in the fifties, Jamaica's integrated athletics teams, with their winning records, were a point of pride for the school. In 1954, Ward was elected the school's first black class president.

He was accepted at Morgan State University, a historically black institution in Baltimore, but his family couldn't afford the tuition, so he played D-League baseball for a few years, then applied to the New York City Police Academy and, in 1960, became one of the first black members of the motorcycle corps. Of the more than three hundred graduates in Ward's Police Academy class, fewer than two dozen were African American. In 1974, he was promoted to a plainclothes unit working out of the 114th Precinct. "Out of sixteen guys, I was the black on the street crimes unit," he told me. His career on the force was, at least demographically, a replay of his experiences at Jamaica, and Ward later credited the school with giving him not only an excellent education but also the skills that allowed him to navigate primarily white environments. "Jamaica being integrated in the fifties was something unusual," he told me. "But it was also a place where I felt I belonged."

South Jamaica's black population continued to grow in the fifties and sixties, though not all of it was as economically stable as Ward's family. In 1947, when the Olympian Bob Beamon was still a baby, his mother died, and he was eventually sent to live with a guardian in a rough part of the neighborhood. After a troubled childhood and a brush with juvenile court, which resulted in his being sent to a remedial school—called "600" schools in New York City after their district number designation—Beamon became convinced that if he could get into Jamaica he could turn his life around. Four decades later, in a memoir, *The Man Who Could Fly,* he wrote of the school in nearly ecclesiastical terms:

> Mr. Louis Schuker, the principal at Jamaica High, had a long talk with me and Coach Ellis. He said the odds of a 600 school student making it in a regular school environment were next to zero. His admonition to me was reminiscent of the one given by the judge who had sentenced me to the 600 school.
>
> "Beamon, any trouble out of you and you are out of here," Mr. Schuker said. "Do I make myself clear?"
>
> "Yes, sir," I answered firmly and clearly. I knew that I wasn't going anywhere but Jamaica High. *This* was where I wanted to be. *This* was where I belonged.

It's easy to wax idealist about the happy spaces of one's childhood, but in Beamon's case the assessment can't be so easily dismissed. He traced his desire to compete in the Olympics to a visit that the track-and-field star Wilma Rudolph, a triple gold medalist in the 1960 games, paid to Jamaica during his sophomore year. The school was a place where someone like him, who grew up poor in a crime-plagued neighborhood, stood a chance of encountering someone like Rudolph.

Beamon and Ward could have been case studies for Kenneth Clark's advocacy of integration. Political salesmanship warranted that advocates speak of integration as a removal of racial strictures and a kind of democratic communion, but, at its core, it was meant to achieve a redistribution of wealth or, at least, of opportunity. If advantage tended to accrue in places inhabited by whites, integrationists like Clark hoped that, by placing black students in physical proximity to whites, the benefits would be spread around.

The Civil Rights Act of 1964 ensured that race could not be used explicitly to prohibit access to public institutions, but there was a big difference in the public's mind between outlawing discrimination and engineering racial diversity. By 1974, when the Supreme Court ruled, in *Milliken v. Bradley,* that school districts could not be compelled to participate in busing programs, the push for integration had already begun to lose momentum. School districts across the country fell back on voluntary integration programs. (The 2007 Supreme Court ruling in the so-called PICS case greatly weakened the ability to do even that.)

Meanwhile, successive tides of immigration in the seventies and eighties transformed Queens into the most ethnically diverse county in the United States. Greek enclaves in Astoria saw an influx of Brazilians, Colombians, Bangladeshis, Chinese, Guyanese, Koreans, Ecuadorans, Romanians, Indians, Filipinos, Albanians, and Bosnians, in addition to Lebanese, Egyptians, Tunisians, Yemeni, and Moroccans. The working-class white areas along Jamaica Avenue became home to Haitian, Jamaican, Dominican, Puerto Rican, Indian, and Pakistani populations. A South Asian community took root south and east of the school. Jamaica High School did not become "integrated" as a consequence of the implementation of a particular set of policy prerogatives. Rather, the school was something more uncommon and more notable: an institution whose diversity simply reflected the entirety of its surrounding communities.

My family moved to Queens about twenty years after John Ward's did, as part of a nascent civil rights–era black middle class. By 1967, my father, who was an electrician, was earning enough to buy a home. He and my mother left a tenement in Harlem for a yellow two-story house in Hollis, far enough into Queens that people referred to Manhattan as "the city." The nearest subway stop was a twenty-minute bus ride away. My father considered the move a validation of his decision, at the age of seventeen, to leave his native Georgia and head north.

My mother, who had left Alabama for New York as a teenager, and took jobs in the city as a domestic and a hotel telephone operator, now no longer needed to work, and she enrolled in night classes, studying for a BA at Queens College. Her American history class was taught by Herb Sollinger, an adjunct professor who was also a full-time social studies teacher at Jamaica High School. Tall and fortyish, Sollinger was a brilliant, quirky figure who wore red socks every day and had an encyclopedic grasp of world affairs. My mother, who deeply resented how limited her educational opportunities had been in Alabama, decided that my sister, who was about to start her freshman year, should attend the high school where Sollinger taught. Hollis was not in the district, so my mother filed a less than accurate change-of-address form with the Board of Education, and the following year my sister enrolled at Jamaica. Three years later, my older brother did, too.

The narrative of individual ascent in America often elides the many frail contingencies that make success possible. In the late seventies, my father found it increasingly difficult to compete with larger electrical contractors. Then, in 1981, my oldest brother— who had served in Vietnam, had come home addicted to heroin, and had been clean for several years—died, one of the earliest victims of AIDS. My father's business collapsed amid the grief that followed. The contingencies piled up. We moved from the yellow house into a second-floor apartment on a dead-end street in Bricktown, a forgettable stretch of South Jamaica alongside the Long Island Rail Road. That part of Liberty Avenue, the northern boundary of the neighborhood, was home to automotive yards, laundromats, bodegas, and a significant number of bad reputations. Bob Beamon recalled seeing, as a boy, one teenager stab another to death there. But Bricktown was zoned for Jamaica High School, and I enrolled as a freshman.

Up to that point, I'd been the type of student who is frequently urged to "apply yourself," but, in a fit of geekdom my freshman year, I developed an obsession with physics—specifically, quarks. A classmate and I started staying behind after science class to discuss subatomic particles with Mr. DeFelice, a wry, mostly grayhaired man who spoke in deliberate cadences that crescendoed at the end of each sentence. He began assigning us additional reading, and eventually recommended us for the honors science track. His affirmation of our potential, coming amid the normal adolescent anxieties and a host of socioeconomic ones, still stands out in my memory.

The school was by then a far more polyglot institution than it had been when Ward or Beamon attended. I played right field on a baseball team that included a Jewish third baseman, a Dominican pitcher, a shortstop from Colombia, and an Indian utility outfielder. We took the field looking as if team tryouts had been held at the Census Bureau. Jamaica remained academically rigorous and was initiating an impressive array of programs designed to prepare students for careers in science and engineering, business and medicine. It was during my sophomore year, when Eileen Petruzillo was principal, that the Department of Education cited the school for its excellence.

In my senior year, the father of my friend Sherman Brown encouraged me and a classmate, Mark Mason, to apply to his alma mater, Howard University. Sherman played first base on the baseball team and lived in Jamaica Estates. His father owned a travel agency. His mother, who held a doctorate in psychology, was the first person I'd ever met with a PhD. Mark was the senior-class president and, like me, the first in his family for whom going directly from high school to college was a possibility. Sherman, Mark, and I wound up as roommates at Howard. My four closest black friends at Jamaica, including Sherman and Mark, earned master's degrees, and two of them were later awarded doctorates. Mark, now a chief financial officer at Citigroup, summarized Jamaica's impact: "We came from neighborhoods where very few people went to college, but went to school with a set of people almost certain to go to college, and the school had a bigger influence."

My high school years had coincided with a train of racially charged events in the city: the death of Eleanor Bumpurs, a sixty-six-year-old woman who was shot in her apartment by a police officer; the death, from injuries sustained in police custody, of the graffiti artist Michael Stewart; the arrest of Bernhard Goetz in the shooting of four young black men who he claimed had attempted to mug him in the subway; and the death of Michael Griffith, in Howard Beach. Griffith's death brought a roiling racial subcurrent to the surface: he was fatally struck by a car as he fled onto a highway to escape a mob of whites who were chasing him. Adults in my neighborhood who had grown up in the South called Griffith's death a lynching, and they warned me to stay out of white working-class enclaves like Howard Beach. Three days after Griffith's death, I saw a group of black teenagers attack a white teenager on Hillside Avenue and rage through the streets shouting, "Howard Beach! Howard Beach!" Yet neither I nor any of the teachers and alumni I spoke to recall those tensions as being particularly prominent at Jamaica. The school continued to represent an educational idyll. But it could not stand entirely outside the times.

Students usually gathered in the first-floor auditorium before the start of classes, but on the morning of Wednesday, November 5, 1986, Principal Petruzillo announced over the PA system that the auditorium was off-limits owing to a construction emergency. Her story held up for just as long as it took for the police and ambulances to arrive. Earlier that morning, Gregory Evelyn, an almost fragilely small sixteen-year-old junior, with whom I had taken swimming class, had shot a sophomore named Stanley Pacheco following what was said to have been a dispute over a girl. Leo Greenfest, a gym teacher certified in first aid, tended to Pacheco, but the bullet had severed his spinal cord and left him paralyzed below the neck. Evelyn ran out of the building and was arrested at his home a short time later.

School shootings were not yet recognized as a common feature of American life, which meant that the incident generated an enormous amount of news coverage, and also that there were no established safety or emotional health protocols with which to respond to it. The shooting and its aftermath hung over us the rest of the school year; for the graduating students, it remained a set of emotional ellipses never quite resolved. Outside the school, the shooting came to be seen as a vector of ill tidings, definitive evidence of an institution in decline. But to the teachers who returned the following year, and the years after, the shooting was a tragedy that presaged the coming violence in American schools more than it spoke to any particular trouble at Jamaica. On the morning of the shooting, Susan Sutera, a gym teacher, was leading a combined class with Leo Greenfest. She continued to teach at the school until the year before it closed. "The shooting was a crazy, tragic day," she told me. "But, terrible as it was, it didn't really define Jamaica as a dangerous place. It was something that we recognized we had to move on from."

As late as 1998, Jamaica held a respectable standing among the city's large high schools. Though it was no longer the elite institution of earlier years, more than 75 percent of the students graduated on time. But, by 2009, the graduation rate had tumbled to 39 percent. A confluence of events brought about the decline. In that period, talented students in northern Queens were given the option of attending two other high schools, both based on college campuses. In 1995, Townsend Harris, a magnet high school on Parsons Boulevard, moved onto the campus of Queens College. With roughly half the number of students as Jamaica, Townsend Harris had graduation rates that fluctuated between 99 and 100 percent. During the eighties and nineties, Jamaica allowed students to enroll in courses at York College, a liberal arts institution about a mile south of the high school. In 2002, York became the location of Queens High School for the Sciences, which granted admission based solely on standardized-test scores.

In 2004, in the name of greater choice, the Bloomberg administration revised the districting rules to allow students to attend any high school in the city. Given the realities of residential segregation, and of school quality as a determinant of real estate values, there was something almost radical in that idea. It's even possible to see the Bloomberg plan as a long-awaited response to Arthur Levitt's claim, in 1954, that the problem in New York was not segregated schools but segregated neighborhoods. But it also meant that students whose parents—owing to language difficulties or work demands, immigration status or a generalized fear of bureaucratic authority—could not or would not pursue other educational options for their children found themselves relegated to increasingly unappealing schools.

The demographic balance that characterized Jamaica during my years became impossible to maintain. In 2011, the year that the city formally decided to close the school, 14 percent of the student population had disabilities and 29 percent had limited English proficiency. In the year before the school closed, it was 99 percent minority, a demographic that would not in itself be a concern were it not also the case that 63 percent of the students qualified as poor.

James Eterno taught social studies at Jamaica from 1986 until it closed and was also a representative of the United Federation of Teachers. A trim, voluble man in his fifties, he speaks in a rapid-fire cadence and with precisely the accent you'd expect of someone who'd spent all but two years of his life in Queens. Eterno agreed with Joel Klein's description of the school's enrollment during its last decade. "We still had plenty of smart kids, but we had many more higher-needs kids, English-language learners," he told me. Concentrations of high-needs students place a strain on schools, and, Eterno said, "We didn't get the support. We were not prepared to deal with the changing population." The tacit belief that large schools were unreformable meant that Jamaica's sliding numbers looked to some experts like predictable educational failure; to the faculty, those numbers looked like what happens when a school is asked to educate a challenging population without the necessary tools. (This is what George Vecsey was referring to when he wrote about "cooking the books.") In the battle over the school's future, many came to see those changing demographics not as happenstance but as a purposeful way of ensuring that the creation of small schools in the building would be a fait accompli.

In a way, the protests over school closure are a bookend to the riots that broke out over busing four decades ago. Like "busing" and "integration," the language of today's reformers often serves as a euphemism for poverty mitigation, the implicit goal that American education has fitfully attempted to achieve since *Brown v. Board of Education*. Both busing and school closure recognize the educational obstacles that concentrated poverty creates. But busing recognized a combination of unjust history and policy as complicit in educational failure. In the ideology of school closure, though, the lines of responsibility—of blame, really—run inward. It's not society that has failed, in this perspective. It's the schools.

In 1954, Kenneth and Mamie Clark's arguments about the pernicious effects of racism on black children implicated white society. Sixty years later, arguments that black students associated studiousness with "acting white" were seen not as evidence of the negative effects of internalized racism but as indicators of pathological self-defeat among African Americans. The onus shifted, and public policy followed. The current language of educational reform emphasizes racial "achievement gaps" and "underperforming schools" but also tends to approach education as if history had never happened. Integration was a flawed strategy, but it recognized the ties between racial history and educational outcomes. A 2014 study by the Civil Rights Project at UCLA found that New York has the most segregated school system in the country, a reflection of the persistence of the housing patterns that Arthur Levitt talked about in 1954 but also of the failure of the integrationist ideal that was intended to address it. From that vantage point, the closure of Jamaica seemed to be less about the interment of a single school than about the impeachment of a particular brand of idealism regarding race and, by extension, American education.

Ninety years ago, the City of New York broke ground on a huge, beautiful building as a symbol of its commitment to public education. Last year, it closed the school that the building housed, purportedly for the same reasons. The people who gathered angrily outside Jamaica High School weren't really protesting its closing; they were protesting the complex of history, policy, poverty, and race that had brought it about.

When I visited the old building on Gothic Drive a few months ago, it was undergoing renovation and was obscured by scaffolding and tarps. It looked as if it were draped in a shroud. Then I drove a mile southeast to my old apartment building in Bricktown. The area had never been beautiful, but now it sagged in a way that it hadn't done in the early eighties when I lived there. Rows of boarded-up properties lined the street. Our building was now windowless and abandoned. For the first time in many years, I understood myself to be from Bricktown, even as the glare from a man across the street, as subtle as an eviction notice, told me that I no longer belonged there.

Education was central to the gamble at the heart of my parents' migration north. My mother began her adulthood cleaning houses for whites in Alabama; she ended it as a holder of two degrees from New York University—a trajectory that said as much about the possibilities she found in Queens as it did about her own determination. Bricktown's declining fortunes said everything about what is at stake in public education—about what happens when a place like Jamaica ceases to be great and then ceases to be at all. It was obvious that a good portion of the homes in Bricktown had been foreclosed. What was less apparent was that so had a key route—the one I took thirty years ago—to get out of there.

II

WINTER IN AMERICA

When the poet and vocalist Gil Scott-Heron released his 1974 album *Winter in America,* he was not remarking on the temperatures in the lower forty-eight. For one thing, the album was released well into the spring of that year, but no matter. His listeners understood the point. After the dissolution or disruption of vital movements and the very ethic of social change that had defined the previous decade, the nation was—politically at least—a colder place by the time Scott-Heron and his collaborator Brian Jackson began work on the release in October 1973. It wasn't until more than a decade later that Scott-Heron recorded the song "Winter in America," which later listeners presumed was the title track of what was, by then, a cult classic album.

I came to empathize with Scott-Heron's perspective in the early morning hours of November 9, 2016, as the electoral returns began pointing toward a victory for Donald Trump, the bombastic political neophyte who had cut his teeth by alleging that Barack

Obama, president of the United States, was not even a citizen of the country he led. The four years that ensued raised profound questions, some of which have yet to be adequately answered. But the most fundamental (and seemingly commonplace, at least among those who were rightfully alarmed by the country's direction) was: *How did we get here?* The following dispatches take up a slightly different concern, chronicling some of what happened while we were there.

Four years is a comparatively short period of time, but so much transpired then that it was difficult to keep up with it all. Two of the individuals profiled here—the politician Stacey Abrams and the preacher Reverend William Barber—represented dynamic reactions to the cold front that swept the nation. Other pieces, particularly reporting on the siege of Charlottesville by right-wing acolytes of Donald Trump and the trial of the mass murderer Dylann Roof, point to just how cold it had gotten. These pieces are not exhaustive—the forthcoming histories will be charged with that responsibility. But they highlight a few things that I suspect will be worth thinking about—now and in the winters to come.

THE MATTER OF BLACK LIVES

March 14, 2016

On February 18, as part of the official recognition of Black History Month, President Obama met with a group of African American leaders at the White House to discuss civil rights issues. The guests—who included Representative John Lewis of Georgia; Sherrilyn Ifill, the director-counsel of the NAACP Legal Defense and Educational Fund; and Wade Henderson, who heads the Leadership Conference on Civil and Human Rights—were intent on pressing the president to act decisively on criminal justice issues during his last year in office. Their urgency, though, was tempered by a degree of sentimentality, verging on nostalgia. As Ifill later told me, "We were very much aware that this was the last Black History Month of this presidency."

But the meeting was also billed as the "first of its kind," in that it would bring together different generations of activists. To that end, the White House had invited DeRay Mckesson, Brittany Packnett, and Aislinn Pulley, all of whom are prominent figures in Black Lives Matter, which had come into existence—amid the flash points of the George Zimmerman trial, Michael Brown's death in Ferguson, and the massacre at the Emanuel AME Church in Charleston—during Obama's second term.

Black Lives Matter has been described as "not your grandfather's civil rights movement" to distinguish its tactics and its philosophy from those of 1960s-style activism. Like the Occupy movement, it eschews hierarchy and centralized leadership, and its members have not infrequently been at odds with older civil rights leaders and with the Obama administration—as well as with one another. So it wasn't entirely surprising when Pulley, a community organizer in Chicago, declined the White House invitation on the ground that the meeting was nothing more than a "photo opportunity" for the president. She posted a statement online in which she said that she "could not, with any integrity, participate in such a sham that would only serve to legitimize the false narrative that the government is working to end police brutality and the institutional racism that fuels it." Her skepticism was attributable, in part, to the fact that she lives and works in a city whose mayor, Rahm Emanuel, Obama's former chief of staff, is embroiled in a controversy stemming from a yearlong cover-up of the fatal shooting by police of an African American teenager.

Mckesson, a full-time activist, and Packnett, the executive director of Teach for America in St. Louis, did accept the invitation, and they later described the meeting as constructive. Mckesson tweeted: "Why did I go to the mtg w/ @potus today? B/c there are things we can do now to make folks' lives better today, tomorrow, & the day after." Two weeks earlier, Mckesson had announced that he would be a candidate in the Baltimore mayoral race, and Obama's praise, after the meeting, for his "outstanding work mobilizing in Baltimore" was, if not an endorsement, certainly politically valuable.

That split in the response to the White House, however, reflected a larger conflict: while Black Lives Matter's insistent outsider status has allowed it to shape the dialogue surrounding race and criminal justice in this country, it has also sparked a debate about the limits of protest, particularly of online activism. Meanwhile, internal disputes have raised questions about what the movement hopes to achieve, and about its prospects for success.

The phrase "Black Lives Matter" was born in July 2013 in a Facebook post by Alicia Garza, called "a love letter to black people." The post was intended as an affirmation for a community distraught over George Zimmerman's acquittal in the shooting death of seventeen-year-old Trayvon Martin, in Sanford, Florida. Garza, now thirty-five, is the special-projects director in the Oakland office of the National Domestic Workers Alliance, which represents twenty thousand caregivers and housekeepers and lobbies for labor legislation on their behalf. She is also an advocate for queer and transgender rights and for anti-police-brutality campaigns.

Garza has a prodigious social media presence, and on the day that the Zimmerman verdict was handed down, she posted, "the sad part is, there's a section of America who is cheering and celebrating right now. and that makes me sick to my stomach. we gotta get it together y'all." Later, she added, "btw stop saying we are not surprised. that's a damn shame in itself. I continue to be surprised at how little Black lives matter. And I will continue that. stop giving up on black life." She ended with "black people. I love you. I love us. Our lives matter."

Garza's friend Patrisse Cullors amended the last three words to create a hashtag: #BlackLivesMatter. Garza sometimes writes haiku—she admires the economy of the form—and in those four syllables she recognized a distillation not only of the anger that attended Zimmerman's acquittal but also of the animating principle at the core of black social movements dating back more than a century.

Garza grew up as Alicia Schwartz in Marin County, where she was raised by her African American mother and her Jewish stepfather, who run an antiques store. Her brother Joey, who works for the family business, is almost young enough to have been Trayvon Martin's peer. That is one reason, she said, that the Zimmerman verdict affected her so deeply. The family was not particularly political, but Garza showed an interest in activism in middle school, when she worked to have information about contraception made available to students in Bay Area schools.

She went on to study anthropology and sociology at the University of California, San Diego. When she was twenty-three, she told her family that she was queer. They reacted to the news with equanimity. "I think it helped that my parents are an interracial couple," she told me. "Even if they didn't fully understand what it meant, they were supportive." For a few years, Garza held various jobs in the social justice sector. She found the work fulfilling, but, she said, "San Francisco broke my heart over and over. White progressives would actually argue with us about their right to determine what was best for communities they never had to live in."

In 2003, she met Malachi Garza, a gregarious, twenty-four-year-old trans male activist, who ran training sessions for organizers. They married five years later. In 2009, early on the morning of New Year's Day, a transit police officer named Johannes Mehserle fatally shot Oscar Grant, a twenty-two-year-old African American man, in the Fruitvale BART station in Oakland, three blocks from where the Garzas live. Alicia was involved in a fight for fair housing in San Francisco at the time, but Malachi, who was by then the director of the Community Justice Network for Youth, immersed himself in a campaign to have Mehserle brought up on murder charges. (Mehserle was eventually convicted of involuntary manslaughter and served one year of a two-year sentence.)

Grant died nineteen days before Barack Obama's first inauguration. (The film *Fruitvale Station*, a dramatic recounting of the last day of Grant's life, contrasts his death with the national exuberance following the election.) His killing was widely seen as a kind of political counterpoint—a reminder that the grip of history would not be easily broken.

Garza had met Patrisse Cullors in 2005, on a dance floor in Providence, Rhode Island, where they were both attending an organizers' conference. Cullors, a native of Los Angeles, had been organizing in the LGBTQ community since she was a teenager—she came out as queer when she was sixteen and was forced to leave home—and she had earned a degree in religion and philosophy at UCLA. She is now a special-projects director at the Ella Baker Center for Human

Rights in Oakland, which focuses on social justice in inner cities. Garza calls Cullors her "twin." After Cullors created the Black Lives Matter hashtag, the two women began promoting it. Opal Tometi, a writer and immigration rights organizer in Brooklyn, whom Garza had met at a conference in 2012, offered to build a social media platform on Facebook and Twitter, where activists could connect with one another. The women also began thinking about how to turn the phrase into a movement.

Black Lives Matter didn't reach a wider public until the following summer, when a police officer named Darren Wilson shot and killed eighteen-year-old Michael Brown in Ferguson. Darnell Moore, a writer and activist based in Brooklyn, who knew Cullors, coordinated "freedom rides" to Missouri from New York, Chicago, Portland, Los Angeles, Philadelphia, and Boston. Within a few weeks of Brown's death, hundreds of people who had never participated in organized protests took to the streets, and that campaign eventually exposed Ferguson as a case study of structural racism in America and a metaphor for all that had gone wrong since the end of the civil rights movement.

DeRay Mckesson, who was twenty-nine at the time and working as an administrator in the Minneapolis public school system, watched as responses to Brown's death rolled through his Twitter feed. He decided to drive the six hundred miles to Ferguson to witness the scene himself. Before he left, he posted a request for housing on Facebook. Teach for America's Brittany Packnett helped him find a place; before moving to Minneapolis, he had taught sixth-grade math as a TFA employee in Brooklyn. Soon after his arrival, he attended a street-medic training session, where he met Johnetta Elzie, a twenty-five-year-old St. Louis native. With Packnett, they began sharing information about events and tweeting updates from demonstrations, and they quickly became the most recognizable figures associated with the movement in Ferguson. For their efforts, Mckesson and Elzie received the Howard Zinn Freedom to Write Award in 2015, and Packnett was appointed to the president's Task Force on 21st Century Policing.

Yet, although the three of them are among the most identifiable names associated with the Black Lives Matter movement, none of them officially belong to a chapter of the organization. Elzie, in fact, takes issue with people referring to Garza, Cullors, and Tometi as founders. As she sees it, Ferguson is the cradle of the movement, and no chapter of the organization exists there or anywhere in the greater St. Louis area. That contentious distinction between the organization and the movement is part of the debate about what Black Lives Matter is and where it will go next.

The central contradiction of the civil rights movement was that it was a quest for democracy led by organizations that frequently failed to function democratically. W. E. B. Du Bois, in his 1903 essay "The Talented Tenth," wrote that "the Negro race, like all races, is going to be saved by its exceptional men," and the traditional narrative of the battle for the rights of African Americans has tended to read like a great-black-man theory of history. But, starting a generation ago, civil rights historians concluded that their field had focused too heavily on the movement's leaders. New scholarship began charting the contributions of women, local activists, and small organizations—the lesser-known elements that enabled the grand moments we associate with the civil rights era. In particular, the career of Ella Baker, who was a director of the Southern Christian Leadership Conference, and who oversaw the founding of the Student Nonviolent Coordinating Committee, came to be seen as a countermodel to the careers of leaders like Martin Luther King, Jr. Baker was emphatically averse to the spotlight. Barbara Ransby, a professor of history and gender studies at the University of Illinois at Chicago, who wrote a biography of Baker, told me that, during the 1940s, when Baker was a director of branches for the NAACP, "she would go into small towns and say, 'Whom are you reaching out to?' And she'd tell them that if you're not reaching out to the town drunk you're not really working for the rights of black people. The folk who were getting rounded up and thrown in jail had to be included."

Cullors said, "The consequence of focusing on a leader is that you develop a necessity for that leader to be the one who's the spokesperson and the organizer, who tells the masses where to go, rather than the masses understanding that we can catalyze a movement in our own community." Or, as Garza put it, "The model of the black preacher leading people to the promised land isn't working right now." Jesse Jackson—a former aide to King and a two-time presidential candidate who won seven primaries and four caucuses in 1988—was booed when he tried to address young protesters in Ferguson, who saw him as an interloper. That response was seen as indicative of a generational divide. But the divide was as much philosophical as it was generational, and one that was visible half a century earlier.

Garza, Cullors, and Tometi advocate a horizontal ethic of organizing, which favors democratic inclusion at the grassroots level. Black Lives Matter emerged as a modern extension of Ella Baker's thinking—a preference for ten thousand candles rather than a single spotlight. In a way, they created the context and the movement created itself. "Really, the genesis of the organization was the people who organized in their cities for the ride to Ferguson," Garza told me in her office. Those people, she said, "pushed us to create a chapter structure. They wanted to continue to do this work together, and be connected to activists and organizers from across the country." There are now more than thirty Black Lives Matter chapters in the United States, and one in Toronto. They vary in structure and emphasis and operate with a great deal of latitude, particularly when it comes to choosing what "actions" to stage. But prospective chapters must submit to a rigorous assessment, by a coordinator, of the kinds of activism that members have previously engaged in, and they must commit to the organization's guiding principles. These are laid out in a thirteen-point statement, written by the women and Darnell Moore, which calls for, in part, an ideal of unapologetic blackness. "In affirming that Black Lives Matter, we need not qualify our position," the statement reads.

Yet, although the movement initially addressed the killing of unarmed young black men, the women were equally committed to the rights of working people and to gender and sexual equality. So the statement also espouses inclusivity, because "to love and desire freedom and justice for ourselves is a necessary prerequisite for wanting the same for others." Garza's argument for inclusivity is informed by the fact that she—a black queer woman married to a trans man— would likely have found herself marginalized not only in the society she hopes to change but also in many of the organizations that are dedicated to changing it. She also dismisses the kind of liberalism that finds honor in nonchalance. "We want to make sure that people are not saying, 'Well, whatever you are, I don't care,'" she said. "No, I want you to care. I want you to see all of me."

Black activists have organized in response to police brutality for decades, but part of the reason for the visibility of the current movement is the fact that such problems have persisted—and, from the public's perspective, at least, have seemed to escalate—during the first African American presidency. Obama's election was seen as the culmination of years of grassroots activism that built the political power of black Americans, but the naïve dream of a post-racial nation foundered even before he was sworn into office. As Garza put it, "Conditions have shifted, so our institutions have shifted to meet those conditions. Barack Obama comes out after Trayvon is murdered and does this weird, half-ass thing where he's, like, 'That could've been my son,' and at the same time he starts scolding young black men." In short, all this would seem to suggest, until there was a black presidency it was impossible to conceive of the limitations of one. Obama, as a young community organizer in Chicago, determined that he could bring about change more effectively through electoral politics; Garza is of a generation of activists who have surveyed the circumstances of his presidency and drawn the opposite conclusion.

I met up with Garza in downtown San Francisco last August, on an afternoon when the icy winds felt like a rebuke to summer. A lively crowd of several hundred people had gathered in United Nations Plaza for Trans Liberation Tuesday, an event that was being held in twenty cities across the country. A transgender opera singer sang "Amazing Grace." Then Janetta Johnson, a black trans activist, said, "We've been in the street for Oscar Grant, for Trayvon Martin, for Eric Garner. It's time for our community to show up for trans women."

The names of Grant, Martin, and Garner—who died in 2014 after being put in a choke hold by police on Staten Island—are now part of the canon of the wrongfully dead. The point of Trans Liberation Tuesday was to draw attention to the fact that there are others, such as Ashton O'Hara and Amber Monroe, black trans people who were killed just weeks apart in Detroit last year, whose names may not be known to the public but who are no less emblematic of a broader social concern. According to a report by the Human Rights Campaign, between 2013 and 2015 there were fifty-three known murders of transgender people; thirty-nine of the victims were African American.

Garza addressed the crowd for just four minutes; she is not given to soaring rhetoric, but speaks with clarity and confidence. She began with a roll call of the underrepresented: "We understand that, in our communities, black trans folk, gender-nonconforming folk, black queer folk, black women, black disabled folk—we have been leading movements for a long time, but we have been erased from the official narrative." Yet, overall, her comments were more concerned with the internal dynamics of race. For Garza, the assurance that black lives matter is as much a reminder directed at black people as it is a revelation aimed at whites. The message of Trans Liberation Tuesday was that, as society at large has devalued black lives, the African American community is guilty of devaluing lives based on gender and sexuality.

The kind of ecumenical activism that Garza espouses has deep roots in the Bay Area. In 1966, in Oakland, Huey P. Newton cofounded the Black Panther Party, which was practically defined by hyperbolic masculinity. Four years later, he made a statement whose message was, at the time, rare for the left, not to mention the broader culture. In a party newsletter, he wrote:

> We have not said much about the homosexual at all, but we must relate to the homosexual movement because it is a real thing. And I know through reading, and through my life experience and observations, that homosexuals are not given freedom and liberty by anyone in the society. They might be the most oppressed people in the society.

The Black Power movement remained steadfastly masculinist, but by the 1980s Newton's words had begun to appear prescient. When I asked Garza about the most common misperception of Black Lives Matter, she pointed to a frequent social media dig that it is "a gay movement masquerading as a black one." But the organization's fundamental point has been to challenge the assumption that those two things are mutually exclusive. In 1989, the race theory and legal scholar Kimberlé Crenshaw introduced the principle of "intersectionality," by which multiple identities coexist and complicate the ways in which we typically think of class, race, gender, and sexuality as social problems. "Our work is heavily influenced by Crenshaw's theory," Garza told me. "People think that we're engaged with identity politics. The truth is that we're doing what the labor movement has always done—organizing people who are at the bottom."

As was the case during the civil rights movement, there are no neat distinctions between the activities of formal organizations and those incited by an atmosphere of social unrest. That ambiguity can be an asset when it inspires entry-level activism among people who have never attended a protest, as happened in Ferguson. But it can be a serious liability when actions contrary to the principles of the movement are associated with it. In December 2014, video surfaced of a march in New York City, called in response to the deaths of Eric Garner and others, where some protesters chanted that they wanted to see "dead cops." The event was part of the Millions March, which was led by a coalition of organizations, but the chant was attributed to Black Lives Matter. Several months later, the footage provoked controversy. "For four weeks, Bill O'Reilly was flashing my picture on the screen and saying we're a hate group," Garza said.

A week after the march, a troubled drifter named Ismaaiyl Brinsley fatally shot two New York City police officers, Rafael Ramos and Wenjian Liu, as they sat in their patrol car, before killing himself. Some observers argued that, although Brinsley had not identified with any group, his actions were the result of an anti-police climate created by Black Lives Matter. Last summer, not long after Dylann Roof killed nine African Americans at the Emanuel AME Church, South Carolina's governor, Nikki Haley, implied that the movement had so intimidated police officers that they were unable to do their jobs, thereby putting more black lives at risk. All of this was accompanied by an increasing skepticism, across the political spectrum, about whether Black Lives Matter could move beyond reacting to outrages and begin proactively shaping public policy.

The current presidential campaign has presented the movement with a crucial opportunity to address that question. Last summer, at the annual Netroots Nation conference of progressive activists, held in Phoenix, Martin O'Malley made his candidacy a slightly longer shot when he responded to a comment about Black Lives Matter by asserting that all lives matter—an evasion of the specificity of black concerns, which elicited a chorus of boos. At the same event, activists interrupted Bernie Sanders. The Sanders campaign made overtures to the movement following the incident, but three weeks later, on the eve of the first anniversary of Michael Brown's death, two protesters identifying themselves as Black Lives Matter activists—Marissa Johnson and Mara Willaford—disrupted a Sanders rally in Seattle, preventing the senator from addressing several thousand people who had gathered to hear him. The women were booed by the largely white crowd, but the dissent wasn't limited to whites. This was the kind of freestyle disruption that caused even some African Americans to wonder how the movement was choosing its targets. At the time, it did seem odd to have gone after Sanders twice, given that he is the most progressive candidate in the race, and that none of the Republican candidates had been disrupted in their campaigns.

Garza argues that the strategy has been to leverage influence among the Democrats, since 90 percent of African Americans vote Democratic. She says that it will be uncomfortable for voters if "the person that you are supporting hasn't actually done what they need to be doing, in terms of addressing the real concern of people under this broad banner." She defended the Seattle action, saying that it was "part of a very localized dynamic, but an important one," and added that "without being disrupted Sanders wouldn't have released a platform on racial justice." Afterward, Sanders hired Symone Sanders, an African American woman, to be his national press secretary. He also released a statement on civil rights that prominently featured the names of African American victims of police violence and he began frequently referring to Black Lives Matter on the campaign trail. He subsequently won the support of many younger black activists, including Eric Garner's daughter.

An attempt to disrupt a Hillary Clinton rally early in the campaign, in New Hampshire, failed when the protesters arrived too late to get into the hall. But Clinton met with them privately afterward, and engaged in a debate about mass incarceration. She has met with members of the movement on other occasions, too. Clinton has the support of older generations of black leaders and activists—including Eric Garner's mother—and she decisively carried the black vote in Super Tuesday primaries across the South. But she has been repeatedly criticized by other activists for her support of President Bill Clinton's 1994 crime bill and, particularly, for comments that she made in the nineties about "superpredators" and the need "to bring them to heel." Two weeks ago, Ashley Williams, a twenty-three-year-old who describes herself as an "independent organizer for the movement for black lives," interrupted a private fundraising event in Charleston, where Clinton was speaking, to demand an apology. The next day, Clinton told *The Washington Post,* "Looking back, I shouldn't have used those words, and I wouldn't use them today."

If Black Lives Matter has been an object lesson in the power of social media, it has also revealed the medium's pitfalls. Just as the movement was enjoying newfound influence among the Democratic presidential contenders, it was also gaining attention for a series of febrile Twitter exchanges. In one, DeRay Mckesson and Johnetta Elzie got into a dispute with Shaun King, a writer for the New York *Daily News,* over fundraising for a social justice group. The far-right website *Breitbart* ran a picture of Mckesson and King with the headline "Black Lives Matter Leaders Just Excommunicated Shaun King."

Last month, it was announced that Garza would speak at Webster University in St. Louis, which prompted an acrimonious social media response from people in the area who are caught up in the debate over the movement's origins. Elzie tweeted, "Thousands of ppl without platforms who have no clue who the 'three' are, and their work/sacrifice gets erased," and said that the idea that Garza is a founder of the movement is a "lie." Garza released a statement saying that she had canceled the event "due to threats and online attacks on our organization and us as individuals from local activists with whom we have made an effort to have meaningful dialogue." She continued, "We all lose when bullying and personal attacks become a substitute for genuine conversation and principled disagreement."

There's nothing novel about personality conflicts arising among activists, but to older organizers, who had watched as federal surveillance and infiltration programs sowed discord that all but wrecked the Black Power movement, the public airing of grievances seemed particularly amateurish. "Movements are destroyed by conflicts over money, power, and credit," Garza said, a week after the cancellation. "We have to take seriously the impact of not being able to have principled disagreement, or we're not going to be around very long."

Almost from the outset, Black Lives Matter has been compared to the Occupy movement. Occupy was similarly associated with a single issue—income inequality—which it transformed into a movement through social media. Its focus on the 1 percent played a key role in the 2012 election, and it likely contributed to the unexpected support for Bernie Sanders's campaign. To the movement's critics, however, its achievements fell short of its promise. Its dissipation seemed to prove that, while the internet can foster the creation of a new movement, it can just as easily threaten its survival.

Black Lives Matter would appear to face similar concerns, though in recent months the movement has tacked in new directions. In November, the Ella Baker Center received a $500,000 grant from Google for Patrisse Cullors to further develop a program to help California residents monitor and respond to acts of police violence. Last year, Mckesson, with Elzie, Brittany Packnett, and Samuel Sinyangwe, a twenty-five-year-old data analyst with a degree from Stanford, launched Campaign Zero, a list of policing policy recommendations that calls for, among other things, curtailing arrests for low-level crimes, reducing quotas for summonses and arrests, and demilitarizing police departments. To date, neither Clinton nor Sanders has endorsed the platform, but both have met with the activists to discuss it.

The announcement of Mckesson's mayoral candidacy, which he made on Twitter—he has more than three hundred thousand followers—is the most dramatic break from the movement's previous actions. (Beyoncé has more than fourteen million followers, but she follows only ten people. Mckesson is one of them.) Mckesson is a native of Baltimore and he grew up on the same side of town as Freddie Gray, whose death last year in police custody sparked protests and riots in the city—at which Mckesson was a frequent presence. His family struggled with poverty and drug addiction, but he excelled academically and went on to attend Bowdoin College in Maine. He will be running against twenty-eight other candidates. One of them, the city councilman Nick Mosby, is married to Marilyn Mosby, the Maryland state's attorney, who is handling the prosecution of the six police officers indicted in connection with Gray's death.

In Baltimore, Mckesson told me that he is using his savings to fund his activist work. "It's totally possible to have Beyoncé follow you on Twitter and still be broke," he said. (*BuzzFeed* reported that a former Citibank executive would host an event at his New York City home to raise funds for Mckesson's campaign.) He wouldn't discuss his candidacy's implications for the movement, but he is very serious about running. Two weeks ago, he released a twenty-six-page report detailing his platform for reforming the city's schools, police department, and economic infrastructure. He has already been attacked for his connection to Teach for America; after he released his plan for improving Baltimore's schools, it was dismissed as a corporatist undertaking along the lines of Michael Bloomberg's and Rahm Emanuel's reforms. He rejects the idea that his lack of experience in elected office should be an obstacle. When I asked how he thought he would be able to get members of the city council and the state legislature to support his ideas, he said, "I think we build relationships. That question seems to come from a place of traditional reading of politics. That says, 'If you don't know people already, then you cannot be successful.' Politics as usual actually hasn't turned into a change in outcomes here."

Garza is tactful when she talks about Mckesson's campaign. "I'm in favor of people getting in where they fit in. Wherever you feel you can make the greatest contribution, you should," she said. But she doesn't see it as her role to define the future of the movement. She told me an anecdote that illustrates the non-centrality of her role. Last month, on Martin Luther King Day, she and Malachi were driving into San Francisco, where she was scheduled to appear at a community forum, when they heard on the radio that the Bay Bridge had been shut down. Members of a coalition of organizations, including the Bay Area chapter of Black Lives Matter, had driven onto the bridge, laced chains through their car windows, and locked them to the girders, shutting down entry to the city from Oakland. Garza had known that there were plans to mark the holiday with a protest—marches and other events were called across the nation—but she was not informed of this specific activity planned in her own city. "It's not like there's a red button I push to make people turn up," she said. In contrast, it would have been inconceivable for, say, the SCLC to have carried out such an ambitious action without the leadership's being aware of every detail.

In January, Garza traveled to Washington to attend President Obama's final State of the Union address; she had been invited by Barbara Lee, her congressional representative. (Lee, who was the sole member of Congress to vote against the authorization of military force after 9/11, has a high standing among activists who are normally skeptical of elected officials.) After the speech, as Garza stood outside in the cold trying to hail a cab, she said that she was disappointed. The president had not driven home the need for police reform. He had spoken of economic inequality and a political system rigged to benefit the few, but had scarcely touched upon the implications of that system for African Americans specifically. From the vantage point of black progressives, his words were a kind of all-lives-matter statement of public policy.

A year from now, Barack Obama will leave office, and with him will go a particular set of expectations of racial rapprochement. So will the sense that what happened in Sanford, Ferguson, Baltimore, Charleston, and Staten Island represents a paradox. Black Lives Matter may never have more influence than it has now. The future is not knowable, but it isn't likely to be unfamiliar.

DONALD TRUMP AND THE DEATH OF AMERICAN EXCEPTIONALISM

November 4, 2016

In the sixteen months since he declared his candidacy, Donald Trump's presidential campaign has elicited comparisons to those of George Wallace and Barry Goldwater, to the hallucinatory paranoia of Joseph McCarthy, to the fascist preoccupations of Charles Lindbergh, and to lesser lights of American demagoguery like Father Coughlin and the Know-Nothings of the nineteenth century.

The unifying theme among these figures, beyond their disdain for democracy, was their common residence in the loser's aisle of American history. McCarthy's conspiratorial manipulation of the public eventually earned him the enmity of both Republicans and Democrats and a vote in the Senate to censure him. Wallace carried just five states and garnered 13 percent of the popular vote. Goldwater lost to Lyndon Johnson by sixteen million popular votes, winning just 52 Electoral College votes to Johnson's 486. Richard Hofstadter's 1964 classic *The Paranoid Style in American Politics* charted the lunatic genealogy of fringe movements dating back to the early years of the republic, but the more sanguine assessment of that lineage is that few of these movements—anti-Catholicism, anti-Freemasonry, or Know-Nothingism, for instance—managed to sustain themselves in the long term or to fully inhabit the political mainstream.

Goldwater is heralded as the father of modern conservatism, but he could occupy that niche only because successive generations of his heirs refined and streamlined his message, buffing away the elements that the public saw as extremist. The modern Republican Party staked its claim on conservatism, not on Goldwaterism.

All this points to yet another reason why Trump represents a unique danger in American politics. Trumpism does not seek simply to make a point and pass on its genes to more politically palatable heirs, nor is it readily apparent why he would need to settle for this. When George Will announced his departure from the GOP last summer, he offered a modified version of Ronald Reagan's quote about leaving the Democrats—"I didn't leave the party; the party left me." But a kind of converse narrative applies to Trump; he didn't join the Republican Party so much as its most febrile elements joined him. Trump is partly a product of forces that the GOP created by pandering to a base whose dilated pupils the party mistook for gullibility, not abject, irrational fear that would send those voters scurrying to the nearest authoritarian savior they could find. The error was in thinking that this populace, mainlining Glenn Beck and Alex Jones theories and pondering how the Minutemen would have fought Sharia law, could be controlled. (For evidence to the contrary, the party needed look no further than the premature political demise of Eric Cantor.) The old adage warns that one should beware of puppets that begin pulling their own strings.

In this light, Trump represents a kind of return to the old-time religion, a fundamentalism that rejects the effete nature of dog-whistle politics the way the religious right defined itself by rejecting the watery tenets of liberal Christianity. Implicit within dog-whistling is enough respect for democratic norms and those outside one's base to speak to that base in terms that the mass populace can't readily decipher. Here, plausible deniability is at least a recognition that there are people with interests different from one's own and that their influence, if not their interests or humanity, warrants a certain degree of respect. Trump is doing the opposite of this. He is an exhorter in a midsummer tent revival: direct, literal, and speaking at a decibel that makes it impossible to misunderstand his intentions. The end result of Trump's evangelism is that a xenophobic, racist, misogynistic, serially mendacious narcissist is poised to pull in somewhere north of fifty million votes in the midst of the most bitterly contentious election in modern American history. The easy analysis holds that Trump's jihad against decency has wrecked the Republican Party, but the damage is far more extensive than this.

Two months ago, the French president François Hollande remarked that Trump's excesses made him "want to retch." It was a notable moment not only for the imagery but also for the implications—a foreign head of state was criticizing a current nominee for president of the United States—and, by association, the millions of Americans who had seen in him a potential leader. It might be said that Hollande, whose own country has witnessed the increasing prominence of Marine Le Pen's reactionary, nativist National Front, has plenty to attend to on his soil. But this is precisely the point. The anti-immigrant, authoritarian, and nationalist movements we've witnessed in Germany, the U.K., Turkey, and France—troubling as they may be—do not violate a broader mandate that those nations have assigned to themselves. The United States' claim to moral primacy in the world, the idea of American exceptionalism, rests upon the argument that this is a nation set apart. In June, Pew reported that 85 percent of Europeans who were polled had no confidence in Trump's ability to "do the right thing" in world affairs (compared with 27 percent who lacked this confidence in Hillary Clinton and 22 percent who saw President Obama this way).

The old presumptions hold that some element of national humiliation and decline predisposes nations toward fascism, or at least the appeals of fascistic movements. But in the United States this movement sprang up on the contrails of the first black presidency—a moment that was, perhaps naïvely at the time, thought to be one of national affirmation and triumph. The unsavory implication here, of course, is that, for the cornerstone elements of Trumpism, that triumph *was* a national humiliation, that the image of an African American receiving the deference and regard that the presidency entails invalidated these Americans' understanding of what the United States is, or at least what it is supposed to be.

In the broader context, Trumpism represents the demise of American exceptionalism, or at least the refutation of the most cogent arguments for it ever having existed in the first place. An exceptional nation would have better reflexes than this, would recognize the communicable nature of fear more quickly, would rally its immune defense more efficiently than the United States has in the past sixteen months. At a quaint moment in the recent past, it was possible to think that a decisive Clinton victory would exorcise Trumpism from public life. But, on the verge of the election, that idea increasingly seems like an indulgent delusion. The problem of Trump is not simply that his opinions far exceed his knowledge; it's that what he does know is so hostile to democracy, not only in the Republican Party or the United States but in the world. Whatever happens on November 8, we are at the outset of a much longer reckoning.

POSTSCRIPT TO "DONALD TRUMP AND THE DEATH OF AMERICAN EXCEPTIONALISM"

There are too many paradoxes associated with the movement surrounding Donald Trump to ever sort through which of them is the most relevant, but here is one that I suspect would be in the top five: in seeking to reaffirm America's status as an exceptional nation—the greatest embodiment of the human aspiration toward freedom—the nation twice elected a man who is a pristine embodiment of the very opposite. The louche, ill-informed, conspiratorial, cynical, belligerent greed of the forty-fifth (and forty-seventh) president of the United States represents the abnegation of democratic values in ways that we will likely be grappling with for many decades into the future. I wrote this piece just ahead of the 2016 election at a point where the threat Trump represented had become apparent enough to be alarming. That danger has been realized in the long years since that day. Among my key aspirations as a writer is a wish to make the obscure more apparent, to think about concerns whose contours have not yet become completely visible, and, through the work of writing, to help elucidate what is happening around us. This is an essay I would not write today. Mainly because the point I was trying to make here is no longer insightful. It's painfully, thoroughly, unexceptionally obvious. But when I returned to it, I still found it useful as an artifact of a moment when we were awakening to something—half in denial, half in paralyzed terror.

BARACK OBAMA IN DEFEAT

November 10, 2016

Twelve years ago, Barack Obama introduced himself to the American public by way of a speech given at the Democratic National Convention in Boston in which he declared, "There is not a black America and a white America and Latino America, an Asian America; there's the United States of America." Few of us believed this to be true, but most, if not all, of us longed for it to be. We vested this brash optimist with our hope, a resource that was in scarce supply three years after the September 11 terrorist attacks in a country mired in disastrous military conflicts in two nations. The vision he offered—of national reconciliation beyond partisan bounds, of government rooted in respect for the governed and the Constitution itself, of idealism that could actually be realized—became the basis for his presidential campaign. Twice the United States elected to the presidency a biracial black man whose ancestry and upbringing stretched to three continents.

At various points that idealism has been severely tested. During his presidency, we witnessed a partisan divide widen into an impassable trench, and gun violence go unchecked while special interests blocked any regulation. The president was forced to show his birth certificate, which we recognized as the racial profiling of the most powerful man in the world. Obama did not, at least publicly, waver in his contention that Americans were bound together by something greater than what divided them. In July, when he spoke in Dallas after a gunman murdered five police officers, he seemed pained by the weight of this faith, as if stress fractures had appeared in a load-bearing wall.

It is difficult not to see the result of this year's presidential election as a refutation of Obama's creed of common Americanism. And on Wednesday, for the first time in the twelve years that we've been watching him, Obama did not seem to believe the words he was speaking to the American public. In the White House Rose Garden, Obama offered his version of a concession speech—an acknowledgment of Donald Trump's victory. The president attempted gamely to cast Trump's victory as part of the normal ebb and flow of political fortunes, and as an example of the great American tradition of the peaceful transfer of power. (This was not, it should be recalled, the peaceful transfer of power that most observers were worried about.) He intended, he said, to offer the same courtesy toward Trump that President George W. Bush had offered him in 2008. Yet that reference only served to highlight the paradox of Obama's presidency: he now exists in history bracketed by the overmatched forty-third president and the misogynistic racial demagogue who will succeed him as the forty-fifth. During his 2008 campaign, Obama frequently found himself—and without much objection on his part—compared to Abraham Lincoln. He may now share an ambivalent common bond with Lincoln, whose presidency was bookended by James Buchanan and Andrew Johnson, two lesser lights of American history.

Even Obama's vast reservoir of grace seemed near the faltering point. "Sometimes we move in ways that some people think is forward," he said, but then had to circumnavigate the phrase "sometimes we go backward." He landed safely by adding, "and others think is moving back," but the implications were clear. Trump is the antithesis of Obama: louche rather than gracious, parochial rather than worldly, conspiratorial rather than pragmatically intellectual. Yet the two are now bound in history, and in perhaps the cruelest subplot, Obama must now show regard and professional courtesy to the man responsible for engineering the doubts about his very citizenship.

In his brief remarks, the president left a great deal unsaid. Perhaps it was better this way. We need not contemplate the fact that his signature policy achievements, the Affordable Care Act and the Iran nuclear deal most notably, will be undone immediately. More distressingly, the very nature of Trump's campaign—its venomous bigotry, its radioactive contempt, its tribalism—may have already diminished Obama's significant cultural achievements. We reveled in the small moments of this presidency: the image of a black man standing behind the presidential seal, quietly broadening our frame of reference for black men in this society; his open adoration of his wife, Michelle; the sight of his two daughters flourishing into young womanhood, recognizing along the way that we, a vast, sprawling, unwieldy entity, had common affinity for these two African American teens. Trump's moment seems to represent an inversion of this. We now occupy an altogether less honorable place culturally. In the short term, at least, it seems that divisiveness has prevailed.

Regardless of the dire moment that has come, the past eight years have meant something. History will have its way with Obama's presidency, and most certainly with the man himself. But if that future assessment is thorough, it will note that he won against long odds, persevered under adverse circumstances, and that we, this divided, fraught collection of tribes, were the better for it.

GWEN IFILL, 1955–2016

November 15, 2016

Long before Monday, when Gwen Ifill, the renowned PBS journalist, died at age sixty-one of cancer, this year had begun to look like a bouquet of hardships. It is a particular cruelty that Ifill, who was a standard-bearer for journalism, a mentor to young reporters, and a profoundly decent colleague, should depart now, when the country has never been more in need of those qualities.

Ifill, who was gracious even with those she strongly disagreed with, managed to calibrate professionalism and warmth, intellect and humility, and a keen sense of humor. She came of age at a moment when the default voice of authority in journalism—male, white, avuncular—was entrenched, and she helped to quietly upend those presumptions. Ifill, the daughter of an African Methodist Episcopal minister, grew up in parsonages and public housing on the East Coast and graduated from Simmons College, in Boston, in 1977. She was part of a generation that emerged in the wake of the civil rights movement, but she was not too distant from the tumult of that era to take its gains for granted.

Ifill began her journalistic career covering the chaotic aftermath of court-mandated busing in Boston. She navigated the conundrum that black journalists then and now confront: how to respond to the need for informed coverage of racial issues without being confined by it. Ifill went on to cover municipal politics in Baltimore, gaining a vantage point on the economic and social changes that were taking root in cities across the country. Those tectonic up-heavals were also producing tensions between the established class of black leaders, many of them alumni of the civil rights movement, and a group of younger voices, who were not beholden to the old way of doing things. In Baltimore, this was reflected in the election of Kurt Schmoke, a Yale University and Harvard Law School graduate, as the city's second black mayor, in 1987. Ifill covered Schmoke's tenure and Jesse Jackson's presidential campaign the following year. Twenty years later, as she chronicled Barack Obama's march toward the White House, she recognized it as the culmination of the story she'd been covering for much of her career.

I first encountered Ifill in 2008, as part of a circle of black journalists who were trying to make sense of the almost unbelievable changes in the political landscape. We spoke briefly as she was working on her book, *The Breakthrough: Politics and Race in the Age of Obama*. Our most sustained interactions came as the euphoria that accompanied Obama's election began to curdle into the resentments that fueled this year's presidential election. In 2014, Ifill moderated a town hall discussion of the crisis in Ferguson and invited me to participate. A year later, we met for another discussion, in Charleston, in the wake of the mass shooting at Emanuel AME Church. What I remember most about that afternoon was the expert way that she guided that conversation—not an easy one—with about two hundred members of the community. Ifill was a humane presence, but nonetheless pushed those gathered in the room to examine the deeper factors that had culminated in yet another racial tragedy.

I last saw her almost exactly a year ago, after joining her on *PBS NewsHour* for a discussion of racism and free speech on college campuses. Two days later, I ran into Ifill on a flight to Chicago. We spoke during boarding, and I was pleasantly surprised to see her waiting on the concourse when I exited. We talked about Obama's final year in office, and about journalism, travel, and the current state of civil rights. Earlier this year, she was selected to receive the

John Chancellor Award for Excellence in Journalism. The awards dinner was to be held this Wednesday night. I was looking forward to seeing her and commending her on the example she had set in her four decades of journalism. Instead, we are summing up her contributions in memoriam. There is a great deal of work ahead of those of us who take democracy seriously. It's heartbreaking to consider that we will have to do it without Ifill at our side.

LIBERALS INVOKE STATES' RIGHTS

November 28, 2016

The wake of the presidential election has stirred an array of reactions—grief, denial, outrage, bewilderment—among the liberals and progressives who supported Hillary Clinton. Her loss, scarcely predicted in the polls, and therefore all the more shocking to the people who voted for her (and who outnumber her opponent's supporters by more than a million and counting), has become a case study in political trauma. Donald Trump's victory inspired another, less noted reaction that may prove more politically significant than the current wave of demoralization: defiance.

On the day after the election, Kevin de León, the pro tempore president of the California Senate, and Anthony Rendon, the speaker of the California Assembly, released a joint statement whose opening sentence—"Today, we woke up feeling like strangers in a foreign land"—perfectly summarized the disorientation that millions of Americans were experiencing. More important, the statement pointed out that Trump's bigotry and misogyny were at odds with California's values of inclusiveness and tolerance, and, the authors vowed, "we will lead the resistance to any effort that would shred our social fabric or our Constitution."

Three days later, Andrew Cuomo, the governor of New York, after initially flirting with the idea that Trump could be a "bonus" for the state, posted a statement on Facebook arguing that New Yorkers "have fundamentally different philosophies than what Donald Trump laid out in his campaign." Cuomo was tacitly accusing the president-elect—who *is* a New Yorker—of a kind of betrayal. He continued:

> Whether you are gay or straight, Muslim or Christian, rich or poor, black or white or brown, we respect all people in the state of New York.
>
> It's the very core of what we believe and who we are. But it's not just what we say, we passed laws that reflect it, and we will continue to do so, no matter what happens nationally. We won't allow a federal government that attacks immigrants to do so in our state.

That line of thought carried down the chain of command. Both Eric Garcetti and Bill de Blasio, the mayors of Los Angeles and New York, vowed to protect vulnerable populations in their cities. (Sanctuary cities across the nation, including Chicago, Seattle, and Denver, did the same, even though Trump threatened to defund them.) Charlie Beck, the chief of the LAPD, added, "We are not going to work in conjunction with Homeland Security on deportation efforts. That is not our job, nor will I make it our job."

These announcements cannot be dismissed as simply the whiny objections of the coastal elites. Thirty-nine million people live in California—12 percent of the population of the United States. The state is home to the economic and cultural axes of Silicon Valley and Hollywood. Last year, its economy became the sixth largest in the world, a spot formerly held by France. Clinton beat Trump by 28 points in California, and by 21 points in New York. Now the two states have triggered an uncommon development in a year that has offered us a great number of them: liberals invoking states' rights.

We have become accustomed to governors denouncing overreach by the federal government. Last year, more than thirty governors released statements opposing President Barack Obama's plan to resettle Syrian refugees in their states, even though federal authority clearly allowed him to do so. In 2012, Republican opponents of the Affordable Care Act based their challenge at the Supreme Court on the ground that it violated states' rights. Later that year, shortly after Obama was reelected, more than a hundred thousand Texans signed a petition requesting that the White House respond to their demand for secession. (This presented a paradox in that the petitioners were recognizing federal authority in an attempt to claim that the federal government did not have authority over them.) It would seem ironic that two of the largest and most consistently Democratic states have now presented states' rights arguments in their cause, were it not for history.

States' rights have a complicated genealogy, which ties the birth of the Confederacy to Southern resistance to civil rights. In 1980, when Ronald Reagan invoked the phrase in Philadelphia, Mississippi—where three civil rights workers had been murdered in 1964—he was offering a kind of absolution, if not for racial violence then for the principle that had been used to justify it. Today, the phrase is often shorthand for opposition to "big government," a term that carries racial implications of its own. Yet the argument for states' rights began in the early years of the republic, in an effort to confront exactly the type of threat to non-citizens that the incoming administration poses.

In 1798, the passage of the Alien and Sedition Acts increased the residency requirement from five years to fourteen years before immigrants could vote and authorized the executive branch to summarily deport immigrants who were deemed dangerous or who had come from hostile nations. In response, James Madison and Thomas Jefferson, whose Democratic-Republican Party was favored by immigrants, wrote the Virginia and Kentucky resolutions, which held that individual states had the right to nullify unconstitutional laws within their borders. They further stipulated that states had the right to "interpose" themselves against the authority of the federal government. George Washington was among those who saw the resolutions as a cure that was worse than the illness of federal overreach. But the notion of states' rights survived.

Trump's hostility toward immigration has taken various iterations, but the common theme is to rid the country of foreign residents deemed dangerous and to prohibit the entry of people from hostile nations. It would appear that, 218 years later, the principles of the Alien and Sedition Acts have sprung, with surprising vigor, from their resting place in history. The political leaders in New York and California have not yet proposed nullifying federal authority on immigration—they are only resisting it, in the service of the higher principle of democracy and inclusion. That alone can't forestall the damage that a Trump administration might do on the issue of immigration. But for the millions of Americans, immigrants and non-immigrants alike, who also woke up last week feeling like strangers in a foreign land, it is as good a starting place as any.

TAKING IT TO THE STREETS

January 9, 2017

On December 6, less than a month after the election, Vice President Joe Biden, who was in New York to receive the Robert F. Kennedy Ripple of Hope Award for his decades of public service, used the occasion to urge Americans not to despair. "I remind people, '68 was really a bad year," he said, and "America didn't break." He added, "It's as bad now, but I'm hopeful." And bad it was. The man for whom Biden's award was named was assassinated in 1968. So was Martin Luther King, Jr. Riots erupted in more than a hundred cities, and violence broke out at the Democratic National Convention in Chicago. The year closed with the hairbreadth victory of a law-and-order presidential nominee whose Southern Strategy of racial politicking remade the electoral map. Whatever innocence had survived the tumult of the five years since the murder of John F. Kennedy was gone.

It was telling that Biden had to sift through nearly a half century of history to find a precedent for the current malaise among liberals and progressives, but the comparison was not entirely fitting. Throughout Richard Nixon's presidency, Democrats maintained majorities in both the Senate and the House of Representatives. The efforts of the antiwar movement to end American involvement in Vietnam had stalled, but Nixon's first years in office saw the enactment of several progressive measures, including the Occupational Safety and Health Act and the Clean Air Act, as well as the formation of the Environmental Protection Agency. In 2016, the Republicans won the White House, maintained control of both chambers of Congress, and secured the ability to create a conservative Supreme Court majority that could last a generation or more. Donald Trump, a man with minimal restraint, has been awarded maximal power.

Last summer, the ACLU issued a report highlighting the ways in which Trump's proposals on a number of issues would violate the Bill of Rights. After his victory, the ACLU's home page featured an image of him with the caption "See You in Court." In November, Trump tweeted that he would have won the popular vote but for millions of illegal ballots cast. This was not just a window into the conspiratorial and fantasist mindset of the president-elect but a looming threat to voting rights. Ten days after the election, the NAACP Legal Defense Fund released a statement opposing the nomination of Senator Jeff Sessions of Alabama as attorney general, based on his record of hostility to voting rights and on the fact that he'd once brought unsubstantiated charges of voter fraud against civil rights activists. But, with a Republican majority that has mostly shown compliance with Trump despite his contempt for the norms of democracy, the fear is that he will achieve much of what he wants. Even if he accomplishes only half, the landscape of American politics and policy will be radically altered. This prospect has recalled another phenomenon of the 1960s: the conviction that "democracy is in the streets."

Movements are born in the moments when abstract principles become concrete concerns. MoveOn arose in response to what was perceived as the Republican congressional overreach that resulted in the impeachment of President Bill Clinton. The Occupy movement was a backlash to the financial crisis. The message of Black Lives Matter was inspired by the death of Trayvon Martin and the unrest in Ferguson, Missouri. Occupy's version of anti-corporate populism helped to create the climate in which Senator Bernie Sanders's insurgent campaign could not only exist but essentially shape the Democratic Party platform. Black Lives Matter brought national attention to local instances of police brutality, prompting the Obama administration to launch the Task Force on 21st Century Policing and helping defeat prosecutors in Chicago and Cleveland, who had sought reelection after initially failing to bring charges against police officers accused of using excessive force.

Last July, when the Army Corps of Engineers gave final approval for the completion of the Dakota Access Pipeline, members of the Standing Rock Sioux Tribe, anxious that the pipeline would threaten their water supply, started an online petition and filed a lawsuit to halt construction. Thousands of activists, including members of Black Lives Matter and two thousand military veterans, went to Standing Rock to protest on the Sioux's behalf; last month, they endured rubber bullets and water hoses fired in freezing temperatures. On December 4, the Army Corps announced that it would look for an alternate route. But since Rick Perry, Trump's choice for energy secretary, sits on the board of Energy Transfer Partners, the company building the pipeline (and in which Trump, until recently, owned stock), protesters are settling in for a long winter.

In that context, the waves of protests in Portland, Los Angeles, Oakland, New York, Chicago, and Washington, D.C., in the days after the election look less like spontaneous outrage and more like a preview of what the next four years may hold. Unlike the specific protests that emerged during the Obama administration, the post-election demonstrations have been directed at the general state of American democracy. Two hundred thousand women are expected to assemble in front of the Capitol on January 21, the day after the inauguration, for the Women's March on Washington. Born of one woman's invitation to forty friends, the event is meant as a rejoinder to the fact that a candidate with a troubling history regarding women's rights—one who actually bragged about committing sexual assault—has made it to the White House.

The first inauguration of George W. Bush in 2001 saw mass protests driven by the sentiment that the election had been stolen. The protests that greet Trump will, in all probability, exceed them: some twenty other groups have also applied for march permits. Given his history with African Americans, Muslims, Latinos, immigrants, unionized labor, environmentalists, and people with disabilities, it is not hard to imagine that there will be many more to come. The Congress is unlikely to check the new president, but democracy may thrive in the states, the courts, the next elections, and—lest the lessons of the sixties be forgotten—the streets.

POSTSCRIPT TO "TAKING IT TO THE STREETS"

Unlike his 2024 reelection, Donald Trump's inaugural presidential campaign victory generated a shock that his brand of mendacious, autocratic, and conspiratorial politics could appeal to enough people to form an Electoral College majority in the United States. That terrible recognition made committed activists of bystanders and inspired, in turn, a wave of reaction that came to be known as "The Resistance." This movement then fed the paranoia that had always abided Trump and culminated in a fervid fear that the federal bureaucracy itself was shot through with Resisters, a shadowy "deep state" of civil service employees bent upon thwarting the president's fascistic will. (In reality, having never governed or held public office previously, Trump came in ill-prepared to move the levers of government in any coordinated or productive way.)

The Trump Resistance had as its operating presumption that the checks upon government—both the internal ones like the courts and the external ones like demonstrations and grassroots organizing—were the only obstacles standing between Trump and his goal of American autocracy. This proved to be largely true. The Resistance shored up the will of otherwise deferential Democratic politicians. The courts produced a more checkered result—allowing, for instance, Trump's purported "Muslim ban" to go into effect and offering him wide latitude in matters of the executive branch. His nominees proved decisive in ending the abortion protections offered by *Roe v. Wade* and affirmative action in higher education, although they blocked him from ending temporary protected status for people from Sudan, Nicaragua, Haiti, and El Salvador and prevented him from spending military funds to build a wall at the southern border of the United States.

This piece was written eleven days before the inauguration when none of this was known but many of us feared the worst. With the president awarded "maximal power" as I noted, the question was whether these mechanisms could be enough to avert the worst possible outcomes. Democracy, such as it was, did indeed exist in the streets and in the hearts of the people occupying them. Eight years later, that question has regained salience as, against the now wearying but no longer shocking vision of Trump being inaugurated to the presidency, a fearful public asks if those same guardrails can offer anything like protection for a second go-round.

PRODIGY OF HATE

February 6, 2017

Early on the morning of December 7, a dozen officers from the Department of Homeland Security were stationed outside the federal courthouse at 85 Broad Street in Charleston, South Carolina. It was warm out, and the officers looked both relaxed and alert, talking among themselves as they kept watch. The federal building is a bunker, all right angles and gray concrete, completed in 1987. Across the street stands the county courthouse, designed by James Hoban, the architect of the White House, and diagonally opposite is the city hall, built in 1801. The federal building would mar what the American Planning Association calls one of the nation's "great streets," except that it is hidden by a redbrick antebellum structure that faces the street—an architectural sleight of hand that says much about the reasons that the Homeland Security officers were on Broad Street that day.

The federal trial of Dylann Roof was commencing, eighteen months after he shot and killed nine African American congregants at the Emanuel African Methodist Episcopal Church during evening Bible study, a crime he had confessed to on video in horrific detail and without remorse. The authorities were concerned that Roof, who repeatedly stated that he had committed the murders as a call to action for persecuted whites, had become a cause célèbre for white nationalists. That movement had been exiled to the political fringes after the murders, but it had regained some visibility during the presidential campaign.

Two days earlier, a jury had deadlocked in the trial of Michael Slager, a North Charleston police officer charged with murder in the death of Walter Scott, an unarmed fifty-year-old black man Slager had shot in the back as he ran from a traffic stop. When the judge declared a mistrial, Scott's mother invoked God's will toward justice, and the state's governor, Nikki Haley, cautioned patience until the state could retry the officer. Now some feared that, despite the confession and the overwhelming forensic evidence, something similar might occur in the Roof trial.

Judge Richard Gergel was presiding. He is an avuncular silver-haired man with a reputation for efficiency and a liberal bent; in 2014, he issued a ruling that same-sex couples have the right to marry in South Carolina, and he was responsible for installing a portrait of Jonathan Jasper Wright, the state's first black supreme court justice, in the court building. The courtroom was solemn as Roof entered, wearing a gray-and-black-striped prison jumpsuit. He is now twenty-two but, with his blond hair in a fresh bowl cut, he appeared younger. He is small to the point of fragility, and his frame swam in the jumpsuit. He was charged with thirty-three felony counts; twelve of them were hate crimes, and eighteen others, including firearm and religious-obstruction charges, were punishable by death.

The family members of the victims, their supporters, the church's new pastor, Eric Manning, and other clergy filled the benches on the right side of the courtroom. Roof's mother and his paternal grandparents sat in the second row on the left. Many people had assumed that Roof was a representative of the disenfranchised white population whose narrative of loss had come to play an unexpectedly central role in the election. Roof dropped out of high school after repeating ninth grade and then dropped out of an online alternative school before later earning his GED, but he did not grow up in poverty. His grandfather is a prominent real estate attorney in Columbia. His father, who attended the trial sporadically, is a building contractor and owned several properties around the state. At the time of the shooting, Roof lived with his mother in a spacious home in Lexington, across the Congaree River from Columbia.

He had chosen to drive two hours to Charleston to commit his crime, he told the police, because the city is "historic." Mother Emanuel, as the church is known, traces its roots to 1816. It was a center of clandestine anti-slavery activity, and in 1822, when city officials discovered that congregants were planning a slave revolt, they burned the church to the ground. The current building was erected in 1891 on Calhoun Street, named for Vice President John C. Calhoun, the intellectual progenitor of secession. The Calhoun monument, a column eighty feet high and topped by a statue of the statesman, is half a block away. The monument and the church, which came to play a central role in the Southern civil rights movement, stand like a statement and its rebuttal. Roof had drawn up a list of half a dozen churches before settling on Mother Emanuel. "I realize these people are not criminal," he said. "They're in church." He chose them, he explained, because killing a black drug dealer would not have generated the same attention.

The lead prosecutor was Jay Richardson, an assistant U.S. attorney based in Columbia. He is a small dark-haired man who speaks in a commanding tone. Roof's mother sank down on the bench as he delivered his opening statement, which contained details of the crime that had previously been withheld from the press. At a certain point, she slumped over. It seemed for a moment that she had fainted, but she was taken to a hospital and it was later learned that she had suffered a heart attack. She survived, but did not return for the remainder of the trial.

Richardson reported that Roof pulled into the church parking lot and sat in his car for some time, "contemplating," before going inside. He had loaded eight clips of hollow-point ammunition for his Glock .45 semiautomatic handgun because, Richardson implied, he wanted to have eighty-eight bullets; the number is white nationalist code for "Heil Hitler."

The most well-known of Roof's victims was Emanuel's pastor, the Reverend Clementa Pinckney, who also served in the South Carolina State Senate. (He became a member of the state House of Representatives in 1996, when he was twenty-three, the youngest African American ever elected to the state's legislature.) Pinckney welcomed the newcomer, gave him a Bible, and offered him a chair next to him in the circle where the twelve attendees of the study group sat. Roof's motive was "retaliation for perceived offenses" against the white race, Richardson said. "He also talked about 'the call to arms,' the hope that his attack would agitate others, worsen race relations, increase racial tensions that would lead to a race war."

Four months before the shooting, the Equal Justice Initiative issued a report on the history of lynching in the United States after Reconstruction. There were 184 recorded lynchings in South Carolina. The last occurred in 1947, when a mob beat, stabbed, and shot to death Willie Earle, a twenty-four-year-old black man who had been accused of murdering a white cabdriver from Greenville. Strom Thurmond, who was then the governor, pushed for those responsible to be brought to trial, perhaps worried that the incident would undercut efforts to recast the state's brutish image. Thirty-one white men were charged; all were acquitted. Richardson, in his opening, seemed to suggest that lynching had not ceased in South Carolina; it had just been on a sixty-eight-year hiatus. Later in the trial, he made that connection explicit, charging that Roof was guilty of "a modern-day lynching."

Few people in Charleston's legal community expressed interest in handling the defense, so the court appointed David Bruck to represent Roof. Bruck is originally from Montreal but attended law school in South Carolina and worked there for more than twenty years, both as a public defender and in private practice. He now teaches law in Virginia, at Washington and Lee University, where he also directs a death penalty defense clinic; he almost exclusively takes on cases that involve the death penalty, which he views as both unjust and racist in its application. In 1983, he wrote a groundbreaking article for *The New Republic* in which he argued that the imposition of capital punishment—a practice that reinforced the value of the lives of white victims over those of black ones—was as troubling as violent crime itself.

In 2015, Bruck served on the defense for Dzhokhar Tsarnaev during his federal trial for the Boston Marathon bombing. Bruck had previously represented Susan Smith, a white South Carolina woman who, in 1994, drowned her two young sons in a lake and blamed the act on a fictional black carjacker. (Tsarnaev was sentenced to death; Smith was given a life sentence.) His thinking appears to be that, if the lives of defendants charged with heinous crimes can be spared, so could the lives of those charged with lesser crimes. If the bar is raised high enough, the death penalty might never be applied.

Bruck's relationship with Roof had been difficult almost from the outset. The defense called for a competency assessment and moved to have Roof declared mentally unfit, which he vigorously resisted. Roof asked Judge Gergel to be allowed to represent himself, which he did, during the jury selection, then asked to have counsel reinstated for the guilt phase of the trial, but not for the penalty phase. That ultimately led to a second competency hearing between the two phases.

In the opening statement for the defense, Bruck, who seems almost congenitally soft-spoken, addressed the jury in such low tones that some family members had to lean forward in their seats in order to hear him. "The story that Mr. Richardson just finished telling you really did occur," he said, referring to the prosecutor's graphic recounting of the murders. Everyone, himself included, Bruck said, expected that the verdict "will be guilty." The jurors may have been wondering why there even was a trial, he said. Roof had offered to plead guilty in exchange for a life sentence, but the Justice Department had not allowed it. Many people in Charleston thought that Loretta Lynch, the U.S. attorney general, should have spared the families—and the city—the ordeal of a trial, but she ruled that the hate crime elements of the case warranted the harshest sentence at the government's disposal. The federal hate crime statute that covers racially motivated crime, however, does not carry the death penalty, which accounts for some of the additional charges. The trial, with its attendant expense and emotional trauma, Bruck intimated, was purely a function of the government's desire to pursue the death penalty.

Shortly after one o'clock, Richardson called the first witness: Felicia Sanders, a longtime member of Emanuel. She escaped harm that night, only to witness the death of her son, Tywanza, a twenty-six-year-old poet, barber, and musician who had planned to start graduate school in the fall. Felicia Sanders is fifty-nine, with deep brown skin and shoulder-length brown hair, and that day she wore a floral-patterned dress with a purple cardigan. She owned—and, until the shooting, had operated—a local salon, where her son had grown up amid a hive of conversation, jokes, and gossip. She speaks with a pronounced Charleston accent, and when Richardson asked her if she was married she looked at her husband, sitting in the front row, and answered "yes" so wearily that the courtroom erupted into laughter.

Then Richardson asked her about Roof's behavior in the church. "Most of the time, he hung his head down just the way he's doing right now," she said. Tywanza was an avid social media user, and he uploaded a video of himself at the church to Snapchat. Roof can be seen in the background, sitting in the Bible circle. "He was there for forty-five minutes to an hour," Sanders continued. "We stood up and shut our eyes to say a prayer." When she heard the first shots, she assumed that the noise stemmed from a problem with a new elevator that was being installed, but then she looked at the defendant. "I screamed, 'He has a gun!' " she said. "By then, he had already shot Reverend Pinckney."

Roof began firing randomly. At one point, he paused to ask Polly Sheppard, a seventy-two-year-old retired nurse, if he had shot her yet. "My son rised up to get the attention off Miss Polly, even though he had already got shot," Sanders told the jury. "He stood up and said, 'Why are you doing this?' " She continued, "The defendant, over there with his head hanging down, refusing to look at me right now, told my son, 'I have to do this, because you're raping our women and y'all taking over the world.'" She added, "That's when he put about five bullets in my son." Sanders lay on the floor, shielding her eleven-year-old granddaughter, holding the girl so tightly that she worried she might smother her.

She went on, "I said, 'Tywanza, please lay down.' He said, 'I gotta get to Aunt Susie.'" Susie Jackson, who was eighty-seven, was the family matriarch, Tywanza's great-aunt on his father's side. She had been shot, but Tywanza managed to crawl over to her and reached out to touch her hair before he died. Sanders began to sob as she recalled her son's final moments. She'd had a difficult pregnancy with him—the doctors warned that she might miscarry—and she had always thought of his birth as a testament to faith. She had come to think of his death in similar terms. Sanders told the court, "I watched my son come into this world and I watched my son leave this world."

The family members sat quietly throughout most of the trial, but Sanders's words left several of them weeping. The sign language interpreters, as they relayed the proceedings to Gary Washington, whose mother, Ethel Lance, was among the dead, were crying. The courtroom sketch artist and many of the journalists present paused to wipe away tears. Judge Gergel called a short recess.

When the court reconvened, Bruck, during his cross-examination of Sanders, asked if Roof had said anything as he left the church. "Yes," she replied. "He said he was going to kill himself, and I was counting on that. He's evil. There's no place on earth for him except the pit of Hell."

Dylann Roof, in writings found during a search of his prison cell, imagined himself the last stalwart of the Lost Cause of the Confederacy. He wrote that "segregation was not a bad thing. It was mostly defensive." (When investigators asked where he got his information, he said, "It's all there on the internet." He had found the Council of Conservative Citizens website, which descended from the old White Citizens' Councils.) The Civil War began in Charleston. The Ordinance of Secession was signed in Institute Hall, on Meeting Street, in December 1860; the first shots were fired at Fort Sumter, in the harbor, a few months later. The reaction of many

Charlestonians to the extraordinary moment, at a bond hearing the day after Roof's arrest, when, one by one, family members stood and forgave him, was an outgrowth of the city's relationship to that past. Forgiveness was not just an example of how to metabolize hatred directed at you, or just a demonstration of Christian faith, though it was both of those things. It stood for a broader redemption, an exoneration from history itself.

One afternoon during the trial, I visited the Confederate Museum, located in Market Hall on Meeting Street. The hall was built in 1841 and served as the headquarters of a market where, the museum's website states, "fruits, meats, vegetables, and fish were sold—no slaves." In 1899, the Daughters of the Confederacy opened the museum in a large room on the second floor. Glass cases display Confederate uniforms, swords, volumes of the military registries of the Confederate States of America, and aged histories of the conflict. Chunks of shrapnel from the Union's assault on the city rest on shelves. A South Carolina secession flag dominates the center of the room.

One of the docents, a red-haired woman in her forties, introduced herself as Jill. She wore an orange Clemson University sweater in honor of its football team, which had clinched the national championship the night before. I told her that I was in town for the Roof trial, and she said, "He's just a crazy nut," adding that the jury shouldn't need to deliberate long before passing a death sentence. Another docent, Barbara, who belongs to a Methodist church near Emanuel, said that she'd been deeply moved by the victims' families: "I was blown away by their faith. It was completely unshakable." When I asked the two women if it was possible to interpret Roof's motives as an extension of the Confederate cause, they both demurred. "We can't control how crazy racists use the symbols," Jill said. "What he's doing isn't connected to anything to do with our heritage," Barbara added. A man visiting the museum agreed, saying that Roof did not understand the Confederacy and had merely retrofitted it to his terrible worldview.

During the recent battles over the appropriateness of flying the Confederate flag from public buildings, some Southerners rallied around the phrase "heritage, not hate." At the museum, it occurred to me that this act of distancing was what Roof most fiercely rejected. Charleston today is a testament to the successful paring of hate from heritage. Herb Frazier, a black journalist who grew up in the city and has attended Emanuel since childhood, told me that black Charlestonians have always hated the Calhoun monument. "He looks down with this scowl on his face," he said. Then, in 1999, Charleston's Holocaust Memorial was erected just fifty feet from the base of Calhoun's column. That proximity suggests either a wishful denial of Calhoun's legacy or a level of irony not typically found among municipal planners.

Last year, Frazier collaborated with Marjory Wentworth, South Carolina's poet laureate, and Bernard Powers, a professor of history at the College of Charleston, on *We Are Charleston,* a book that puts the church murders in the context of the city's racial history and records the responses to it. A week after the shooting, following a vote in the legislature, Governor Haley called for the removal of the Confederate flag that had flown at the State House since 1961, an act that was widely praised. But Wentworth pointed out that the decision was at least partly pragmatic. "We've been boycotted ever since it went up," she said. "You don't read much about that. There were a lot of business leaders that wanted it down." It was a recognition not altogether distinct from the one that Strom Thurmond may have reached sixty-eight years earlier: that racism, at least in its most overt forms, is bad for business.

But for Roof and the fraternity that he sought out on websites like Stormfront, where he operated under the user name LilAryan, this paring was a contradictory undertaking. What is the point, he seemed to reason, of commemorating the Confederacy if you ignore the reason that it existed in the first place?

The second day of the trial began with a debate between the defense and the prosecution about the velocity with which Roof's soul might arrive in hell. Bruck had filed a motion for a mistrial, arguing that the jury might construe Sanders's statement that "there's no place on earth for him" as a plea for the death penalty. Richardson objected. "She was not commenting on the punishment," he said, but rather on where Roof would have gone if he had killed himself. He added, "That is also where he's going if he dies of natural causes or the state does it."

For many people in Charleston, being asked to decide whether Roof should be executed amounted to what older Southern blacks refer to as being "put in a trickbag": a circumstance in which there are no good options and one must reconcile with the bad ones. It had been noted that the family members and the congregation were averse to having Roof put to death, but they were not unanimous in their views. Eric Manning, the pastor, told me that the AME church opposes the death penalty: "We are called to be the light of the world, so life is sacred." Carey Grady, a senior pastor at Reid Chapel AME Church in Columbia, had known Pinckney from childhood. The two friends kept in touch regularly and often texted. Grady showed me the message he'd sent Pinckney when he first heard about the shooting. "I know you're getting dozens of calls right now," it said. "You and the Emanuel Church family are in our prayers." Pinckney, Grady said, almost to himself, "never replied." The criminal justice system was unfair to African Americans, Grady told me, then added, "I hate to say it, but, if the system is unjust, the most just thing to happen in that system is for Roof to get the death penalty, because otherwise you make the statement that black lives really don't matter."

Malcolm Graham is the youngest brother of Cynthia Hurd, one of the victims. She had worked for more than thirty years as a librarian for the public and the university systems. Graham, a former state senator from North Carolina, recently ran for Congress—something that his sister had encouraged him to do. He concurred with Grady: why have the death penalty if it wasn't used in this instance? Sharon Risher's mother, Ethel Lance, was a lifelong member of the church. She died that night, too, but Risher thought it preferable that Roof live out every day of his natural life in full knowledge of what he had done. Rose Simmons's father, Daniel, an assistant pastor at the church, was shot when he ran to help Clementa Pinckney; he died in the hospital a few hours later. Simmons told me that her own views were irrelevant, because Roof had "sentenced himself to death by his actions."

Those moral calculations, as with everything else associated with the case, were refracted through the lens of race. In a statewide poll, two-thirds of African Americans favored sentencing Roof to life in prison, while 64 percent of whites believed that the death penalty was warranted. That result mirrored the general division between blacks and whites on the issue of capital punishment, which is driven, at least in part, by the fact that it has disproportionately been used against black defendants. It had to be said that excising Roof's presence from the world would change little about black Charlestonians' perspective on what happened at the church that night. Their white counterparts, meanwhile, were eager to reject Roof's overtures to them. Joe Riley, the city's mayor at the time, emphasized that the suspect was not from Charleston, a point that Riley's successor, John Tecklenburg, reiterated, as did other whites with whom I discussed the trial. If race offered a reluctant commonality between Roof and white Charleston, geography provided at least a literal distancing.

Then there was the fact that, during the past forty years, 81 percent of those given the death sentence in South Carolina had been convicted of killing white victims. A death sentence for Roof would add a patina of fairness to a practice steeped in the racial disparities of the criminal justice system. A life sentence, on the other hand, would seem to suggest that, whatever the opaque mathematics of race, a black life was worth less than one-ninth of a white one.

For David Bruck, Roof's case represented another chance to address the unjust imposition of the death penalty. At certain moments in the trial, though, his belief that he could diminish a racist practice by saving the life of a white supremacist appeared idealistic to a fault. During his cross-examination of Joseph Hamski, the FBI's lead investigator in the case, Bruck asked, "What became of Denmark Vesey?" Vesey, a slave who had bought his freedom and become a carpenter, was the lead plotter of the 1822 revolt at the church. "He was hung," Hamski replied. Bruck was suggesting that the death penalty is irrevocably tainted by racism, but he had seemed to equate Vesey, a man who was prepared to kill for the cause of black freedom, with Roof, a man who had killed because he thought that blacks were too free. The families murmured uneasily at the comparison.

The abstract morality of the sentencing contrasted with the concrete particulars of the crime, which were presented on the second day of the trial. Brittany Burke, who had served as an agent with the South Carolina Law Enforcement Division, testified that seventy-four shell casings had been recovered from the scene, and that fifty-four bullets had been removed from the nine bodies. Clementa Pinckney was shot three times; Sharonda Coleman-Singleton, a dynamic young preacher at the church, was shot five times. DePayne Middleton-Doctor, a minister and an admissions coordinator at a local learning center, was shot eight times; Cynthia Hurd, six times. Tywanza Sanders was shot four times; Ethel Lance, seven; Myra Thompson, who had received her preaching certificate that evening and was excited about leading Bible study for the first time, eight times. Daniel Simmons was shot four times. Susie Jackson, the oldest of the victims, was shot eleven times.

Judge Gergel had suggested that the family members give strong consideration to whether they would return to the courtroom after the morning recess. The prosecution was going to walk the jury through the shooting, with photographs of the crime scene, and there was no shame in wanting to avoid that spectacle. But the families returned, escorted by two court-appointed advocates, who were there to offer support. The photographs showed a spacious room with a small altar and several round tables and chairs, as if in preparation for a reception. A bulletin board read, in large red letters, "2015 Congrats Grads!" A Bible rested undisturbed on one of the tables, but most of the furniture was riddled with gunfire. The dead lay in an obscene array about the room. Many in the courtroom wept, again, at that sight.

I watched Roof during the prosecution's presentation, and it seemed possible that he had not fully realized the extent of his actions prior to that moment. In his confession, when the police officers asked him how many people he had shot, he said, "If I was gonna guess, five," and he appeared surprised to learn that he had actually killed nine. But, in the courtroom, he sat impassively—as he did throughout the trial—his response to the atrocities as inscrutable as his capacity to have committed them in the first place.

On December 15, when it was time for Bruck to present his closing argument, he stood facing the jury with his hands clasped behind his back. He described Roof as "really a boy, who gives his whole life over to a belief that there is raging in our society a fight to the death between black people and white people that is being concealed and covered up by some sort of vast conspiracy." Bruck added, "He doesn't seem to think that anybody but him really understands this."

Bruck pointed out that Roof had no escape plan. He used seven clips of ammunition during the attack, but kept the eighth with him as he departed, planning—as he'd said in the church and also during his confession—to kill himself if escape proved impossible. When he was arrested the day after the shooting in Shelby, North Carolina, he had been driving toward Nashville. When the police asked him why, he replied, "Why not? I've never been to Nashville." Because Roof had refused to have his mental health history discussed, Bruck was left to portray him as an alienated young man, not fully capable of distinguishing between the real world and the hyperbolic paranoid clamor that he found on the internet.

Bruck's emphasis on Roof's age wasn't entirely lost on the court. Andy Savage, the lawyer who represented several of the families in a separate lawsuit against the federal government for allowing Roof to purchase a firearm despite a drug arrest—and who had also, incidentally, represented Officer Michael Slager in his trial—told me that the families initially suspected that Roof hadn't acted alone. "That changed after watching the confession," Savage said. Roof was not the product of sinister manipulation: his biggest complaint was his inability to find like-minded patriots—he dismissed other white nationalists as being all talk. He was, instead, a prodigy of hate.

The jurors withdrew just after one o'clock. That afternoon, Roof was convicted of all thirty-three charges. Felicia Sanders nodded silently each time Judge Gergel uttered the word "guilty."

The court recessed until the new year, when the penalty phase of the trial started. Roof was representing himself again, and, as his defense sat nearby, he offered a disjointed opening statement in which he told the jurors that he would not lie to them, reiterating that "there was nothing wrong with me psychologically," and asked them to ignore everything that they had previously heard from the defense. He spoke for barely three minutes. He called no witnesses and offered no evidence.

During the next few days, Richardson called twenty-three witnesses to attest to the character of the victims and to the impact of their deaths. The first of them, Jennifer Pinckney, the widow of the pastor, spoke for nearly three hours about the life they had shared since meeting as college students. Anthony Thompson talked about the strength of the bond between him and his wife, Myra; he sighed as he looked at their wedding photograph, still awed by her beauty. "She was the one I prayed for," he told the court. At Judge Gergel's prodding, Richardson had the subsequent witnesses testify for shorter periods. But nearly all of them brought photographs of their loved ones, each of which had to be approved by the defense, which, in this case, was the defendant. The testimonies became a surreal processional, in which Roof became privy to the personal achievements and intimate family moments of the deceased. Killing the nine people was one crime. Being allowed to posthumously get to know them seemed an altogether different one.

On the afternoon of January 10, the prosecution rested, and Roof made a brief closing statement in which he said, "I felt like I had to do it. I still feel like I had to do it." The jurors withdrew to deliberate. They did not, in fact, need long. When the court reconvened, just three hours later, they recommended the death penalty for Roof. Gergel thanked the jurors for their service and dismissed them. The next day, he allowed those family members who had not yet had a chance to deliver their statements to address the court; most of the jurors returned to hear them. Gary Washington, through his sign language interpreters, told of a sense of foreboding that had hung over him on the day of the shooting and how he had anxiously tried to reach his mother that night. The news of her death hit him so hard that he had to be hospitalized. "You don't know anything about us," he said to Roof. "You don't know anything about who we are."

Cynthia Hurd's brother Melvin Graham, a retired laboratory technician, also spoke. He is taller and thinner than Malcolm Graham, but he has the same features and the same note of sadness in his eyes. In the tone of a man who had marshaled the entirety of his will toward self-control, Melvin told Roof, "You tried to kill my sister, but you failed." Instead, Roof had immortalized her. As a librarian, she had helped generations of students and readers, and her death had spurred an outpouring of recognition for that work: "the Cynthia Graham Hurd Fellowship, University of South Carolina; the Cynthia Graham Hurd St. Andrews Regional Library, Charleston, South Carolina; the Cynthia Graham Hurd Memorial Scholarship, College of Charleston." Graham named nearly a dozen such tributes. "And that's just what I could remember off the top of my head," he said. The stories served to remind the court of what had been lost, but they also must have reassured Roof that these were indeed the type of blameless, decent people he had set out to hurt.

Judge Gergel then turned to the final sentencing. "This trial has produced no winners, only losers," he said. "This proceeding cannot give the families what they truly want, the return of their loved ones." He sentenced Roof to death eighteen times and handed down an additional fifteen life sentences for the hate crimes and other charges. It took Gergel ten minutes to read the entire sentence. Roof then stood and requested new counsel to handle an appeal. When Gergel asked him on what basis he was making the request, Roof smirked and said of Bruck, "I just don't trust him." The request was denied.

The State of South Carolina is also due to try Roof, but that trial has been postponed indefinitely. Last summer, Scarlett Wilson, the local state solicitor, balked at the federal trial's taking precedence over the state prosecution, noting that the federal government hadn't carried out an execution since 2003. The fate of Dylann Roof will likely wind through thickets of legal appeals and an equally onerous state trial before it is ultimately resolved.

The day after the sentencing, I flew to San Francisco. As I checked in to a hotel, I made small talk with the bellman, Aaron Thames, an African American in his early forties. I asked if he was a native of the Bay Area, and he replied, "No, I'm originally from Charleston, South Carolina." When I told him that I'd just come from the Roof trial, he looked stricken. He said, "My family knew Reverend Pinckney and Cynthia Hurd since I was a child. Miss Cynthia is one of my mother's oldest friends, and when we would visit the library she would always have books set aside for me and my brother to read."

I had flown almost as far from South Carolina as I could get without leaving the continental United States but had encountered the consequences of Roof's crime in the transparent grief of the first person I'd spoken with in a new city. The immensity of the pain that Roof has inflicted upon Charleston is not contained by geography. It conforms perfectly to the contours of the nation that produced him.

BEN CARSON, DONALD TRUMP, AND THE MISUSE OF AMERICAN HISTORY

March 8, 2017

Earlier this week, Ben Carson, the somnolent surgeon dispatched to oversee the Department of Housing and Urban Development on behalf of the Trump administration, created a stir when he referred to enslaved black people—stolen, trafficked, and sold into that status—as "immigrants" and spoke of their dreams for their children and grandchildren. In the ensuing hail of criticism, Carson doubled down, saying that it was possible for someone to be an involuntary immigrant. Carson's defenses centered upon strict adherence to the definition of the word "immigrant" as a person who leaves one country to take up residence in another. This is roughly akin to arguing that it is technically possible to refer to a kidnapping victim as a "houseguest," presuming the latter term refers to a temporary visitor to one's home. Carson had already displayed a propensity for gaffes during his maladroit presidential candidacy, and it might be easy to dismiss his latest one as the least concerning element of having a neurosurgeon with no relevant experience in charge of housing policy were it not a stand-in for a broader set of concerns about the Trump administration.

A week earlier, Betsy DeVos, the secretary of education, had described historically Black colleges and universities as pioneers in "school choice"—a view that can only coexist with reality if we airbrush segregation into a kind of level playing field in which ex-slaves opted to attend all-black institutions rather than being driven to them as a result of efforts to preserve the supposed sanctity of white ones. The Trump administration is not alone in proffering this rosy view of American racial history. Last week, in a story about changes being made at Thomas Jefferson's estate, Monticello, *The Washington Post* referred to Sally Hemings, the enslaved black woman who bore several of Jefferson's children, as his "mistress"—a term that implies far more autonomy and consent than is possible when a woman is a man's legal property. Last fall, the textbook publisher McGraw-Hill faced criticism for a section of a history book that stated, "The Atlantic Slave Trade between the 1500s and 1800s brought millions of workers from Africa to the southern United States to work on agricultural plantations." The word "worker" typically carries the connotation of remuneration rather than lifelong forced labor and chattel slavery.

One part of the issue here is the eliding of the ugliness of the slave past in this country. This phenomenon is neither novel nor particularly surprising. The unwillingness to confront this narrative is tied not simply to the miasma of race but to something more subtle and, in the current atmosphere, more potentially treacherous: the reluctance to countenance anything that runs contrary to the habitual optimism and self-anointed sense of the exceptionalism of American life. It is this state-sanctioned sunniness from which the view of the present as a middle ground between an admirable past and a halcyon future springs. But the only way to sustain that sort of optimism is by not looking too closely at the past. And thus the past can serve only as an imperfect guide to the troubles of the present.

In his 1948 essay "The Gangster as Tragic Hero," Robert Warshow wrote about the midcentury efforts to pressure studios to stop producing their profitable gangster movies. The concerns focused partly upon the violence of the films but more directly upon the fear that these films offered a fundamentally pessimistic view of life and were therefore un-American. There is a neat throughline from those critics to Ronald Reagan's "Morning in America" idealism to the shopworn rhetoric of nearly every aspirant to even local public office that the nation's "best days are ahead of us." We are largely adherents of the state religion of optimism—and not of a particularly mature version of it, either. This was part of the reason Donald Trump's sermons of doom were seen as so discordant throughout last year's campaign. He offered followers a diet of catastrophe, all of it looming immediately if not already under way. He told an entire nation, in the most transparently demagogic of his statements, that he was the only one who could save it from imminent peril. And he was nonetheless elected president of the United States.

Strangely enough, many of us opted to respond to Trump's weapons-grade pessimism in the most optimistic way possible, conjuring best-case scenarios in which he would simply be a modern version of Richard Nixon, or perhaps of Andrew Jackson. But he is neither of these. Last summer, as his rallies tipped toward violence and the rhetoric seemed increasingly jarring, it was common to hear alarmed commentators speak of us all being in "uncharted waters." This was naïve and, often enough, self-serving. For many of us, particularly those who reckon with the history of race, the true fear was not that we were on some unmapped terrain but that we were passing landmarks that were disconcertingly familiar. In response to the increasingly authoritarian tones of the executive branch, we plumbed the history of Europe in the twentieth century for clues and turned to the writings of Czesław Miłosz and George Orwell. We might well have turned to the writings of W. E. B. Du Bois and James Baldwin for the more direct, domestic version of this question but looked abroad, at least in part, as a result of our tacit consensus that tragedy is a foreign locale. It has been selectively forgotten that traits of authoritarianism neatly overlap with traits of racism visible in the recent American past.

The habitual tendency to excise the most tragic elements of history creates a void in our collective understanding of what has happened in the past and, therefore, our understanding of the potential for tragedy in the present. In 1935, when Sinclair Lewis wrote *It Can't Happen Here,* it already *was* happening here, and had been since the end of Reconstruction. In 1942, the NAACP declared a "Double V" campaign—an attempt to defeat fascism abroad and its domestic corollary of American racism.

Similarly, it was common in the days immediately following September 11 to hear it referred to as the nation's first large-scale experience with terrorism—or at least the worst since the 1995 Oklahoma City bombing, staged by Timothy McVeigh. But the nation's first anti-terrorism law was the Ku Klux Klan Act of 1871, designed to stall the attempts to terrorize emancipated slaves out of political participation. McVeigh's bombing, which claimed the lives of 168 people, was not the worst act of terrorism in the United States at that point—it was not even the worst act of terrorism in the history of *Oklahoma*. Seventy-four years earlier, in what became known as the Tulsa Race Riot, the city's black population was attacked and aerially bombed; as many as three hundred African Americans were killed. Such myopia thrives in the present and confounds the reasoning of James Comey, who refused to declare Dylann Roof's murder of nine black congregants in a South Carolina church, perpetrated in hopes of sparking a race war, as an act of terrorism—a designation the then FBI director did not hesitate to apply to Omar Mateen's murderous actions in the Pulse nightclub in Orlando a year later.

The American capacity for tragedy is much broader and far more robust than Americans—most of us, anyway—recognize. Our sense of ourselves as exceptional, of our country as a place where we habitually avert the worst-case scenario, is therefore a profound liability in times like the present. The result is a failure to recognize the parameters of human behavior and, consequently, the signs of danger as they become apparent to others who are not crippled by such optimism. A belief that we are exempt from the true horrors of human behavior and the accompanying false sense of security have led to nearly risible responses to Trumpism.

It has become a cliché each February to present the argument that "black history is American history," yet that shopworn ideal has new relevance. A society with a fuller sense of history and its own capacity for tragedy would have spotted Trump's zero-sum hustle from many miles in the distance. Without it, though, it's easy to mistake the overblown tribulations he sold his followers for candor, not a con. The sense of history as a chart of increasing bounties enabled tremendous progress but has left Americans—most of us, anyway—uniquely unsuited to look at ourselves as we truly are and at history for what it is. Our failure to reckon with this past and the centrality of race within it has led us to broadly mistake the clichés of history for novelties of current events.

THE BATTLE OVER CONFEDERATE MONUMENTS IN NEW ORLEANS

March 12, 2017

The adage holds that history is written by the victors, but, as the masked, bulletproof-vested municipal workers who assembled in New Orleans at three o'clock in the morning on Confederate Memorial Day might attest, the most indelible version of the American past was authored by those who lost the Civil War. The workers were there to remove an obelisk dedicated to the Crescent City White League and the Battle of Liberty Place of 1874. Clashes over American history are typically fought with dueling sets of footnotes and the subjective shade of historiographic essays. This one, which involved death threats issued to the mayor and the contractors bidding on the project, risked being fought using tools with considerably higher stopping power.

Four monuments in all, including those memorializing Robert E. Lee, P. G. T. Beauregard, and Jefferson Davis, were slated to be removed, and on Sunday protests and counterprotests broke out over the removal. In the dark early morning hours of Thursday, the statue of Davis was removed as dueling demonstrations cheered and denounced the action. But the obelisk carried particularly fraught implications. The cause of the Confederacy, even before its participants were all dead, was edited into a more palatable abstraction—"states' rights," a phrase whose meaning was ambiguous enough that it might actually pass for virtue. In his memoirs, Davis, the president of the Confederacy, wrote that slavery was "in no wise the cause of the conflict." This was a breathtaking act of self-absolution and deception. Consider the language of South Carolina's declaration of secession from the Union. Speaking of Lincoln's Republican government, the state wrote:

On the 4th day of March next, this party will take possession of the Government. It has announced that the South shall be excluded from the common territory, that the judicial tribunals shall be made sectional, and that a war must be waged against slavery until it shall cease throughout the United States. . . . We, therefore, the People of South Carolina, by our delegates in Convention assembled, appealing to the Supreme Judge of the world for the rectitude of our intentions, have solemnly declared that the Union heretofore existing between this State and the other States of North America, is dissolved.

Yet the denial of slavery's role allowed for the South's actors and their motives to be thought of as "complex." This became the first line of defense for their apologists. Still, no such complexity, manufactured or otherwise, extends to the Crescent City White League. In September 1874, the group revolted against the interracial Reconstruction government of Louisiana, killing eleven police officers in what came to be known as the Battle of Liberty Place. In 1932, a plaque was added to the base of the monument recognizing the revolt explicitly as a noble act in support of what it unabashedly called "white supremacy," referring to Reconstructionist officials as "usurpers."

If the history of the Civil War and its causes remain strikingly unfamiliar to certain Americans, the story of Reconstruction is virtually an enigma. This is not an accident. The story of Reconstruction is that of interracial government and white terrorism that brought it to an end. It sits awkwardly in the narrative of an America defined by continual progress and the inevitable triumph of good over evil. The Civil War is the central axis of American history, cleaving the past between that of a fledgling union and that of a scarred but mature nation that understood the notion of tragedy. Reconstruction, however, has largely been disparaged as a failure, though for wildly divergent reasons.

During the eleven-year period between the end of the Civil War and the disputed election of 1876, the United States inaugurated a bold experiment in actual democracy. Between 1865 and 1870, the ratification of the Thirteenth, Fourteenth, and Fifteenth Amendments successively abolished slavery, established black citizenship and equal protection of laws, and extended the vote to African American men, resulting in the election of more than six hundred black local, state, and federal officeholders, many of whom were themselves former slaves. Even before the period ended, however, a body of literature was being created to disparage it as the calamitous era of "Negro rule" in the South. In 1909, when the historian W. E. B. Du Bois delivered a paper to the American Historical Association on the benefits of Reconstruction, he was swimming against the tide of an entire body of scholarship proclaiming the period as a uniquely disastrous experiment that had proved the folly of racial equality. Six years later, that perspective was cemented in popular perception by D. W. Griffith's white supremacist melodrama *The Birth of a Nation*. In 1935, when Du Bois published *Black Reconstruction*, a 746-page tome in defense of the interracial governments of the South, he identified the true disaster as the political horse-trading that had ended Reconstruction and left emancipated blacks at the mercy of their former enslavers. Thus, to one set of eyes, Reconstruction failed at the moment it was abandoned; to another, the failure lay in its ever being undertaken in the first place.

This has everything to do with the tumult that emerged in New Orleans last week, and which will likely persist as the city maintains its secret schedule of removals. When I spoke to Mayor Mitch Landrieu and mentioned that there was a lot going on in New Orleans, he replied, "Well, it's been going on for three hundred years." The New Orleans City Council voted to remove the monuments in the wake of Dylann Roof's murderous assault on the Emanuel AME Church in June 2015—an act he tied to the Confederate cause. In response, South Carolina removed the Confederate flag from the grounds of the state capitol; other monuments to the Confederacy have been removed since then.

The Southern Poverty Law Center noted in 2016 that there were more than seven hundred Confederate monuments throughout the South and as far away as Arizona and Massachusetts. The Union cause is sequestered in textbooks; the cause of insurrection, of states' rights, of the unalloyed brutality of human enslavement—that cause still towers in the region where the war was fought.

As with much else in Trump's version of America, the protesters who lined up to defend the monument wish to maintain an à la carte relationship with history. They have cloaked their defense of the monuments by presenting it as a recognition of the valor of the men who fought for the Confederate cause. But that excuse falls flat when recognizing, for instance, that there is no monument in New Orleans to the mass slave revolt that took place there in 1811, when some two hundred men who had endured the brutality of bondage marched on the city, killing two white men and burning plantations as they went. This is not the version of valor recognized by the crowd before the Lee memorial, or by those phoning in death threats to the mayor's office.

At the same time, there is a valid, if lesser, risk in removing the Confederate monuments: the possibility that their absence is too neatly exculpatory—that future generations may know little about the acts of inhumanity that took place in the South, and even less about the misguided impulse that glorified those incidents for more than a century. The monuments are not relics of a bygone era; they're indicators of the one we're still living in.

POSTSCRIPT TO "THE BATTLE OVER CONFEDERATE MONUMENTS IN NEW ORLEANS"

Years ago, during a Fulbright fellowship in Moscow, I visited the Red Army Museum. As one would expect, the facility celebrates the long history of Russia's military—the appellation "Red" predates the rise of the Bolsheviks by more than a century. Every object in the museum's vast holdings is carefully contextualized and positioned. There is, however, one notable exception to this respectful and deliberate curation: the materials seized from the Reichstag building following the surrender of the Nazi army in May 1945. Those objects were placed on the museum floor. That inauspicious placement solved an underlying question: what is to be done with objects that should be retained for historical purposes but do not merit the respect of those charged with the preservation? The monuments to the Confederacy that proliferated in the long aftermath of the American Civil War and against the backdrop of the civil rights movement received a very different treatment. The epic, heroic scale of the monuments that dot the nation's landscape connotes vast esteem for these men and their ignoble cause. That esteem—based on calcified lies about history—has gotten in the way of any reckoning with the morality of honoring people who fought a war for the right to buy, sell, rape, abuse, and exploit other human beings.

The idea of removing those monuments inspired a different set of objections from people who, for a broad array of reasons, were "opposed to removing history." Even opponents of the monuments sometimes worried that their removal would whitewash the history of whitewashing history. The whole thing became very meta. I eventually struck upon a novel solution to that problem, rooted in my experiences in Russia: the monuments should not be taken down; they should be knocked over. Like a vanquished king at the end of a chess game. This solution would have solved the problem of the "honor" afforded to those posthumous slavers and reminded a justifiably confused public as to who actually lost the war. Presuming enough time has gone by for us to know the answer to that question ourselves.

CHARLOTTESVILLE AND THE TROUBLE WITH CIVIL WAR HYPOTHETICALS

August 16, 2017

Even before the insipid forces of radical whiteness had withdrawn from Charlottesville, Virginia, one heard the beseeching protestation "This is not us." That sentiment blossomed into a hashtag, exculpating our society after some of its citizens had seemingly forgotten our standing position against fascism. The truth, though, is that there has never been a time when what we saw in Charlottesville has *not* been us. The present is bequeathed to us by the past, and seldom was that relationship more apparent than it was at the base of the Robert E. Lee statue that was at the center of the violent clashes in Charlottesville. Last month, HBO inspired an avalanche of criticism when it announced that it planned to produce a series called "Confederate," which would explore a hypothetical world in which the South had won the Civil War. The events in Charlottesville illustrated a problem with that idea: only by the most specific, immediate definition can we consider the Confederacy to have lost the Civil War, and its legacy has defined a great deal of our history since then.

With the exception of the brief interval of Reconstruction, the states of the former Confederacy have been able to exert as much influence on national affairs and on matters of race as they had before the Civil War, and possibly more. Having lost the quest to maintain slavery, they put in place sharecropping—a system of agricultural serfdom—which was dominant for the next eight decades. Prior to the Civil War, slaveholding states held a disproportionate influence in Congress because the census counted 60 percent of the enslaved population—people who could not vote—in apportioning representation. After the Fourteenth Amendment was adopted, the census counted the entire black population, but the regime of white terrorism that followed Reconstruction ensured that these African Americans could not vote, either. Thus, Southern white political power was amplified after the war by the mere existence of disfranchised African Americans living in Southern states.

Deference to Confederate racial preferences could be seen even before the war had ended. Late in the summer of 1862, when, bruised by more than a year of internecine bloodshed, Abraham Lincoln's administration had begun to seriously consider emancipating the entire enslaved population, the president invited a group of African American leaders to visit him at the White House. Lincoln wanted to discuss with them a now little-recalled premise of his plan for emancipation: the emigration of the free black population. Lincoln rationalized the measure by telling them:

> You and we are different races. We have between us a broader difference than exists between almost any other two races. Whether it is right or wrong I need not discuss, but this physical difference is a great disadvantage to us both, as I think your race suffer very greatly, many of them by living among us, while ours suffer from your presence. In a word we suffer on each side.

The remarkable part of this statement is not that Lincoln could alchemize a sense of white victimhood from a situation in which four million black people were being bought, sold, bred, whipped, and raped, but that, in the midst of a civil war, he proposed the removal not of the belligerents attempting to overthrow the government but of a people he planned to recruit to save it. Political pragmatism eventually forced Lincoln to relinquish the colonization scheme, but the point remains that he recognized a fraternal bond with the white men of the Confederacy that extended beyond his reckoning with the humanity of those who had most egregiously suffered under its thumb.

Seventy-four years later, Walter White, the executive secretary of the NAACP, met with Franklin D. Roosevelt at the White House to discuss his organization's hopes for federal legislation to outlaw lynching. Roosevelt, however, demurred. A few months later, Eleanor Roosevelt wrote to White, explaining that the president shared his concerns but felt that the surest path forward was to simply educate Southerners not to lynch—an effort that the president would hinder by association. "If it were done by a Northerner, it will have an antagonistic effect," she wrote. More precisely, it might have jeopardized support for the New Deal among members of Congress from the former Confederate states.

In 1963, a full century after the Emancipation Proclamation, a group of African Americans, including James Baldwin, Harry Belafonte, and Lorraine Hansberry, met with Robert F. Kennedy, then the attorney general, to press the administration on civil rights issues. Kennedy countered that the impetuous pace of the movement had already jeopardized his brother's position with Southern Democrats. President John F. Kennedy notably sought a "cooling-off period," to decrease the fractious tensions that the movement had produced between African Americans and the Southern wing of the party.

Roosevelt and Kennedy were making politically pragmatic decisions, but the fact is that the attitudes of the former Confederate states remained a part of political calculations on matters of race. Nixon's Southern Strategy and the partisan realignment of the 1960s was a product of this dynamic. The system of for-profit incarceration in the South, which had essentially replaced slave labor with the labor of convicts, is an ancestor of the current era of mass incarceration. The white nationalists who marched through Charlottesville bearing torches last Friday night were, on some level, the culmination of decades of politics that had validated their worldview, albeit tacitly and in coded language.

Three months ago, New Orleans's decision to remove four statues dedicated to the Confederacy brought armed protesters to that city from hundreds of miles away. Mayor Mitch Landrieu received death threats, the workers removing the statues were forced to wear masks, and the city had to hire a safety-and-intelligence firm to monitor the situation. There may come a time when it's reasonable to create hypotheticals about a world in which the Confederacy won the war. But that time would surely be at a point when that hypothetical no longer resembles the world in which we're actually living.

FROM LOUIS ARMSTRONG TO THE NFL: UNGRATEFUL AS THE NEW UPPITY

September 24, 2017

Sixty years ago, Central High School in Little Rock, Arkansas, became a flash point in the nascent civil rights movement when Governor Orval Faubus refused to abide by the Supreme Court decision in *Brown v. Board of Education*. Faubus famously deployed the state's National Guard to prevent nine African American students from attending classes at the high school. In the midst of the crisis, a high school journalist interviewing Louis Armstrong about an upcoming tour asked the musician about his thoughts on the situation, prompting Armstrong to refer to the Arkansas governor as several varieties of "motherfucker." (In the interest of finding a printable quote, his label for Faubus was changed to "ignorant plowboy.") Armstrong, who was scheduled to perform in the Soviet Union as a cultural ambassador on behalf of the State Department, canceled the tour—a display of dissent that earned him the scorn and contempt of legions of whites, shocked by the trumpeter's apparent lack of patriotism. As the historian Penny Von Eschen notes in *Satchmo Blows Up the World*, a history of the American usage of black culture as a tool of the Cold War, students at the University of Arkansas accused Armstrong of "creating an issue where there was none" and they joined the procession of groups canceling Armstrong's scheduled concerts.

The free-range lunacy of Donald Trump's speech on Friday night in Alabama, where he referred to Colin Kaepernick—and other NFL players who silently protest police brutality—as a "son of a bitch," and of the subsequent Twitter tantrums in which the president, like a truculent six-year-old, disinvited the Golden State Warriors from a White House visit, illustrates that the passage of six decades has not dimmed this dynamic confronted by Armstrong, or by any prominent black person tasked with the entertainment of millions of white ones. We again witness outrage over events that shock the conscience among people who sincerely believe, or who have at least convincingly lied to themselves, that dissenters are creating an issue where there is none. Kaepernick began his silent, kneeling protest at the beginning of last season, not as an assault against the United States military or the flag but as a dissent against a system that has, with a great degree of consistency, failed to hold accountable police who kill unarmed citizens. Since he did this, forty-one unarmed individuals have been fatally shot by police in the United States, twelve of them African American, according to a database maintained by *The Washington Post*. The city of St. Louis recently witnessed days of protests after the acquittal of Jason Stockley, the former officer who, while still working for the city's police force, fatally shot Anthony Smith, a twenty-four-year-old African American motorist who had led officers on a chase. Stockley emerged from his vehicle having declared that he would "kill the motherfucker," then proceeded to fire five rounds into the car. Later, a firearm was found on the seat of Smith's car, but the weapon bore only Stockley's DNA. The issue is not imaginary.

Yet the belief endures, from Armstrong's time and before, that visible, affluent African American entertainers are obliged to adopt a pose of ceaseless gratitude—appreciation for the waiver that spared them the low status of so many others of their kind. Stevie Wonder began a performance in Central Park last night by taking a knee, prompting Congressman Joe Walsh to tweet that Wonder was "another ungrateful black multi-millionaire." Ungrateful is the new uppity. Trump's supporters, by a 24-point margin, agree with the idea that most Americans have not got as much as they deserve—

though they overwhelmingly withhold the right to that sentiment from African Americans. Thus, the wonder is not the unhinged behavior of this weekend but rather that it took Trump so long to exploit a target as rich in potential racial resentment as wealthy black athletes who have the temerity to believe in the First Amendment.

It's impossible not to be struck by Trump's selective patriotism. It drives him to curse at black football players but leaves him struggling to create false equivalence between Nazis and anti-fascists in Charlottesville. It inspires a barely containable contempt for Muslims and immigrants but leaves him mute in the face of Russian election intervention. He cannot tolerate the dissent against literal flag-waving but screams indignation at the thought of removing monuments to the Confederacy, which attempted to revoke the authority symbolized by that same flag. He is the vector of the racial id of the class of Americans who sent death threats to Louis Armstrong, the people who necessitated the presence of a newly federalized National Guard to defend black students seeking to integrate a public school. He contains multitudes—all of them dangerously ignorant.

It has been convenient and politically profitable for Trump to paint the black athletes' protests as an inane attack upon the symbols of the United States, but he is deeply implicated, and is increasingly aggravating the actual cause of this discord. It was Trump who urged police officers in Brentwood, New York, to treat the suspects in their charge with casual brutality. Trump's Department of Justice has overseen the dismantling of the community policing initiative, which was meant to encourage greater rapport between law enforcement and the neighborhoods they patrol. It is the president's DOJ that has displayed disdain for the federal consent decrees that had been used to reform dysfunctional police departments.

A week and a half ago, Sarah Huckabee Sanders, the White House press secretary, assailed the black ESPN journalist Jemele Hill for referring to Trump on Twitter as an "ignorant white supremacist." She asserted that Hill's tweets were a "fireable offense." Several days later, Trump attacked the sports network on Twitter and demanded that it "apologize for untruth." After Trump rescinded his White House invitation to the Golden State Warriors, Hill tweeted, "Hey @stephencurry30, welcome to the club, bro." LeBron James tweeted that Trump was a "bum"—which inspired criticism that he had crossed a line. (James was, it should be noted, considerably kinder than Louis Armstrong might have been.) The club of Trump dissidents grew larger on Sunday, when dozens of players from the Baltimore Ravens and the Jacksonville Jaguars took a knee, and Shad Khan, the owner of the Jaguars, locked arms with players and coaches who remained standing during the national anthem. All but one of the Pittsburgh Steelers opted to remain in their locker room during the playing of the national anthem ahead of their game against the Chicago Bears. Both the Seattle Seahawks and the Tennessee Titans decided to do the same for their game. If Trump's intention was to stigmatize such displays, his words have had the opposite effect. He is perhaps the greatest example of the law of unintended consequences this side of the Darwin Awards.

Amid Trump's nuclear brinksmanship and social media provocation toward North Korea, amid the swollen gorges of water streaming through Puerto Rico, amid the craven and indefensible attempts to gut healthcare, amid the slower-moving crises of voting access, economic inequality, and climate change—amid all these things, Trump yet again found a novel way to diminish the nation he purportedly leads. He has authored danger in more ways than there are novel ways to denounce it. This is his singular genius. When this moment has elapsed, when some inevitably unsatisfactory punctuation has concluded the Trump era, we will be left with an infinitude of questions. But Trump, we will assuredly understand, is a small man with a fetish for the symbols of democracy and a bottomless hostility for the actual practice of it.

POSTSCRIPT TO "FROM LOUIS ARMSTRONG TO THE NFL: UNGRATEFUL AS THE NEW UPPITY"

While Colin Kaepernick's kneeling act of civil disobedience harked back to a long tradition of athletic activism in the United States, its impact seemed largely symbolic. It momentarily roiled the NFL and the ranks of its interested parties—fans, owners, television networks, and the players themselves—but at the time appeared to succeed only in forestalling his own football career. Kaepernick himself was at cross-purposes, wanting both to protest the league's complicity in the state of affairs that devalued black lives and to procure another position as a quarterback within that league. The condescending line of criticism that I highlight here was part of a broader hostility toward both Kaepernick and the idea he was articulating—that black lives in the United States were uniquely vulnerable to violence from the state. That hostility did not face substantial blowback until the death of George Floyd, at which point Kaepernick had already been out of the league for more than three years. The NFL, along with entire swaths of the country, grudgingly recognized that Kaepernick had a point. But that did not translate into another opportunity to play professional football, nor did it facilitate lasting changes in the situation he'd been trying to highlight. This ultimately says more about us than it does about him.

HARVEY WEINSTEIN, BILL COSBY, AND THE CLOAK OF CHARITY

October 14, 2017

The great mystery of evil is not that it persists but, rather, that so many of its practitioners wish to do so while being thought of as saints. Consider the fact that such a bizarre, oxymoronic accolade as the International Stalin Prize for Strengthening Peace Among Peoples once existed—and that it was created after his plans for agricultural collectivization resulted in the deaths of some four million Ukrainians. Once considered a hallmark of Soviet ineptitude, the starvation now appears, Anne Applebaum writes in her new book, *Red Famine,* to have been the deliberate result of a plan to rid the state of a rebellious peasantry. Or think of Leopold II, the nineteenth-century Belgian king who carefully cultivated a reputation for outsized philanthropy and Christian devotion while overseeing the ruthless subjugation of the population of the present-day Democratic Republic of Congo, and commanding an army that committed massacres and routine disfigurements of locals. These are hypocrisies on the grand brutal scale, but, as the past week has demonstrated once again, there is no shortage of smaller tyrannies and compromised altruism in our times and in our midst.

In a matter of days, Harvey Weinstein went from being heralded as a formidable media titan to being accused as a serial sexual predator. The charges of sexual harassment leveled against him last Thursday in a *New York Times* report, followed by further allegations in Ronan Farrow's article published by *The New Yorker* five days later, bracketed a period that saw a maelstrom of social media outrage and Weinstein's firing from the prestigious film company that he had helped found. There have since been reports that his wife is leaving him, and he has come under investigation by police in New York City and London as well as been accused of rape by a fourth woman. Last Saturday, in a statement that appeared to prove that, like Einsteinian space-time, irony is capable of bending to dimensions that we cannot fully grasp, Donald Trump remarked that he had known Weinstein for a long time and "I am not at all surprised." Game, as the adage says, recognizes game.

What is perhaps more notable than the fact that Weinstein's alleged transgressions could persist for so long with so little scrutiny is that they coexisted with his reputation as a stalwart of progressive causes. Weinstein's films generated more than three hundred Oscar nominations and earned Best Actress honors for several women in films that he produced. In any other context, this would be a banner legacy of helping women achieve standing and power in an industry that, as the director Ava DuVernay has said, was "created by men, for men, to tell stories about men." Last week, it was reported that Weinstein had pledged $5 million to the University of Southern California film school toward a scholarship fund for female filmmakers. (The school is reportedly rejecting the pledge.) He also championed Hillary Clinton's bid to be the first female president of the United States and donated to the campaigns of a number of other women, including Senator Elizabeth Warren. (Both women are now donating the money to charities.)

Weinstein's palette of giving earned him the standing as a man who was, if not an embodiment of male progressivism, at least someone willing to stand on its periphery. In that way, Weinstein's public demise recalls Hugh Hefner's mortal one, last month. Hefner, whose great realization, as my colleague Adam Gopnik has pointed out, was that virtually anything, even pornography, can be mainstreamed in America if it is paired with a measure of upperclass aspiration, contained contradictions similar to Weinstein's, though they were a great deal more transparent. Critics maintained that Hefner innovated the tradition of female objectification and hijacked the idea of women's sexual autonomy for his own agenda of furthering male prerogatives. His defenders claimed that he "empowered" women—a vague term that can be deployed to camouflage the fact that one group of people is getting rich while the "empowered" group is getting hustled—and was a strong advocate of women's reproductive rights and of civil rights. The reality, though, is that it's possible, maybe even typical, for all these things to be true.

It's not uncommon for people to tangentially benefit groups that they're simultaneously exploiting. Note that of the boldface names recently associated with charges of sexual harassment or assault—Bill Cosby, Donald Trump, Roger Ailes, Bill O'Reilly, and Weinstein—every one of them could, and some did, argue that they'd hired and promoted women in their professional enterprises. None of this obviates the possibility that any of them harassed or assaulted women in those same enterprises.

It is striking that a former temporary employee at the Weinstein Company reported to Farrow that Weinstein had said that "he'd never had to do anything like Bill Cosby"—apparently a reference to the fact that some of Cosby's accusers have said that he drugged them prior to assaulting them—though otherwise there are distinct similarities in the accounts of how both men used their positions of power against vulnerable women whose careers they purported to help. Another commonality extends to their relationships with philanthropy.

Bill Cosby was particularly hailed for his largesse in the 1980s, when he paid college tuition for students in need who wrote to him, created scholarships, and gave broadly to causes connected to African Americans. The donation that cemented his status as a minor deity among African Americans came when he and his wife, Camille, donated $20 million to Spelman College in Atlanta in 1988. At the time, it was the largest single donation ever given to a historically black college. The fact that Spelman is also a women's college seemed to certify Cosby as a man whose credentials as a humanitarian were beyond impeachment. (Amid the swirling controversy over Cosby's behavior, the college terminated a professorship endowed in his name and returned related funds in 2015.)

One view is that philanthropy can operate as a kind of penance mechanism. The individual who recognizes that he has done wrong attempts to make good in equal measure, to place a thumb on the scale of karma. This kind of moral licensing—do-gooding to offset wrongdoing—is not unusual. We routinely celebrate the annual awarding of the Nobel Peace Prize, which was created by a man who grew rich from the sales of dynamite and the attendant war munitions. Many of the great name-brand foundations were created in honor of individuals whose personal character or wealth was connected to deeply morally compromising actions.

Yet this is not quite what seems to be happening here. Both Weinstein and Cosby gave publicly and visibly, and that inevitably created situations that also left their beneficiaries vulnerable. When Fareed Zakaria interviewed Hillary Clinton earlier this week, she denied any knowledge of Weinstein's alleged history of predation, which prompted Anthony Bourdain, who is currently in a relationship with one of Weinstein's accusers, to suggest on Twitter that Clinton's claim strained credulity. (Clinton seems fated to be in close proximity to men who both assist her career and undermine it through their alleged sexual impropriety.)

A Weinstein Company executive told Farrow that she was particularly disturbed that Weinstein seemed to use female employees as "a honeypot to lure these women in, to make them feel safe." In that light, the philanthropy can be seen as a sort of honeypot scheme, in which a concern for social issues lulls people into seeing only one side of the giver. In some cases, charity doesn't contradict monstrosity. It enables it.

HARD TESTS

January 8, 2018

One morning last February, not long after Donald Trump had been inaugurated as president but long before many people had reconciled themselves to that fact, students at Howard University awoke to find a bold message written on a walkway of the campus's central plaza, known as the Yard. Spray-painted in blue block letters, it read "WELCOME TO THE TRUMP PLANTATION, OVERSEER: WAYNE A. I. FREDERICK." The message was aimed at the heart, the character, and the conscience of Howard's president, a reserved, deliberative oncologist and surgeon whom the board of trustees had unanimously elected to the position in 2014. Frederick is pure Howard: he earned his undergraduate and medical degrees and a master's in business administration there. At forty-six, he has held a number of titles, but "overseer"—a derisive term for black proxies of white authority—was hardly one he was seeking.

There was an additional layer of shade visible to those familiar with the school's history. When Howard—one of the largest of the roughly one hundred historically black colleges and universities, or HBCUs, in the United States—was founded in 1867, it was supported by the Freedmen's Bureau, the federal agency charged with helping emancipated black people navigate the world that awaited them after the Civil War. The author of the spray-painted message was clearly suggesting that the school—and, specifically, Frederick—no longer represented a disruption of the nation's racial hierarchy but was a bulwark of it.

The message was a response to a series of events that began on February 9, when Betsy DeVos, the Trump administration's newly appointed secretary of education, made Howard, which is located in Washington, D.C., the site of her first official campus visit. Trump had long been unpopular with African Americans—on account of his company's discriminatory real estate practices and his racist pronouncements, to begin with—but the bigoted rhetoric of his campaign has made him more so. (When Talladega College, a historically black school founded by two former slaves in Alabama, announced that its band would march in Trump's inaugural parade, alumni started a petition in protest and inundated the college's web page with complaints.)

Trump's nomination of DeVos, a billionaire businesswoman—whom Chuck Schumer, the Senate Minority Leader, called the "least qualified nominee in a historically unqualified cabinet"—was seen as another affront. Frederick told me, "She was confirmed at noon, and at two o'clock I had a call saying she wants to have a conversation." A provision of Howard's governance automatically makes the secretary of education an ex officio member of the board of trustees, but many on campus felt that DeVos was using Howard as a convenient backdrop for a show of broadmindedness. Why else would she make the visit such an immediate priority? As a former Howard administrator told me, "It's not like she was there to announce a multimillion-dollar grant."

Then, on February 27, Frederick and sixty-eight other presidents of black institutions went to the White House to meet with various officials in the hope of laying the groundwork to secure additional funding from the federal government. Howard, in a unique arrangement, receives 40 percent of its operating budget—$221 million in 2016—from a congressional appropriation. This makes its administrators accountable not only to its donors, its alumni, and its students—as all college administrations are—but to the national political leadership. At a meeting that day, DeVos further angered many educators by referring to HBCUs as pioneers of "school choice"—a perspective akin to viewing Jim Crow as an empowering opportunity for black people to drink from race-specific water fountains. As John Silvanus Wilson, then the president of Morehouse College in Atlanta, wrote after the meeting, "HBCUs were not created because the four million newly freed blacks were unhappy with the choices they had. They were created because they had no choices at all."

Omarosa Manigault, a graduate of two black universities—Central State in Ohio as well as Howard—was then the director of communications for the White House Office of Public Liaison. She had reportedly pushed Trump to schedule a meeting with the university presidents in the Oval Office, and pushed them to attend it. Frederick told me, "I was probably the last person to enter the room. I knew there would be a photo op." In one of the photographs from the meeting, Kellyanne Conway, the counselor to the president, knelt on a sofa in what seemed inappropriate informality. But many African Americans were more offended by another photograph, which featured Trump smiling broadly with the African American leaders standing around him. It seemed like a tableau from plantation days and served as a succinct summary of the fraught transition from Barack Obama—the first black president and Howard's 2016 commencement speaker—to Trump, who had smeared Obama by trafficking in birtherism and who now embraced the support of white nationalists. Frederick stayed near the door, out of the camera's view. Nonetheless, his presence became an incendiary element in the post-election mood at Howard. The message appeared the next morning.

Juan Demetrixx, a political science major and leader of a student activist group called HU Resist, told me that he didn't know who had written it, but added, "We agree with the sentiment." Another student told the *Hilltop*, the campus newspaper, "Frederick doesn't care about us, only money." Other local media reported that additional messages had appeared, such as "Wayne Frederick doesn't care about black people" (a spin on the accusation that Kanye West leveled at George W. Bush after Hurricane Katrina) and "Make Howard black again." Mark Mason, an alum who is a chief financial officer at Citigroup and a vice co-chair of the university's board of trustees, was protective of Frederick, telling me that the graffiti "was inappropriately personalized and should not have happened." He added, "Howard has always been a place where people have been able to offer a difference of views, and Wayne continues that aspect of our legacy, but there's a respectful way to do that."

I enrolled at Howard in 1987, a year before Frederick, though I didn't know him there. I met him briefly a year ago, but our first substantial conversation took place last spring, at his office, in a corner suite on the fourth floor of the main administration building. The room looked very different from the last time I had been in it, in my sophomore year, when students occupied the building during a protest. Frederick's office is composed and serene, much like his demeanor. That day, he wore a blue suit, a crisp white shirt, and a pin commemorating Howard's recent 150th anniversary. He is trim and somewhat formal, and speaks softly, with a trace of the accent of his native Trinidad. (Frederick's father, a policeman, died when he was two; he was raised by his mother, a nurse, and his step-father, a prison officer.) He lives in suburban Montgomery County, Maryland, with his wife, Simone, a fellow Trinidadian he met at Carnival and who previously worked in healthcare information technology. They have two children.

Frederick might best be described as a pragmatic optimist. James Comey, the former director of the FBI, is spending the year as a fellow at Howard, and he told me that he found Frederick to be both kind and tough. Effective leaders, Comey said, "are nice people who listen well, but they're not going to get run over." The day the message appeared, Frederick asked that it not be removed: "I said, 'Let the rest of the campus see it.' There's a freedom of expression that we're going to uphold." (Graduate students cleaned it up the next day.) But he was clearly shaken by the incident, particularly when a white classmate of his twelve-year-old son mocked him, saying that Frederick was "running Trump's plantation" and would soon be fired. He told me, "I'll be honest with you. That probably was one of the lowest points not just in my being president but in my life."

Part of Frederick's frustration stems from the fact that, although he is more conservative in his actions and in his manner than most students and faculty members, both groups had previously regarded him favorably. A number of people told me how impressed they had been by the speech he gave at the 2016 convocation ceremony. The night before, the university marshal, who traditionally leads the parade of faculty, emailed Frederick to say that, in light of the anti-racist and anti-police-brutality demonstrations being staged across the country, she would not stand when the national anthem was played. She offered to step down as marshal or to resign, but Frederick said no. At the ceremony, others followed her example, and during his remarks Frederick paused to ask those who had sat during the anthem to stand and be recognized. He told them, "While I intend to stand when the national anthem is played, I also will respect and celebrate your interests in protesting." For many college presidents, this would be a straightforward embrace of free speech, but, for one whose campus is so susceptible to the fluctuations of national politics, it was an audacious position to take.

Then circumstances changed. In April, members of the faculty senate passed a vote of no confidence in Frederick's leadership due to, according to the chair at the time, "ineffective fundraising" and a failure to incorporate faculty perspectives in decision-making. No one who voted against him would speak to me on the record, and no further actions were taken. Some faculty members disputed the validity of the vote on procedural grounds. Also last year, six women filed suit against Howard, alleging that the university had been slow to respond to reports of sexual assault and that, in at least one instance, this had allowed a perpetrator to commit additional offenses. The university filed a motion to dismiss the lawsuit, which has not yet been ruled on. In the meantime, Howard announced a new set of policies to clarify the handling of sexual assault complaints, following an internal review.

In addition, despite the federal funding, Howard has faced particular financial challenges. It is responsible for the administration of the undergraduate college and seven graduate and professional schools, with a combined enrollment of ten thousand students, more than half of whom come from low-income families. It also runs Howard Hospital, a six-story, four-hundred-bed facility built in the 1970s. In March, *The Washington Post* reported that the hospital was suffering a financial and organizational crisis that threatened the well-being of the broader institution. (It is currently ranked sixth out of seven major hospitals in the District of Columbia, and it operated at a $19 million loss in 2015.)

"There's a reason the other two universities in D.C."—Georgetown and George Washington—"don't fully own their hospitals," Frederick told me. "It's a business with a very small margin, and an industry unto itself." The issue is further complicated by the hospital's history: not only does it provide critical care for low-income, predominantly African American residents of the city, but it was founded, as the Freedmen's Hospital in 1862, to care for black soldiers wounded in the Civil War. Although Howard did not take over the hospital until 1967, the school has used it for teaching since 1868, and it represents a central part of the school's mission. More than a hundred positions have been eliminated, and the university says that there has been a surplus in the annual budget for two consecutive years. Even so, it is exploring options to sell the hospital or to share its ownership.

Frederick hopes to one day return to surgical practice full-time, and he still occasionally operates at the hospital. I visited him there in early July, when he had volunteered to be on call. He had also invited a recent graduate named Shakira Jarvis, who was considering applying to the medical school, to accompany him on his rounds. At the hospital, a different side of Frederick's personality emerged: he was at ease and even, at times, jovial. He first checked in on a patient he'd operated on two days earlier for a perforated ulcer. Then he looked in on a twenty-five-year-old man with familial adenomatous polyposis, a disorder that begins in adolescence and is characterized by the growth of tumors in the large intestine. Those with the condition are at a high risk of developing colon cancer. The recommended treatment, Frederick explained later, is the removal of the intestine at around age sixteen. This patient, who lived in one of the poorest areas of the city, had received only sporadic treatment, and a cancerous growth had gone unnoticed. Frederick was there to discuss end-of-life care with him.

When Frederick came out of the patient's room, he talked to Jarvis about how medicine cannot be separated from the social context in which it is practiced. His long-term plan is to send not only medical students but also social work students and nutrition majors to chronically underserved communities in the district, in an effort to step in where the healthcare system has failed. It's easy to see how the demands of Howard's social mission might outstrip its resources.

The issue confronting Howard and the other HBCUs is not whether they still have a role in a society where the formal segregation of higher education no longer exists; that is something commonly asked about black colleges, not by them. In the years immediately following the *Brown v. Board of Education* decision in 1954, many worried that the colleges would be unable to compete against prestigious, better-resourced, mostly white schools in order to attract talented black students. Yet the schools' core mission, their cultural traditions, and, increasingly, their capacity to provide a sense of community for a significant subset of black students who grew up in largely white environments gave them durability in the new landscape. If part of the terrible yield of racism has been the reduction of human complexity to flat caricature, then Howard's objective— pedagogically, socially, demographically—has been the opposite. As Jacob Hardman, a senior finance major who grew up in a predominantly white community, told me, "Howard was the first opportunity I had to not just be the one exceptional black person."

The resilience of the HBCUs is even more striking given the fate of women's colleges in the United States, which have declined in number by 80 percent in the past fifty years. (There are currently just forty-four.) A study in the 1990s found that three-quarters of African Americans with doctoral degrees and four-fifths of black federal judges hold at least one degree from a historically black institution. The question that looms over the HBCUs is not "why" but "how."

The "big four" among HBCUs includes Morehouse and Spelman, both in Atlanta, and Hampton, in Virginia, but Howard, situated in the nation's capital, holds a central status. A study from the Equality of Opportunity Project ranks it in the top 8 percent of elite schools in terms of impact on the social mobility of students. Its list of alumni includes luminaries in politics (Thurgood Marshall, Doug Wilder, Andrew Young, David Dinkins, Kamala Harris); arts and letters (Zora Neale Hurston, Lucille Clifton, Donny Hathaway, Ossie Davis, Amiri Baraka, Roberta Flack, Jessye Norman, Toni Morrison, Ta-Nehisi Coates); business and science (Walter Lincoln Hawkins, Bill Bell, Kelly Miller); and academia (E. Franklin Frazier, Thomas Sowell, Marjorie Lee Browne). In my time there, such people were held up not simply as case studies in achievement but as a kind of categorical validation of the ideal of black institutions. They were data points of possibility to counter the roster of pessimisms arrayed against black America and, tragically, even subscribed to at times by members of our own communities.

Faculty and alumni refer to Howard as "the mecca," in part because it has historically attracted students from throughout the African diaspora. It is held in particularly high regard in Frederick's native Trinidad. Eric Williams, who became the nation's first prime minister after independence in 1962, taught in the social science department. Stokely Carmichael, who was a student activist at Howard before becoming a leader of the Student Nonviolent Coordinating Committee and, later, the Black Power movement, was also Trinidadian. Shaka Hislop, a former English Premier League soccer player, was a star of Howard's team in the late 1980s and had been a schoolmate of Frederick's in Trinidad. "I left to attend Howard on a soccer scholarship," Hislop told me. "I fell in love with the place and encouraged him to come." Hislop went so far as to cover the twenty-five-dollar application fee in a bid to ensure that Frederick applied.

Frederick's decision was complicated by the fact that he has sickle cell anemia, a condition that causes fatigue and painful blockages of the blood flow. Cold weather can worsen the symptoms, and Frederick worried about winters in Washington, D.C. But the appeal of Howard's history prevailed. He arrived on campus a sixteen-year-old freshman weighing less than a hundred pounds. Frederick and Hislop were a study in contrasts: the tall, popular athlete and the diminutive introvert so dedicated to his studies that he earned his undergraduate and medical degrees in just six years. In 2014, Hislop completed an executive master's in business administration; his degree bears the signature of the friend he all but coerced into applying.

Most of the HBCUs are in the South, where they were the product of an ethic of social uplift adopted after the Civil War, when resistance to the education of blacks was almost as fierce as it had been during slavery. W. E. B. Du Bois, in his history of Reconstruction, published in 1935, quotes a Louisianan to the effect that white Southerners were "more hostile to the establishment of [black] schools than they are to [blacks] owning lands." Theories about what social roles best befitted the four million black people in the United States in 1865—a sixth of the population—varied, and so did the mission of the schools. Many focused on agricultural and technical education, such as Tuskegee Institute in Alabama and North Carolina A&T University. Others, such as Morehouse, Spelman, and Howard, aimed to build a broadly educated segment of black America that would open the doors of opportunity for the remainder of the race. And, for decades to come, admission to white-dominated universities remained so segregated, at least in the de facto sense, that without the HBCUs higher education would have been an impossible aspiration for formerly enslaved people and their descendants.

Howard was first envisioned during a series of dinner conversations among political brokers in downtown D.C. The organizer was Oliver Otis Howard, who, as a general in the Union Army, had fought at Gettysburg. In May 1865, Howard was appointed the commissioner of the Freedmen's Bureau. In his memoirs, published in 1907, he wrote that he had experimented with organizing primary schools for black children in the South, but that the white teachers he hired were too indoctrinated with racism to be effective educators. The dinner group came up with the idea of establishing a college to train black teachers. But General C. H. Howard, Oliver's brother, suggested that educators alone could not safeguard the civil rights of such a vulnerable population. Lawyers were also needed, so a law school should be established, too. Over the course of a month, a plan to create a full university came together.

Oliver Howard's experience in the war had given him a higher regard for African Americans than that held by many of his contemporaries, including President Andrew Johnson, who generally resisted the Freedmen's Bureau initiatives. By the standards of the era, Howard's proposal was wildly idealistic, even if today it appears notably tentative. "A brief experience showed us that the Negro people were capable of education, with no limit that men could set to their capacity," he wrote. "What white men could learn, or had learned, they, or some of them, could learn."

In the spring of 1867, Howard authorized a transfer of funds from the bureau to cover the cost of building the main campus, on 150 acres of farmland that he and others—the new trustees—had purchased. Charles Boynton, a clergyman who also served as the chaplain for the U.S. House of Representatives, was selected as the first president. Although John Mercer Langston, the great-uncle of Langston Hughes, had served as interim president from 1873 to 1875, it was not until 1926 that the university appointed its first black president, Mordecai Wyatt Johnson, a thirty-six-year-old theologian. Johnson, whose parents had both been enslaved, was so light-skinned that he could be mistaken for white. He presided over Howard's first great expansion and modernized the law school, with a focus on civil rights law, hiring Charles Hamilton Houston, the first African American to make the *Harvard Law Review,* to run it. Houston became a mentor to Thurgood Marshall, and together they initiated much of the key litigation to integrate American schools in the 1950s.

Howard also attracted an overtly political student body. A famous photograph from 1934 shows a line of students, wearing nooses around their necks, standing across the street from the Daughters of the American Revolution Memorial Hall, where a national conference on crime was being held. The students demanded that the attorney general, Homer S. Cummings, take action to halt the dozens of lynchings that were still occurring across the nation. The following year, members of the House Appropriations Committee called on Johnson to answer questions about radicalism on campus. He said that he would sooner send the students and faculty "back to the cornfield" than prescribe what they could read or how they could think. Johnson's audacity made him a legendary figure in Howard's history—the main administration building is named for him—but many at Howard saw his statements and his actions as irresponsible, even reckless.

In *Invisible Man,* published in 1952, Ralph Ellison, who was a student at Tuskegee Institute in the 1930s, described the tense dynamic between black colleges and their leadership. The first section of the novel is set at an unnamed Southern school where the protagonist, a student, runs afoul of the president, Dr. Bledsoe, who is as dictatorial toward blacks as he is deferential to whites. When white benefactors, whose noblesse oblige blinds them to their own racism, gather for dinner, Bledsoe discreetly excuses himself rather than offend their sensibilities by dining with them.

Bledsoe was based, in part, on Booker T. Washington, the founder of Tuskegee, but he represents a broader character type in HBCU history. In 1963, Albert Manley, the president of Spelman, fired Howard Zinn, then the chair of the history department, for encouraging his students—Alice Walker and Marian Wright Edelman among them—to participate in the burgeoning civil rights movement. Manley worried that student activism would upset the white goodwill upon which the school depended.

In Ellison's time, Tuskegee was dedicated to the proposition that personal dignity and character were the antidotes to racism. Du Bois, one of Washington's most ardent ideological opponents, criticized him for practicing the "old attitude of adjustment and submission." Howard was always intended to be a more forward-thinking institution, though the delicate political positioning of the school made that a complicated undertaking, particularly for its administration.

Over and over again at Howard, the conflict between conciliation with the white world and a more assertive form of politics animated campus activism. In 1968, when students shut down the school and demanded a greater prominence in the curriculum for African American studies, they posted a sign reading "Black University" on the front of the administration building.

In 1987, when I arrived at Howard from Jamaica, Queens, to become the first college student in my family, James Cheek had been the president for eighteen years, following a successful stint in that role at Shaw University in North Carolina. (Mark Mason, the Howard trustee, was also from Jamaica, and was my freshman roommate.) During my sophomore year, in a display of the kind of racial pragmatism that so incensed Ellison, Cheek recruited the Republican political operative Lee Atwater to the board. Atwater, a specialist in employing racially coded rhetoric to discredit and defeat Democratic opponents, had run George H. W. Bush's 1988 presidential campaign, where he used the notorious Willie Horton ad to portray Michael Dukakis as "soft on crime." For Cheek, the virtue of Atwater's political access outweighed his actions. For the students, the move heightened a fear, bequeathed to us by the protesters in 1968, that Howard was not a black university but merely a university with black people.

At the annual Charter Day ceremony in 1989, at which Bill Cosby was given an honorary degree, a group of protesters led by April Silver, who now runs an arts agency, and Ras Baraka, the son of Amiri Baraka and now the mayor of Newark, confronted Cheek about the Atwater appointment. Cheek dismissed their concerns. A few days later, more than two thousand students occupied the administration building, shutting down the university. Atwater resigned from the board four days later. Cheek was widely criticized for his decision to deploy the D.C. police in an attempt to remove the students from the building, and he stepped down soon afterward.

But Frederick, who did not participate in the protests, regards Cheek in far less stark terms than I do, in part because Cheek presided over the largest modern expansion of Howard's campus—including the construction of the new hospital building—and of its student population. Where some saw in Cheek a figure willing to sacrifice self-respect in pursuit of revenue, others saw a brilliant tactician navigating a minefield of white antipathy. Frederick is not unaware that the same debate colors the way his own presidency is seen.

The intertwined sense of the weight of Howard's history and its current implications has typically inspired a kind of racial omertà—a reticence to openly speak ill of your own in a society that is always ready to use your shortcomings against you. This made the circumstances surrounding Frederick's selection as president all the more noteworthy. In June 2013, Renee Higginbotham-Brooks, the vice chair of the board of trustees, published an open letter warning that, under the leadership of Sidney Ribeau, a communications scholar who became president in 2008, Howard was on the verge of financial collapse. It had also undergone a worrisome decline in prestige: its credit rating had fallen and its standing in the annual *U.S. News & World Report* rankings had dropped for several years running. Some of Ribeau's supporters disputed the claims, but he announced his retirement later that year, which led to the appointment of Frederick, a physician with a master's degree in business.

I visited Frederick again on campus late last summer. He'd arrived at the office at seven, and I sat in on several meetings he had scheduled with his "cabinet" of executive officers and new faculty members. One of them was Justin Hansford, an attorney and Howard alum whose parents and maternal grandparents also graduated from the university. I had first met him in Ferguson in 2014 when he helped bring a human rights complaint to the United Nations against the United States in response to the events surrounding the death of Michael Brown. He was coming to Howard to lead a civil rights institute at the law school. "Social justice is in the DNA of this institution," Frederick said, and he hoped that Hansford would help revitalize the tradition. Given all the recent criticism that Frederick has been too conciliatory, the remark seemed somewhat pointed. Hansford, though, felt that Frederick was sincere. "There's a huge gap between the way the students view him and the way the faculty views him," he later told me. Students, in his estimation, are far more critical. Yet Frederick's relationship with the faculty is not without problems, as the vote of no confidence, valid or not, made plain.

Frederick thinks that his difficulties are partly due to a bias that some African Americans have against West Indian blacks. "I'm the first non-American-born president of the university," he said. "There's an undercurrent of 'Does he really relate to black people?'" I was struck by his forthrightness, even though I wasn't sure I believed it, given Howard's history as a crossroads of the African diaspora. But later, when I asked a retired senior administrator about Frederick's decision to attend the White House meeting, she said, "It may be that, as someone from outside this country, he doesn't know the various cultural markers, doesn't have an absolute understanding of racism the way we do." That "we" she conscripted me into was as loathsome a designation as the "they" that has so often been the lens through which black people are viewed. (Her argument also failed to explain why so many black American college presidents attended the meeting.) Clarence Lusane, who chairs the political science department, echoed Frederick's impression: "There's an idea that there is a West Indian faction and a black American one, and that Frederick favors the former." The idea had no real basis, Lusane said, and no one I spoke to could identify any specific instance of favoritism, but the perception nonetheless complicates Frederick's reputation on campus.

Frederick knows that alumni will judge him largely on the university's financial footing at the end of his tenure. Harvard, with an endowment of $36 billion, has a policy that students whose families earn less than $65,000 a year are awarded free tuition, fees, and housing. Stanford, which has an endowment of more than $22 billion, has a similar policy for families earning less than $125,000. Howard, which competes against these institutions for students, cannot come anywhere close to such largesse. In 2015, the financier John Paulson gave Harvard a gift of $400 million. Howard is the only HBCU with an endowment larger than Paulson's gift—around $600 million. The largest gift to the university during Frederick's tenure so far is a $4 million donation from the media executive Cathy Hughes and her son, Alfred Liggins III. Frederick also secured $10 million in pledges for need-based scholarships last year.

I also sat in on a meeting in the admissions office, where the staff was celebrating the record number of commitments the school had received from accepted applicants for the 2017–2018 year. That presented new challenges, though, in terms of housing and classrooms; most of all, the administrators were concerned with the number of academically high-achieving applicants from low-income families. "We've got an incoming class with an average GPA of 3.54 and 1210 SAT scores," Frederick told me later. "But, when they run the analyses, probably 60 percent of those kids can't afford to be here." This meant that those students would struggle with finding financial aid and paying it off. It was the main difficulty confronting all the HBCUs: a crisis not of purpose but of means.

Last year, the Howard administration sent out a fundraising email requesting donations for a "Senior Year Fund" for students who had managed to pay tuition for three years but could not cover their senior year. I understood the problem intimately—that circumstance had forced me to drop out of Howard in the fall of 1990. I owed $3,000 in back fees, and therefore couldn't register for the upcoming year. I stayed in Washington, working in bookstores, attending lectures, and writing bad short fiction. Three years later, when Carmen James, the bursar, and Elizabeth Clark-Lewis, a history professor, discovered that I had not graduated, the registrar's office allowed me to reenroll and to pay off the outstanding fees in monthly hundred-dollar increments. Everything that followed—graduate school, a doctorate, a career in academia—was thanks to that intervention, a step that the school took in keeping with its sense of mission. But this is precisely the kind of thing that makes it possible for a university to receive a substantial budgetary appropriation and still find itself chronically strapped for funding. Howard's outstanding tuition fees currently amount to $18 million.

The HBCU system has become a sort of longitudinal study of how the racial wealth gap plays out in higher education. Still, Frederick notes, "Howard produces more black people who go on to complete PhDs in STEM fields than any other college or university in the country. Nine of the top ten producers of black people with undergraduate degrees in physics are all historically black colleges." He added, "One of the things I feel is a real challenge is communicating what we accomplish not in comparison with each other but with all colleges and universities in the country."

He has some ideas to that end. In an effort to become a crucial player in the diversification of industries where African Americans are underrepresented, the university launched Howard West, which grew out of a program that brought in Google engineers to serve as computer science faculty. Through Howard West, twenty-five students were selected by faculty to take a twelve-week course on coding at Google's San Francisco campus this past summer. The company funded the program, which was initiated by Bonita Stewart, a Google vice president and Howard alum. There are plans to expand it to a full academic year.

Another idea has reconnected Frederick with Ben Carson, the secretary of the Department of Housing and Urban Development. Frederick originally applied to medical school because he wanted to work on a cure for sickle cell anemia, which afflicts a hundred thousand people in the United States. Once he began his studies, he decided that he wanted to be a surgeon, though he wasn't sure that he had the physical stamina the job requires. In 1993, Frederick cold-called Carson, then a celebrated neurosurgeon at Johns Hopkins University and the author of several bestselling books, to ask his advice. Carson invited him to Baltimore, took him to lunch, and persuaded him to pursue surgery.

Frederick does not share Carson's political views, but he is still grateful for the advice that Carson gave him twenty-four years ago. He recently called him again, to talk about how HUD's loan programs might help with a potential new plan to finance the hospital. But, Frederick joked, "that doesn't mean I'm going to say he needs to be on my board of trustees."

James Comey declined offers from many universities in favor of Howard's. He was looking to engage in the conversation about law enforcement and race, he said, and "I thought maybe the hardest, most stimulating, and for me most beneficial place to have that would be at the mecca." Some on campus interpret his presence as a sly gesture on Frederick's part. Having been criticized for attending the White House gathering, he hired the man whose firing triggered an ongoing, potentially existential threat to Trump's presidency. But Frederick denies any political motivation: he met Comey last year, before the White House meeting, when he gave a black history talk at FBI headquarters, and the fellowship offer came out of discussions they had afterward.

In any event, Comey's hiring sparked a campus backlash. Students from HU Resist released a statement saying that Comey "represents an institution diametrically opposed to the interests of Black people domestically and abroad." Frederick met with the students, who later told me that they objected to Comey's use of the term "Ferguson effect" to describe an alleged uptick in violent crime that followed the national protests against police brutality because police officers felt powerless to do their jobs effectively. They also criticized the reported monitoring of members of Black Lives Matter during Comey's tenure, and lodged wide-ranging, historical complaints against the FBI for its treatment of Martin Luther King, Jr., and Malcolm X and its role in the 1927 deportation of the black nationalist leader Marcus Garvey.

Convocation typically draws a respectable but far-from-capacity crowd, yet on the morning of last September's ceremony, where Comey was due to deliver the convocation address, students and faculty packed the auditorium. Shortly after he began to speak, students started chanting protest slogans and singing "We Shall Not Be Moved." The clamor suggested that at least some students believed that Howard had once more chosen political accommodation over principle. But an apparently larger group began shouting that Comey should be allowed to finish. He continued, saying that "Howard has always been different, which is why I wanted to be part of it. It was designed that way and it has remained that way. A safe space, especially for those who face the oppression and the challenge of being black in America." He ended his comments to sustained applause. When I asked him later about the event, he laughed and said, "I've never given a speech where people were shouting 'Comey is not my homie.'" Then he added, "Howard is dealing with this, like a lot of universities: How do you both embrace energy and protest and dissent and maintain an open environment where people can have hard conversations?"

Frederick was no less sanguine. "Institutions like the FBI and the White House have a tortured history among minorities," he said. "But we didn't blame Barack Obama for every ill of the White House's history. It's the same with Comey." Frederick had brought him to campus not despite the strained relationship between minority communities and law enforcement but because of it. "The dialogue is important because minorities are being killed by law enforcement, and I thought it important for my students to be asking him about that directly."

The protest and counterprotest reminded me yet again of the apparent paradox at the heart of HBCUs, where pragmatists are in the business of producing new generations of fierce idealists. Ralph Ellison's Bledsoe delighted in the idea that he might alchemize power from deference. Booker T. Washington denounced racial equality to powerful segregationists, but he also secretly funded efforts to defend black civil rights. Howard's militancy has been underwritten by its compromises.

One afternoon, when I spoke to Frederick by phone, he told me about a student who had harshly criticized his decision to attend the White House meeting but who later came to his office seeking financial assistance to pay for his final year. To Frederick's mind, the connection between his trip to the White House and his ability to aid the student was obvious. To his critics, such connections either are opaque or come at a cost that betrays the school's founding mission. "People think we're doing God's work, on God's time, with God's money," Frederick said. "The problem is, we don't have access to the latter two."

BLACK *PANTHER* AND THE INVENTION OF "AFRICA"

February 18, 2018

The Maison des Esclaves stands on the rocky shore of Gorée Island, off the coast of Senegal, like a great red tomb. During the years of its operation, the building served as a rendezvous point for slavers trafficking in a seemingly inexhaustible resource: Africans, whose very bodies became the wealth of white men. A portal known as the "Door of No Return," leading to the slave ships, offered the forlorn captives a last glimpse of home before they were sown to the wind and sold in the West. For nearly four centuries, this traffic continued, seeding the populations of the Caribbean, Brazil, Argentina, Mexico, and Central and North America and draining societies of their prime populations while fomenting civil conflict among them in order to more effectively cull their people. On the high seas, the vessels jettisoned bodies in such terrible numbers that the poet Amiri Baraka once wrote, "At the bottom of the Atlantic Ocean there's a railroad made of human bones."

I visited Gorée Island in 2003 with a group of black academics just days after George W. Bush had come to the island and offered platitudes about the cruelties of human history but stopped short of apologizing for the United States' role in the transatlantic slave trade. Residents of the island greeted us in the markets like long-lost kin. We repeatedly heard some version of "Welcome home, my black brothers and sisters!" But later, over dinner, a Senegalese guide casually informed us that we were neither their siblings nor even distant kin to Africa, implying that the greetings in the market had been merely a clever sales tactic directed at gullible black Americans who travel to the continent in search of roots, as if they were abused foster kids futilely seeking their birth parents. "You are Americans. That is all," she said. This exchange took place fifteen years ago, but I can still recall the way her words hung in the air like a guilty verdict. The policy of "No Return," she suggested, applied to distant descendants, too.

There is a fundamental dissonance in the term "African-American," two feuding ancestries conjoined by a hyphen. That dissonance—a hyphen standing in for the brutal history that intervened between Africa and America—is the subject of *Black Panther*, Ryan Coogler's brilliant first installment of the story of Marvel Comics' landmark black character. "I have a lot of pain inside me," Coogler told an audience at the Brooklyn Academy of Music on Wednesday night. "We were taught that we lost the things that made us African. We lost our culture, and now we have to make do with scraps." Black America is constituted overwhelmingly by the descendants of people who were not only brought to the country against their will but were later inducted into an ambivalent form of citizenship without their input. The Fourteenth Amendment, which granted citizenship to all those born here, supposedly resolved the question of the status of ex-slaves, though those four million individuals were not consulted in its ratification. The unspoken yield of this history is the possibility that the words "African" and "American" should not be joined by a hyphen but separated by an ellipsis.

Our sensibilities are accustomed to Marvel films offering clear lines of heroism and villainy, but *Black Panther* dispatches with its putative villain, Ulysses Klaue, a white South Africa–based arms dealer, halfway through the film. Chadwick Boseman's T'Challa, the Black Panther and the King of Wakanda, confronts Erik Killmonger, a black American mercenary, played by Michael B. Jordan, as a rival, but the two characters are essentially dueling responses to five centuries of African exploitation at the hands of the West. The villain, to the extent that the term applies, is history itself.

Wakanda is a technologically advanced kingdom in Central Africa that was never colonized by any Western power. T'Challa, the noble leader of an unvanquished people, upholds the isolationism that has always kept the kingdom safe; Killmonger, driven by the horrors that befell those who were stolen from the continent, envisions a world revolution, led by Wakanda, to upend the status quo. When Killmonger arrives there after the death of King T'Chaka (the father of T'Challa), he sets in motion a reckoning not only with his rival but with broader questions of legitimacy, lineage, and connection. Black Panther, as Ryan Coogler pointed out in Brooklyn, has been an inherently political character since his inception during the Black Power era of the 1960s. He is a refutation of the image of the lazy and false African promulgated in the white world and subscribed to even by many in the black one. Coogler told Marvel up front that his version of the story would remain true to those political elements. It is shot through with the sense of longing and romance common to the way that people of a diaspora envision their distant homeland.

Like the comics on which they are based, the Marvel movies, in general, have not shied away from political concerns. *Captain America: The Winter Soldier,* released in 2014, grapples with ideas of preemptive warfare, drones, and the surveillance state as elements of the war on terror. The first *Iron Man* film, from 2008, addressed war profiteering and arms contractors at a time when the United States was still heavily involved in Iraq.

Yet nothing in Marvel's collection of films is or could be political in the same way as *Black Panther,* because in those other stories we were at least clear about where the lines of fantasy departed from reality. *Captain America* is a fantastic riff on the nation's idealism, filtered through the lens of the Second World War, a historic event whose particulars—however horrific and grandly inhumane—are not in dispute. *Black Panther,* however, exists in an invented nation in Africa, a continent that has been grappling with invented versions of itself ever since white men first declared it the "dark continent" and set about plundering its people and its resources. This fantasy of Africa as a place bereft of history was politically useful, justifying imperialism. It found expression in the highest echelons of Western thought and took on the contours of truth. In 1753, the Scottish philosopher David Hume wrote, "I am apt to suspect the Negroes, and all other species of men . . . to be naturally inferior to the whites. There never was any civilized nation of any complexion other than white." Two centuries later, the British historian Hugh Trevor-Roper wrote, "Perhaps, in the future, there will be some African history to teach. But at present there is none, or very little: there is only the history of the Europeans in Africa."

Africa—or, rather, "Africa"—is a creation of a white world and the literary, academic, cinematic, and political mechanisms that it used to give mythology the credibility of truth. No such nation as Wakanda exists on the map of the continent, but that is entirely beside the point. Wakanda is no more or less imaginary than the Africa conjured by Hume or Trevor-Roper, or the one canonized in such Hollywood offerings as *Tarzan*. It is a redemptive counter-mythology. Most filmmakers start by asking their audiences to suspend their disbelief. But, with Africa, Coogler begins with a subject about which the world had suspended its disbelief four centuries before he was born. The film is a nearly seamless dramatic chronicle of the threat created when Killmonger travels to the African nation he descends from. Yet some of the most compelling points in the story are those where the stitching is most apparent. Killmonger is a native of Oakland, California, where the Black Panther Party was born. (In an early scene, a poster of Huey P. Newton, the co-founder of the party, hangs on a wall next to a Public Enemy poster.) In an impeccably choreographed fight sequence, T'Challa and General Okoye, the leader of Wakanda's all-female militia (brilliantly played by Danai Gurira), alongside Nakia, a wily Wakandan spy (played by Lupita Nyong'o), confront a Boko Haram–like team of kidnappers. At the same time, it is all but impossible not to notice that Coogler has cast a black American, a Zimbabwean American, and a Kenyan as a commando team in a film about African redemption. The cast also includes Winston Duke, who is West

Indian; Daniel Kaluuya, a black Brit; and Florence Kasumba, a Ugandan-born German woman. The implicit statement in both the film's themes and its casting is that there is a connection—however vexed, tenuous, and complicated—among the continent's scattered descendants. Coogler said as much in Brooklyn when he talked about a trip that he took to South Africa as research for the film: after discovering cultural elements that reminded him of black communities in the United States, he concluded, "There's no way they could wipe out what we were for thousands of years. We're African."

There is a great deal more that differentiates *Black Panther* from other efforts in the superhero genre. The film is not about world domination by an alien invasion or a mad cabal of villains but about the implications of a version of Western domination that has been with us so long that it has become as ambient as the air. When Shuri, Wakanda's chief of technology and the irreverent younger sister of T'Challa, is startled by a white CIA agent, she says, "Don't scare me like that, colonizer!" When I saw the movie, the audience howled at the inversion, "colonizer" deployed as an epithet rather than a badge of cultural superiority. In addition, Marvel has been criticized for failing to center a film on any of its female characters, but it is the female characters in *Black Panther* whose ideas and determinations dictate the terms on which the rivalry between the male protagonists plays out. T'Challa engages with his female counterparts as equals; Killmonger kills two women and assaults a third. Their political positions may be equally compelling; their ideas about gender are not.

Coogler's commentary on the literal tribalism of the African diaspora, his devotion to a glorious vision of Africa, and, most provocatively, his visceral telling of the pain of existing as an orphan of history—as seen in the story of Killmonger, whose separation from Africa is not simply historical but also paternal—is striking but not unique. The narrative of Africa as a tragic tabula rasa in world history exists in dialogue with another version, equally imaginary, but idealized, and authored by descendants of those Africans who passed through the Maison des Esclaves and the other structures like it. In 1896, after Ethiopian forces defeated an invading Italian army in the Battle of Adwa, black people across the globe celebrated the country as the last preserve on the continent free from the yoke of colonialism and as a sign of hope for the black world—the Wakanda of its day. In the 1930s, after Mussolini invaded Ethiopia, Depression-era black Americans and West Indians scraped together pennies to send to fund the resistance of a country they had never visited. In the late nineteenth century, the West Indian educator and diplomat Edward Wilmot Blyden envisioned and promoted a kind of black Zionism in which people of African descent in the West would return to work on behalf of African redemption. What Blyden, and what Marcus Garvey—a Jamaican who, in the 1920s, organized a global pan-Africanist effort to end European colonialism—and what the organizer Audley Moore and the scholar John Henrik Clarke, and what the entire lineage of that pan-African tradition insisted on was a kind of democracy of the imagination. If the subordination of Africa had begun in the minds of white people, its reclamation, they reasoned, would begin in the minds of black ones.

I understand this story intuitively and personally. In my twenties, I consumed volumes of African history and histories of the slave trade, seeking out answers to the same questions that Coogler asked in South Africa, a fugitive from the idea that I descend from a place with no discernible past. I dropped my given middle name and replaced it with an African one in an effort to make transparent that sense of connection. On Gorée Island, I patiently listened to the guide's argument before pointing out to her that we were conducting our conversation in English, in a building constructed by the French, in a country that had been a colony of France, and that the issue was not whether black Americans retained any connection to Africa but whether history had left anyone on the continent still in a position to pass judgment on that question. Superheroes are seldom tasked with this kind of existential lifting, but that work is inescapable in the questions surrounding Wakanda and the politics of even imagining such a place. Marvel has made a great many entertaining movies in the past decade, but Ryan Coogler has made a profound one.

POSTSCRIPT TO "*BLACK PANTHER* AND THE INVENTION OF 'AFRICA'"

There was no way to know at the time of writing this piece that *Black Panther* would become the highest-grossing film in the history of black cinema, catapulting director Ryan Coogler into the elite ranks of Hollywood auteurs. Across the span of years since its release, the accomplishment only becomes more notable. The classic dichotomy of cinema—really, that of all art—is the tension between work that is commercially viable and work that is aesthetically complex or advances a particular set of artistic or societal conversations. The presumption is that these two pursuits are mutually exclusive. Moreover, the Marvel cinematic universe in which *Black Panther* is situated had grappled with thorny questions of patriotism, war, and technology, but nothing so divisive as the themes of race, colonialism, and the legacy of slavery that are central to Coogler's film.

Black Panther's $1.3 billion box office haul also made it the fourteenth highest-grossing film in Hollywood history and raised anticipation for the sequel. Those hopes were vastly complicated in August 2020 when Chadwick Boseman, who played T'Challa, the titular Black Panther, died unexpectedly of colon cancer at age forty-three. Boseman's death cemented a kind of singularity for the film. There would surely be subsequent films and additions to the comic lore of the character, but his was the original—the only version that would include that full, unmatchable cast. The sequel, *Black Panther: Wakanda Forever*, continued the narrative of the mythological African kingdom but also bore the weight of grieving and memorializing Boseman.

Reality intruded in other ways. The diamond company

De Beers named Lupita Nyong'o, the actress who played Nakia, the head of Wakanda's intelligence services, as a global brand ambassador ahead of the film's release. De Beers, deeply implicated in the colonization and subordination of South Africa's black population, had managed to engineer the representation of their gems—and their bloody legacy—at the film's premiere. The point was inescapable: the fantasy of Wakanda existed within the reality of a world in which the prerogatives of white power still held sway.

In a comparatively short period of time, the original film began to seem like a hallmark of a more innocent era, one not freighted by mortality's capriciousness or how easily the veil of black empowerment can be pierced by the historic agents of black subordination. That alone makes Coogler's film worth revisiting.

THE SOUTHERN STRATEGIST

May 14, 2018

At first glance, the crowds of people congregating on a block of Mulberry Street, a stretch of squat brick buildings near downtown Memphis, on the morning of April 4, might have been there for a variety of reasons. The street vendors selling T-shirts and posters and the jumbotron set up near a parking lot suggested the start of a music festival; delegations of men and women dressed in their union best pointed to a labor rally. But the plaintive notes of gospel music drifting from speakers and the black bunting draped over a balcony of the building at the center of the activities indicated a more somber occasion. The space behind the bunting had begun as an overlook, became a crime scene, and is now a historic site. The hundreds of people, most but by no means all of them black, were gathering at the Lorraine Motel and the National Civil Rights Museum to mark the moment when, fifty years earlier, Martin Luther King, Jr., was assassinated as he stood on the balcony outside Room 306. The past five years have been a season of semi-centennials: 2013, 2014, and 2015 brought anniversaries of the triumphs of the March on Washington, the Civil Rights Act, and the Voting Rights Act. This year recalls losses: King's death and, with it, the hopes of a signal phase of the civil rights struggle.

Speeches, some of them from associates of King's, went on all day. James Lawson, who, at eighty-nine, is nearly as dynamic as he was when he helped organize the Freedom Rides of 1961, spoke about the landmark strike of black sanitation workers, which was called in Memphis in early 1968 to protest unsafe work conditions and unequal pay. It was Lawson who had invited King to Memphis, to lend his support. (A sanitation worker at the commemoration who had traveled with a group from New York City told me that it was important to reclaim King's connections to organized labor.) Jesse Jackson, who was with King when he was shot, movingly recounted the final moments of his life. Gina Belafonte, the daughter of King's close friend Harry Belafonte, runs Sankofa, an organization that connects the arts with activism, and she spoke about the imperatives of culture in the service of social change. But the day was warm and, by the afternoon, the crowd was beginning to grow restless. As with any rite that is repeated at regular intervals, even for an event so consequential, the speeches began to seem rote. The comparisons between the past and the present and the inevitable declarations that we still have "so far to go"—which tend to reinforce how creative and distinctive those monumental events of the past were—sometimes raised the dispiriting question of whether anything being done in the present would warrant such celebration in the future.

All this added to the anticipation surrounding one of the final speakers of the day. The Reverend Dr. William Barber, a pastor of Greenleaf Christian Church in Goldsboro, North Carolina, has become, in the past few years, an indispensable figure in the civil rights landscape and, perhaps, the individual most capable of crafting a broad-based political counterpoint to the divisiveness of Trumpism. Charismatic, tireless, eloquent, and yet resistant to an excessive nostalgia for the glory days of the movement, he has presence. At around five o'clock, he came out on the balcony. A tall, heavyset, handsome man with the kind of face that people describe as being "of indeterminate age"—he is fifty-four—Barber was dressed in a black suit, a magenta shirt with a clergyman's collar, and a white clerical stole that read "Jesus Was a Poor Man." He has an ursine bearing and moves methodically, which gave the applause a moment to build.

Allotted just five minutes to speak, Barber began by addressing not King's victories but the burdens that he bore. "The weight of these years, by the time he got to Memphis, to stand with black men who were organizing a garbage strike, were heavy," Barber said. "By the time he got to Memphis, he had racists, moderates, politicians, a president, and even jealous criticism from black leaders, who used his position against the Vietnam War as an excuse to diminish his status in the eyes of liberal white America while raising their own. And then the bullet rang. And his body fell." But what was more important than mourning King's suffering, Barber said, was honoring the work that he undertook in the last months of his life: confronting racism, to be sure, but also militarism and poverty.

Barber speaks in a resonant baritone with precise phrasing, but he is a true thespian of the pulpit: his eyes widen in mock surprise or squint in faux confusion at an act of outrage or injustice. Sometimes, after making a point, he whirls around, looking over his shoulder as if to see whether anyone has overheard him. From the balcony, he boomed, "We don't need a commemoration, we need a *reconsecration*." He had blown past the five-minute mark, but the crowd was with him. He warned, "The Bible says woe unto those who love the tombs of the prophets." The duty of the living, he said, is not simply to recall the martyrs of the movement but to continue their work. "We've got to hold up the banner until every person has healthcare, we've got to hold it up until every child is lifted in love, we've got to hold it up until every job is a living-wage job, until every person in poverty has guaranteed subsistence." He finished to loud and sustained applause. Shortly afterward, at a minute past six, the time that King was shot, an enormous bell in the motel courtyard rang thirty-nine times—once for each year of King's life—and the crowd on Mulberry Street began to disperse.

Barber had offered the most concrete answer that day to the question King asked in the title of his last book, *Where Do We Go from Here?*, and he wasn't speaking rhetorically. For the past three years, Barber and the Reverend Liz Theoharis, a co-director of the Kairos Center at Union Theological Seminary in New York, who stood next to him as he spoke in Memphis, have led an effort to revive King's most radical project: the 1968 Poor People's Campaign. At the commemoration, Jesse Jackson spoke about how King, after shepherding the movement to the Civil Rights Act and Voting Rights Act, had begun to wonder if he had achieved enough. Despite the pivotal new laws, he knew that the structures of racism, inequality, and injustice had hardly crumbled. So he proposed to broaden the movement's targets from the race-specific concerns of fighting Jim Crow to an assault on the plight of the impoverished across racial lines.

The Poor People's Campaign demanded full employment, a guaranteed basic income, and access to capital for small and minority businesses. King's decision to support the Memphis strike was a way of recognizing labor struggles as part of the movement. The campaign called on people across the country to travel to Washington, D.C., where, for six weeks over the summer, protesters occupied tents on the National Mall in a camp called Resurrection City. The idea had roots in both the 1963 March on Washington and the 1932 Bonus Army marches of First World War veterans who, left destitute by the Great Depression, set up a camp in the capital and insisted that their pensions be paid early. The centerpiece of the 1968 campaign was a mule cart procession of people from Marks, Mississippi, the poorest town in the poorest county of the poorest state in the country.

Barber and Theoharis met in 2013 at the opening of the Kairos Center, where he was one of the speakers. (The center advocates a grassroots approach to ending poverty, in which poor people are the key elements of leadership.) At the time, he was launching his Moral Monday movement in North Carolina, enlisting a broad-based alliance of Christians, Muslims, Jews, nonbelievers, blacks,

Latinos, poor whites, feminists, environmentalists, and others to protest the conservative agenda of the state legislature. Theoharis, an ordained Presbyterian minister, had spent twenty-five years doing organizing and social justice work among domestic workers and Native Americans and advocating for the rights of the homeless. The new project is called the Poor People's Campaign: A National Call for Moral Revival. This time, the demands include federal and state living-wage laws, equity in education, an end to mass incarceration, a single-payer healthcare system, and the protection of the right to vote.

Beginning on Mother's Day and continuing until June 23—the last full day of the 1968 campaign—thousands of people in some forty states are expected to commit acts of civil disobedience and protest against policies enacted at the federal and, especially, the state level that have disproportionately affected poor people. "If you have bad voting laws in your state," Barber told me, "that's not done in Congress, that's something done at the local level." The movement is largely intended to be an independent undertaking of community groups, but it is aided by Theoharis's indefatigable organizing efforts and Barber's ability to project his charisma from the pulpit and the TV screen—he is a regular presence on CNN and, in particular, MSNBC.

On the left, Barber tends to inspire unsolicited testimonials. Last winter, I found myself seated in front of Senator Elizabeth Warren of Massachusetts on a train from New York to Boston. We started talking, and I mentioned that I was writing a story about Barber. She said that she had participated in an event with him years earlier and had followed his work since. She was impressed by his intelligence and his commitment. "He's the real thing," she said. A few weeks later, at a restaurant in Cambridge, Cornel West used the same words when he saw that I had a copy of Barber's book *The Third Reconstruction,* which is partly a memoir of his activism and partly an elucidation of his ideas for the movement that he is attempting to build. "That brother is the real thing," West told me. Theoharis has also heard the phrase applied to Barber. "He has really given his life and all that is in it to the struggle," she said.

"And I don't think that happens every time. I don't think that, in this society, that actually is heralded, or valued, or upheld as what you're supposed to do. But he embodies this."

His work has been made more difficult by the fact that he suffers from ankylosing spondylitis, an arthritic condition that causes him chronic pain and forces him to lean forward when he stands, as if he were poring over a book or speaking to a child. Last year, on an icy night in Boston, I watched as he arrived in an SUV at Trinity Church on Copley Square, where he was scheduled to speak. He had been resting, fully reclined, in the passenger seat, but, in a ritual that came to be familiar to me, he hoisted himself up, swung his legs out the door, shifted his weight onto a cane, stood, and slowly made his way across the pavement and up the church steps. I asked him how he copes with his condition, given the schedule that he keeps. He chuckled and told me that once, when he was visiting an encampment of homeless people, a woman offered him her chair, one of her few possessions. He was moved by the gesture. "I first had to put my own struggle in perspective," he said. "I had to turn my ankylosing into a testimony, in this sense: every time I'm fighting for healthcare, I'm reminded I have it. How many people are there that have this disease but don't have healthcare? It gives you a sense of deep—not just sympathy but empathy, right?" He reminded me that Harriet Tubman suffered from epilepsy and that Franklin Roosevelt commanded the country for thirteen years, through the Depression and global war, despite having been stricken with polio—and that all the heroes of the Bible had some physical or mental challenge. As Barber sees it, the challenges that he confronts are shared by many who are called to serve; it would be indecent to complain.

Barber's career has veered between the political and the religious, but the two paths often intersect: he argues politics from a theological perspective, while his sermons are informed by the lessons of the streets. When he mentions "the good book," he is as likely to be referring to Howard Zinn's progressive primer *A People's History of the United States* as he is to the one that contains the Old and New Testaments. He learned both traditions at home.

Barber was born on August 30, 1963, in Indianapolis. His mother, Eleanor, a government clerk, had gone into labor forty-eight hours earlier—on the day of the March on Washington, he likes to point out. His father, for whom he was named, was an ordained minister in the predominantly white Disciples of Christ denomination, and he held degrees in physics and social work as well as in theology. Like millions of African Americans in the first half of the twentieth century, Barber's father had left the South—North Carolina, in his case—as part of the Great Migration to Northern and Midwestern cities. He met Eleanor in Indiana, and they settled there.

Despite having achieved a middle-class stability that would be infinitely more difficult to maintain in the South, in 1968 the couple heeded the call of E. V. Wilkins, a high school principal and family friend who asked them to help him with a school integration movement that he was attempting to build in Roper, a small town in the eastern part of North Carolina near where Barber's father had grown up. When Barber was in second grade, his parents enrolled him as one of the first black students in the local elementary school. He told me jokingly, "My first foray into activist work was not of my choice." It was a family undertaking: his mother worked in the high school office and his father taught science. Eleanor, who is now eighty-five, still works at the school.

In *The Third Reconstruction,* Barber writes that his father could have secured a prestigious position as the pastor of a large urban church, but that coming home to Roper "was a vow of poverty" for him. He was respected in clerical circles—when he wasn't teaching, he traveled the state as an itinerant preacher—but he was such an uncompromising and fervent critic of racism that some black congregations were hesitant to host him. As a child, Barber accompanied his father on his travels. He learned that the concerns of religion could hardly be distinct from those of earthly matters, like racial injustice. He remembers visiting a friend of his father's, a bishop who had run afoul of some local whites, and praying together in the man's yard that he might be kept safe. As night fell, the friend went inside and placed shotguns by the windows. "What's that for?" Barber asked. His father answered, "That's an extra precaution in case the prayers don't work."

In 1978, at the age of fifteen, Barber was elected president of the local NAACP Youth Council. Three years later, he enrolled in North Carolina Central University, a historically black institution in Durham. In his senior year, he met a first-year nursing student, Rebecca McLean, when she joined a march he had organized to support Jesse Jackson's 1984 presidential bid. They married three years later and had five children; she works as a psychiatric nurse. Barber is hesitant to talk about his family, because death threats are still an occupational hazard for civil rights leaders. "I believe he is doing what the Church as a whole, all of us, are called to do," Rebecca Barber told me. "And that is do justice, love mercy, and walk humbly with God." That sense of abiding purpose, she said, has allowed her not to dwell on the threats, which, in recent years, have grown in number.

Initially, Barber resisted entering the clergy; he wanted to be a civil rights lawyer. "I had developed a distaste for the Church," he told me. "I always believed in God, but I was struggling with the Church piece of it." He chose Central in part because there was no religious course requirement. But in his senior year he had a crisis of conscience over the question of what he could do with his life versus what he was called to do with it. In March 1985, he discussed his dilemma with his father, who urged him to distinguish between the failings of the Church and the perfection of God. Three weeks later, Barber preached his first sermon, on the Good Samaritan. The Samaritan, he noted, was not concerned about how to get into Heaven—the focus of too much of religion, in his opinion. Instead, "he chose to go down into the ditch, he chose to go down to where people were hurting." After graduating, Barber enrolled at Duke

University to earn a master's degree in divinity. His father died in 1988, but Barber still often mentions him when talking about his understanding of Christianity.

At Duke, Barber studied with C. Eric Lincoln, the acclaimed scholar of the black church whose work explored the ways that race had shaped American Christianity—rendering the religion, for example, entirely capable of reconciling fidelity to its creed with slavery and racism. He also read the works of Reinhold Niebuhr, whose concept of Christian realism led Barber toward a practical theology, a way of faith that is rooted in the struggles of common people and seeks justice and mercy against unfavorable odds. His studies gave him an intellectual scaffolding that was no less important than what he had learned from his father about the moral and practical obligations of faith. Later, he met the theologians Paul Tillich and James Cone, whose thinking also became a major influence on him. His approach to faith, however, put him at odds with the Moral Majority version of evangelicalism that was ascendant in the 1980s. He told me on the phone one evening that those Christians "say so much about areas where the Bible says very little"—abortion, homosexuality—"and speak so little about the issues where the Bible says so much," like poverty, empathy, and justice.

Meanwhile, Barber's belief in the possibility of an alliance of poor people across racial lines was beginning to take shape. The idea may seem radical, particularly in the era of Donald Trump, but it isn't novel; it had a long history even when King proposed it. A number of such alliances formed during Reconstruction in a grand, if short-lived, experiment in inclusive populism. In North Carolina, the Fusion movement came together to protest the Democratic Party's monetary policy, which hurt both black and white small farmers, and for a time it created one of the most progressive governments in the state's history. In 1894, a Fusion-Republican alliance won every state office up for election, and it sent George Henry White, a black Republican, to the U.S. House of Representatives in 1896. It all came to an end just two years later with the Wilmington race riots, in which an estimated two thousand white men attacked black residents, burned black businesses, and unseated Fusionist officials, replacing them with white Democrats in what was essentially a coup d'état. The movement of resurgent white nationalists, unironically referred to as "redemption," had triumphed in North Carolina. Nevertheless, the inspiration of the Fusionists has stayed with Barber throughout his career.

After Duke, Barber was hired as the chair of the North Carolina State Human Relations Commission in Durham. He traveled around the state investigating instances of discrimination in housing and employment. He was committed to the work, but in the summer of 1993, when he was thirty, Greenleaf Christian Church in Goldsboro, which is part of the Disciples of Christ denomination, asked him to be its pastor, and he decided to accept the offer. A month later, he awoke unable to move. Ankylosing spondylitis causes joints and vertebrae in the spine to fuse; Barber's neck, hips, and the base of his spine had essentially frozen in place. He had played football in high school, and the pain and stiffness in his back that signaled the onset of the disease had been misdiagnosed as a bad disk. There is no cure for ankylosing spondylitis, but therapy and medication can alleviate some of its symptoms.

He spent nearly three months in the hospital and began an intensive, painful process of regaining mobility. He sank into a depression and encouraged Greenleaf to find an able-bodied pastor—a request the church rejected. With the assistance of a walker, Barber was eventually able to take a few tentative steps. He continued to preach at Greenleaf, mastering a technique of swinging the walker behind him in the pulpit and bracing himself against it. One morning in 2005, he managed to walk to the bathroom unassisted. Later that day, he bought a white wooden cane for the blind, which he painted black. He still uses it; battered and weathered, it is a testament to his twelve years of trial and endurance.

In Goldsboro, a city of some thirty thousand, he threw himself into local issues, securing funding to build a community daycare center and housing for low-income families and seniors. He had remained active with the NAACP, and in 2005 he was elected president of the North Carolina State Conference, which had a history of frontline activism and outsized personalities. Ella Baker, whose work was key to the successes of the Southern Christian Leadership Conference, had organized branches of the NAACP in North Carolina in the 1940s. Barber remembers his father speaking about Baker's work whenever the topic of political organizing came up. "She was a hero in my family," he said. Robert F. Williams, the president of the Union County branch, was known for his defense of two young boys falsely accused of rape in the infamous 1958 "Kissing Case." The next year, Williams urged blacks to take up arms in self-defense, a suggestion that alarmed not only the chief of police, Jesse Helms, Sr., the father of the future Republican United States senator, but also Roy Wilkins, the organization's staid, pacifist national president, who suspended him for six months. In 1961, facing a false kidnapping charge, he and his wife fled the country for several years, first to Cuba and then to China; the charges were eventually dropped. He became a legendary figure and was widely credited with anticipating Malcolm X's statements about the right to self-defense. "Some choose to only focus on Williams's decision to have armed guards," Barber told me, but that overshadowed his contributions, such as his willingness to defend the poorest African Americans, even those other blacks considered "not high enough on the social ladder."

Barber pushed to return the state conference to its dynamic roots. He steered it into a battle in Wake County, where a school board had gutted guidelines promoting racial diversity in classrooms. The organization set about organizing protests and mobilizing voters. The following year, every member of the board who had tried to resegregate the schools was voted out. Barber also built a coalition of social justice organizations, NAACP chapters, and youth groups from around the state called Historic Thousands on Jones Street, named for the street where the North Carolina General Assembly meets. The idea was to influence legislators' priorities around fourteen key issues, including criminal justice, healthcare, immigrants' rights, and voting rights.

Unlike most of the South, which reliably gives Republican candidates big majorities, North Carolina is a purple state. When Barack Obama managed a slim win there in the 2008 presidential election—becoming the first Democrat to carry the state since Jimmy Carter—conservatives worried that North Carolina could become a beachhead for Democrats and progressives in the region. Two years later, after the Supreme Court's *Citizens United* decision allowed a massive infusion of campaign cash from the retail heir James Arthur Pope—the Raleigh *News & Observer* once called Pope "the Knight of the Right"—Republicans took control of both houses of the legislature for the first time in more than a century. They immediately redrew voting districts, eliminated the earned-income tax credit, introduced a bill that would allow residents to carry firearms in public parks and restaurants, cut funding to prekindergarten education, and engineered a voter ID bill that would have made it disproportionately difficult for African Americans to vote. (In 2016, the Fourth Circuit Court of Appeals struck down the voter ID law, saying that it targeted black voters "with almost surgical precision," and earlier this year it declared the redistricting map unconstitutional.)

In 2012, a Republican, Pat McCrory, was elected governor, displacing Beverly Perdue, a Democrat. The McCrory-era legislature passed restrictions on abortion, loosened environmental regulations, and refused Medicaid expansion under the Affordable Care Act in a state where 20 percent of the residents lacked health insurance. McCrory also signed a law preventing transgender individuals from using the bathroom that conforms to their gender identity. Conservatives in the state exulted in their ability to fulfill their agenda—and to raise the funds to do so—but there was a boomerang effect: they encouraged a diverse group of dissenters to recognize a common cause.

On April 29, 2013, a Monday, Barber led a group of some seventy-five people, including members of the Historic Thousands coalition, to the state legislature to protest what Barber has said was the legislature's attempt to persecute minorities and the disadvantaged. As he once put it, "We said if they were going to crucify the poor, the sick, the children, the unemployed, the immigrants, the LGBT, and the women, and then on top of that crucify voting rights, then every crucifixion, as Billy Kyles"—a Tennessee civil rights leader—"would say, needs a witness." The protesters disrupted the legislature's deliberations and confronted Thom Tillis, the Republican speaker of the House. Police arrested Barber and sixteen others. This was the start of Moral Mondays.

The group returned the following week, and nearly twice as many people were arrested. By the end of the term, fourteen weeks later, more than a thousand protesters had been arrested. The Moral Monday demonstrations continued for four years, with tens of thousands of participants. The protests are largely credited with helping Roy Cooper, a Democrat, narrowly defeat McCrory in the 2016 gubernatorial race.

Barber has a particular disdain for politicians who use racial rhetoric and voter suppression in order to win elections but whose agenda is broadly damaging to poor whites as well as blacks. "They get elected using racial gerrymandering, then enact policies that affect everybody," he said. He sees the current political polarization as a result of a deception that has driven a good deal of American politics since at least the 1968 presidential election, when Richard Nixon exploited the resentment of white Southerners in an attempt to draw them into a Republican coalition. The so-called Southern Strategy was, in many respects, the antithesis of King's campaign. "Poverty has been so racialized," Barber told me, "that most people don't even know that, in raw numbers, the majority of poor people are white."

Marian Wright Edelman, the founder of the Children's Defense Fund, which was an outgrowth of the original Poor People's Campaign, also sees a cyclical history of racial division at play. The country "sold poor white men on their skin and denied them basic opportunities," she said. "Their resentment flares up every half century. And you have to constantly fight it back." Demagogic politicians, economic malaise, and racism, she told me, often lead people to "vote against their own interests." The dueling populism of Senator Bernie Sanders and Donald Trump during the 2016 campaign—inclusiveness versus tribalism—was another replay of this conflict. Sanders told me that he thinks Barber "is doing some of the most important work in the country." More precisely, he and Barber share the same theory of social change: "What he understands is that real change never takes place from the top on down," Sanders said. "It is always from the bottom on up, and that's what he is trying to do and what he understands and what he preaches."

I spoke to Barber by phone one night and asked if the prospect of rekindling a Fusion-style alliance is, at this moment, far-fetched. He responded, as he often does, with a story. He met Jonathan Wilson-Hartgrove, an evangelical minister, twenty years ago. Wilson-Hartgrove had once been a Senate page for Strom Thurmond of South Carolina, who ran for president in 1948 on a platform of segregation despite having fathered a child with a black domestic worker employed in his family's home. But, in 1998, Wilson-Hartgrove heard Barber speak at an event organized by the state's Human Relations Commission in Raleigh and invited him to visit his all-white Southern Baptist church in Stokes County. The area was known as a stronghold of the Ku Klux Klan. Barber visited anyway, and the two men developed a friendship that pushed Wilson-Hartgrove to question the racial assumptions he had grown up with and the ways that they were connected to conservative theology. Eventually, he collaborated with Barber on *The Third Reconstruction*. In the afterword to the book, Wilson-Hartgrove wrote, "I can trust a man who embraces his enemy and then trusts him to tell his story." Later that night, Barber texted me images from recent Poor People's Campaign rallies in Appalachia, with hundreds of people, most of them white, in the audience.

Moral Mondays brought Barber to the attention of both progressives and Democratic Party officials—the model of large-scale protests against legislative assaults on civil rights was followed in Georgia, Alabama, and Missouri—but it was not until the summer of 2016, when he spoke in a prime-time slot at the Democratic National Convention in Philadelphia, that he became a nationally recognizable figure. He touched on now familiar themes: the common ground of the disenfranchised and the attenuated brand of morality that has been marketed by religious conservatives. "I worry," Barber said, "about the way that faith is cynically used by some to serve hate, fear, racism, and greed." His message harked back to the politics of King in 1968 and to a kind of liberation theology: "Pay people what they deserve. Share your food with the hungry. Do this and then your nation shall be called a repairer of the breach." This last phrase was a reference to the Book of Isaiah and an admonition to leaders who abuse their authority and deprive the poor. (The reference was strategic: since 2015, Barber has also led an organization called Repairers of the Breach, which seeks to reclaim the notion of morality for progressive activism.) He concluded with an extended riff on the heartlessness of Republican policies and those who would "harden the heart" of American democracy, and called on the assembled Democrats to be "the moral defibrillators of our time," a phrase that brought them to their feet. "We must shock this nation with the power of love, we must shock this nation with the power of mercy," he said. "We can't give up on the heart of our democracy, not now, not ever!" The speech was so rousing and so well received that a headline on an article by Janell Ross in *The Washington Post* read, "The Rev. William Barber Dropped the Mic."

The activist contingent in the NAACP hoped that Barber would become the organization's national president, but instead, the following year, he stepped down from the North Carolina conference (he is still on the national board of directors). There doesn't seem to have been a great deal of acrimony surrounding the departure, although Barber's independent streak and his growing national profile—he had not consulted with the organization before he spoke in Philadelphia—had apparently provoked some discord in the upper ranks. Jotaka Eaddy, who served as a senior adviser to several presidents of the NAACP, including Ben Jealous, told me that Barber's departure was "in alignment with his worldview." He left, she said, "to create space for someone else to lead, and he focused on where he was being naturally pulled." Barber told me, "I left after twelve years—that's four years longer than the president of the United States serves." He turned to his work with Repairers of the Breach and to the idea of rebuilding King's coalition.

Barber had already begun talking with Liz Theoharis about creating a national platform to address the intersecting effects of poverty. They then started a Moral Revival tour, which eventually led to a series of discussions including people such as Roz Pelles, the executive director of Repairers of the Breach; Traci Blackmon, the executive minister of justice for the United Church of Christ and a pastor of a church in Florissant, Missouri; Alan McSurely, an attorney and organizer now based in North Carolina who had worked with the original Poor People's Campaign; and the civil rights historian Timothy Tyson, who wrote a biography of Robert F. Williams. McSurely, who is eighty-one, had advised Barber on the Moral Monday movement and serves on the steering committee for the new project. This working group set the agenda, and Barber and Theoharis began traveling across the country, speaking and leading workshops on organizing and civil disobedience training. Barber has created a structure that allows him to oversee Greenleaf and the Repairers of the Breach despite his constant travels. He begins each day on conference calls with the officers of the Repairers and then with the leadership of the church. "I don't believe a pastor should be doing everything," he told me. "I believe in power-sharing."

Barber won't discuss the particulars of any of the actions planned for the campaign, since a number of them will involve civil disobedience. But he told me, "I can say we intend to nonviolently confront our government and its policies and we will refuse to give up our constitutional right to protest." The campaign has attracted the support of organizations such as the Service Employees International Union (SEIU), the Fight for $15, and the United Food and Commercial Workers International Union (UFCW), but Barber considers the grassroots network the crucial part of what the group has accomplished. "Our movement is a national call for moral revival," he told me. "Sometimes people will only think of something as national because you have the presence of national organizations. Our focus has been to go to the people first, in the states, on the ground, and build a network of coordinating committees." The campaign approached the larger community organizations only after it had support from local people affected by issues of poverty.

After King's death, the 1968 Poor People's Campaign foundered, dogged by federal surveillance and the infiltration efforts of J. Edgar Hoover. It also strained under the logistical demands of transporting to the nation's capital thousands of people who, by definition, lacked resources to meet their needs. The assassination of Robert F. Kennedy on June 5 deprived the campaign of one of its most important allies. The number of people in Resurrection City dwindled from three thousand to about five hundred. On June 24, the police forcibly removed the last occupiers, and later that day, the mayor, fearing a repeat of the unrest in the capital that followed King's death, called in the National Guard (thirty-six years earlier, the Army had been called in to evict the Bonus Marchers). The Poor People's Campaign was over before it had achieved any of its objectives. The movement's most ambitious undertaking became its most conspicuous failure.

The Moral Monday movement captured the imagination of activists across the country and achieved tangible results in North Carolina, but it remains to be seen whether its tactics can succeed nationwide. Marian Wright Edelman is sanguine about the prospects of the new initiative. Barber, whom she described as "brilliant," is in a position to help finish the work that was begun fifty years ago, she told me. When I asked Barber how he hoped to translate protest into progress, he said, "The civil disobedience is just one part of the plan." A second phase of the campaign will focus on voter registration, building a broader network, and creating a detailed list of policy demands, which will be released late in the summer. "We surely want to influence the 2018 midterm elections and the 2020 presidential election," Theoharis told me. But they do not plan to endorse candidates or cast their lot with either of the major political parties. They want to change the political conversation around poverty, to create a climate in which it is impossible for any candidate or party to continue ignoring the subject. In this they have as much in common with the Occupy movement as with the original Poor People's Campaign. Barber and Theoharis seem to see history as a guide, not a script.

Three weeks after the commemoration in Memphis, Barber spoke at the Performing Arts Centre in Montgomery, Alabama, for the opening of the National Memorial for Peace and Justice, a monument to the more than 4,400 African Americans who were lynched between the end of Reconstruction and the beginning of the modern civil rights movement. At the site, a project of the Equal Justice Initiative led by Bryan Stevenson, hundreds of metal markers list the locations of lynchings and the names of the people who died there. The impact is traumatic, and not simply in a historical sense. Barber told me, "We should be traumatized by the idea that something like this can be seen as normal, and think about the wrongs we've become accustomed to today."

He had spent the previous two days discussing the Poor People's Campaign with Apache activists in Arizona and with representatives of the UFCW in Las Vegas. But, despite the long journey, in Montgomery he delivered the best speech I have heard him give, before an audience of about a thousand. It was a sprawling oration, citing the historian Nell Painter, the Constitution, the crusading journalist Ida B. Wells-Barnett, the lyrics to "Strange Fruit," and the speech that King delivered in Montgomery at the end of the march from Selma in 1965. That speech, which Barber encouraged the audience to listen to in its entirety, contains King's recitation of the history of populism and the ways that racism disadvantaged both black and white poor people—the points that Barber has been reiterating across the country. (Segregation, King said, was "a simple thing to keep the poor white masses working for near-starvation wages in the years that followed the Civil War.")

Barber touched on his usual themes of inequality and the mistaken priorities of the Church, but the audience erupted in applause when he turned to the monument itself, declaring that "Jesus was lynched—an innocent victim of mob hysteria." He again charged his listeners with avoiding the hypocrisy of commemorating the victims of the past while failing to build a movement to address the present. We must pay homage, he said, "to all those who continued to fight, even after they saw the bodies swinging from trees. But there are all kinds of things swinging in the air today"—hunger, police violence, hundreds of thousands of deaths each year linked to poverty-related causes. He was interrupted six times by standing ovations, and the crowd was on its feet and applauding long after he'd stopped speaking.

As he walked off the stage, I detected, just for a moment, a rare note of fatigue. Reverend Barber is, it occurred to me, relentless, not tireless; determined, not indefatigable. He is driven by a fugitive hope that an ancestral breach might finally be cemented. Backstage, organizers praised him for the speech, but he didn't linger. He had a nine-hour drive ahead of him, to North Carolina, where he would tend to his church and, after a brief respite, head out on the road again.

FROM CHARLESTON TO PITTSBURGH, AN ARC OF PREMEDITATED AMERICAN TRAGEDY

November 1, 2018

On the afternoon that the first of the funerals for the eleven people killed at the Tree of Life synagogue, in the Squirrel Hill neighborhood of Pittsburgh, were held, a crowd began to spill over the street and onto the sidewalks and lawns along a stately stretch of Beechwood Boulevard. There is not a word in the American lexicon for such gatherings—the semi-spontaneous assembly of people in the wake of tragedy who are united by both grief and anger and whose public mourning serves to reaffirm their civic bond to one another. But we need such a word, because this ritual happens frequently enough to be familiar—so frequently that its purpose need not be explained to those in attendance. "Are people here to protest against Donald Trump?" I asked a man in the crowd. "They're here because of *everything*," he answered.

"Everything," in this instance, meant the entire sequence of events that had preceded the shooting deaths of Rose Mallinger, Melvin Wax, Joyce Fienberg, Bernice and Sylvan Simon, Daniel Stein, Irving Younger, Cecil and David Rosenthal, Jerry Rabinowitz, and Richard Gottfried; the factors that had enabled them; and the subsequent ways in which the murders have been woven into the larger rubric of premeditated American tragedy. Tree of Life now enters a glossary of such events; among them, the Emanuel AME Church in Charleston, South Carolina, the site of another mass shooting, on June 17, 2015, in another house of worship, committed by another white nationalist, became the closest case study.

Jamie Gibson, the senior rabbi at Temple Sinai, which is not far from the Tree of Life synagogue, had helped to organize a vigil three years ago for those who died in Charleston. The attack in Pittsburgh on Saturday brought recollections of that vigil back into focus. "I think that the people who devise these plans and get hold of these murderous weapons have created an entire world in their mind where it makes sense," he told me. "They have an enemy. The enemy is an African American, the enemy is a Jew. And they can only feel safe if they protect themselves." Malcolm Graham, whose sister Cynthia Graham Hurd was killed at Emanuel, told me that hearing about Pittsburgh "was like a punch in the gut." The news had pulled him back to the moment when he learned of his sister's death. J. A. Moore, whose sister Myra Thompson was also killed at Emanuel, told me, "My first thought was how this was going to affect all the family members in that community. It immediately flashed me back to June of 2015."

In Charleston, a member of Emanuel had told me that the process of healing was made doubly difficult by the fact that the attack had claimed the lives of people who would otherwise have steered the church through difficult times, including its pastor, Clementa Pinckney, who also served as a state senator. Those who died at Tree of Life were said to be among its most faithful attendees, part of the nucleus of a larger congregation. The attacks also share an inscrutable dissonance of heavily armed men firing rounds at utterly defenseless targets: the oldest victim in the synagogue was the ninety-seven-year-old Rose Mallinger; the oldest in the church was the eighty-seven-year-old Susie Jackson.

The architects of these atrocities are white men whose fury was amplified in the echo chamber of the internet. Notably, both shooters conceived of their actions as a form of self-defense. Robert Bowers, the man accused of the Pittsburgh shootings, reportedly wrote in his last post on Gab, a social media network favored by the alt-right, that he would not stand by while his people were "slaughtered." In Charleston, just before Tywanza Sanders, a twenty-six-year-old member of Emanuel AME, died, he asked the gunman, Dylann Roof, why he was committing murder. Roof replied, "You are raping our women and taking over the country." Roof's language was striking because, just a day earlier, in a gaudy, absurdist spectacle in Manhattan, Trump had declared his presidential candidacy, citing a scourge of Mexican "rapists" as part of his motivation.

Albeit in vastly different ways, Trump and Roof were responding to a common zeitgeist of racial paranoia. Bowers had reportedly expressed disdain for Trump in social media posts, fueled by his belief that the president viewed Jews too favorably. But Bowers shared Trump's terminology for the caravan of Central American migrants winding its way north through Mexico: the migrants are, in the estimation of both men, "invaders." Trump has both promoted and profited from the racial siege mentality. The other significant overlap between what transpired in Charleston and the morass of horror in Pittsburgh lies less in what the murderers did than in the responses of the wider culture that surrounded them.

It was necessary, and therefore predictable, that Roof would be understood as a singularly troubled youth rather than as a vector of a broader ill or as a reflection of a set of mores deeply rooted in American history. He posed for photographs holding the Confederate flag, yet people I spoke with in the Confederate Museum in Charleston rejected the idea that his actions could be seen as a logical extension of valorizing an army that had fought primarily for the preservation of white supremacy. In Pittsburgh on Tuesday evening, a tall white man in his fifties, with long hair and a tan windbreaker, jabbed his finger at a young protester and rebuked him for suggesting that Bowers may have felt validated by Trump's anti-immigrant rhetoric. The president was "*not responsible* for this!" the man shouted. "You're *politicizing* this tragedy!" He was the embodiment of a minority opinion on that street at that moment, but, beyond the liberal preserves of Pittsburgh, in the broader precincts of America, he was not alone in this thinking. "The president is not responsible for these acts," said Sarah Huckabee Sanders, the White House press secretary, two days after the shootings.

This is part of a broader paradox in which Trump's heroism—to that portion of the public that deems him a hero—derives from his projection of a particular version of masculine authority. The country had fallen far from its pinnacle, he told the delegates at the Republican National Convention in 2016. "I alone can fix it," he said. The election thereby became an exercise in a kind of circular logic: Trump is powerful, so he should be given more power. Yet he is simultaneously exonerated from responsibility for the myriad failures that have occurred on his watch by the idea that he is powerless to affect such matters.

The biggest indictment of the moral calibration in Trump's presidency is found in the sheer frequency by which he is absolved by his most ardent supporters. The man who sent explosive devices to men and women Trump had named as enemies of the nation, or had scorned as rogues skirting the consequences of their actions, was not someone prompted by the president's words but, rather, a lone lunatic. The shooter who reportedly preyed upon a mostly elderly group of worshippers, in part because the synagogue housed a congregation that supported work on behalf of refugees, was not responding to a corrupted dialogue about immigration but was simply drunk on the ancient bias of anti-Semitism. Yet the arithmetic is inescapable—all the singulars become a plural, and that plural is the collective face of a volatile white nationalist movement whose ascent corresponds closely to Trump's, who took comfort in his equivocating over the moral lines in Charlottesville, and who understood his declaration "I am a nationalist" last month as evidence that he had forgone his dog-whistle appeals to them in favor of sounding a bullhorn.

As I spoke with people in Pittsburgh, "shock" was the word I heard most often. Barbara Burstin, a member of the history faculty at both Carnegie Mellon and the University of Pittsburgh who studies the history of Jews in that city, told me she was shocked to learn of such an attack occurring not just in Pittsburgh but in Squirrel Hill, as idyllic a multiethnic setting as a big city could aspire to achieve. Sonja Wimer, who teaches at the Hillel Academy of Pittsburgh and was attending a bar mitzvah service at a nearby synagogue when the attack occurred, expressed her "shock" at the killings, as did Nate Itskowitz, the boy whose bar mitzvah it was. (The synagogue where the ceremony took place was in lockdown mode, with information parceled out from people in the building who were not prohibited from using their smartphones on the Sabbath. Nate's parents, Robert and Shelly, told me how proud they were that their son, unflustered despite the cacophony of sirens blaring in the streets outside, completed the service perfectly.)

By contrast, people in Charleston spoke to me this week mostly of a numbness—more specifically, of a fear of becoming numb to the kind of tragedy that they have endured, and which is now being visited upon others. The difference in perspectives—what people feel in the immediate aftermath and what they fear three years on— is not only a commentary on how humans metabolize trauma but also a measure of how much hurt has transpired in the interim.

When Barack Obama arrived in Charleston in June 2015, he was visibly wearied by another rite of mourning needlessly dead Americans, and perhaps pondering how his own identity as the first black president of the United States had factored into the hatred ricocheting through Dylann Roof's psyche. But he came as a voice of reconciliation. He eulogized Pinckney, who had been slain in his own sanctuary, and he sang a hymn in the old tradition. On Tuesday, Trump arrived in Pittsburgh to a headwind of his own making, derived from his own words and from the symphony of fearmongering and divisiveness that he has conducted from the Oval Office. What this meant in more practical terms was that, three days after the attacks, a few thousand people were marching and carrying signs that read "Pittsburgh Builds Bridges Not Walls" and "President Hate Leave Our State." The crowd that assembled on Beechwood Boulevard had turned onto Forbes Avenue, the thoroughfare that connects Squirrel Hill to the campuses of Carnegie Mellon University and the University of Pittsburgh, about a mile to the west. Then they marched along Shady Avenue to Wilkins Avenue, where the Tree of Life is located. A banner at the front of the procession read: "President Trump, You Are Not Welcome in Pittsburgh Until You Fully Renounce White Nationalism."

Rabbi Jeffrey Myers welcomed Trump to Tree of Life—given his position, it would have been difficult for him to do anything else—but that sentiment was not prevalent. "As president, it would be inappropriate for him not to come, but, given his role in spreading hate against refugees and the other, I'm not comfortable with it," Mark Hetfield, the president of the Hebrew Immigrant Aid Society, told me. Hetfield said that HIAS, which had reportedly been the subject of angry posts written by Bowers, had not yet received a word of condolence or sympathy from any official in the State Department, despite the fact that the organization's refugee resettlement work operates in partnership with it. Students I talked to at the University of Pittsburgh thought of Trump's visit as a kind of trolling.

You're politicizing this. Arguably, every aspect of what happened last Saturday was political, from the reason that Gab exists to the fact that Bowers was able to purchase an assault rifle and three handguns legally, to the fact that he was able to download extreme rhetoric that amped his paranoia by a magnitude, to the fact that he reportedly targeted a congregation that was guilty only of subscribing to an idea—*welcome the stranger*—that is allegedly part of the national writ. The preface to this mass homicide was never *not* political; its aftermath could not help but be the same.

At the same time, the local context of what happened on Saturday matters.

Barbara Burstin, who has lived in Squirrel Hill for more than forty years, told me that the community had represented a benchmark of social progress for Jews, particularly those of the generation who immigrated to the United States in the late nineteenth century. "You had the German Jews, who came earlier," she told me. "Then, beginning in the 1870s, you had the Eastern European Jews. The poorer Eastern European Jews lived on what was called the hill." As the community grew and successive generations rose economically, the neighborhood became home to Reform, Orthodox, Reconstructionist, and Conservative synagogues, all nestled in an enclave that is walking distance from the university centers of Pittsburgh. Tree of Life occupied a central niche in the cultural and religious life of the community—there are thirty-three references to it in the second volume of *Steel City Jews,* Burstin's history of Jewish Pittsburgh. The area was not immune to bias, though: in the 1940s, an America First rally drew 2,800 people to the Soldiers and Sailors Memorial Hall on Fifth Avenue near Carnegie Mellon. "Jews have been very much involved in the fabric of Pittsburgh," Burstin told me. "It's not to say that there hasn't been subtle discrimination in the past."

On Monday, Burstin drove me the short distance from her home to Tree of Life. En route, she pointed out the Middle Eastern, Indian, Greek, Italian, and Asian restaurants along Forbes Avenue that reflect the diverse community. In just the past five years, the Jewish Family and Community Services organization, which works on refugee resettlement in conjunction with HIAS, has helped eight hundred refugees—among them Nepalis, Iraqis, Burmese, Somalis, Syrians, and Congolese—move into the area. (The numbers are dropping, Mark Hetfield told me, because the Trump administration has aggressively lowered the number of refugees allowed into the country.) As we got closer to the synagogue, we saw people carrying flowers to lay at the memorial. About fifty people stood near the entrance, some of them crying, others singing and praying in the autumn chill. A black man in his sixties named Ernest Bey was wearing a jacket emblazoned with "MAD DADS," the name of a national grassroots organization seeking to end urban violence. "Me and my brother served with MAD DADS, as these two brothers"—Cecil and David Rosenthal—"served this congregation," Bey told me. "It just impacted me that I gotta get out and lay some flowers at their site."

The next day, I visited a class that Burstin is teaching this semester at Carnegie Mellon called "The American Jewish Experience." Over the weekend, the course had seemingly changed from history to current events. Burstin showed me a journal entry in which she asked, "What do I say to students who have just spent weeks learning about the frightening levels of anti-Semitism in the United States in the 1930s, who have been immersed in the horrendous history of the Holocaust? And what will they say to me?" Earlier in the semester, the class had read about Madison Grant and the nativist strain of anti-Semitism that he promoted in the early twentieth century. "It seems like there are people who believe the exact same things Grant thought a century ago," Duncan Covell, a junior, told me.

That collision between past and present reminded me of the historian Timothy Snyder's argument that fascism has a tendency to exist outside history. It is never entirely interred in the past; it's an ailment that may go into remission but never entirely disappears. We are currently witnessing in some corners of American life the reemergence of a fascistic political culture that has allied itself with the president of the United States. But Trump is a man who leaves no fingerprints. No forensic accounting of his culpability is sufficient; he benefits from a sort of implausible deniability. He courts the favor of anti-Semitic nationalists but points to his Jewish family members and his support of Israel as evidence of his equanimity. He traffics in the worst misogynistic ideas but boasts of the number of women he hired in his businesses. He lied about the birthplace of the first black president and discriminated against African Americans in apartment buildings that his family owned, but he once dated a biracial model and has sought the company of black celebrities throughout his public life. These contradictions were apparent on Tuesday when he visited Tree of Life with his Jewish son-in-law and daughter while a largely Jewish crowd protested his presence, some holding signs that accused him of harboring neo-Nazi sympathies. These matters appear to be complicated, but they're merely conveniently contradictory. Yet contradictions are not the same as absolution. Trump is not, as the students suspected, trolling Pittsburgh; he is trolling American democracy.

Sixty years ago, the KKK bombed the Hebrew Benevolent Congregation Temple of Atlanta. No one was killed, but the damage was estimated at more than $100,000. The attack was meant to serve as both a warning and a punishment for the synagogue's support of civil rights. Six decades have not dimmed the utility of that brand of contempt, its efficacy as a weapon against the American creed. Burstin mentioned George Santayana's dictum that those who cannot remember the past are doomed to repeat it. But the events in Pittsburgh, and those three years earlier in Charleston, suggest that the problem is not that certain people among us cannot remember history. The terror has emerged precisely because they do.

THE NEW ZEALAND SHOOTING AND THE GREAT-MAN THEORY OF MISERY

March 20, 2019

The macabre harvest of innocents, this time claiming fifty lives in two mosques in Christchurch, New Zealand, is a double-edged form of madness. It is both the product of an absence of human empathy and a drain on the reserves of those who possess it: decency these days requires the ability to stare barbarism in the face, repeatedly, randomly, intensely, without ever becoming inured to the ugliness of its features. Terrorism hopes to inspire fear and confusion, but its most pernicious impact begins the moment that people no longer feel either of those things but, rather, simply a grudging acknowledgment that this is the way we now live.

We have seen so many of these atrocities that they can be put into subcategories. The attack in Christchurch exists in the company of other attacks on houses of worship: the Sikh temple in Oak Creek, Wisconsin, in 2012; the Emanuel African Methodist Episcopal Church in Charleston in 2015; the Islamic Cultural Center in Quebec City in 2017; the Tree of Life synagogue in Pittsburgh in 2018. Live like this for long enough and you end up with a sample size sufficient to discern patterns among the antagonists: the circular reasoning of their rationales and the shared sense of themselves as vectors of great change.

In 1840, Thomas Carlyle declared that the course of history was set by humanity's great men, and for a great while that view of the past held sway. But as the nineteenth and twentieth centuries progressed, the influence of Marxism and other strands of social history inverted that narrative: it was the mass of people and their collective interests, not the whims of a small number of extraordinary individuals, which drove history. Still, recent years have seen something of a resurgence of the belief in the supreme role of "great men"—of heroes—and it seems to have taken a particular, perverse hold among zealots, notably those of the white nationalist persuasion.

Most of the men who committed these recent acts of terror composed manifestos, like self-decreed heroes setting down their own origin stories. A sense of history turning on the fulcrum of a single man's actions is a theme within them. The authors also rely on the distortion of facts to support their homicidal crusades. Brenton Tarrant, the twenty-eight-year-old Australian who is accused of the killings in Christchurch, reportedly traveled to New Zealand to attack an immigrant population he described as "invaders." He cited as inspirations Dylann Roof, the then twenty-one-year-old South Carolinian who killed nine African Americans in the basement of Emanuel AME Church, and Anders Breivik, who in 2011 murdered seventy-seven people in Norway, many of them members of the governing Labour Party's youth wing, because he thought that they were encouraging a "Muslim invasion." Tarrant wrote that he hoped his actions would incite violence and retaliation in a cycle of conflict that would stoke division between white Europeans and immigrants.

On a blog titled "The Last Rhodesian," Roof lamented that there were not enough proactively violent white people in the world. He raged at the thought of imperiled whites in suburbs, hiding from the growing black populace of the cities. He wrote that he chose to attack Charleston because the city "at one time had the highest ratio of blacks to whites in the country." Robert Bowers, who is accused of murdering eleven people in the Tree of Life synagogue last October (he has pleaded not guilty), posted a message on the social media network Gab, saying, "I can't sit by and watch my people get slaughtered." He, too, rued the unwillingness of white people to act. He purportedly attacked the synagogue as a means of intimidating Jewish charities involved in refugee resettlement efforts and he indulged the widely disseminated but utterly false claim that white Americans are being murdered wholesale by immigrants.

Tarrant fulminated about hordes at the gate from Australia, where white settlers first established a colony in 1788 and, over the next century, proceeded to murder, kidnap, and subjugate the Aboriginal population. He apparently felt compelled to go to New Zealand in order to protect whites there from the actual fate that had befallen the Maori when white Europeans arrived in the mid-nineteenth century. Roof fretted about being outnumbered by the descendants of people who had been brought to the United States against their will. The ratio of blacks to whites in Charleston was the product not of black invasion but of the colonial greed of white slave traders.

This skewed sense of history is not unrelated to a fixation with reproduction. Like earlier versions of white nationalism, the current strain is obsessed with fertility and birth rates—and the so-called replacement theory—a tendency that, as *The New York Times* reported, provides a segue to the anti-feminism that is prominent in far-right circles. There are no plans afoot to "replace" white people—an undertaking as absurd as it is impossible—but that fact has not interfered with the hysteria raging in white nationalist circles. Tarrant began his screed with the words "It's the birthrates. It's the birthrates. It's the birthrates." Roof suggested that white women who have children with black men are "victims." As Adam Serwer has written, such concerns about population have often reinforced other forms of prejudice. The assorted racists who gathered in Charlottesville in 2017, for instance, wed their demographic anxieties to anti-Semitism, chanting, "Jews will not replace us," even though Jews represent only a small percentage of the U.S. population and, of course, many of their forebears came here specifically to escape persecution and murder at the hands of white Europeans.

The demographic paranoia is simply another form of projection that is starkly at odds with actual history. Indeed, it's not as much paranoia as a fear of a specific kind of historical karma—one that sees in immigration a mechanism by which what has been sown now will be reaped. Aboriginals constitute just 3 percent of Australia's population. The Maori are just 15 percent of the population of New Zealand. (The Charlottesville marchers might have taken a moment to consider the American equivalents: native Hawaiians account for just 6 percent of Hawaii's population; Native Americans represent just 2 percent of the United States'.)

The supposed defense of white people in New Zealand—or in Pittsburgh or in Charleston—highlights another presumption of the white nationalists: the right of whites to exist in safety anywhere in the world and the simultaneous belief that no non-white group should have that same right. The nationalist convulsions in France, Germany, and elsewhere embrace the same contradiction, and a steadfast refusal to recognize that Europe's current diversity is, in some measure, a product of its centuries of colonial rule around the globe.

The significance of what happened in Christchurch cannot be understood outside the context of a growing transnational movement of epidermal fanaticism. It is the kind of fury that was foreshadowed two years ago when a man who made racist statements and was lauded by white nationalists was elected president of the United States. It is the validation of the alarms that sounded for those who looked at Charlottesville, where esprit de corps grew among zealots led by charlatans, and recognized that they would be further emboldened. It is difficult to overestimate the threat that this poses. The individual does not drive history, but the actions of individuals have consequences for the rest of us—sometimes devastating ones. Rather than share the world, the extremists would content themselves with the lion's share of its ashes.

HOW THE TRAIL OF AMERICAN WHITE SUPREMACY LED TO EL PASO

August 6, 2019

A century ago this week, the city of Chicago, its air tinged with smoke, was conducting a body count. It had just endured eight days of arson and violence, which had claimed the lives of thirty-eight people—fifteen of them white, twenty-three of them black—including John Simpson, the sole police officer killed during the unrest. More than five hundred people were injured. Ostensibly, the violence began when Eugene Williams, a seventeen-year-old African American, went swimming and rafting with his friends on Lake Michigan and drifted toward a part of the beach used only by whites. A white man named George Stauber began hurling stones at Williams, who eventually slipped beneath the water and drowned. Racial skirmishes broke out along the beach and spread across the city, lighting kindling that had been laid throughout the previous year. Thousands of black soldiers returning from the First World War competed against white workers for employment and housing. The veterans brought with them a renewed intolerance for discrimination, an attitude summarized in an editorial by W. E. B. Du Bois in the magazine *The Crisis*. "By the God of Heaven," Du Bois wrote, "we are cowards and jackasses if now that the war is over, we do not marshal every ounce of our brain and brawn to fight a sterner, longer, more unbending battle against the forces of hell in our own land." Other African Americans, migrants from the South newly arrived as part of what became known as the Great Migration, were viewed as interlopers whose willingness to work for low pay undercut the wages of white men. As the poet Eve Ewing notes in her searing collection *1919*, white Chicagoans attributed the violence to a "Negro invasion" of previously white enclaves. The world had been made safe for democracy; Chicago had not.

This past Saturday, the Chicago Race Riot of 1919 Commemoration Project held events across the city, including a bike tour and panel discussions, to memorialize the dead and to detail the legacy of that week of chaos and terror. The same day, fifteen hundred miles to the south, in El Paso, Texas, there was a different commemoration taking place, one more akin to a dramatic reenactment than a somber reflection—the past climbing out from its shallow grave to place its claim on the present. Twenty-two people died at the hands of a man armed with a semiautomatic rifle and a list of grievances yellowed by a century of repetition. A manifesto believed to be written by the shooter cites the "Hispanic invasion of Texas"—a contortion of history if ever there was one—as a motive for the murders. Another section of that document offers a disclaimer meant to indemnify Donald Trump. "My ideology has not changed for several years," it states. "My opinions on automation, immigration, and the rest predate Trump and his campaign for president." This is notable, in the sense that unsolicited denials often sound like direct admissions. In the past month, Trump has urged four sitting members of Congress—Ilhan Omar, Ayanna Pressley, Alexandria Ocasio-Cortez, and Rashida Tlaib—all women of color, to "go back" to where they came from, and he attacked a fifth representative, Elijah Cummings, an African American, by claiming that his district is "disgusting," rat-infested, and beneath human habitability. Trump followed that with a tweet appearing to jeer when Cummings reported that his home had been burglarized. The language of the alleged El Paso shooter's screed bears resemblance to Trump's rhetoric, particularly in the martial description of undocumented people as an "invasion." If the immediate conversation in the aftermath of El Paso—and the massacre of nine people thirteen hours later in Dayton, Ohio—has tended toward the accessibility of weapons of war in civilian life, the word "invasion" becomes even more telling. We are not, the killers seem to be telling us, living in peacetime. An AK-47 is a tool created to address enemy invasions.

In remarks delivered at the White House on Monday, Trump explicitly denounced white supremacy—just as he eventually did after first praising the "very fine people" at the "Unite the Right" rally in Charlottesville two years ago, before reverting to form a few months later by referring to Haiti and African countries as "shitholes." Similarly, after criticizing the people who'd chanted "Send her back!" at Ilhan Omar at a rally three weeks ago, he again quickly returned to form launching more racist tweets a week later. Trump's mindless belligerence, his perilous and ignorant worldview, and, particularly, his use of inflammatory racist rhetoric are rightly seen as alarming. The presidency is the most esteemed and powerful platform in the country, and it is reasonable to see a relationship between the president's imprimatur and the ballistic bedlam that regularly erupts and targets people and groups for whom he has expressed contempt. Cesar Sayoc, who on Monday was sentenced to twenty years in prison for sending sixteen homemade pipe bombs to people he deemed enemies of the president, argued that his perspective was skewed by mental illness—and also by his obsessive admiration of Trump. This, for the record, is why people in public life are supposed to be mindful of their rhetoric. Their words reach a wide swath of the public, which has varying abilities to interpret their meaning and their nuance or to parse what is said in earnest from what is meant facetiously. Trump is particularly troublesome in this regard, as his most incendiary words are frequently explained away as humor lost on his uptight critics.

The more difficult possibility is that the alleged shooter's manifesto is truthful, and that there is no causal or suggestive link between Trump's words and his actions. The Chicago Race Riot of

1919 exists within a constellation of violence known as the Red Summer. Two dozen riots erupted in the summer and fall of that year, overwhelmingly targeting black people, particularly those who had migrated to urban areas in the North and Midwest. In that pre-internet age, there was no need for central coordination. In Elaine, Arkansas; Washington, D.C.; Omaha, Nebraska; Charleston, South Carolina; Wilmington, Delaware; Chicago, and elsewhere, mobs of whites, confronted with the possibility of black people gaining a share of the housing, employment, and democracy that they enjoyed, independently reached the same conclusion about the proper recourse. As the historian Linda Gordon points out in her book *The Second Coming of the KKK,* the Klan, which had become moribund at the end of the nineteenth century, was resurrected during that time, adopting a broader set of hatreds, adding Jews and immigrants to its enemies list. Racial charlatans such as the lawyer and eugenicist Madison Grant, who wrote *The Passing of the Great Race,* and the journalist Lothrop Stoddard, the author of *The Rising Tide of Color Against White World-Supremacy,* whipped up public fears that the white population was being subsumed in a tide of inferior bloodlines. Exclusionary, racist immigration laws were passed. And black people in cities were pursued and attacked, leaving an estimated 250 fatalities. Invasions, after all, are to be met with overwhelming force.

Trump declared his presidential campaign on June 16, 2015, citing the presence of Mexican "rapists" as part of his rationale. A day later, Dylann Roof killed nine black people in the basement of a church in Charleston, citing the threat of black rapists as his rationale. The former did not cause the latter—Roof, in fact, had been planning the attack for months. But Trump and Roof were responding to the same racial zeitgeist, one in which the elevation of a black president meant that the value of whiteness had been correspondingly diminished. History, we're told, repeats itself. But this phrasing has always troubled me, as if we are beholden to an inanimate application designed to produce similar situations again and again. A more precise assessment is that people respond in familiar ways to the same dynamics across time. There is no law mandating that our futures bear some familial resemblance to the worst of our present. Humans may learn from history. But we'll invariably find ourselves locked in conflict with dangerous men intoxicated with their own sense of mission, and drunkenly believing that the only problem with the past is that we ever departed from it at all.

STACEY ABRAMS'S FIGHT FOR A FAIR VOTE

August 19, 2019

Among the many issues currently polarizing American politics—abortion, climate change, healthcare, immigration, gun control—one of the most consequential tends to be one of the least discussed. The American electorate, across the country, is diversifying ethnically and racially at a rapid rate. Progressives, interpreting the shift to mean that, following traditional paths, the new voters will lean Democratic, see a political landscape that is turning blue. Conservatives apparently see the same thing, because in recent years many of them have supported policies, such as voter ID laws and voter roll purges, that have disproportionately affected people of color.

The issue has become more pressing with the approach of the 2020 presidential election. In June, the Supreme Court ruled that federal judges do not have the power to address partisan gerrymandering, even when it creates results that "reasonably seem unjust." Last month, President Donald Trump was finally forced to abandon his effort to add, in defiance of another Supreme Court ruling, a citizenship question to the census—an idea that Thomas B. Hofeller, the late Republican strategist who promoted it, believed would aid the GOP in further redistricting. But, days later, the president was telling four American women of color, all elected members of the House of Representatives, to "go back" to where they came from.

The nation got a preview of the battle for the future of electoral politics last year in Georgia's gubernatorial race. The Republican candidate was declared the winner by a margin of less than 2 percentage points: 55,000 votes out of nearly 4 million cast—a record-breaking total for a midterm election in the state. Many Georgians, though, still use the terms "won" and "lost" advisedly, not only because the Democrat never technically conceded but also because of the highly irregular nature of the contest. The Republican, Brian Kemp, was Georgia's secretary of state, and in that role he presided over an election marred by charges of voter suppression; the Democrat, Stacey Abrams, has become the nation's most prominent critic of that practice.

Although she has only recently come to wide attention, Abrams, a forty-five-year-old tax attorney, romance novelist, and former state representative, has been working on electoral reform—particularly on voter registration—in Georgia for some fifteen years. In that regard, some Georgians view her campaign as a success; she won more votes than any Democrat has ever won for statewide office. Georgia is representative of the nation's demographic changes. The population is 10.5 million, and, according to *The Atlanta Journal-Constitution*, it was 57.5 percent white in 2008, fell to 54.2 percent white in 2018, and will be 53.6 percent white next year. It will be majority-minority by 2033. Democratic leaders from red states in the South and beyond with shifting populations—they include the presidential candidates Mayor Pete Buttigieg of South Bend, Indiana; former representative Beto O'Rourke of El Paso, Texas; and the former agriculture secretary Mike Espy, who is considering a second run for the U.S. Senate in Mississippi—have examined Abrams's campaign to see how they might adopt its strategies. Espy described his discussion with her as "a graduate course in politics."

Abrams has yet to decide if she will run for office again. For now, she is focused on addressing the irregularities that her campaign identified. Within days of the election, she formed an organization called Fair Fight Action, which, with Care in Action, a domestic worker advocacy group, filed a federal lawsuit alleging that Kemp had impaired citizens' ability to vote and thereby deprived them of rights guaranteed under the First, Fourteenth, and Fifteenth Amendments. (Abrams is the group's chair; her former campaign director, Lauren Groh-Wargo, is the CEO.) The suit seeks changes to the entire structure of Georgia's electoral system, from the number of polling stations and the kind of voting machines used to policies on registration. In May, a federal judge for the Northern District of Georgia ruled that the case may proceed.

The clash between Kemp and Abrams drew national attention again in May as a result of another issue shaping the 2020 race. Kemp campaigned as an anti-abortion stalwart, and for his first major piece of legislation he signed House Bill 481. A so-called heartbeat bill, H.B. 481 prohibits abortion once "embryonic or fetal cardiac activity" can be detected, which can happen as early as six weeks after conception, before a woman may even know that she is pregnant. Opponents, Abrams among them, call it the "forced-pregnancy bill." It is scheduled to go into effect in January. Six other states have passed similarly restrictive bills this year. Many opponents say that the laws were designed to push legal challenges to them to the Supreme Court, which, with the appointments of Neil Gorsuch and Brett Kavanaugh, many conservatives believe would now be willing to, in effect, reverse *Roe v. Wade*.

A week after the signing, Abrams warned, in a minute-long video on Twitter, that "right now, across the South, and around the country, a woman's right to control her body, and a doctor's ability to give the healthcare we deserve, is under attack." Senators Kirsten Gillibrand, Elizabeth Warren, Amy Klobuchar, and Kamala Harris— all of whom are running for president—also appeared in the video, urging viewers to support organizations working to protect access to safe, legal abortion.

Pro-choice activists called for an economic boycott of Georgia, like the one directed at North Carolina in 2016 after it passed a law prohibiting transgender people from using the public bathroom corresponding to their gender identity. (That law was partly repealed in 2017.) A number of television and movie production companies have shot on location in Georgia in recent years. But Abrams, who describes herself as a "pragmatic progressive," discouraged any boycott by those companies, out of concern for workers who would suffer as a result. "I think the superior opportunity for Georgia," she told the *Los Angeles Times,* is to "use the entertainment industry's energy to support and fund the work that we need to do on the ground, because Georgia is on the cusp of being able to transform our political system." Jordan Peele and J. J. Abrams, the producers of the HBO horror series *Lovecraft Country,* which was scheduled to shoot in the state, announced that they would continue production but donate "100% of our respective episodic fees" to the ACLU of Georgia and to Fair Fight Action. They added that they wanted to "stand with Stacey Abrams and the hardworking people of Georgia." (In June, the ACLU of Georgia, with the Center for Reproductive Rights and Planned Parenthood, brought a suit against the state, arguing that the abortion law was unconstitutional. Last month, the groups sought a court injunction to stop it from taking effect.)

I spoke to Abrams about H.B. 481 when it was still making its way through the legislature, and she framed it as part of a larger set of reproductive health issues. Georgia has "one of the highest maternal mortality rates in the nation," she said, adding that half the counties lack an ob-gyn practice and that, overall, the quality of reproductive care is poor. So she saw an obligation to think about "abortion as one of the tools in the medical tool kit to address reproductive health." I spoke with her again after Kemp signed the bill, and she made a direct connection between reproductive rights and civil rights. The law is not only radical, she said; it also carries no more legitimacy than the election that gave Kemp the authority to sign it. "This is a perfect example of what the consequences of not having free and fair elections can have," she said.

In another conversation this spring, Abrams told me, "I live my life with an assumption that I have the right to do the things I think I should do, and that my gender and my race should not be limitations." Two black United States senators are currently running for president; the Congress is the most diverse ever seated; and an African American woman, Maxine Waters, serves as the chair of the powerful House Financial Services Committee. In the presidential elections of 2008 and 2012, black women had the highest voter participation rate of any demographic group. Yet they are among the least likely to hold elected office. (Women of color constitute just 4 percent of statewide elective executives.) Abrams is the first black woman to be nominated for the governorship of Georgia—if she had won, she would have been the first black female governor in the country.

In the spring, she reissued a political memoir, *Lead from the Outside*. The protocols of mainstream American politics generally frown on the word "power." Abrams sees that as precisely the issue. "Minorities rarely come of age explicitly thinking about what we want and how to get it," she writes. By contrast, "people already in power almost never have to think about whether they belong in the room." Abrams is characteristically direct, but such statements are also an attempt to upend the presumptions of what leadership in this society is expected to look like. She goes on, "For most people from the outside, every story you read, every narrative you're told, except for a couple months out of the year, is about how you're not supposed to be one of these people." The net effect, she writes, is that people view themselves as "ancillary, not essential" to the decision-making processes.

Dalton, Georgia, is a city of some thirty thousand people located in Whitfield County in the foothills of the Blue Ridge Mountains near the Tennessee border. It's a place earnest enough that it claims Marla Maples, Donald Trump's second wife, as a famous daughter—even though, technically, she is from nearby Cohutta. The county is overwhelmingly white, though the Latino population, in particular, is growing. In 2016, Hillary Clinton lost there to Trump by 45 points; in 2018, a non–presidential election year, Abrams lost it to Kemp by a similar margin, though the Latino turnout increased. Conventional wisdom would hold that time spent by a Democratic politician in Whitfield County is a seed tossed onto arid soil. Abrams would say that, according to that kind of thinking, she never should have run for governor in the first place. Last year, she campaigned in every county; now that she is no longer a candidate, she wants to keep every county engaged with her electoral reform campaign.

So, on a chilly afternoon on the last day of March, Abrams, who lives in a gentrifying section of Atlanta's east side, made the ninety-minute drive to Dalton as part of a tour that she has been conducting around the state. She was ebullient, even though the Dalton appearance would be her second event of the day. She had risen early to speak at the Antioch AME Church in Stone Mountain, a middle-class suburb of Atlanta. "I'm not a glad-hander," she told me. "I'm a good responder, but I'm also very comfortable sitting in silence." Abrams is, nevertheless, an effective speaker. Her speeches are short on grand metaphors, long on blunt declarative sentences. "Voters aren't dumb," she said. "They can tell if you mean what you say." Cynicism "comes about because people don't tell you the truth."

The Dalton Convention Center is a sprawling complex just off Interstate 75 near the site where, a historical marker notes, Confederate forces temporarily repelled William Tecumseh Sherman's troops as they marched on Atlanta. About 150 people had shown up for Abrams's event, which had been organized by Fair Fight Action. Many of them were older white people, and some had volunteered for her campaign.

Abrams was wearing a navy blue sheath dress and a braided strand of pearls, and her hair was in her signature twists. When she took the stage, she looked like an attorney about to make an opening argument. She began by thanking the volunteers, the Georgia Democratic Party, and its LGBTQ caucus; her campaign actively courted gay and lesbian voters—a month before the election, she became the first nominee of a major party to march in the Atlanta

Pride Parade. Then she repeated a line that she uses often, to the irritation of Georgia's Republican leadership. She said, "I'm gonna tell you what I've told folks across this state, and this is not a partisan statement, it's a true statement: we won."

She added, "In this election, we tripled Latino turnout, we tripled the Asian–Pacific Islander turnout." Between 2014 and 2018, according to Fair Fight Action, African American participation also rose, by 40 percent. (The organization says that its voter figures are more accurate than census data, which show smaller, though still significant, increases.) For Abrams, the point of continuing to try to organize in places like Whitfield County is to create a cross-racial coalition that can make the state more competitive for Democrats. In that sense, her efforts look less like a Hail Mary than like a pass hurled downfield toward a specific receiver no one else has noticed.

Abrams may be a symbol of the new Georgia, but her roots are elsewhere. She was born in 1973 in Madison, Wisconsin—where her mother, Carolyn, was earning a master's degree in library science at the University of Wisconsin—and she grew up in Gulfport, Mississippi. Carolyn met Abrams's father, Robert, in their hometown of Hattiesburg, Mississippi, when they were in high school, and in the late sixties they enrolled in Tougaloo College, which had been a center of the student civil rights movement. Politics has always been a part of the family's life. In the eighties, Carolyn told me, when she worked as a librarian and Robert had a job as a dockworker, the family picketed a Shell Oil gas station for the company's refusal to divest from South Africa.

Stacey is the second of six children. Each of the three oldest children was assigned responsibility for one of the three youngest. She was paired with her brother Richard, who is now a social worker in Atlanta. Her older sister, Andrea, has a doctorate in anthropology; Jeanine has a doctorate in biology. Leslie is a federal judge for the Middle District of Georgia. Walter, who attended Morehouse College, has struggled with bipolar disorder and addiction, and has served time in jail. Earlier this year, at the 92nd Street Y in New

York, Abrams spoke about his difficulties, as she has done in the past, with his permission, to raise awareness about addiction and mental health issues. "If our leaders are ashamed to tell real stories, how can we trust them to have real answers?" she said.

In her junior year of high school, the family moved to Atlanta, where both of her parents enrolled in the master of divinity program at Emory University's Candler School of Theology. (They are now retired elders of the Mississippi Conference of the United Methodist Church.) In 1991, Abrams began attending Spelman College, a historically black women's institution, founded in Atlanta in 1881. (I taught history there from 2001 to 2011.) Johnnetta Cole, an anthropologist who was the first black female president of the college (and later became the director of the Smithsonian's National Museum of African Art), met Abrams and her parents at the start of her freshman year. Cole remembers that Robert told her, "I want you to know that I am leaving my baby girl Stacey here, but, if anything happens, I'm coming to find you." She said, "I took a deep breath and told the Right Reverend that it was my responsibility to make sure that Stacey and all her sisters in that class were as safe as possible, and that we stretched them so they learned how to fly."

Abrams had grown up with college-educated parents, but she had never known kids whose families socialized with presidential cabinet members or flew on private jets. Cole encouraged her to run for campus office—by her senior year, she'd been elected student government president—and allowed her to sit in on meetings of the board of trustees. The idea was to give Abrams, who frequently told Cole how she thought Spelman should be run, insight into the workings of a university. Abrams says that the experience provided her with her first lessons in raising and allocating funds.

A turning point in her understanding of politics came in the spring of 1992 when four Los Angeles police officers were acquitted in the beating of Rodney King, an African American construction worker. Los Angeles exploded into riots, and there was unrest on campuses across the country. Students from several schools gathered at the Atlanta University Center to protest the verdict.

Atlanta's civic leadership, unlike that of Los Angeles, was largely black—a legacy of the civil rights movement—and included Mayor Maynard Jackson and Police Chief Eldrin Bell. That fact heightened the indignation of the protesters when the police began teargassing them.

Incensed by sensational portrayals of the protest in the local news, Abrams organized students to call the networks repeatedly to complain, and that led to a meeting with Mayor Jackson. In her memoir, Abrams writes, "With a boldness that surprised me, I excoriated his record and scoffed at his leadership. If I'd thought more deeply before I stood, I might have held my tongue. . . . In this moment I had access to power, a voice, and a question. Sometimes the why of ambition can only be discovered in a nervy action that cuts against our natural instincts."

After graduating from Spelman and then earning a master's degree in public policy from the University of Texas, she entered Yale Law School. It was there that Abrams began writing novels. (She has published eight, under the pseudonym Selena Montgomery, the last of them, *Deception,* in 2009. They feature professional women caught up in romance and intrigue.) "The act of writing is integral to who I am," she told *The Washington Post* last year. But fiction was a sideline; she'd specialized in tax law, and decided to go back to Georgia. She knew that she wanted to pursue a career in government, and in 2002, when she was twenty-nine, she became a deputy city attorney for Atlanta. Four years later, she won a seat in the Georgia House representing the Eighty-Fourth District, which encompassed part of the east side of Atlanta.

In 2004, the Democrats had lost control of the Georgia House for the first time in more than a century, and DuBose Porter, then the leader of the Democratic caucus, was struggling to define its role as the minority. He saw an asset in Abrams. "When Stacey was first elected, she was somewhat reserved," he told me, but "she instantly gained credibility, because she was kind of like our Google. If you needed some answers on something, you would go ask Stacey."

Abrams also earned a reputation for being willing to oppose the Republican leadership, though she is not a radical by nature. Her emergence as a national figure has coincided with the left's ascendancy in the Democratic Party, and many have portrayed her as part of that movement. But colleagues repeatedly point to her ability to forge compromises. Porter ran for governor in 2010—he lost in the primary, and Nathan Deal, a Republican congressman, was elected—and when Abrams made a bid to replace him as minority leader, Porter supported her. She won, becoming the first woman to lead either caucus in the Georgia House.

That year, Kemp, then a forty-six-year-old state senator from Athens, became the secretary of state. After the 2010 census, the Republicans redrew the district lines. The GOP was expected to pick up seats in the 2012 races, and it was Abrams's job to try to prevent the party from winning a supermajority in the legislature. Lauren Groh-Wargo, then a thirty-one-year-old activist turned strategist from Cleveland who had worked on Democratic campaigns in Ohio, including Governor Ted Strickland's unsuccessful 2010 bid for reelection, was looking for candidates to support. She had heard about Abrams and spoke with her a few times by phone, and they met for lunch in early 2012 when Groh-Wargo was visiting Atlanta. Abrams hired her as a consultant. Groh-Wargo, who is white and a lesbian, and Abrams represented voices that had never been at the center of Georgia politics, and, together, they pursued a plan to blunt the effects of redistricting through voter mobilization.

Abrams surprised the state GOP by raising more than $300,000 to support Democratic candidates that year. The money was spent not on expensive television and radio ads but on voter turnout strategies, like organizing canvassing teams and volunteer networks. In the end, the Democrats held on to four redistricted seats. "It was a really big deal that the Republicans didn't get the supermajority they had drawn for themselves," Groh-Wargo told me.

But Abrams had also discovered how fractious party politics can be. The previous year, as part of a round of budget cuts, Governor Deal considered severely curtailing the state's popular HOPE

Scholarship, which had used funds from the Georgia Lottery to pay the tuition and cost of books for hundreds of thousands of qualifying students at certain Georgia colleges. A plan called for full scholarships to be made contingent on SAT scores, which meant that many students would no longer be eligible for them. Abrams agreed to a compromise: a second tier of partial tuition funding was made available to tens of thousands of students who met the previous standard of a 3.0 GPA. (Porter pointed out that the compromise spared Georgia's pre-K program, which was also funded by the lottery.) Liberals criticized the deal, largely because tying the funds to SAT scores would favor suburban, mostly white students. Abrams still sounds stung by the experience. In February, during an interview with MSNBC host Chris Hayes, she said, "I was accused of selling out the students because they got 10 to 20 percent less. To me, 80 percent is a lot more than zero."

Then came the 2013 Supreme Court decision in *Shelby County v. Holder,* which struck down as unconstitutional a provision of the Voting Rights Act that had required Georgia and other states with a history of discriminatory voter suppression to get "preclearance" from the Justice Department or from a federal court before changing their voting regulations. Legislatures and elected officials in the South and elsewhere immediately embarked on efforts to disenfranchise voters. (Earlier this month, the Brennan Center for Justice reported that seventeen million Americans had been purged from the voter rolls between 2016 and 2018, and that the largest increases in purges were in states that had previously been under preclearance.) Abrams launched, and became a part-time CEO of, the New Georgia Project, a nonprofit organization devoted to registering overlooked constituencies: young people, women, people of color.

There were conflicts early on—critics noted Abrams's $177,000 salary, and in 2014 Kemp's office, acting on reports that the group was submitting fraudulent registration forms, began an investigation of more than eighty thousand forms. The Lawyers' Committee for Civil Rights Under Law filed a suit on behalf of the New Georgia Project and the state NAACP, alleging that the state had wrongfully held up thousands of forms submitted by the group; a judge found that the suit lacked sufficient evidence. Ultimately, Kemp's office identified fifty-three registrations as potentially fraudulent; all of them had been submitted by canvassers who were hired and paid by outside companies that the New Georgia Project had contracted. Kemp's investigators found no evidence of wrongdoing by the group, and the matter was referred to the state attorney general's office, where it still awaits possible civil action. The battle proved to be a prelude to 2018.

By 2018, Republicans had won the previous four gubernatorial races in the state, but political strategists were beginning to think that a black candidate who could perform respectably in rural areas and overperform in the Democratic strongholds around the cities could win. Abrams decided to run on a platform of Medicaid expansion, affordable housing, criminal justice reform, and gun control. She defeated the former state representative Stacey Evans in the primary, in a contest cast as the "Battle of the Staceys."

Kemp had also decided to run, and he campaigned on an anti-immigration, pro-gun platform, supporting tax cuts and opposing Medicaid expansion. Trump endorsed him, and after a primary runoff he became the Republican nominee. But he didn't resign his office, which meant that he oversaw an election in which he himself was a candidate—a conflict of interest that Abrams likened to a boxing match in which one fighter is also the referee and one of the judges.

Kemp, who described himself as a "politically incorrect conservative," did not endear himself to the emerging electorate. He appeared in campaign ads with a truck he said he drove in case he needed to round up "criminal illegals." Another ad accused Abrams of "dancing around the truth" of her financial history while showing a clip of tap-dancing feet. Some viewers saw this as a racist reference to minstrelsy. (Abrams had disclosed that she was $200,000 in debt, citing student loans and the costs of helping support family members. She also owed the IRS more than $50,000 in deferred tax payments, which she said she was repaying. She noted that three-quarters of Americans are in debt and that it shouldn't prevent them from running for office.)

Kemp's office declined to comment on the election for this piece, though he has called reports of voter suppression "a farce." A spokesperson pointed to a new report from the U.S. Election Assistance Commission that lists Georgia as the leading state for voter registration through its motor vehicle department. But there was a broad range of complaints during the campaign. In July 2017, according to a study by American Public Media, the secretary of state's office, under a "use it or lose it" policy and allegedly as part of an effort to prevent voter fraud, canceled the registrations of a hundred thousand voters who hadn't voted in seven years. Kemp also enacted an "exact-match" policy, which required information on voter registration applications to precisely match information on other official records. Something as minor as a missing hyphen could put a registration on hold. The registrations of 53,000 voters, 70 percent of whom were African American, were set aside for review. The race drew national attention as more complaints were lodged, including reports that residents who had become citizens were wrongly informed that they could not vote. Voters who requested absentee ballots said that they never received them. The state Democratic Party reported that 4,700 absentee ballot requests from DeKalb County, which is more than 50 percent black, had gone missing.

Four days before the election, U.S. District Court Judge Eleanor Ross ruled that the exact-match policy presented a "severe burden" for voters, and allowed 3,000 new citizens whose registrations had been held up to vote. The day before the election, the Brennan Center brought a lawsuit on behalf of Common Cause Georgia, a nonprofit, nonpartisan organization that focuses on election integrity, alleging that a vulnerability in the registration database left it open to hacking, and requested that Kemp's office ensure that provisional ballots be properly counted. On Election Day, November 6, there were numerous reports that polling places ran out of provisional ballots; residents of Gwinnett County, a heavily minority district outside Atlanta, had to wait in lines for hours to vote.

Lawyers for the Abrams campaign sought more time for ballots to be examined; a margin of less than 1 percent would have triggered a recount. The next Monday, U.S. District Court Judge Amy Totenberg ordered Kemp to open a hotline so that voters could determine if their provisional ballots had been counted. The state had planned to certify the results the next day, but Totenberg ordered that no certification occur before 5 P.M. that Friday. By the end of the week, though, it became clear that there would not be a recount. On the night of November 16, Abrams gave a speech in which she said, "I acknowledge that former Secretary of State Brian Kemp will be certified as the victor of the 2018 gubernatorial election. But to watch an elected official—who claims to represent the people of this state—baldly pin his hopes for election on the suppression of the people's democratic right to vote has been truly appalling. So, to be clear, this is not a speech of concession."

Many people in and outside Georgia believe that, without the irregularities, Abrams would have won. In early June in Atlanta, Joe Biden, the front-runner for the 2020 Democratic presidential nomination, told the African American Leadership Summit that "voter suppression is the reason Stacey Abrams isn't governor." Addressing the same event, Pete Buttigieg said, "Stacey Abrams ought to be governor right now."

In March, I interviewed Abrams for an event at the Brookings Institution in Washington, D.C., and asked her why she thought voter suppression—an issue most closely associated with the civil rights era—had reemerged as a pivotal concern across the country. She replied, "We've never not been in this situation." Historically, Georgia's gubernatorial elections, in particular, have highlighted the nexus between racism and voter suppression. In 1906, the Democratic primary race—between Hoke Smith, a former publisher of *The Atlanta Journal,* and Clark Howell, the editor of *The Atlanta*

Constitution—became a competition over who would do more to disenfranchise the African American population. The escalating rhetoric, amplified by the candidates' newspapers, set off a riot that left at least twenty-five blacks and two whites dead. In 1946, Governor Eugene Talmadge, a noted segregationist, lost the popular vote in the Democratic primary to James V. Carmichael, an Atlanta businessman who was a moderate on racial issues. But Talmadge was declared the winner, owing to Georgia's notorious "county unit" system, which gave disproportionate weight to rural areas. In 1966, Lester Maddox, an Atlanta restaurant owner, won the office after refusing to serve black customers, in open defiance of the 1964 Civil Rights Act.

In 1971, Maddox was succeeded by Jimmy Carter, but even Carter, who would become an icon of Southern liberalism, was not immune to the contortions of Georgia politics. He had lost a bid for the governorship in 1966 when he was a state senator, in part for appearing insufficiently conservative on matters of race. (He had worked to repeal voter restrictions.) In 1970, he courted the support of white conservatives, and Maddox, who was running separately for lieutenant governor, endorsed him. But Carter announced, in his inaugural address, that "the time for racial discrimination is over," and he set about integrating the state government. In the 1976 presidential election, he carried every state of the former Confederacy except Virginia, winning just 45 percent of the white vote but 95 percent of the black vote.

Beginning in the 1970s, Georgia—particularly Atlanta—became a destination for a growing number of educated African Americans repatriating to the South. Between 2000 and 2010, the state's black population grew by 25 percent, and the Latino population almost doubled, to nearly 9 percent. By 2010, Asian Americans accounted for 3 percent of the population. But those changes were not entirely reflected at the polls. In 2016, 600,000 African Americans who were eligible to vote remained unregistered. Many people viewed this fact as a reflection of the Democratic Party's pessimism toward the potential of the black electorate in the state. In 2008, Ben Jealous, then the director of the NAACP, told me that Democrats were ignoring a political bounty by failing to allocate sufficient money to organize and register black Georgians.

Shortly before Abrams announced her candidacy, she told me in a phone conversation that, if she ran, her campaign strategy would rely on registering those 600,000 people. During our Brookings discussion, I said that she probably could have heard my eyebrow raise over the phone. "More like I could hear your eyes rolling," she said. In her public appearances, Abrams often rattles off statistics about the election. But one statistic stands out: 925,000 African Americans voted in the 2014 gubernatorial race; in 2018, 1.4 million African Americans voted—94 percent of them for Abrams.

The fact that her campaign had conceived of a plan that, at least in theory, made Georgia look like a purple state has not gone unnoticed. "The path to victory as a Democrat here is you have got to build a multiracial, multiethnic coalition," Groh-Wargo told me. "You have got to get super intellectually curious about African American voters, about Latino voters, about Asian American voters, about millennials, and white suburbanites." When I asked Abrams if the national party had invested too heavily in those communities in 2016 at the expense of the lower-income white electorate and ushering in Trump's victory, she rejected the framing of the question. "I think where the Democratic Party has gotten into trouble is that we've created a binary, where it's either the normative voter we remember fondly from 1960"—the working-class white male—"or it's the hodgepodge. The reality is that we are capable as a society of having multiple thoughts at the same time. That's one of the reasons why I went to the gay pride parade," she added. "I know that, as an ally, I'm responsible for making certain that the LGBTQ community is seen and heard." Most elections are framed as a referendum on the future; Georgia's race was about how much of the past had been dragged into the present.

All this leaves open the question of what Abrams will do next. Chuck Schumer, the Senate Minority Leader, tried to persuade her to run against David Perdue, Georgia's junior senator, who is up for reelection in 2020. In May, she announced that she would not run next year, a decision that was met with disapproval from observers who think that it's incumbent on prominent Democrats to help the party win control of the Senate. Abrams defended her decision to me by saying, "I was following the protocol that I set for myself, making sure that I take on jobs and roles because they are the right thing for me, and not simply because they're available." Strategists thought that she could beat Perdue; Trump's approval rating in Georgia has dropped 17 points since his inauguration, and Perdue's close ties to the president may make him vulnerable in the suburbs, where Abrams fared well. She was less sanguine about the part that would come next. The prestige of the Senate does not, in her estimation, offset its torpid pace of change. "It is a more indirect approach than the one I see for myself," she said. "When I thought through who would be the best advocate in the U.S. Senate for Georgia, under the structure of the Senate, that was not me."

Yet Republican control of the Senate has been key to some of the issues that most concern her. If it weren't for the confirmation of Kavanaugh to the Supreme Court, an imminent challenge to *Roe v. Wade* would be much less likely. Similarly, the Supreme Court ruling in *Shelby County v. Holder* left open the possibility that Congress could create an updated standard for voter protection. One such effort is the Voting Rights Advancement Act of 2015, which was co-sponsored by John Lewis, the longtime Georgia congressman and civil rights leader. The bill, among other things, calls for any jurisdiction that's been found to have committed repeated voting rights violations in the past twenty-five years to be resubjected to preclearance for ten years. Abrams has testified twice this year before Congress in support of such measures. (The Fair Fight Action lawsuit calls for Georgia to be put back under preclearance requirements.) A new voter protection standard has almost no chance of passing the Senate now. It could, though, if Democrats gain control of the chamber.

Then there is still the question of the governorship. Abrams could run against Kemp again in 2022, though some aspects of the past campaign are still being fought. In April, Kemp signed two significant bills that addressed some of the issues raised by Democrats and the Common Cause lawsuit, such as extending the "use it or lose it" period and ensuring protections for voters using absentee and provisional ballots. New voting machines will be installed by next year, though there are concerns about security. And the new secretary of state, Brad Raffensperger, has opened an investigation into the 4,700 absentee ballot applications that were reported missing.

But, also in April, David Emadi, the new head of the Georgia Ethics Commission, subpoenaed financial records and correspondence from Abrams's campaign to investigate contributions from four groups that, according to the subpoenas, may have exceeded the limit for statewide candidates. Groh-Wargo called the move "insane political posturing" and pointed out that Emadi was a donor to Kemp. (He contributed $600 to Kemp's 2018 bid.) Emadi said in a statement that audits and investigations of all the campaigns are ongoing and that "all of these candidates enjoy the presumption of innocence in these matters unless and until evidence indicates otherwise."

There is also the question of whether Abrams will run for president. Supporters have been calling on her to do so since last year. In January, she delivered a well-received response to Trump's State of the Union—an honor generally afforded to a high-ranking officeholder. A few months ago, she was mentioned in the press as a potential running mate for Biden—a development that caught her off guard. She had met with him, but they did not discuss a joint ticket. When I asked her about that possibility, she promptly shut it down: "I don't believe you get into a race to run for second place."

Abrams defended Biden earlier this year against allegations of inappropriate behavior with women, saying, "We cannot have perfection as the litmus test. The responsibility of leadership is not to be perfect but to be accountable." She was equally politic when I asked her about Biden's dispute with Kamala Harris over his history of opposing busing: "While America must reckon with its past, my focus is on how the next president will address the persistent issue of inequity in public education." Her name will likely continue to show up on various shortlists for the vice presidency.

What is not likely to change, at least in the short term, is the dynamic of the contest between two political directions, one of inclusion, one of resentment. Abrams told me, "What we did in our campaign was realize that the fundamentals are true for everyone. Everyone wants economic security. Everyone wants educational opportunity for their children and for themselves." It's an optimistic view—a belief that people are motivated more by their common aspirations than they are by their tribal fears. Abrams's own future, no matter what she does next, hinges on that being true.

BACK TO SCHOOL REFORM

September 8, 2019

The New York City Department of Education, the sprawling bureaucracy headquartered at 52 Chambers Street in lower Manhattan, has stewardship of more than a million students—a number larger than the total population of San Francisco, Boston, or Denver. Public education in the five boroughs encompasses not only schools divided by grade but also vocational schools, specialized schools, charter schools, alternative schools, and an extensive array of programming within the schools. The temptation is to speak of the system itself in the plural, and to a lot of people that is exactly what it is—a system of many unequal parts. Three-quarters of the children in the city's schools are poor, and more than 70 percent of black and Latino children attend schools in which most of the students live in poverty. While 43 percent of the city's population is white, white students account for only 15 percent of the public school population.

This school year was met by two particularly contentious reform issues. One began in June 2018 when, as part of an effort to combat the enduring problem of segregation, Mayor Bill de Blasio announced his intention to discontinue the testing requirement for admission to the city's eight selective "elite" high schools, which have long been the capstones of the system. A bill that would have eliminated the tests failed to pass in the state legislature, but de Blasio has the authority to remove five of the schools from the entrance exam requirement.

Then, late last month, the School Diversity Advisory Group, which de Blasio had created to address the problem of integrating schools, released a report suggesting that the city rethink its entire approach to identifying and educating high-achieving children. The reductive discussion of the report described it as a plan to eliminate initiatives for these children. The gifted-and-talented programs, in which admission is based on a single test given to four-year-olds—they must score in at least the 90th percentile to qualify—offer a more rigorous curriculum to advanced learners. More accurately, the advisory group criticized the racial and socioeconomic bias of the test and recommended replacing the programs with new initiatives, modeled on those in San Antonio, Chicago, Washington, D.C., and Montgomery County, Maryland, which challenge precocious children without relying on a test or academic tracking.

But the alarmist headlines, following on the plan for the specialized high schools, seemed to indicate that, as the mayor waged a lonely crusade in Iowa to rise above 1 percent in the Democratic presidential polls, his administration had declared war on smart children. The ensuing uproar recalls some of the most fraught moments in the recent history of the system: the battles over integration in the fifties, local control of schools in the sixties, busing in the seventies, and school closures during the mayoralty of Michael Bloomberg. The current clashes, too, are shot through with questions of race and equity.

The proposed changes to the specialized-high-school admissions came in response to the declining numbers of black and Latino students enrolled in them: this year, African American students qualified for just seven of the nearly nine hundred places at Stuyvesant High School, the most selective in the system; Latino students got thirty-three. Black and Latino students together make up almost 70 percent of the public school population but just 10 percent of the population of the specialized high schools.

There was further controversy in August of last year after the

Department of Education announced that it would expand its Discovery program, which provides additional resources and coursework for students who fall just short of the test score cutoff for specialized high schools and was intended to help increase black and Latino enrollment. The Pacific Legal Foundation, representing community groups and Asian American parents who feared that the expansion would disadvantage their children, filed a lawsuit to block it. Asian American students account for 16 percent of the overall school population but 62 percent of the enrollment at specialized high schools. Earlier this year, a federal judge ruled that the expansion could proceed.

The allure of testing lies in its apparent neutrality—its democratic indifference to a student's background and wealth. But this is not how the current system functions. Success correlates closely to socioeconomic advantages and access to test preparation. Pricey services offer tutoring to ever younger children. (There is a niche industry of consultants who help two-year-olds ace their preschool admissions assessments.) Yet many defenders of testing believe that more subjective forms of evaluation present their own unfairness. As the Students for Fair Admissions lawsuit, filed against Harvard University in 2014, has demonstrated, Asian American students tend to receive lower scores on the most subjective parts of college admissions evaluations—often in ways that correspond to personality stereotypes attached to Asian Americans.

It's not clear what the result of the current debate will be. The mayor has not yet eliminated the entrance exam for any of the specialized high schools, and last week the schools chancellor, Richard Carranza, indicated that no changes will be made to the gifted-and-talented programs this year. One thing, however, is certain: the competition for slots at New York's elite schools is driven, in part, by a lack of faith in the quality of education in other parts of the system. Outside the neutral language of policy reports, the issue of testing is debated in a context of winners and losers, of model minorities and problematic ones. A less primitive view sees the conflict as being between different groups fighting for a system in which their children are the least likely to be hampered by discrimination.

Because discrimination functions in different ways across lines of race and ethnicity, the issue is not simply the fairness of testing; it's that people on either side of the question can reasonably describe their position as an attempt to fight against discrimination.

The success of Asian American students, some from low-income families, doesn't imply that the system is fair; it suggests that unfairness can be mitigated by extraordinary effort. There is a vast difference between an equal system and one in which it is possible to succeed. Rather than commit the tremendous resources, time, and will that would be required to create a fair education system, we have settled on one in which success is possible, in which the obstacles are sizable but also surmountable, and one that—provided you don't look very hard—passes for actual democracy.

HOW ROBERT FRANK'S PHOTOGRAPHS HELPED DEFINE AMERICA

September 11, 2019

A nation that is premised on an idea—not on an alleged shared bloodline or eons of history on common acreage—is prone to periodically question exactly who and what it is. The matter that binds Americans, as much as any doctrine or document, is the pursuit of a definition of who Americans are. There are facile adjectives applied to us—optimistic, volatile, swaggering—but they more often seem to apply to pretensions that we wear before the world. Who we are in our unguarded moments, and even what portion of people are included in the word "we," is another matter entirely. This is part of the reason that Robert Frank's photographic essay *The Americans,* published in France as *Les Américains* in 1958 and released in the United States a year later, is both an indelible reflection of American culture and one of the works that helped define it. To produce it, Frank, who died this week at the age of ninety-four, spent two years scouring the country in a used car, courtesy of a Guggenheim grant, a contrail of dust his most constant companion.

Frank was born in 1924 in Switzerland to a Swiss mother and a German Jewish father. His family remained safe throughout the Second World War, but he became part of the postwar exodus from Europe, departing in 1947 for New York, where he settled; later in life, he began dividing his time between Manhattan and Nova Scotia. His early magazine work in *Harper's Bazaar* gained him a reputation in New York arts circles, but it wasn't until 1955, when he undertook the work that became *The Americans,* that his capacity as a photographer and chronicler became widely apparent. Frank evolved as an artist, eventually turning to film and directing—most notably *Cocksucker Blues,* a cinematic record of the Rolling Stones's 1972 U.S. tour, which became the subject of a protracted lawsuit. (The Stones attempted to suppress the film, partially out of fear over how its illicit contents would be received in the United States. On Tuesday, the band put out a statement calling Frank "an incredible artist whose unique style broke the mould.") But *The Americans* remained Frank's best-known work, a reference point for both him as an artist and the medium in which he created it.

It's often difficult to gauge the importance of a work long after its initial appearance, because the groundbreaking ideas of one generation tend to become the accepted conventions of those that follow it. *The Americans,* however, was compelling as a contemporary document when it was released and it remains so as an archival representation six decades later. The eighty-three photographs in the book were culled from more than twenty-seven thousand that Frank took in Nebraska, Montana, Connecticut, South Carolina, Georgia, New York, California, and various points in between. The original cover features a gracefully composed image of a trolley car in New Orleans, the passengers gazing directly out as if deliberately holding eye contact with the viewer. It is a document of a mid-century American conveyance, but also a subtle testament to much more. The implications of the arrangement of those passengers—the black travelers are seated in the back—and the trolley's metaphorical depiction of an entire set of social relations are simply hinted at. Frank succinctly, subversively places all these people—who are literally heading in the same direction—under the title line of the book. They are the Americans.

The array of moments that Frank captured and presented is a statement on the broad, unwieldy idea of America itself: a lone Jehovah's Witness standing in Los Angeles, his face weathered and intense; a Miami dowager mid-conversation, a stole draped casually about her shoulders; a woman and child in a packed car in Butte, Montana, both so weary and concerned that they seem like real-life Joads, heading off in pursuit of better fortune. The American flag appears randomly in the series, affixed to a building during a parade in Hoboken, New Jersey; at a Fourth of July celebration in Jay, New York; in a bar in Detroit. A man in Venice, California, fashions one into a canopy to shelter himself from the sun. The motif points to the varied undertakings here, the staggering diversity of lives coexisting in forty-eight contiguous states.

When Frank was working, photography had already been integrated into the media, but its universal acceptance as art, hastened by John Szarkowski's tenure as the director of photography at New York's Museum of Modern Art, was still years away. Americans might see images from other parts of the country in newspapers, and projects such as the New Deal's Works Progress Administration had created an archive of invaluable documentary photography, but the idea of essentially introducing America to itself through images, as Frank endeavored to do, was still an ambitious use of the craft. He was also working before the Federal-Aid Highway Act of 1956 had transformed the road trip into an American rite. When Jack Kerouac's *On the Road* appeared, a year before *The Americans,* the idea of driving across the country still carried a frisson of audacity and adventure. Fittingly, Kerouac wrote the introduction to Frank's book, in which he noted that Frank had "sucked a sad poem right out of America onto film." Even decades later, that is a remarkable assessment of what Frank achieved, even if those words don't resonate the way they might have in 1958.

Earlier this year, I visited the Pier 24 Photography gallery in San Francisco to see an exhibit called *This Land,* a portrait of the United States as witnessed by eighteen photographers. It's a project that clearly finds Frank's work in its genealogy. The collection included Alessandra Sanguinetti's compelling images of Black River Falls, Wisconsin, and Richard Misrach's stark, beautiful photographs of the California desert. But it also included evidence of American decline: Brian Ulrich's images of defunct shopping malls, Dawoud

Bey's picture of the shuttered Lenox Lounge in Harlem, portraits of random Americans from Bruce Gilden's *Citizen* series, each of their faces portending, like a bad weather forecast. If Frank captured the visages of people who look as if they just punched out from a double shift, Gilden's subjects look as if the plant had shut down three years prior and nothing has opened in its place. Declension is a conspicuous theme in *This Land* in a way that is absent from *The Americans*.

It is a strange and ironic form of achievement to craft outstanding work at age thirty-four and live to see that work define you as an artist for the next sixty years. Yet Frank's book, and thereby his statement about the country, still warrants consideration, albeit for reasons that are very different than when it initially appeared. We know how many of the themes that Frank touched on in the book have played out, yet we're no closer to answering many questions they raised about American identity—and are perhaps more belligerently confused by them now even than we were in 1958. Kerouac saw sadness in Frank's collection, but what is most notable about the staid, unburnished faces now is their comparative sanguinity. The passage of time does to emotion the same thing that inflation does to prices; yesterday's extravagance seems a steal today. And sadness, like exorbitance, depends entirely upon what it's being compared to.

WHAT ELIJAH CUMMINGS MEANT TO BALTIMORE

October 18, 2019

By the time Representative Elijah Cummings left the pulpit during the funeral services for Freddie Gray on April 27, 2015, he had delivered *a word*, as the church elders are prone to call it. "I've often said our children are the living messages we send to a future that we will never see," the congressman told the congregation of New Shiloh Baptist Church in Baltimore. "But now our children are sending us to a future that *they* will never see. There's something wrong with this picture." Gray, who died on April 19 at the age of twenty-five one week after sustaining injuries while in police custody, had become a symbol for the relationship between black people and the police in Baltimore, and beyond. (Charges against officers who were involved were later dropped.) When I visited the city two days before his funeral, it seemed to be edging toward detonation. Not long after I arrived, a protest march wound through downtown, then past the courthouse and the Inner Harbor, before concluding in sporadic rioting just outside Camden Yards, where the Orioles play. I watched from an overpass as groups of young men smashed the windows of police cars and officers in riot gear marched toward the demonstrators. The violence there resulted in two people being injured and a dozen arrested.

At Gray's funeral, Cummings reminded the audience that he knew intimately the loss they were experiencing. "Family, there are those who will tell you, 'Don't cry.' I'm not gonna say that. I put my nephew in a grave four years ago," he told them. "Blasted away— still don't know who did it. I mourn every day." Cummings's ability to speak to that moment and its indelible hurt underscores the reason that Baltimore itself began grieving on Thursday morning as its residents awoke to the news that the congressman, aged sixty-eight, had died a few hours after midnight.

Pay attention to the responses to outrages involving police and African Americans and you begin to see patterns, especially among elected leaders. Some seize on the national spotlight, making scripted displays of unity. Others tend toward bureaucratic responses and a reflexive defense of flawed institutions. A small number possess both the honesty and the insight to speak truthfully. Cummings belonged to that number. He was seemingly everywhere in the chaotic aftermath of Gray's death: on the streets, cautioning people to protest peacefully; in the pulpit, offering a balm to the people Gray left behind; and chastising those who set fires in protest of the state of affairs that allowed situations like those surrounding Gray's death to arise in the first place. Mostly, though, he was present, a powerful politician who still spoke like a concerned neighbor, a man who was so identifiably and devoutly a product of the communities he represented that at times he seemed to be the only person capable of credibly speaking to the hostilities that Gray's death had brought to the surface.

The obituaries made note of his achievements on the national stage: that he was a twelve-term representative of Maryland's Seventh District and that he chaired the crucial House Oversight and Reform Committee, one of the committees directed to conduct an impeachment inquiry of President Donald Trump. Cummings grew up in Baltimore, graduated from Howard University with honors before earning a law degree at the University of Maryland, and then served for fourteen years in the state legislature before running to replace Representative Kweisi Mfume when he left Congress to head the NAACP in 1996. What most struck me about Cummings, however, was the role he played in shepherding Baltimore through the aftermath of Gray's death. In the past decade, the city's population has shrunk by 18,500 people; more than 16,000 houses stand empty. The poverty rate is nearly 24 percent. The city was immortalized in *The Wire,* which was the most nuanced and profound meditation on the decline of American cities and a catalog of the reasons people were fleeing cities like Baltimore. In short, it is a place that, like the rest of America these days, is badly in need of visionaries.

In July, when Trump assailed Baltimore, in typically crude and hyperbolic fashion, as a "rodent-infested mess" where no human would want to live, he was providing an object lesson in the very stereotypes that Cummings had devoted himself to fighting. He invited Trump to visit his district and offered to spend an entire day chaperoning him around Baltimore and its suburbs to clarify the president's vision of what the place was all about. (Trump did not take him up on the offer.)

One other thing: democracy. Cummings, in his speeches, particularly those he gave in the past few years, insistently invoked it, and not in the inert way that elected officials tend to. He spoke of democracy as something vital and fragile and valuable, an inheritance that had to be safeguarded for future generations. When he spoke of H.R. 1, the exhaustive election protection bill that the Democrats introduced in January as their first piece of legislation of this Congress, he mentioned his ninety-two-year-old mother, who had died a year earlier. She was a former sharecropper who implored him, "Do not let them take our votes away from us." He viewed his chairmanship of the House Oversight and Reform Committee as part of the battle to protect voting rights. His death unleashes a flurry of speculation about whom the Democrats will choose to next lead the committee—Representative Carolyn Maloney of New York will serve as the acting chair—and how that person will oversee its portion of the impeachment inquiry. Those matters will be resolved at a future date. What remains clear is the void that Cummings's absence leaves in his district and his country.

This would have been the case at nearly any point in his quarter century in Congress. But it's even more acute in this one. In a fiery bit of oratory delivered at the introduction of H.R. 1, he pledged to "fight to the death" in defense of voting and, thereby, of democracy. It was a promise that he made good on.

THE POWERFUL PERSPECTIVE OF *QUEEN & SLIM*

November 27, 2019

Last month, five days after the former police officer Amber Guyger was sentenced in the fatal shooting of Botham Jean, an unarmed twenty-six-year-old black man, whom she shot in his home, and five days before Atatiana Jefferson, a twenty-eight-year-old black woman, was killed in her home by the police officer Aaron Dean, *Queen & Slim* began previews in a small theater just off Bryant Park in Manhattan. The film is the product of the vision of two black women: Lena Waithe, who wrote it, and Melina Matsoukas, who directed it. (Waithe collaborated on the story with James Frey, the shamed memoirist.) It means something that a movie that was conceived years ago could land so squarely in the midst of dual tempests involving firearms, police, and black people whose lives expired violently, prematurely, at the hands of white people who were sworn to protect them. The fact that both Jean and Jefferson were at home when they were killed underscores a central conceit of the film: that a system capable of dispensing such arbitrary deaths cannot be trusted in any context, least of all to administer justice on behalf of those it also victimizes.

The recognition of this fact changes the implications of the story that Waithe and Matsoukas tell with this film: about a couple on a first date who kill a police officer in self-defense and their subsequent life as fugitives. Early buzz around the movie pegged it as a *Bonnie and Clyde* tale for the Black Lives Matter set, but that would be an entirely different film from *Queen & Slim*. *Bonnie and Clyde* is the story of two outlaws who are fleeing justice; *Queen & Slim* is a meditation on a system of justice that treats innocent people as outlaws. This is not a novel undertaking. It's hard to overlook, for instance, that this movie arrives in theaters in the same year as the thirtieth anniversary of Spike Lee's *Do the Right Thing*.

That film follows the events of a single day in Bedford-Stuyvesant and culminates in the death, at the hands of the NYPD, of a neighborhood fixture named Radio Raheem. In 2014, in the aftermath of Eric Garner's death from a choke hold administered by a New York City police officer, Lee spliced together video from Garner's and Raheem's deaths, one cinematic, one chaotically real, both somehow true—a diptych of life and art relaying the same subject matter. As I wrote at the time, however, Lee conceived of the Radio Raheem scene after the death of Michael Stewart, a black graffiti artist who died in police custody in 1983, possibly as the result of a choke hold. *Do the Right Thing* was not prescient in forecasting Garner's death; it was archival in rendering a version of Stewart's. Eight years before Stewart's death, the film *Cornbread, Earl and Me*, which features a fourteen-year-old Laurence Fishburne, tells the story of a rising basketball star, played by Jamaal Wilkes, who is shot by police in a case of mistaken identity, and it shows the ways in which the system protects the officers who killed him. And so it goes, act and depiction, tumbling all the way back to some unknown original insult. The capricious loss of black life is so common a reality as to have inspired an entire body of art addressing its implications.

The story of *Queen & Slim* is propelled by an arbitrary traffic stop in which a white officer detains a couple, whose names we do not know yet, played by Daniel Kaluuya and Jodie Turner-Smith. When the officer fires his gun to prevent Turner-Smith's character from recording the incident on her cellphone, we are anticipating a scenario that has become a dispiriting cliché of social injustice, the indefensible but somehow bureaucratically justifiable death of a black civilian. But the gun is wrestled away and goes off during the struggle, killing the officer. The shooting, captured on the squad car's camera, is a Rorschach test that asks all subsequent characters, and by extension the audience, what they see when they look at the incident. The officer himself is like Patient Zero in an outbreak: his actions set in motion the decisions made by everyone else we encounter en route to the film's finale. Each television screen or cellphone upon which the footage plays serves as a kind of exposure to a pathogen, as everyone reacts to a different reading of the situation. Everyone is moral but no one is right.

Matsoukas has touched upon these themes previously. She directed the much-lauded video for Beyoncé's "Formation," which was criticized by police groups for provocative imagery of a police car sinking underwater in a Hurricane Katrina–like flood. In *Queen & Slim*, the system is inundated by a metaphorical flood. In the opening scene, Turner-Smith and Kaluuya are on an awkward first date. She, we learn, is an attorney whose client was sentenced to death earlier that day. It's the intimacy of her relationship to the criminal justice system that makes it all the more damning when she demands that they go on the run rather than attempt to explain to other officers what happened. The hypothetical implicit in the scene itself is: What would have happened if someone like Eric Garner had fought back? What would have happened had Botham Jean or Atatiana Jefferson shot first? And what are the probabilities that anyone fighting back against unsanctioned police violence could be thought of as anything beyond a thug or murderer by the greater public?

The connections between *Cornbread, Earl and Me* and Michael Stewart and *Do the Right Thing* and Eric Garner form a daisy chain in which the question is less about whether art or life is imitating the other and more about the ways in which art serves as a bridge between tragedies that occur at irregular intervals but with such similarities that they have formed a canon of the wrongly dead. This is part of what makes *Queen & Slim* such a brilliant, indelible departure, and it's most of the reason that I continued to think about it obsessively in the weeks after I saw it in that theater in midtown.

There is an accidental homicide, but it is not committed by a police officer. There is no template of bureaucratic responses, no corps of surrogates deployed to dispel the innocence of the victim in the media, no hedging of the deaths with reminders of how dangerous the shooter's line of work is and what he means to the rest of society.

When the eighteen-year-old Michael Brown was killed by the police officer Darren Wilson five years ago in Ferguson, *The New York Times* ran a piece that led with the description of Brown as "no angel," to which outraged critics in Ferguson and beyond shouted that they didn't know he had to be. The system here is no angel. It is the story of two people—a black everyman, played with sublime reserve by Kaluuya, and an attorney who is both sincere and cynical in equal measure, compellingly brought to life by Turner-Smith.

There are a great number of other implications to this story: the brilliant inversion of a slave narrative in which two people flee from a Northern free state into the Deep South to seek freedom; the thorny and complicated ways in which other African Americans respond to them en route; a twist in the middle of the film that unsettles any sense of moral simplicity that the viewer might have indulged up to that point. Most provocatively, the incident at the heart of *Queen & Slim* is framed in the context of a May 1973 incident on the New Jersey Turnpike in which members of the Black Liberation Army, including Assata Shakur, were involved in a shootout in which the police officer Werner Foerster was killed. Shakur, who is referenced multiple times in the film and serves as a kind of historical inspiration for the decisions Turner-Smith and Kaluuya make after the shooting, escaped from prison in 1979 and has remained a fugitive in Cuba for nearly four decades. The State of New Jersey and the FBI maintain rewards for her capture; she has been denounced by successive New Jersey governors. At the same time, her memoir, *Assata,* is a mainstay of African American studies courses and has remained in print for thirty years.

This is not a divergence in the responses to Shakur; it's a divergence in people's views about the credibility of the system that arrested and imprisoned her and of its representative who pulled her

over that day. These different points of view are implicit in *Queen &
Slim*—it is emphatically told from the vantage point of people with
the vindicating view of Shakur. If we're unaccustomed to grappling
with these questions in film, it is because it's been so long since they
were raised. Matsoukas did not create a gangster-moll story for the
modern era; she created a Blaxploitation movie. The reference is
not *Bonnie and Clyde;* it's *Sweet Sweetback's Baadasssss Song.* Melvin
Van Peebles's indie film, released in 1971, is another audaciously
black story that grapples with an African American who attacks police officers and goes on the run. It, too, was a movie that took its
audience's understanding of systemic injustice as a given. It, too,
recalled history, albeit not the strand of it we prefer to highlight in
the United States.

It was raining the night I saw *Queen & Slim* and, after the screen-
ing, I stood outside the theater beneath a construction scaffold to
sort through the layers of the film. The movie reminded me of a
historical reference buried deep in my memory. A hundred and
nineteen years ago, a black man named Robert Charles sat with a
friend on the steps of a building in New Orleans near where his
girlfriend lived, waiting for her to get ready for a date. He was approached by several police officers, one of whom grabbed him. A
fight ensued in which he and the officer both opened fire. Charles
then fled. Police tracked him to his apartment, where he killed two
officers. A police manhunt terrorized black communities in New
Orleans, but Charles evaded capture for several days until he was
tracked to an empty building where, in the course of a standoff, he
shot more than twenty other white men. The official versions of this
story held that the men who set the building on fire and shot
Charles as he exited were heroes. Black people chose a different
protagonist. The journalist Ida B. Wells-Barnett wrote of Charles
that "white people of this country may charge that he was a des-
perado, but to the people of his own race Robert Charles will always be regarded as the hero of New Orleans." People subject to
the same abuses Charles suffered were unconcerned with whether
he was an "angel." What mattered was the number of white men
who would now think twice before trying to pull the same stunt.

Queen & Slim is an extrapolation of thoughts that run through the heads of black people each time we're called upon to mourn publicly, to request justice like supplicants, to comfort ourselves with inert lies about this sort of thing stopping in the near future. That kind of insular honesty is rare in any kind of art but is particularly perilous in cinema. This is a film that stands as strong a chance of being hailed and lauded as it does of being denounced and picketed, but it understands the inescapable fact that heroism is entirely a matter of context, that heroes need not be concerned with explaining themselves, and that it—like the characters at its center, like the history it draws upon—stands a great likelihood of being misunderstood. And, gloriously, neither its writer nor its director appears to give a damn.

HISTORY LESSENS

In the early days of the Covid pandemic, as the world seemed to contract to the precise dimensions of our living arrangements, I took to slipping out of my apartment late in the night, while my daughter and infant twin sons were asleep, to ride my bike around the silent streets of Manhattan. We had by then become almost accustomed to a city whose streets were as bereft of human activity as the famous scene of a desolate Times Square in the movie *Vanilla Sky.* What I recall most clearly is the way that the quiet would periodically be broken by the distant wails of ambulances ferrying the Covid-infected to overcrowded emergency rooms and the subtle, almost imperceptible hum of bicycle tires as food delivery workers carried takeout seemingly throughout the night.

In the moment, 2020 seemed like one of those crucible years that, like 1968, 1939, or 1914, warranted being chronicled in a history of its own. A presidential election year in which a deadly global pandemic emerged, the national economy tanked, and the murder of an unarmed man by a police officer sparked the largest protests in the nation's history. Schools closed, sending students fortunate enough to possess computers into virtual learning pods and leaving the others yet further behind. Businesses shuttered and a grim tally of pandemic fatalities became a regular feature of our lives. The pandemic and the inept way in which the federal government handled it most certainly factored in to the polls that year, influencing the margin by which Joe Biden defeated Donald Trump. In Harlem, word of the election results sent jubilant crowds of people to the statue of Frederick Douglass at the intersection of 110th Street and Central Park West. The mad vitriol of the preceding years and the chaos conductor responsible for it seemed, at least in that moment, to be an anomaly of history. But the story was far more complicated. Only months later, just on the other side of a new year, a Trumpist mob laid siege to the United States Capitol, wrongly convinced that the election had been stolen. The specter of that mob would linger in the years that followed. It became clear that the celebrations were premature: nothing was vanquished.

The lessons of history implicit within that eerie, empty spring of 2020 seemed to fade nearly as soon as the calendar scrolled into the new year. The following pieces touch upon some of the people and events that might help that moment make slightly more sense. The past, we're told, is prologue. These pieces are the closest prefaces to where we are now and wherever we might find ourselves next.

D-NICE'S CLUB QUARANTINE IS WHAT YOU NEED

March 22, 2020

The odd irony of the current plague is that we are experiencing it at once collectively and entirely by ourselves. The governors and mayors who oversee various swaths of the country have ordered their residents to stay indoors, and we have bristled and mostly complied. But it took Derrick Jones, professionally known as DJ D-Nice, to give us a reason to want to.

For *nine* hours on Saturday night, D-Nice oversaw a spectacle that was part dance party, part social media therapy, and a health policy initiative cleverer than anything the government has put together. Chaka Khan showed up. Lenny Kravitz was there. So were Diddy, Timbaland, Alicia Keys, Ava DuVernay, MC Lyte, Halle Berry, Rihanna, Jamie Foxx, and Kerry Washington. Michelle Obama popped in for a minute and caused a record skip as D-Nice froze, trying to decide what to play for the former FLOTUS—he went with a Beyoncé set. The virtual party, broadcast over Instagram Live, featured a simple webcam shot of D-Nice—bopping in a white T-shirt, wire-framed glasses, and a rotating array of wide-brimmed hats—standing at his digital DJ setup in Los Angeles and curating sets of classic R&B, soul, old-school hip-hop, dance music, nineties pop, and the occasional salsa or Afrobeat offering. Somewhere in the fifth hour, Mark Zuckerberg dropped in like a club owner swinging by to check out the revenues before heading home for the night. Like any great impresario, Jones made sure his audience knew why it wanted to be there: hyping his next set, shouting out friends and new celebrity arrivals. In between, he offered the occasional public health gem of the corona era: "Wash your hands!" and "We're in Club Quarantine, but we ain't gonna let corona stop us!"

The night was the latest step in an artistic journey for Jones, who is forty-nine and started out in the late eighties as a minor member of the hip-hop group Boogie Down Productions. (His 1990 single "Call Me D-Nice" is a semi-obscure gem of rap's golden era.) In the wake of his career as a rapper, he reinvented himself as a photographer and gained enough of a following to become a brand ambassador for Leica, only to then generate even more acclaim as a DJ. He played for Barack Obama's farewell party at the White House on October 26, 2016—a little more than a week before Donald Trump was elected president of the United States. So there was a symmetry to what he did on Saturday night, offering music as a balm, this time in the midst of calamity, not as preface to it. And there was an overlapping guest list: Michelle Obama, Naomi Campbell, and Usher had been at the White House that night and were in the virtual room on Saturday evening.

Typically, DJs feed off the energy of the crowd, and that was part of what made D-Nice's performance exceptional: he stood, in all likelihood, in an otherwise empty room and became the architect of a vibe washing over thousands of people around the world he could not see. On the first night of Club Quarantine, on Wednesday, he had about 200 listeners. By 7 P.M. eastern time on Saturday, the crowd was hovering around 19,000. The audience size was all the more impressive because Instagram ended D-Nice's live stream after sixty minutes, meaning he had to start again from scratch each hour. What could have been an impediment instead became an hourly affirmation that the crowd wanted more. At the peak, around 10:30 P.M. eastern time, he hit 105,000 listeners. There were other forms of endorsement. People sent liquor to his hotel room—by the end of the night, he could've stocked a wet bar with donations alone. Others searched for him on Venmo, trying to pay a "cover charge" as tribute.

The set at Club Quarantine followed the arc of all good things that become a little too popular: First, a small number of people intimately connected to the cause and familiar with the references—people who know exactly why he'd play Meli'sa Morgan's "Fool's Paradise" early on and Frankie Beverly's "Before I Let Go" late in the game. Then a bigger, more diverse set of folk show up, drawn by word of mouth—the scroll of A-listers popping into the room tends to have that effect. Finally comes the list of people—Joe Biden, Bernie Sanders, a Kardashian—who might not know where exactly they are, just that there's some cachet to being there. And some of these people were certainly represented by social media managers who had tuned in on their behalf. (Still, it was fun to imagine that Sanders might actually be out there with a casual slouch in his bearing, one hand grasping a Guinness stout and the other thrown in the air as salute during the Buju Banton dancehall set.)

D-Nice ended around two in the morning on the East Coast, and there was a sense that people who joined the live stream had witnessed a thing, that they might talk about his set on Club Quarantine the way older partygoers reminisce about nights spent at the Paradise Garage in the eighties. In the currency of social media, D-Nice took in a haul—600,000 new Instagram followers—but, more significantly, he took people's minds off the invisible peril that surrounds us. If our physical worlds have contracted, our virtual ones, D-Nice seemed to be pointing out, retain far broader horizons. As the set wound down, the digital crowd drifted away, back to their bottles of hand sanitizer and stockpiles of toilet paper, back to monitoring every sneeze as an omen of ill health. The virus is still around, but so is Club Quarantine. Before D-Nice signed off, he told his stragglers that he'd be spinning again at 6 P.M. on Sunday.

AMERICAN SPRING

June 22, 2020

onsider for a moment how the events of May 25 through
June 9—the days of democratic bedlam in the streets, bracketed
by the death and burial of George Floyd—would appear had they
occurred in some distant nation that most Americans have heard of
but might not be able to find on a map. Consider that, in the midst
of a pandemic whose toll was magnified by government incompe-
tence, a member of a long-exploited ethnic minority was killed by
the state, in an act defined by its casual sadism. Demonstrators pour
into the streets near the site of the killing, in a scene that is soon
repeated in city after city. The police arrest members of the media
reporting the story. The president cites a threat to law and order,
and federal agents are dispatched to disrupt protests in the nation's
capital, using tear gas and a military helicopter. These acts further
erode his already tenuous position, prompting church leaders to
rebuke him and decorated generals to question his fitness for office.

In such a scenario, the lines of conflict gain new clarity, the abuses
more unqualified horror. American commentators would compare
the successive nights of protests to the Iranian uprisings of 2009
and the Arab Spring of 2011. The U.S. State Department, depending on its allegiances, might surreptitiously aid the protesters. We

would all recognize the moment as the product of a traumatized society.

Now consider a different scenario, that the death of George Floyd did occur in another country: the traumatized version of America inhabited by black people. Fifty-two years ago, following the storm of riots that swept through 1967 and 1968, the Kerner Commission report noted: "Our nation is moving toward two societies—one black, one white, separate and unequal." Today, the weight of grief and poverty in this country still falls disproportionately on black shoulders. The eight minutes and forty-six seconds during which a Minneapolis police officer killed George Floyd as three others looked on cannot be understood outside the context of a pandemic in which African Americans have died at three times the rate of white Americans. The chaotic, angry, defiant tableaux in the streets of Minneapolis, Seattle, Los Angeles, New York, Philadelphia, Oakland, Atlanta, Chicago, Houston, Louisville, San Francisco, Indianapolis, Charleston, Detroit, Baltimore, and beyond represent a reckoning, a kind of American Spring, one long in the making and ignited not just by a single police killing. In death, George Floyd's name has become a metaphor for the stacked inequities of the society that produced them.

Race, to the degree that it represents anything coherent in the United States, is shorthand for a specific set of life probabilities. The inequalities between black and white Americans are documented in rates of morbidity and infant mortality, wealth, and unemployment, which attest that, although race may be a biological fiction, its reality is seen in what is likely to happen in our lives. The more than forty million people of African descent who live in the United States recognize this reality, but it's largely invisible in the lives of white Americans. As with men who, upon seeing the scroll of #MeToo testimonies, asked their wives, daughters, sisters, and co-workers, "Is it really that bad?," the shock of revelation that attended the video of Floyd's death is itself a kind of inequality, a barometer of the extent to which one group of Americans have moved through life largely free from the burden of such terrible knowledge.

At a congressional hearing last Wednesday, Philonise Floyd said that he hoped his brother would be "more than a face on a T-shirt, more than a name on a list that won't stop growing." The Reverend Al Sharpton cited that list, of the wrongfully dead, in the eulogy that he delivered at Floyd's funeral, naming Ahmaud Arbery, Breonna Taylor, Eric Garner, Trayvon Martin. He could have gone on: Jordan Davis, Rekia Boyd, Freddie Gray, Tamir Rice. A sentiment common among many African Americans is that these people lived and died in Black America, which is a different place from America at large—and that their deaths, most of which came at the hands of law enforcement, represent a broader reality, even though a significant number of white Americans were skeptical of its existence.

The demographics of the protests that followed those deaths tended to reflect this disparity, with overwhelmingly black crowds turning out to demand justice. But Floyd's death, and the agonizing, protracted manner in which it occurred, has produced a different reaction. Seventy-one percent of white Americans now say that racial discrimination is a "big problem." They, too, rushed into the streets. In Salt Lake City, where the black population stands at just 2 percent, huge, raucous protests stretched on for days.

Confronted with this challenge, the system went on a self-incrimination spree. In Atlanta, police officers used stun guns against two college students as they sat in a car; in Buffalo, officers shoved a seventy-five-year-old man to the ground, while others walked past as he lay bleeding; in Brooklyn, two NYPD SUVs drove into protesters. Images of such incidents spurred protests and acts of solidarity in dozens of countries. For many people, what they saw was astonishing not because it was contrary to what they'd heard of this nation but because it was similar to the repression they'd experienced at home.

Policing is inescapably a metaphor for governmental power. The impunity of the American police has been achieved by slow accretion through the decades, and with the tacit understanding that it would be deployed in great disproportion against black people. But, whatever ensues now, we are in a different moment. Officers in Atlanta, New York City, Buffalo, and Philadelphia have been charged with assault for their actions against protesters. Calls to "defund the police," stripping them of all but their core law enforcement functions and allocating resources to other community institutions, are being taken seriously; in Los Angeles, Mayor Eric Garcetti has proposed cutting up to $150 million from the police budget. Last week, Democrats in the House of Representatives announced the Justice in Policing Act, which would ban choke holds, mandate body cameras, and establish a national registry of police misconduct. In Minnesota, Governor Tim Walz endorsed a package of comprehensive police reforms. The Louisville city council passed Breonna's Law, for Breonna Taylor, banning the "no knock" warrants that enabled the police to shoot her in her home.

There have been other developments. The argument once mired in pointless circumambulation, between "All Lives Matter" and "Blue Lives Matter," has been settled. Muriel Bowser, the mayor of Washington, D.C., renamed a street leading to the White House Black Lives Matter Plaza, emblazoning the phrase on the asphalt in gigantic yellow letters. The near ubiquity of those words in the past three weeks—Amazon, Apple, and Airbnb all added some version of it to their home pages—has prompted a consideration of what this means in practical terms. Critics on social media were quick to assert that the truest endorsement of Black Lives Matter lies not in what you say on your website but in what you do for your black employees.

The American Spring has not toppled a power, but it has led to a reassessment of the relationship between that power and the citizens from whom it is derived. It has resolved any remaining questions regarding Donald Trump's utter ineptitude as president; it has laid bare the contradictory and partial democracy that the United States holds before the world as exemplary. Most significant, it has clarified our terms. Floyd's life is the awful price we have paid for a momentarily common tongue, a language that precisely conveys what we are speaking of when we say "American." Fourteen successive days of protest opened the possibility that George Floyd died in America, not simply in its black corollary. The task that remains is to ensure that more of us might actually live there.

POSTSCRIPT TO "AMERICAN SPRING"

Among the most resonant images of the tragic, brutal spring of 2020 was that of six-year-old Gianna Floyd, daughter of the slain George Floyd, stating, "Daddy changed the world." Her words recall the old Marxist aphorism that men make history but not under the circumstances of their own choosing. No one would have wanted to change the world in the way he purportedly did—as an exhibition of its capricious cruelty and calcified bias, as an object fatally acted upon in public. But it was also apparent that the child had been given those words as an insufficient solace, a ballast against the grief of his absence from all her subsequent days. There was a prevalent hope in those days that a new consciousness had been forged amid the traumatic spectacle of Floyd's death, that the little girl would be correct in her proclamation. There was good reason for this belief. Public pressure pushed Congress to take up the issue of police reform with a degree of urgency not seen since the aftermath of the 1992 Rodney King riots. Books that explored the fraught history of race in the United States rocketed to the top of the *New York Times* bestseller list. Fortune 500 companies issued pledges to initiate or expand efforts at diversifying the ranks of their employees and suppliers. Magazines promised to diversify the ranks of their contributors. Two major publishing houses appointed black women as publishers. Joe Biden's endorsement of Juneteenth as a national holiday the following year was understood as part of the remedial moment that came in the wake of those massive George Floyd protests. What ensued, however, was much more complicated.

No significant federal reforms in policing came out of the Floyd protests. The scholars whose books were eagerly read that year found themselves targets of public derision and campaigns to discredit their work. The diversity pledges that were issued in the febrile summer of 2020 were frequently slow-walked or downgraded. In retrospect, it is apparent that the assault upon black market share in American civic life began at the precise moment when the cause of racial equality seemed most ascendant. The right-wing war on anything progressive that could be tainted with the label "woke" took on added seriousness with the return of Donald Trump to the White House four years later. The net result is that, five years after Officer Derek Chauvin murdered George Floyd on South Chicago Avenue in Minneapolis, we inhabit a nation that has slid further to the right—one in which another incident like that one is more likely, not less so. Floyd did in fact change the world, but neither in the way he would have chosen nor in any way that we, immersed in the righteous, chaotic energy of that spring, might ever have imagined.

THE ESSENTIAL AND ENDURING STRENGTH OF JOHN LEWIS

July 18, 2020

B y the time John Lewis made his exit from this realm, on Friday, his life had been bound so tightly and for so long to the mythos of the movement for democracy in America that it was difficult to separate him from it. For this reason, a friend who texted me "John Lewis is gone, what are we going to do now?" was not only reacting to grief but expressing a real and common sentiment. Lewis, who spoke at the March on Washington, chaired the Student Nonviolent Coordinating Committee, and served seventeen terms in Congress representing Georgia's Fifth District, succumbed to pancreatic cancer, a ruthless and efficient plague whose diagnosis is fatal around 95 percent of the time. When he revealed his condition last December, hope persisted despite those odds, in part because, for many people, the thought of confronting the reactionary, racist, and anti-democratic realities of the Trump era without one of the nation's most potent symbols of decency was too difficult to countenance.

Those contrasts were not merely hypothetical. In 2017, when President Trump announced that he would attend the opening of the Mississippi Civil Rights Museum, Lewis said that he would not. The then White House press secretary, Sarah Huckabee Sanders, seemed to accuse Lewis of failing to show proper respect for the movement. Months earlier, Trump had attacked the Fifth District as "crime-infested" and suggested that the blame lay with Lewis. I wrote at the time that Trump's disdain for Lewis betrayed a theme: having never grasped the concept of sacrifice, the president is contemptuous of people whose lives have been defined by it. No criticism that Lewis issued about Trump was as strong an indictment as the simple facts of his life: born to Alabama sharecroppers, leader of SNCC, exemplar of humility.

The civil rights movement is best understood as a collaboration between two groups of people: the martyrs who died for the cause, and the stalwarts who were tasked with living for it. The first group is most commonly associated with Martin Luther King, Jr., whose death at the hands of an assassin cleaved an entire section of American history into before and after. But a different, strange, and particular burden befell the second group, the people who survived the manifold dangers of Albany, Anniston, Jackson, and Little Rock and were then witness to the incipient plagues of crack and AIDS, spiraling homicide rates, and mass incarceration. The survivors were tasked with institutionalizing and defending the movement's hard-won gains against the slow accretion of power by people who hoped to remake the present in the image of the past. Lewis, like his peers Andrew Young, Marion Barry, and Eleanor Holmes Norton, transitioned into elected office as the post from which he would approach this work. It was not an easy undertaking.

John Lewis ran for Congress in 1986 in a race that pitted him against his former SNCC colleague Julian Bond, by then a Georgia state senator who was well connected in the district and heavily favored to win. Lewis prevailed in a bitter contest in which, reportedly to make fighting drug abuse an issue in the campaign, he challenged Bond to take a drug test. (Bond said that it would trivialize the issue.) The bare-knuckles politicking was a departure for Lewis, who, throughout his tenure in the civil rights movement and his time as the chairman of SNCC, had been thought of as "too nice." The fact was, though, that there had always been political infighting in the movement. In 1966, Lewis was ousted as SNCC chairman by Stokely Carmichael, a brilliant orator whose militant politics were to the left of Lewis's and more reflective of the emerging radical zeitgeist. Even decades later, Lewis referred to the move as "almost like a coup."

The politics of the movement surfaced again in 2008, when I interviewed Lewis about the possibility of the first black president being elected. The conversation turned to Lewis's role in the 1963 March on Washington. He was by that time the last surviving speaker from the event, and he recalled how his speech—a firebrand condemnation of the Democratic Party that culminated in a pledge to "march through the South, through the heart of Dixie, the way Sherman did" and "burn Jim Crow to the ground—nonviolently"— had alarmed the other participants so much that several refused to participate if he gave it. The impasse was resolved when King personally oversaw a more conciliatory edit of the address.

The story was significant as part of Lewis's first-person narrative of the movement, but it also implicitly served another purpose. Lewis had been harshly criticized in his district for supporting Hillary Clinton over Barack Obama during the 2008 Democratic presidential primaries. Lewis was a superdelegate and not bound to support the same candidate as his district, which voted overwhelmingly for Obama. The old criticism of Lewis being too moderate for the moment had resurfaced and, in reminding me of that moment in 1963, he was subtly pointing to the fact that he had not been too moderate to nearly get himself killed on behalf of his constituents before many of them had even been born. It was not insignificant that Lewis was associated with a specific theater of the struggle and a particular instance of brutality. He was among the marchers attacked at the Edmund Pettus Bridge during the "Bloody Sunday" demonstrations in Selma, Alabama, that were part of the campaign for a national voting rights act. He wrote of the moment in his memoir *Walking with the Wind*, from 1998:

> The first of the troopers came over me, a large, husky man. Without a word, he swung his club against the left side of my head. I didn't feel any pain, just the thud of the blow, and my legs giving way. I raised an arm—a reflex motion—as I curled up in the

"prayer for protection" position. And then the same trooper hit me again. And everything started to spin.

Lewis, who was bleeding badly, somehow made it back across the bridge. He returned to the church that had been a staging area for the march and gave a speech denouncing Lyndon B. Johnson's priorities. "I don't know how President Johnson can send troops to Vietnam, I don't see how he can send troops to the Congo, I don't see how he can send troops to *Africa,* and can't send troops to Selma," he said.

The footage of brutal bedlam in Selma pressured Johnson to support what eventually became the Voting Rights Act of 1965. There had already been a great deal of blood spilled in pursuit of justice: two years earlier, the SCLC activist Annell Ponder and SNCC activist Fannie Lou Hamer had been arrested along with three others and beaten, Hamer by male prison inmates at the behest of the white guards; Andrew Goodman, James Chaney, and Michael Schwerner had already been murdered near Philadelphia, Mississippi; and Jimmie Lee Jackson, an activist with the Selma campaign, had been killed by an Alabama police officer just a month earlier.

In the ensuing years, it fell to Lewis to serve as the guardian of this legislation each time it came up for renewal in Congress. It is therefore difficult to reconcile the present state of the Voting Rights Act—gutted by the Supreme Court's 2013 *Shelby County v. Holder* decision—and the posthumous praise for Lewis that has emanated from the Republicans who have refused to support his signature cause. The Senate Majority Leader, Mitch McConnell, tweeted his fond remembrance of singing "We Shall Overcome" with Lewis, a claim that immediately suggests that McConnell should have been singing that song in the second person. Lewis was too good a man to be praised by Mitch McConnell.

The question posed as the news of Lewis's death broke remains: What exactly *does* one do when a figure of his stature departs? The answer may be in the last public image we have of Lewis. Last month, weakened by illness but still standing, his face obscured by a mask but still unmistakable as himself, he inspected the huge words painted on the street in front of the White House: "BLACK LIVES MATTER." Terminal cancer could not stop him from paying homage to the movement that was continuing the work to which he'd devoted his life. The answer, he seems to be telling us, is that you do more of the same.

POSTSCRIPT TO "THE ESSENTIAL AND ENDURING STRENGTH OF JOHN LEWIS"

John Lewis died in the summer of 2020 amid the Covid-19 pandemic and the pitched competition of that year's presidential election. In the moment, it was easy to recognize that his death represented the symbolic close of an era, but it was not yet possible to divine what that might mean in practical terms.

Notably, a blitz of lawsuits over voting regulations made their way through the courts that summer and fall, all of them with the hope of either dilating or constricting access to the ballot. Earlier that year, Wisconsin Republicans, fearful of the presumed Democratic edge in mail-in ballots, sued to prevent the state from enacting an extended deadline for absentee voting. The suit forced residents, particularly those in overwhelmingly blue areas of the state, to vote in person despite the ravages of the pandemic. Similar efforts took place among Republicans in Michigan, Arizona, New Mexico, and Minnesota. References to the phantom concern of "voter fraud" became increasingly prominent as Republicans tried to rationalize this pursuit. The move contained both echoes of the past and harbingers of the immediate future. The language of "election integrity" likely registered with the ailing congressman as a throwback to the rhetoric of the Southern officeholders who sought to maintain black disenfranchisement in the 1950s and 1960s. Those words also forecast what we would see in the upcoming presidential election. In the wake of his electoral defeat that November, Donald Trump immediately bandied accusations of voter fraud. Notably, he alleged that the results in Fulton County, Georgia, which largely overlaps with the city of Atlanta, Philadelphia, Pennsylvania, and Milwaukee, Wisconsin, required further examination. Those areas contained—not coincidentally—the largest concentrations of black voters in their respective states. His supporters launched a campaign of intimidation and harassment directed at poll workers in precincts that voted overwhelmingly for Biden. The eventual Trumpist efforts to overturn the results of the presidential election by interrupting the certification of votes centered on the canard of voter fraud.

John Lewis did not live to see all this transpire, but he knew better than most how volatile the forces seeking to restrict black suffrage could be. We find ourselves once more standing amid the bedlam of the Edmund Pettus Bridge, struggling to find our way to the other side of it.

WHAT BLACK HISTORY SHOULD ALREADY HAVE TAUGHT US

November 5, 2020

As the rites of settling the 2020 presidential election stretched past Tuesday night and into Wednesday morning, the weary analysts on cable news began sounding a similar theme. The presidency would be decided not simply by a handful of swing states but by a small grouping of districts within those states. That responsibility fell largely to Milwaukee, Detroit, Philadelphia, and Atlanta—places with disproportionately black and Democratic voting populations. Two of the four cities, Philadelphia and Atlanta, experienced high-profile shootings of black men by police in the months leading up to the election; a third, Milwaukee, is just forty miles north of Kenosha, Wisconsin, where a third such incident took place. "Democracy is on the ballot," we have heard ceaselessly since the beginning of the presidential primary season. The nation could not come back, many warned repeatedly, from a second term under Donald Trump. The fact that a congenitally moderate figure such as Joe Biden could draw this conclusion gave ballast to an idea that many people have recognized from the moment that Trump's 2016 campaign began to gather momentum: that he represents an existential threat to the nation's democratic traditions. And, if this is true, it also means that, to a great degree, the future of American democracy hinges on the actions of black people living in places that this system has consistently failed.

This year marks the centennial of the ratification of the Nineteenth Amendment and the 150th anniversary of the ratification of the Fifteenth Amendment. Between them, the two acts enshrined the franchise for women and for black men—an expansion of the compact of democracy that seems even more notable given that, in this election, black women, a population that required two constitutional amendments and the Voting Rights Act to gain the franchise, have voted for Biden at a rate of 91 percent. The Nineteenth Amendment, which came in the midst of Progressive Era reforms to American society, was the yield of an interracial movement that pushed for suffrage as a fundamental right of citizenship—and its significance has been rightly commemorated this year. But the animating principles of the Fifteenth Amendment have gone comparatively unnoticed. The amendment was part of an audacious Republican plan to create a new—and, likely, Republican—black electorate to counterbalance the white, mostly Democratic voting bloc in the South. In 1860, Southern Democrats, flush with the disproportionate power granted to them by the Electoral College, had torn the Union in half and instigated four years of bloody internecine warfare. Mindful of this history, in December 1868 Senator Aaron Cragin of New Hampshire and Representative William Kelley of Pennsylvania introduced drafts of what eventually became the Fifteenth Amendment. Black voters were meant to be a bulwark against a similar regime arising to again threaten national unity—which is to say that people who had scarcely ever experienced democracy were now among its chief safeguards. The lynching campaigns and terrorism that disenfranchised black people in the South in the decades that followed weren't only an expression of racism, though they were very much that; they were an attack on the mechanisms that were put in place to inhibit one of the nation's worst habits: a gleeful expression of defiance toward a government that dared try to uphold democracy.

The symmetry of the two moments, then and now, is nearly too heavy-handed to be believed. But here we stand, a century and a half later, biting nails and trading internet memes about which OutKast song best describes the undeterred tide of black voters in Fulton County, Georgia—part of the late John Lewis's district—who, it had been hoped, would deliver the state to Biden and put the election in the history books. On Tuesday night, in an overt attempt at voter suppression, the president tweeted that the ongoing tallying of votes was a "fraud" and an attempt to steal the election from him. The next day, the administration filed suit to prevent the counting of votes in Michigan and Pennsylvania, a move that echoed the lawsuit filed by Texas Republicans to throw out 127,000 votes in Harris County, Texas, which happens to be among the most ethnically diverse counties in the country.

Two weeks ago, FBI agents showed up at the homes of Alicia Garza and Patrisse Cullors, two founders of the Black Lives Matter movement, and informed them that their names were on what appeared to be a hit list that was discovered during the arrest of a suspected white supremacist in Idaho. Garza tweeted, in response, "This is why this president is so dangerous. He is stoking fires he has no intention of controlling." Later that week, the journalist Nikole Hannah-Jones noted that antagonism toward *The New York Times Magazine*'s "1619 Project"—which she oversaw and which, in some corners, has been widely assailed for asserting that racism is foundational to the United States—had become so intense that she received threats that her and her mother's homes would be burned to the ground. The injustice here is not simply the fact that three black women were given cause to fear for their safety for having done work intended to further the cause of democracy but that such work falls so disproportionately to them in the first place.

The parameters of American democracy correlate neatly with the parameters of the nation's racial hypocrisy. This is not a secret; it helps explain why, for instance, a large part of Russian disinformation during the 2016 election sought to exacerbate racial divisions within the country. From the time of the abolitionists, the attempt to point out the fault lines in our democracy—for all our good—has been greeted with violent hostility. But our commitment to democracy was never as unblemished as our national vanity supposed, and our institutions were always more vulnerable to the kinds of corruption that Trump has enacted with astonishing speed. And America's margins have often been the best vantage point from which to survey the weaknesses.

To be black in the first week of November 2020 is to yet again have the feeling of being called off the bench and being told that the whole game is riding on you. Trump is a dangerous man, but he is not nearly as dangerous as the history that animates him. He has retained the allegiance of more than sixty million voters despite a shattered economy and the deaths of nearly a quarter million American victims of Covid-19. He still has a chance to be reelected, and Biden's proposition about how much of him democracy can withstand might yet be put to the test. "Either the United States will destroy ignorance or ignorance will destroy the United States," W. E. B. Du Bois said in a speech to the Niagara Movement. The enduring value of the history that black people have amassed is to facilitate the former proposition. But it is particularly hard, this week, to not look around and suspect that ignorance still has more than a puncher's chance at the title.

WHY IMPEACHMENT DOESN'T WORK

February 22, 2021

Last weekend, forty-three members of the United States Senate voted to acquit former president Donald J. Trump of inciting the insurrection at the Capitol on January 6, which claimed the life of a police officer and four protesters and could have resulted in the deaths of members of Congress. Fifty Democrats and seven Republicans voted to convict Trump, but they fell far short of the sixty-seven votes that would have made him, in addition to being the only president to be impeached twice, the first president to be convicted in a Senate trial. The Republicans who sided with the Democrats are already facing intense blowback from their party, and some are facing it from their own state delegations. As it stands, weaponizing a mob to lay siege to a coequal branch of government, and standing idly by as it ransacks Congress and hunts for elected officials, is apparently consistent with the presidential oath to "preserve, protect, and defend" the Constitution. Or, at least, a president's weaponizing a mob is apparently not ground for keeping him out of office.

Back in December 2019, during Trump's first impeachment for abuse of power and obstruction of Congress, House Speaker Nancy Pelosi repeated a question that Representative Elijah Cummings, who had died just two months earlier, had told her would be asked of them: "What did we do to make sure we kept our democracy intact?" Pelosi answered her friend by saying, "We did all we could. We impeached him." It was then inconceivable that, exactly a year later, the House of Representatives would be taking a second vote for the same purpose. It is possible that the two impeachments will remind posterity of the Democratic Party's intransigent opposition to the corruption, authoritarianism, and bigotry that defined the Trump administration. But it is equally possible that Trump's matching set of trials will establish another point: the overall weakness of impeachment as a device to rein in the presidency. If a weapon is truly potent, you probably don't have to use it twice.

Still, impeachment holds the aura of nuclear authority in politics; it's so fearsome that its mere existence serves as a deterrent. Prior to Bill Clinton's impeachment in 1998, only one other president, Andrew Johnson, had been subjected to the process, and just the prospect of it was evidently sufficient to force Richard Nixon's hand toward resignation in 1974. Trump's dual acquittals have been seen as a product of the Republican Party's obsequious fealty to him. But, although much was made of Senator Mitt Romney's having the courage to be the sole Republican defector in Trump's first trial—he voted to convict on the article of abuse of power—it was even more notable that Romney was the first senator ever to vote for the conviction of a president from his own party. That fact suggests that the bar for conviction would not likely have been met for any president in our current political climate. By contrast, Nixon *might* have represented an exception to this pattern. In 1974, the Democrats controlled the House by a significant margin and held fifty-seven seats in the Senate—not enough to convict on a strict party-line vote. But Nixon's advisers warned him that a conviction might be possible; we'll never know, since he resigned before the House could vote. But, long before Donald Trump's extremism took hold, there was reason to be skeptical of impeachment's power.

Impeachment has a long history, dating back to fourteenth-century England. The framers of the United States Constitution adopted it as part of counterbalancing measures meant to prevent any one branch of government from gaining too much power. The supermajority requirement of a two-thirds vote in the Senate (as opposed to the simple majority required to confirm Supreme Court justices) ensured that the practice would be less likely to be abused. And, as with all the provisions of the Constitution, impeachment was designed before American political parties had become a force in electoral politics. There was no way to consider the ultimately dominant effect that partisanship would have on the process, since the partisans had not yet officially emerged.

Partisanship not only explains the dynamics of last weekend's vote; it has also been a crucial factor in each presidential impeachment that preceded it. No president has been impeached while his party held a majority in the House, and only a very small number of representatives have ever crossed over and voted to impeach a president from their own party. Impeachment is, at best, a tool that can deliver justice when a president's party is a congressional minority and, at its worst, a mechanism whose bar for success is so high as to nullify its own utility.

When Bill Clinton was impeached for perjury in grand jury testimony and obstruction of justice, Republicans held 228 seats in the House of Representatives to the Democrats' 206. Both articles passed with nominal bipartisan support: five Democrats supported each measure, while five Republicans voted against the perjury charge, and twelve opposed the obstruction of justice charge. In the Senate, forty-five Democrats—the entire caucus—and ten of the fifty-five Republicans voted to acquit Clinton of perjury. Five Republicans joined the unified Democratic caucus to acquit him of obstruction of justice. In the days following the second Trump impeachment, Pelosi and Joe Biden called the vote bipartisan, which it technically was; ten Republicans had voted with them. But, given the scale of difference between Clinton's offenses—evidence of his character flaws and his self-preserving prevarications—and Trump's attempt to incite a coup at the cost of human lives, the ten crossovers in the House seem astoundingly meager.

In 1868, when Andrew Johnson was impeached on charges that included violating the Tenure of Office Act by firing Edwin Stanton, the secretary of war, there were forty-five Republicans in the

Senate and just nine Democrats—most of the states of the former Confederacy had not yet been readmitted to the Union. Though Johnson had served as vice president to the most noted Republican in U.S. history, he was a lifelong Democrat who detoured into the National Union Party during the Civil War, in 1864, in order to run with Abraham Lincoln, who had done the same. Johnson's former Democratic colleagues in the Senate voted as a bloc to acquit him of all three charges, as did ten Republicans, resulting in a tally that fell one vote short of the two-thirds required, even in that diminished chamber, for conviction and removal from office.

There's a belief that congressional censure of presidential wrongs, rather than impeachment, might create less partisan outcomes, but history doesn't suggest that it would. Four presidents—Andrew Jackson, James Buchanan, Lincoln, and William Howard Taft—have been subjected to censure attempts that resulted in the adoption of a resolution, and none of the measures were introduced by members of their own parties. Jackson's fellow Democrats eventually expunged the censure directed at him. The fact is that there is precious little that can be expected to check the behavior of presidents when their parties control Congress. Last week, in a passionate summation of the case against Trump, Representative Jamie Raskin asked, "What is impeachable conduct, if not this?" It is the question that has been lodged in the consciousness of every reasonable American since the scenes of bedlam began to play out on January 6. The answer, as difficult as it might be to countenance, is: "Maybe nothing."

POSTSCRIPT TO "WHY IMPEACHMENT DOESN'T WORK"

In the winter of 2021, it was possible, though decidedly optimistic, to think of the issues raised in this piece as concerns for some crisis in the distant future. Congress's second consecutive failure to convict Donald Trump had removed any illusions about the potency of impeachment as a tool for political reform, but

Trumpism itself seemed like a spent movement. The normally invertebrate South Carolina senator Lindsey Graham had publicly broken with Trump; Republican officeholders who had been forced to scramble into hiding when MAGA mobs stormed the U.S. Capitol and attacked dozens of police officers could no longer credibly turn a blind eye to the volatility at the core of Trump's movement. The tradition of the peaceful transfer of power between two rival parties, dating back to Thomas Jefferson succeeding John Adams in 1800, had been irrevocably interrupted at the behest of an egomaniacal demagogue.

While a congressional conviction would have prohibited Trump from holding elected office in the future, it seemed possible that he had rendered himself politically unviable. This viewpoint vastly underestimated the persuasive power of outrageous lies in public life. In short order Republicans who had witnessed the worst of the attack on January 6, 2021, began to refer to the events of that day as a "peaceful protest," despite more than a hundred Capitol police officers requiring medical attention as a result of the mob attacks. By the preliminary stages of the 2024 election, the insurrection had been so sufficiently memory-holed that Trump could speak openly of pardoning the hundreds of participants who had in the interim been convicted of federal crimes related to their actions that day.

Pollsters and political scientists will parse the precise dynamics that allowed Donald Trump to win reelection in November 2024, but at least one of them is already obvious: the partisan cowardice on display in the second impeachment vote. Throughout the campaign season, Joe Biden and then Kamala Harris made the case of Trump's unfitness for the Oval Office. A more fundamental concern should have asked why he was still eligible for it in the first place.

SHAKA KING GRAPPLES WITH HOLLYWOOD AND HISTORY

February 25, 2021

Earlier this month, *Judas and the Black Messiah,* Shaka King's chronicle of commitment, love, and betrayal inside the Illinois chapter of the Black Panther Party, opened in theaters and began streaming on HBO Max. The film arrives at a charged moment, during a Black History Month in which the traumatic memories of the summer of reckoning are still fresh and questions raised by the deaths of George Floyd and Breonna Taylor at the hands of the police remain unresolved. King started work on *Judas and the Black Messiah* four years ago, but those same contemporary questions are an inescapable subtext to the film and the killing at the center of it. The thriller is also a stark departure from King's début feature, *Newlyweeds,* an exploration of weed culture through the lens of a couple whose love of each other is equaled only by their love of marijuana. By contrast, *Judas and the Black Messiah,* which depicts the relationship between Fred Hampton, the charismatic leader of the Panthers' Illinois chapter, and William O'Neal, an enigmatic FBI informant who infiltrates the party, is thematically darker and weightier.

King, who is forty, was immediately drawn to the comedy duo Keith and Kenny Lucas's pitch for the movie, which they described as "*The Departed* inside the world of COINTELPRO." But he also recognized that, for a film about a twenty-one-year-old black radical murdered by the police, the politics of securing studio backing would be as daunting as the artistic challenge of telling Hampton's story well. During our recent conversation, which has been edited for length and clarity, we spoke about the complexities of making black biopics (and why this isn't one), the politics of casting black British actors to play black Americans on screen, and how he situates himself inside this moment of creative ferment for black filmmakers and artists.

Let me start with the fundamental question, which is: how much did you know about Fred Hampton before you started this project?

I knew how he passed away. Knew that he was a Black Panther. Knew he was twenty-one years old. Knew that the FBI had assassinated him, and knew that he was the head of the chapter in Chicago. But that's about it. Didn't know anything about William O'Neal at all. Didn't know he was drugged the night of the assassination. And didn't know anything about the way he lived whatsoever.

Hampton occupies this niche where he's exceptionally well-known to the people who know him, and not at all known to people outside of that. And I wonder if that presented challenges in approaching this story.

Only in the sense of getting a "Fred Hampton biopic"—and I put that in quotes—made. And that's why you couldn't do it. Maybe after this movie, if it's successful, you could—truth of the matter is, you need a limited series to do it any justice. If you want to tell the story in full, you can't do it in a movie. It's too dense, too expensive. That's really the primary reason that you couch that movie in genre.

You've said that this is a kind of seventies crime thriller film.

Yeah. But you have to couch it in genre—like, you are only touching upon the name recognition, which is the biggest hurdle. First of all, there are fewer biopics being made now, because most of the movies being made are tentpole franchises: existing properties, remakes, and sequels. So, the window for what people call quote-unquote adult movies is shrinking. And you also have to take into account that if you're talking about a biopic of someone like Fred Hampton, you're talking about a period piece. So, automatically, your minimum budget is probably going to be somewhere in the $10 to $15 million range. And it's a movie with set pieces, so you're going to go up north of that. And once you go north of that, then you're talking about, where's the Louis Armstrong, Joe Louis, Rosa Parks? People who are iconic, across the globe. Taught in schools. On stamps. No biopic. Doesn't exist for them. So, the likelihood of you getting a traditional Fred Hampton biopic made is minimal.

Did you know that going in? Or was there a point after you started the project when you realized, OK, we have to make this a genre film?
I knew it, and it came to me that way. The Lucas brothers [Kenny and Keith Lucas] brought the idea to me. They said, "We want to make a movie about Fred Hampton and William O'Neal that's *The Departed* inside the world of COINTELPRO." I'd spent long enough *trying* to get into the industry, and long enough in it, to know that that was the only way you'd get a movie like that made. And that was the genius appeal of it. *Panther* has a similar conceit.

You mean the Mario Van Peebles movie, from 1995, about the Panther party?
Yeah. It wouldn't surprise me if that's part of the reason that he has that element in there, because that's how you get the movie made in Hollywood.

How long did it take for you to come up with the script, and what process did you go through to create it?
The Lucas brothers came to me with an outline. I started working with them on that. And then I was introduced to Will Berson, my co-writer on the screenplay, via Jermaine Fowler. Will Berson had a traditional Fred Hampton biopic that he'd written and he'd been trying to attach a director to, and I grabbed him and I said, "Hey, do you

want to collaborate with myself and the Lucas brothers on making the movie this way?" And so, he and I sat down and started working on a script. And the draft we showed Ryan [Coogler], we probably took about four to six months to write it. And then Ryan Coogler and Charles King came on board. And they developed several drafts with us—way more than several. And then Warner Bros. came on board, and then we developed some more drafts with Warner Bros. Altogether, it took about three and a half to four years to write. I mean, we were still writing while we were shooting, so four years.

I read that, as part of your research, you read Alondra Nelson's *Body and Soul*, about the Black Panther Party's medical work and the health disparity work that the party did. I happen to have spoken to Alondra Nelson not long ago—she was a colleague of mine at Columbia for a long time—and she'd watched the movie and really had high praise for it.
That's excellent to me. I'm happy to hear that. There's a high bar, rightfully so, for people who have been passionate about this story and this history for a long time. And so, I'm always curious, and very accepting of critique. I think I know the film's shortcomings artistically and politically. I'm certainly the most aware, having gone through it, of what is possible within the industry. And I hope that I can help illuminate that, because I think, for a lot of people who watch movies, and even people who critique films, there's a real disconnect between their understanding of what they watch and their understanding of how it gets made.

So, what do you think those are, when you say there are artistic or political shortcomings?
Well, I think, just from an artistic standpoint, it's tough to make that much story fit within the confines of a two-hour movie, which is the movie we had the budget to make. We weren't afforded the luxury of making a three-hour biopic. We didn't get the money that you got to make *Lincoln* or *Once Upon a Time in Hollywood* or most period pieces of this scope. What we pulled off is quite miraculous. But also, it was so important to us to make sure that the family specifically was

comfortable with us making this film. Fred Hampton, Jr., and Akua Njeri were cultural consultants on the movie, which took about a year and change for us to get to that space.

Everything I had heard about William O'Neal prior to meeting the family, and meeting the Illinois chapter members personally, had stated that he was Fred Hampton's bodyguard, but that's a total lie. It's not true. And our scripts until that point were far more traditional, in the sense that you had these two guys' relationship, this friendship—there are scenes that were cut from the movie, that we shot, that convey a closeness, or that up the drama of the movie, the tension of the movie, that are not historically accurate, that are actually damaging the legacy of Chairman Fred Hampton. And they're not in there. They make a better movie, but they fuck up the history. We made the choice to not pollute the history. Not everybody does that.

The argument that people make on the other side is that this is a film, it's a work of art, there's license. I talked with one filmmaker about another period piece relating to African Americans. And he said to me, straight up, "It's not my job to teach history." And so, it's interesting that you made that decision.
I'm not gonna fault that individual, because I think that's a subjective choice. But you're talking about a group of people who were deeply traumatized, and to not acknowledge that trauma just to make a piece of entertainment is fucked up to me. I don't think that that's fair, to not engage them. And the thing is, I feel almost hypocritical, because it wasn't like we engaged *everyone* who went through that experience. But we definitely made an attempt to talk to anybody who was willing to talk to us about this, who had been through it. But, on a personal level, I don't think of public domain the same anymore. You form relationships with these people. Ultimately, the movie overall is far better off for it. But, at the same time, artistic license—you have it, but you don't fully have it.

In terms of the politics of the film, I actually don't think those take a great hit. We don't get a chance to really touch on their anti-imperialism stance. I wish I'd had that third hour to incorporate some of that. Another thing is, when you couch a political movie in genre, you have to keep the people who came to the movie for the genre invested in the genre while also trying to give them the politics of it. So, it's tricky. And we tried. I mean, the first words you hear Fred Hampton speak are "We're not gonna fight capitalism with black capitalism." We were intentional with that. Like, OK, say it, but then let's see it practiced. What does a socialist lifestyle look like? There's this coalition-building, people living together, always talking about the people, the people, the people—versus, in O'Neal, someone who's embraced a more capitalist ideology. What's that look like? Individualistic, self-interested: "I want this. I will attain this by any means necessary." And so, we tried to express up top and then personify throughout. And I think we threaded the needle pretty damn well.

What's interesting about this artistically is the emphasis on O'Neal. I remember when O'Neal killed himself—and he always struck me, even in the history of the Panthers and the oral history of what happened, as a kind of enigmatic figure—not really knowing where he comes from, what his motivations are, how he sees himself. In that clip at the end of the film, where he talks about himself as being part of the struggle, it almost seems delusional.
That's exactly what it is. He's lying to himself. The interviewer so, so wisely keeps trying to make him talk about going to the apartment afterward and seeing the carnage. And O'Neal is, like, "I can't, I can't, I can't do it." And you see him crack. So he was affected by it. The entire interview, he says "us" and "we," and he's interchangeably talking about the FBI and Black Panthers. So he's a man without a country up until the end. And that last line—one of the reasons we include it is because it feels like a guy trying to lie to himself, and lie to you, and, in my opinion, not doing that great a job. And that postscript says, "See? It didn't work."

Your first film, *Newlyweeds,* was a kind of exploration of weed culture as understood through two people. This film is a radical

departure from that. Were you at all intimidated by doing something so different, and something that was so overtly political, with stakes that were so much higher?

I wasn't intimidated, because I'd watched so many—my favorite genre of movie is seventies crime dramas. And I've made a lot of different kinds of stuff. I make movies, yes, but I've made shorts over the years, and I've directed TV. I've always felt incredibly comfortable directing actors and telling stories visually. The only thing that maybe intimidated me a little bit was the action, because I had no experience doing action. But I felt equipped in my crew. I had Sean Bobbitt, who is incredible at action, as my director of photography, and I had Larnell Stovall, who's also incredible at action, as my stunt coordinator. And I knew what I wanted.

This is also a film about the criminal justice system—in part federal, but also, in Fred Hampton's death, the local Chicago PD. And I think the scene where we see Hampton's death recalls Breonna Taylor's death, for a lot of people. Was what was going on in the country, with George Floyd's and Taylor's deaths, in your mind as this film was being completed? Did you know that it would be the context that the film would be released into?

I did know that. And, I mean, it's been a wave, you know? When the rebellions were jumping off across the country, it was trippy. I'm a very pessimistic person, generally. I remember hearing elders— like, my friend's mom was involved with Angela Davis. And she called my friend this summer, crying with joy, optimistic about the change that she thought was maybe on the horizon, like, "I've never seen anything like this." You had all these young white kids out in the street, but knowing their position was, like, "Look, I'm gonna let black folks lead out here." Because of a family member's health issues, I couldn't risk leaving my house during quarantine. But my friends who were out, they were just, like, "Yo, it's crazy." So, there was a part of me that wondered what the relevance of the film would be, in the sense of, Will it feel like we're out of step in terms of the politics of this country? Will the world be more radical than the film?

It's wild that that would even be a question with a film about Fred Hampton.

[*Laughs*] I mean, three days later, I was, like, "Nah, I don't think so. I'm not so worried about that."

Three days is a long time, comparatively speaking!

I eventually got to a place where I just said, "Well, the movie's coming out at the time it's supposed to come out." When I think of the sheer impossibility of something like this even getting made, and the amount of people who tried in the past to get a movie about Fred Hampton out there, and the challenges that they faced, and the fact that we were able to make it happen—and one of the reasons is because the family said yes. That was a big deal. They said no a lot of times—a *lot* of times.

What made them say yes to this?

I think there's a number of factors. But you'd have to ask them, because they know the full truth. I can't say that I could tell you why.

There were references, which stood out to me, about the internal factionalism in the party, and some of the violence that was happening among Black Panther Party members. And it was interesting, because you have Jesse Plemons's character, Roy Mitchell, describing the Black Panther Party as the counterpoint to the KKK, which is a false analogy. But, at the same time, you do make reference to the fact that there were violent and pretty much indefensible things that were happening within the party itself.

We make reference to [the alleged FBI informant] George Sams, who many say organized the murder of this individual who he labeled an informant. But, you know, it's really interesting—I read about George Sams, and he, it seems, had real serious mental health issues. He was not just a danger to himself but very dangerous to others. And I remember reading an article in *The New York Times,* when researching for the film, just about how the FBI would intentionally seek out individuals with a history of mental health issues as informants, partially because they could always be, like, "Well, this person is crazy. Not true. They're crazy." William O'Neal did things that aren't in the movie—people think they're not in the movie to protect William O'Neal's image. They're actually to protect the Panthers' image. You know, he built an electric chair.

Wow.

And he threatened to use it on anyone who he'd claimed was a rat. It was ultimately destroyed. They talked about kicking him out as a result. He was not kicked out, for whatever reason. But that's a deranged thing to do. I also think that, to view the rise and fall of the party, on a national scale—you read books by some of the members of the Oakland and LA chapters, who talk about some of the really dangerous rough patches that Huey Newton went through toward the end of the party, and you realize the toll that trauma takes. Just constantly in prison. Comrades getting killed left and right. Your house being raided, your phone being tapped—you don't know who to trust. And I think that that trauma led, in some instances, to interpersonal violence. Trauma contributed to that significantly.

There was the gigantic shoot-out in Los Angeles between the Panthers and the LAPD. And two other Black Panthers, John Huggins and Bunchy Carter, were killed at UCLA. Hampton was one of multiple people who died in that same spell in 1969.
There's a direct connection between the Chicago and LA raids. It was a concerted effort during that time period, specifically the month of December, to wipe out the party on a national level. There were a bunch of different raids like that, chapter by chapter, around the country. Which is how you know this was a government-led conspiracy.

Coordinated, right. It's also interesting that this film comes out within weeks of Sam Pollard's documentary, *MLK/FBI*. There's really this explosion of black cinema now—and a lot of it exploring political themes. *Get Out*, Ryan Coogler's *Black Panther*, but also, clearly, *Fruitvale Station*, his first film. We've had the biopic

of Harriet Tubman, and Regina King's film *One Night in Miami* just came out. Do you see yourself as being part of a flourishing of black film?

Yeah, I mean, whether I see myself as part of it or not, I am without question part of it. My friend Mtume Gant, who's a filmmaker, he came up with one of my favorite phrases: "the black-excellence industrial complex." And it's not exclusively related to movies or television. Even hashtags, you know? The rise of, like, Black Girl Magic. For a really long time, outside of probably music, and maybe a little bit of fashion, the things that we made, on a cultural level, were dismissed. Not worth nothing, but worth less. I know this for a fact because I literally had a sales agent, when my movie got into Sundance, tell me that the reason I wasn't going to sell my movie was because there were no famous black actors in it.

You're talking about *Newlyweeds*?

Yeah. And I was, like, "But Sundance breaks actors! I don't know any of these white actors." And he was, like, "Yeah, but they're white." He just told me that, flat out.

Wow.

And I deeply appreciate that man's honesty, because when I came away from Sundance, even though I was sad, I didn't blame myself. And right around that year, things changed. I think *Fruitvale Station* was one of the movies that jump-started the black-excellence industrial complex. *Selma* was another. *Moonlight. Atlanta.* Certain pieces of pop culture moved it along and galvanized the studios' interest, because they saw the profitability. And not just the studios. Everybody got it. It was, like, yeah, we can make money on Black History Month, or we can make money twelve months a year.

I read that Barry Jenkins and Ava DuVernay—and, of course, Ava is as responsible for this moment as anybody in terms of her pioneering work—that they gave you feedback on early versions of this project. It's fascinating that there's a critical mass of people that now have at least some shared cultural references to know where you're coming from on a project.

The upside is that I get to make movies. I get to help other people make movies; other people help other people make movies. There's more stuff being made. Our success—this movie literally stands on the shoulders of *Black Panther*. It doesn't get made if *Black Panther* doesn't get made. And, hopefully, a movie will stand on our shoulders at a certain point. That's a great thing. The fact that I could have Barry Jenkins and Ava DuVernay watch a cut of my film and give me not just artistic guidance but intentional, political guidance: "What are you trying to say here? What do you want people to take away from this?" We have thoughtful, intelligent people who've been through this process and not only know how to make a movie but know how to get people to watch a piece of material and understand it. That's major.

Yeah, I was looking at this body of work and wondering if people would be studying this ferment of black cinema and black creativity, at this moment, in the way that people are studying the directors of the 1970s—heralding a particular moment in American cinematic history.

At some point, it wouldn't surprise me. I mean, it's the same way that we talk about, like, "Look at those great Mexican directors, and the work they've done to support one another, and how their movies are incredible." As treacherous as this industry can be, you really need community as a non-white artist. And it can be treacherous with everybody. It's like a battleground. But, obviously, it's always harder for us.

Previously, with *Harriet* and in a couple of other instances, there's been this murmur of criticism about casting black British actors as characters that are black American. Did you give that any thought? What do you think of those criticisms?

Oh, I have so many thoughts. I thought about these things a little bit prior, 'cause *Harriet* came out when I was still writing it. Daniel [Kaluuya] and I have talked about it at length. He actually brought it up to me the first time, and he was surprised at how little I cared. [*Laughs*] But to start with, for me—my mom's from Queens, right? Her dad was from Panama. Her mom was from Barbados. My father's from Panama. They named me after a South African king. And my house is full of African art. My parents are very Afro-centric parents. So, I come from a very diasporic way of thinking. Growing up, all I knew was, we're black. We're African. So, foundationally, that wasn't a big issue for me.

On top of that, from an artistic perspective, I have a very high intuitive artistic intelligence. I trust that instinct when I cast. Every casting decision I made, it was an intuitive choice. Many people didn't even audition. Most, we had no rehearsal. It was just: "This is the person. I know it." But I've thought a lot about this. Because the subtext of all that is not just that we don't want black British actors playing black American icons. It's really "black British actors are taking over." Personally, I don't think that's the case at all, because there are a lot of black American actors who have high visibility, who are thriving. And I think to a large degree, when you hear people talk about that, what they're really speaking to, even if they're not aware of the fact that they're doing so, is that there's a dearth, even now, of material being frontlined by black actors, period. So there's a bit of a too-many-fish, small-pond situation.

But let's also look at Hollywood math, and how Hollywood makes movies. I remember one time, one executive, the first weekend we met was the weekend of *BlacKkKlansman*'s opening, and he told us that it was going to bomb, and we told him it was gonna be a success. We saw the way people were talking about it, the culture, everything. And he was, like, "We crunched the numbers, and it's gonna bomb." And you and I both know that movie was a tremendous success. Later, when he lowballed us, I reminded him that he predicted that *BlacKkKlansman* was going to bomb because of the algorithm. And that he was using the same algorithm to determine that our movie was not going to make enough money at the box office to give us the money requested. That proved to me that even the math in Hollywood is racist.

I recognize that the reason we were lowballed is because there's still a widely held mistruth that movies headlined by black actors don't do well overseas. The reason why I think they're more comfortable attaching British black actors to movies in that mid-budget range is because those black actors, in their minds, can at least sell you the U.K. They can maybe even sell you former U.K. colonies. It could be coincidence, but it could also be financials. What I know is it isn't this sort of cultural "black British actors have more training" nonsense that you hear spouted about. That is COINTELPRO. [*Laughs*] Like, are you familiar with ADOS?

Yeah. [*American Descendants of Slavery is a controversial movement that advocates specifically for reparations for black descendants of slaves, rather than for the black community as a whole.*]
I really do think that there's some people who believe that, and, like most movements, there's some intelligent discourse in there. But there are also people in there who literally are getting paid to sow discord amongst black people.

Mm-hmm. The very thing that you're talking about in the film.
Yes, that is absolutely the case happening there.

How has the film been received?
I've hardly looked at any of the reviews. I've read the ones that pan it. Some people just didn't agree with our approach. Some people, I think, want readership. And people, by and large, like the movie. There've been some critiques of the film, just from a craft standpoint, that have been interesting to read, and I understand what they want. Some of them, I wouldn't want to give you that anyway, because I don't agree with that aesthetic. And others, we just couldn't tell it that way because it didn't happen that way. We made the choice to move forward with the people who this mattered to most. We couldn't cut corners in places; we had to lay it out as it went. And I'm cool with it. I like the movie. As much as I look back at *Newlyweeds,* and there's so many things in that movie that don't work, at the end

of the day, I'm, like, "That was me then." I've never made a movie, whether I liked it or not, and said, "That's not me." And I never want to. For you to come away from that and not be able to see yourself in it would just be devastating. And so, above all, I came away from a studio movie, and my people who know me are, like, "Yo, that fucking movie feels like you." And I'm so happy that I could say I had that experience.

I'll wrap up with this one question. Walter Mosley, years ago, said that his artistic mission statement, his objective, was to create worlds inhabited by black male heroes. He felt like there was a dearth of recognition of black male heroism in the world as it was, and he wanted to create a corrective to that. Do you have a defining ethic as a director, a reason that you feel you're here to make film?

No. I'm motivated by the thing that captures me and takes me on a ride. I try to be as open as possible. The one thing I will say is that, when I came to recognize that I had an ability to make things that capture people's senses, and can then influence their thoughts and choices, I did feel like I should not be exploitative, and I should seek to make things that had some utility. I come from a perspective of, everything is propaganda. And since that's the case, for example, I'll never direct a commercial. I intentionally say that publicly, so that even if I needed money and times got hard, I would have to embrace the hypocrisy of it, because I really never, ever want to do that. I recognize my power as a visual storyteller, and I don't want to do harm with that ability. But I do want space to remain creative and tell anything that comes to my mind. When I say utility, people always think, Oh, political. *Curb Your Enthusiasm* has tremendous utility to me. As does *Rick and Morty*. Watching those shows puts me in a great mood. That's utility! There is great utility to escapist art. Because life is hard, and sometimes you just need to get out of here and not think about anything related to the world. If I had any kind of parameters, it'd be that.

HOW PARTIES DIE

March 15, 2021

One of the oldest imperatives of American electoral politics is to define your opponents before they can define themselves. So it was not surprising when, in the summer of 1963, Nelson Rockefeller, a centrist Republican governor from New York, launched a preemptive attack against Barry Goldwater, a right-wing Arizona senator, as both men were preparing to run for the presidential nomination of the Republican Party. But the nature of Rockefeller's attack was noteworthy. If the GOP embraced Goldwater, an opponent of civil rights legislation, Rockefeller suggested that it would be pursuing a "program based on racism and sectionalism." Such a turn toward the elements that Rockefeller saw as "fantastically short-sighted" would be potentially destructive to a party that had held the White House for eight years, owing to the popularity of Dwight Eisenhower, but had been languishing in the minority in Congress for the better part of three decades. Some moderates in the Republican Party thought that Rockefeller was overstating the threat, but he was hardly alone in his concern. Richard Nixon, the former vice president who had received substantial black support in his 1960 presidential bid against John F. Kennedy, told a reporter for *Ebony* that "if Goldwater wins his fight, our party would eventually become the first major all-white political party." *The Chicago*

Defender, the premier black newspaper of the era, concurred, stating bluntly that the GOP was en route to becoming a "white man's party."

But, for all the anxiety among Republican leaders, Goldwater prevailed, securing the nomination at the party's convention in San Francisco. In his speech to the delegates, he made no pretense of his ideological intent. "Extremism in the defense of liberty is no vice," he said. "Moderation in the pursuit of justice is no virtue." (He delivered that famous line shortly after the delegates had defeated a platform plank on civil rights.) Goldwater's crusade failed in November 1964 when the incumbent, Lyndon Johnson, who had become president a year earlier after Kennedy's assassination, won in a landslide: 486 to 52 votes in the Electoral College. Nevertheless, Goldwater's ascent was a harbinger of the future shape of the Republican Party. He represented an emerging nexus between white conservatives in the West and in the South, where five states voted for him over Johnson.

The reason for the shift was clear. Many white Southern Democrats felt betrayed by Johnson's support of civil rights. The civil rights movement had learned how to translate grassroots activism into political power. Among government leaders, LBJ was singularly important to the passage of the Civil Rights Act of 1964, and he stood firmly behind the Voting Rights Act of 1965. In both cases, he pressed on white Southern Democrats in Congress who had long supported the racist culture and strictures of Jim Crow. Until the mid-twentieth century, it was the Republican Party, founded a century earlier by Northerners enraged by the expansion of slavery—the "party of Lincoln"—that looked more favorably upon the rights of black Americans. In 1957, it was a Republican president, Eisenhower, who deployed troops to intervene on behalf of black students in the school integration crisis in Little Rock. Goldwater's rise proved the catalyst for change. As the historian Ira Katznelson told me, Goldwater opposed the Civil Rights Act mainly for libertarian reasons: "Nonetheless, it was a signal, and opened up possibilities for a major realignment."

Establishment leaders of the GOP were concerned that Gold-water had opened up the party, which had barely emerged from the shadow of McCarthyism, to fringe groups on the far right, such as the John Birch Society—people Nixon referred to as "kooks." (Robert H. W. Welch, Jr., the founder of the society, claimed that the goal of the civil rights movement was to create a "Soviet Negro Republic.") Marsha Barrett, a historian at the University of Illinois Urbana-Champaign, who chronicles the evolving relationship be-tween civil rights and the Republican Party in her book *Nelson Rockefeller's Dilemma: The Fight to Save Moderate Republicanism*, notes that, before Rockefeller issued his broadside, George W. Lee, a black civil rights activist, businessman, and lifelong Republican, wrote to Robert Taft, Jr., the Ohio Republican who ran for Con-gress in 1962. Failing a significant intervention, Lee said, "the Re-publican Party will be taken over lock, stock, and barrel by the Ku Kluxers, the John Birchers and other extreme rightwing reactionar-ies."

Yet, once it became clear that Goldwater could win the nomina-tion, shock at his extremism on a number of issues, including the potential use of nuclear weapons, began to morph into compliance. Taft's behavior was typical of the trend. Although his family had long been a mainstay of the Republican Party—his grandfather had been president; his father, a senator—he endorsed Goldwater. Bar-rett told me that Goldwater's rise was facilitated by the fact that "some moderate Republicans were simply trying to protect their own political prospects."

In the contemporary Republican Party, the resonance is obvious. Mitch McConnell, the party's leader in the Senate, has long played this game, despising Donald Trump but knuckling under to the real-ity of his immense popularity among Republican voters. At Trump's second impeachment trial, McConnell voted to acquit but, after the vote, delivered an excoriating speech about Trump's incitement of the January 6 riot at the U.S. Capitol and the effort that day to reverse the results of the 2020 election. Days later, when asked whether he would support Trump if he was nominated by the GOP in 2024, McConnell responded, "Absolutely."

The most widely debated political question of the moment is: what is happening to the Republicans? One answer is that the party's predicament might fairly be called the revenge of "the kooks." In just four years, the GOP, a powerful, 167-year-old institution, has become the party of Donald Trump. He began his 2016 campaign by issuing racist and misogynistic salvos, and during his presidency he gave cover to white supremacists, reactionary militia groups, and QAnon followers. Trump's seizure of the party's leadership seemed a stunning achievement at first, but with time it seems more reasonable to ponder how he could possibly have failed. There were many preexisting conditions, and Trump took advantage of them. The combination of a base stoked by a sensationalist right-wing media and the emergence of kook-adjacent figures in the so-called Gingrich Revolution of 1994 and in the Tea Party have redefined the party's temper and its ideological boundaries. It is worth remembering that the first candidate to defeat Trump in a Republican primary in 2016 was Ted Cruz, who, by 2020, had long set aside his reservations about Trump and was implicated in spurring the mob that attacked the Capitol.

One of the most telling developments of the 2020 contest was rarely discussed: in August, the Republican National Convention convened without presenting a new party platform. The convention was centered almost solely on Trump; the events, all of which took place at the White House, validated an increasing suspicion that Trump himself was the Republican platform. Practically speaking, the refusal to articulate concrete positions spared the party the embarrassment of watching the president contradict them. In 2016, religious conservatives succeeded in getting an anti-pornography plank into the platform, only to be confronted by news of Trump's extramarital affair with the adult film performer Stormy Daniels. Now there would be no distinction between the Republican Party and the mendacity, bigotry, belligerence, misogyny, and narcissism of its singular representative.

Or consider the events of the past six months alone: during a presidential debate, a sitting commander in chief gave a knowing shout-out to the Proud Boys, a far-right hate group; he also refused to commit to a peaceful transfer of power, and subsequently attempted to strong-arm the Georgia secretary of state into falsifying election returns; he and other Republican officials filed more than sixty lawsuits in an effort to overturn the results of the election; he incited the insurrectionists who overran the Capitol and demanded the lynching of, among others, the Republican vice president; and he was impeached, for the second time, then acquitted by Senate Republicans fearful of a base that remains in his thrall. The fact that that behavior is commonplace does not mean it should be mistaken for behavior that is normal.

But the character of the current Republican Party can hardly be attributed to Trump alone. On January 6, even after being forced to vacate their chambers just hours earlier, 139 House Republicans and eight senators voted against certifying some of the Electoral College votes. A week later, 197 House Republicans voted against Trump's impeachment, despite his having used one branch of government to foment violence against another. Liz Cheney of Wyoming, the most senior of the ten Republicans who voted to impeach, survived an effort to remove her from her post as chair of the House Republican Conference but was censured by her state's party organization. In the House, more Republicans voted against Cheney than voted to remove Marjorie Taylor Greene of Georgia, the extremist Trump stalwart and QAnon promoter, from her committee posts. She lost those assignments, but only because the Democrats voted her out. Then, on February 13, all but seven Republican senators voted to acquit Trump in his impeachment trial.

The Trump-era Republican Party does occupy a very different niche from the party of 1964. When Trump was sworn into office, the GOP held both houses of Congress. In 2018, the Democrats won back the House; the Senate is now a fifty-fifty split. But the party still controls thirty state legislatures and twenty-seven governorships. In November, Trump, facing multiple, overlapping crises—all of them exacerbated by his ineptitude—won seventy-four million votes. Still, the Republican Party confronts a potentially existential crisis. Last year, Thomas Patterson, a political scientist at Harvard's Kennedy School of Government, argued in his book *Is the Republican Party Destroying Itself?* that, over time, the party has set a series of "traps" for itself that have eroded its "ability to govern and acquire new sources of support." The modern Republican Party was built upon the Southern beachhead that Goldwater established more than half a century ago. Johnson rightly worried that his embrace of civil rights would lose the South for the Democrats for at least a generation. In 1968, Richard Nixon won the presidency, employing the Southern Strategy—an appeal to whites' racial grievances. By 1980, the GOP had become thoroughly dependent on the white South. In 2018, some 70 percent of "safe" or "likely Republican" districts were in Southern states. Prior to last year's election, Southerners composed 48 percent of House Republicans and 71 percent of the party's ranking committee members. The South remains the nation's most racially polarized region and also the most religious—two dynamics that factor largely both in the party's political culture and in its current problems. "The South," Patterson writes, "is a key reason why the GOP's future is at risk."

In addition, the GOP's steady drift toward the right, from conservative to reactionary politics; its dependence on older, white voters; its reliance on right-wing media; its support for tax cuts for the wealthiest Americans; and its increasing disdain for democratic institutions and norms all portend increasing division and a diminishing pool of voters. Republicans, Patterson said, have been depending on a "rear-guard strategy" to "resist the ticking clock of a changing America." Time may be running out for the party, as its base ages and dwindles. "Its loyal voters are declining in number and yet have locked the party in place," Patterson writes. "It cannot reinvent itself without risking their support and, in any event, it can't reinvent itself in a convincing enough way for a quick turnaround. Republicans have traded the party's future for yesterday's America."

The marginalization of moderate Republicans has accelerated in the past decade, since the advent of the Tea Party. Moderates in Congress recognized that, if they hewed to a centrist position, they would face serious primary challenges. In 2010, conservatives revolted against the Obama administration's bailout of the banks during the housing crisis. In theory, that uprising could have spawned a cross-partisan populist alliance of the anti-corporate left and fiscal conservatives, but it was quickly subsumed by paranoid, racist currents. The same year, as debates over the Affordable Care Act came to dominate American politics, Tea Party gatherings began to resemble proto-Trump rallies, at which the first black president was sometimes lampooned as a monkey. That blend of populist rage and overt racism was the active ingredient in what eventually became the Trump movement. In the 2014 Republican primary in Virginia, when David Brat, with the support of state Tea Party activists, defeated Eric Cantor, the House Majority Leader, the GOP took note that even the most powerful conservatives faced a threat from far-right upstarts.

Some of the few remaining Republican centrists, such as Jeff Flake of Arizona, Rob Portman of Ohio, and Pat Toomey of Pennsylvania, are leaving politics entirely. Last month, Reuters reported that dozens of Republicans who had served in government during the George W. Bush era were abandoning the party. Jimmy Gurulé, who was undersecretary of the treasury for terrorism and financial intelligence, said that the Republican Party he knew "no longer exists," that what exists in its place is simply "the cult of Trump." Trump's centrality has so far survived his loss to Joe Biden and the spectacle of the Capitol riot. In states across the country, local Republican officials are working against leaders they deem disloyal to the former president. The Arizona party even censured Cindy McCain, the widow of the state's six-term senator. The result is that the party leadership sees no popular incentive to move toward the center, even as the warning signs of decline accumulate. Last year, for the first time, the number of registered independents exceeded the number of registered Republicans. In the eight presidential contests since 1988, Republicans have won the popular vote only once, in 2004.

The emergence of Trumpism as the Republican brand has also borne out the warning that the GOP would become a white man's party. In a now famous autopsy of Mitt Romney's loss to Barack Obama in 2012, analysts for the Republican National Committee argued that the party had to expand its appeal to people of color if it hoped to be competitive in future national elections. "Nothing happened," Patterson told me, speaking of the GOP's response to the report. "Right-wing media said, 'You're going to ruin America if we take the advice of the Republican National Committee.'" Today, the Republican electorate is whiter and more male by far than its Democratic counterpart. By 2020, 81 percent of Republican voters were white, and 50 percent were male.

Last November, compared to 2016, Trump made gains among some minorities, particularly Latinos, although minority groups remain overwhelmingly supportive of the Democratic Party. The gender gap between voters for Biden and those for Trump was the most pronounced in recent history: 57 percent of women voted for Biden; 42 percent voted for Trump. The GOP has also gained increasing shares of decreasing constituencies. White conservative Christians remain prominent in the party, but they are a dwindling segment of the electorate: in 2007, thirty-nine states had white Christian majorities; today, fewer than half do. In 1996, non-Hispanic whites made up nearly 85 percent of the electorate; by 2018, they were just 67 percent. In the six presidential elections since 2000, Democrats have lost the white vote every time, but prevailed in half of them even without it. The day before the 2020 election, Benjamin L. Ginsberg, a longtime Republican election lawyer who represented the George W. Bush campaign in 2000 and 2004, published an op-ed in *The Washington Post* warning that the party could find itself a "permanent minority."

The fraught discussions over the GOP's future are really debates about whether the current party is capable of adapting to modern circumstances again—or whether it will turn into a more malign version of itself, one even more dependent on white status anxieties. As Heather Cox Richardson, a historian at Boston College and the author of *To Make Men Free: A History of the Republican Party,* told me, "When you see the collapse of parties, it is usually because you have some problem of the existing party system coming up against a major new change."

The Republican Party itself was built on the ruins of the Whigs, a party that broke apart in the tempests leading up to the Civil War. Marsha Barrett mentioned a passage to me from Herbert Hoover's address to the 1936 Republican Convention, four years after he had lost the White House to Franklin Roosevelt, in which he issued a warning about what becomes of parties that fail to navigate the critical issues and circumstances of their time. "The Whig Party," Hoover said, "temporized, compromised upon the issue of slavery for the black man. That party disappeared. It deserved to disappear." Hoover was speaking in the midst of the Great Depression, but his larger point was that parties are not necessarily permanent political fixtures. Considering that history, it's worth asking whether the party of Lincoln, now the party of Trump, is engaged in conflicts so intense that it will go the way of the Whigs.

The GOP's travails echo a historical pattern. Despite the United States' reputation as the most stable democracy in the world, most of the political parties born in this country, including major ones, have ceased to exist. In addition to the Whigs, the list of those that have collapsed includes the Federalists, the Democratic-Republicans, the American Party (also called the Know-Nothings), the Free Soil Party, the Populist Party, the National Republicans, the Anti-Masonic Party, and three iterations of the Progressive Party. (The Socialist and the Communist Parties also briefly commanded public attention.) What we refer to as the two-party system has collapsed twice before. The Democratic and Republican Parties have endured as long as they have because they have significantly altered their identities to remain viable; in a sense, each has come to represent what it once reviled.

America's political parties and the party system are, in fact, accidents of history. The founders were suspicious of "factions," as parties were then called, fearing that powerful blocs would put their own regional or commercial interests above the common good and endanger the fragile union of the new nation. But, as Richard Hofstadter wrote in his 1969 book *The Idea of a Party System,* the founders' "primary paradox" was that they "did not believe in parties as such, scorned those that they were conscious of as historical models, had a keen terror of party spirit and its evil consequences, and yet, almost as soon as their national government was in operation, found it necessary to establish parties."

George Washington reluctantly ran for the presidency in 1788. He remains the only independent elected to that office. His farewell address of September 19, 1796, provides the framework for the peaceful transfer of power. (It is read aloud in the Senate every year; this year, that event occurred a week after Trump's impeachment trial had concluded there.) In the address, Washington, like a father chiding his bickering children, advised his countrymen, no matter what their political passions, to consider the fundamental bonds that connected them as Americans. Political parties were useful to check the worst instincts of a monarch, he wrote, but, in a democracy, a party

> agitates the community with ill-founded jealousies and false alarms, kindles the animosity of one part against another, foments occasionally riot and insurrection. It opens the door to foreign influence and corruption, which find a facilitated access to the government itself through the channels of party passions.

Nevertheless, that fall the nation held its first partisan election. Divisions evident in Washington's administration had solidified into formal categories: the Federalists, who supported a strong central government and favorable relations with Great Britain, coalesced around John Adams and Alexander Hamilton. The Democratic-Republicans adopted Thomas Jefferson's arguments for a decentralized government and a national alliance with France. Adams beat Jefferson in the race to succeed Washington, but, as a result of a quirk in the Electoral College at the time, Jefferson became vice president. Not only had parties come into existence; even James Madison, who had charted their dangers in Federalist No. 10, had joined one—Jefferson's Democratic-Republicans. Each side rationalized its existence by pointing to the excesses of the opposition. After Jefferson won the White House in 1800, the Federalists opposed his signature act, the Louisiana Purchase of 1803. When Madison succeeded him, they opposed the War of 1812. But both events stoked popular support across the country, which was expanding rapidly, and the elitist-oriented Federalists, nestled largely in the Northeast, soon ceased to be contenders in national politics.

The first two-party system was over, but the victor, despite having essentially unchecked one-party rule, didn't survive for long. In the 1824 election, Senator Andrew Jackson, Democratic-Republican of Tennessee and a hero of the War of 1812, won the popular vote, but no candidate achieved a majority in the Electoral College. Two of the runners-up, John Quincy Adams, the son of the first Federalist president, and Henry Clay, the Speaker of the House, formed an alliance that handed the presidency to Adams and made Clay the secretary of state. In the uproar that ensued, the party split, with each side laying claim to a portion of its name: the smaller faction, led by Adams, became the short-lived National Republicans; the larger, led by Jackson, became the Democratic Party.

Crucially, Jackson's populist allure, along with his pioneering campaigning practices, such as hosting barbecues and cultivating a national network of affiliates, meant that people did not simply vote Democratic; they began to identify as Democrats. Parties were becoming a fixture not just in America's politics but also in its social life. In 1828, Jackson defeated Adams in a landslide, and, four years later, was easily reelected. He was succeeded by his vice president and former governor of New York, Martin Van Buren, a wily political operator with consequential ideas about national affairs. Having witnessed single-party rule and the collapse of the Democratic-Republicans, he essentially turned Washington's warning on its head: a contest between parties, rather than jeopardizing democracy, could be the key to its survival, he maintained, precisely because there were so many potential economic and geographic dividing lines in the nation.

A viable second party was already in place. Henry Clay had been building a broad and loosely affiliated coalition of Jackson's opponents; they came to be known as the Whigs, and by 1836 they were in control of the main Senate committees. (Two Whigs were elected to the White House: William Henry Harrison in 1840 and Zachary Taylor in 1848.) As the historian Eric Foner wrote in *Politics and Ideology in the Age of the Civil War,* "Van Buren and many of his generation of politicians had been genuinely frightened by the threats of disunion" in earlier years. "They saw national two-party competition as the alternative to sectional conflict and eventual disunion."

Yet, to a remarkable degree, the history of political partisanship and the trajectory of American parties has been bound up with the history of race in this country. Just as the two major parties of the mid-twentieth century recognized the polarizing effect that civil rights legislation would have, the Democrats and the Whigs sought to prevent slavery from becoming the axis of national politics. Both parties were internally divided on the issue and were largely successful in keeping it at the margins of national discourse. But, in 1854, Senator Stephen Douglas, Democrat of Illinois, in an effort to build a cross-regional alliance that he hoped would help him win the presidency, introduced the catastrophically divisive Kansas-Nebraska Act, which allowed new states to decide for themselves whether they would permit or prohibit slavery. Douglas's act posed a defining dilemma to the parties, much as the Voting Rights Act of 1965 did a century later. The Democratic Party aligned firmly around its pro-slavery wing. The Whigs could neither finesse the issue nor establish a unified opposition to it, and the party dissolved. The second two-party system had ended, with stark implications for the nation, and civil war on the horizon.

Abraham Lincoln, who had returned to legal practice after serving in the House as a Whig, was so incensed by the Kansas-Nebraska Act that he decided to reenter politics. The party he joined got its start at a meeting in a schoolhouse in Ripon, Wisconsin, attended by a small group of disaffected Whigs, alienated Democrats, and Free Soilers, all of whom were furious about the act. The new Republican Party immediately possessed an asset that its predecessor lacked: clarity on the fundamental political and moral issue of the day, the expansion of slavery.

The Federalists collapsed because they failed to expand their demographic appeal; the Whigs because of internal incoherence over what they stood for in the nation's most crucial debate. Among the more striking dynamics of the Trump-era GOP is the extent to which it is afflicted by both of these failings.

The arc of political movements in this country has never been predictable. The Democratic Party, confronted with a changing nation, chose to adapt, evolving over time from a bastion of pro-slavery sentiment in the nineteenth century and of volatile racism for the first half of the twentieth to its current status as a multiracial coalition emphasizing civil, women's, and immigrants' rights. That transformation mirrors the narrative that the country likes to tell about the growth of American democracy. The Republican Party, which had a firmer grasp on that ideal at its outset, rose from a passionate opposition to the spread of slavery to become a redoubt of Confederate sympathizers and racial reactionaries, and home to the twice-impeached former president who cultivated them. Jennifer Horn, the former chair of the New Hampshire Republican Party, told me that the GOP, in its current incarnation, is "the most open embrace of an anti-democracy movement that we have seen in our country in a very long time."

Horn quit the party in December and, until recently, worked with the Lincoln Project, a group of Republicans dedicated to preventing Trump's reelection. She added, "This Republican Party cannot win a national election. Everybody will say, 'But look, Trump brought more people out than they did before.' Yes, but the opposition brought out even more people." The Republican Party appears to have decided in the wake of Trump's defeat that, particularly at the state level, it will pursue tactics, such as gerrymandering and voter suppression, that will enable it to wield power even from a minority position. Since the Civil War, Van Buren's ideas about the stabilizing effects of partisan competition have held sway in American politics. But it is increasingly reasonable to revisit Washington's perspective that, under the right circumstances, a party could become antagonistic to the health of democracy.

In the past decade, gerrymandering has taken on renewed prominence, especially as software has become more sophisticated and analytical tools make it easier to predict how individual households will vote. The Brennan Center for Justice reported that the redistricting put into effect after the 2010 census provided the GOP with at least sixteen additional seats in the House of Representatives. In 2013, the Supreme Court's decision in *Shelby County v. Holder* eviscerated a key provision of the 1965 Voting Rights Act and allowed changes to voting laws that, in the name of preventing "voter fraud"—something that has repeatedly been proved to be a nonexistent problem—made voting more difficult, particularly for minorities. Those laws were overwhelmingly passed in state legislatures controlled by Republicans. (The Brennan Center is tracking more than 250 bills, pending in forty-three states, that would restrict voting.) Last Tuesday, in *Brnovich v. Democratic National Committee,* the Supreme Court heard oral arguments on an Arizona law that effectively restricts voting access for people of color in a case that could undermine remaining protections of the Voting Rights Act; the conservative justices appeared ready to uphold the restrictions.

Michael Steele, the first black chair of the Republican National Committee, told me that these efforts are a losing strategy. We spoke in mid-January, when the images of the Capitol insurrection were still fresh. Early in our conversation, he pointed to the decades when the Democrats controlled Congress in the middle of the twentieth century as a product of the GOP's operating as a regional party, based in the Northeast, rather than as a national one. Making inroads in the Southern states was key to the party's growing influence, but the modern party, Steele told me, "is not really prepared for the ways that the country is changing"—including, again, in the South. "Virginia was a blood-red state," he said. "It was actually sort of the model of Republican strength and political power, by virtue of how the Republicans controlled the state. But what happened? By 2006, that was done. And you could see the trend line heading down 95 into North Carolina, Georgia, bringing it over into the rest of the South." Referring to the defeat of Trump, followed in January by that of the senators David Perdue and Kelly Loeffler, Steele said that the Republicans "lost Georgia not once but three times."

Steele's assessment is akin to conclusions that Rockefeller and other moderates drew in the past century. Between 1940 and 1970, about five million African Americans left the South for industrial centers in Northern and Midwestern states, which were largely Democratic strongholds. The influx changed the political calculus. Black voters had begun abandoning the Republican Party during Franklin Roosevelt's first term; now their increasing numbers in those cities meant that their concerns would carry more weight with Democrats at the state and municipal levels. "Politically, the Democrats repositioned themselves," Steele said. That process happened in fits and starts, but the Democrats' overall shift toward greater reliance on black voters and more attention to their concerns opened a breach with the party's powerful Southern wing, which Goldwater filled.

Conversely, Republicans have moved further away from emerging groups in the electorate, resurrecting political tactics that are reminiscent of the segregation-era South. "If your base is 90 percent white, and you're losing Asian Americans by two to one, the black vote by nine to one, and the Hispanics by two to one," Thomas Patterson told me, "voter suppression becomes the only viable strategic option." Just since the Senate and presidential losses in Georgia, the Republican-controlled state legislature has introduced twenty-two proposed laws that would make voting more difficult in that state; the most restrictive would limit absentee voting and early voting on weekends. (Last Wednesday, the House of Representatives passed H.R. 1, a huge reform package that would expand voting rights; no Republicans voted for it.)

Amid the storm of canards about the presidential vote tally last year, an easily discernible pattern emerged: the Trump administration contested the results in Milwaukee, Detroit, Philadelphia, and Atlanta—all of them cities with significant black populations in states that he lost. The party, Horn told me, has to admit that "we did a terrible thing. We tried to disenfranchise American voters. We targeted minority voters in Georgia and Michigan and Pennsylvania, trying to overturn democracy in America." Yet a reckoning seems nowhere in the GOP's near future. The party offered Donald Trump as its platform, and there's no indication that this state of affairs has changed since he reluctantly moved out of the White House.

Two weeks ago, attendees at the Conservative Political Action Conference, or CPAC, convened in Orlando to rally the right wing of the Republican Party. When Trump took the stage, on the last day, he was received in a manner typically reserved for politicians who have won an election. Matt Schlapp, the conference organizer, referred to Trump as "the President of the United States." Trump cycled through the now familiar grievances about "cancel culture" and bad trade deals and, unsurprisingly, flogged the false tale that his fortunes are the result of election fraud—all to rounds of raucous applause. According to a recent study conducted by the American Enterprise Institute, nearly 80 percent of Republicans hold favorable views of Trump, and two-thirds of them believe that there was widespread voter fraud in November despite clear evidence to the contrary. CPAC featured sessions that included "Protecting Elections: Part 2: Other Culprits: How Judges & Media Refused to Look at the Evidence" and "Fraudulent 2020 Elections in South Korea and the United States."

The idea that the nation would thrive with two parties was contingent upon both of them holding a shared version of reality. It's also the case that a demographic clearly in the thrall of radicalizing conspiracy theories, and convinced that it stands no chance of exercising its will through electoral politics, will potentially turn to violence as a regular form of expression. The American Enterprise Institute study found that 56 percent of Republicans believe that the use of force may be necessary to save "the traditional American way of life." The obvious concern should be that January 6 was not a culmination but, rather, a preface to more violence conducted under the same banners.

At CPAC, Trump shot down the idea that he would form a separate MAGA party, making it clear that the GOP will be cast in his likeness for the foreseeable future. "We have the Republican Party," he told the crowd. There's also the question of Trumpism's having intergenerational potential. Observers are wondering what Ivanka Trump's future looks like, and whether Lara Trump, the former president's daughter-in-law, will run for the seat of Senator Richard Burr, Republican of North Carolina, when he leaves office in 2022. (Burr voted to convict Trump in the second impeachment trial.) Jennifer Horn told me, "I maintained this hope that, if we could just beat Donald Trump, then others in the party would see that as their opportunity to come forward and say, 'OK, let's put that behind us.'" She did not anticipate the durability of Trump's version of Republicanism even after his defeat. "The party," she told me, said, "'You may have defeated Trump, but we're all in for Trumpism. Full steam ahead.'"

THE FREE STATE OF GEORGE FLOYD

July 12 and 19, 2021

Just before dawn on a warm night in early June, a line of city vehicles pulled into a four-block area in South Minneapolis that has come to be known as George Floyd Square. Groups of workers fanned out in the darkness and started removing barricades and other structures that, for nearly a year, had cut off the flow of traffic on two major thoroughfares: Chicago Avenue and East Thirty-Eighth Street. The reaction to what looked like a cross between a covert op and a public works project was immediate; residents of the mixed-income neighborhood began texting and posting a flurry of messages on social media as they streamed out of their homes. Across town, one of those texts reached Jay Webb, a gardener and caretaker of the Square. He got dressed and hustled out the door. Another observer said in a video on Instagram, "Greetings from GFS. They're coming! They're coming!"

Since last summer, the barricades had told visitors that, as a hand-painted sign announced, "YOU ARE NOW ENTERING THE FREE STATE OF GEORGE FLOYD." At the center of the area was the intersection outside the Cup Foods grocery store, where Floyd died on May 25, 2020, after the police officer Derek Chauvin knelt on his neck for nine minutes and twenty-nine seconds during an arrest while three other officers stood by. In the chaotic fury that swept the nation in the days afterward, hundreds of businesses in Minneapolis were vandalized and 150 buildings, including the Third Precinct, where Chauvin worked, were set on fire. There were protests in the intersection, but mourners, activists, tourists, and community members soon turned the area into a sort of shrine, leaving messages, flowers, and candles. A painted silhouette marked the spot where Floyd had died.

One night, a week after his death, law enforcement officials drove through the makeshift memorial. In response, residents dragged cinder blocks, furniture, and even an old refrigerator into the streets to block traffic. Mayor Jacob Frey, who at one point referred to the area as "sacred ground," had concrete construction barriers placed at the intersection, ostensibly to protect pedestrians. But the barriers also deepened the sense that George Floyd Square was now a place unto itself. An ad hoc committee of activists and residents erected and staffed guard shacks at entrances. An abandoned Speedway gas station was repurposed as the People's Way, and an improvised firepit, set up between empty pumps, became a gathering place. Webb collected the detritus of the protests—bricks and plywood that had covered windows—and used it to build a roundabout structure in the middle of the intersection. It included a platform where visitors could leave flowers and messages, and a nine-foot-tall steel sculpture of a fist that the artist Jordan Powell Karis had designed, as a replica of an earlier wooden sculpture, and that residents helped assemble. The Square was becoming more than a shrine to Floyd's life; it was a monument to others who had died in encounters with police and a headquarters for an emergent movement.

Then, on April 20 of this year, Chauvin was convicted of two counts of murder and one count of manslaughter. On June 25, Judge Peter Cahill sentenced him to twenty-two and a half years in prison. The three other officers will be tried next year, and federal indictments have been handed down against all four of them. Many Americans saw the verdict as a just resolution to a public tragedy. The Square's reopening seemed part of a general spirit of relief and a desire to move on from the horror of Floyd's death and the tensions that had turned Minneapolis into a microcosm of the national debate about race and policing.

But another view, held with at least equal resolve, considered the trial only one concern in a constellation of many that needed to be addressed before there could be anything resembling closure. During the trial, Webb, who stands six feet nine inches tall and looks to be about fifty (though he said that he considers himself just a day old—the day he's living), told me he was concerned that "when the flowers die and the helium is gone from the balloons, people will forget the entire case." The monument that he built was intended to prevent that from happening. "This cannot just be another corner," he said. His implication was that, although the world saw Floyd's death as a singular incident of spectacular violence, people in parts of Minneapolis, particularly in the Square, were more likely to connect his death to a long genealogy of events that both preceded and followed it, and which few outside of that community knew much about.

The disparity in the reactions to the Chauvin conviction can be partially explained by the fact that, despite the clear evidence, the verdict was never a given. When I arrived in Minneapolis in April, at the start of the second week of the trial, the downtown was deserted, devoid of the scenes of rage and bedlam that had played out there last summer. Every so often, an almost empty tram slipped into the Government Plaza station near the Hennepin County courthouse, released two or three passengers, and then departed. Yet a cluster of satellite trucks, military transport vehicles, and National Guard troops stationed at the courthouse entrance suggested that the city was prepared for every contingency.

Early on, though, a consensus emerged: the prosecution was handling its case impressively. The attorneys, led in the courtroom by Jerry Blackwell and Steve Schleicher, elicited mesmerizing testimony from the witnesses, including a nine-year-old girl who had been on her way to Cup Foods just before Floyd's death; her seventeen-year-old cousin, Darnella Frazier, who shot the video that sparked global outrage at the murder; and Charles McMillian, a sixty-one-year-old man who broke down while recalling his help-lessness as Floyd cried out, "Mama, they killing me."

The prosecutors also called Medaria Arradondo, the first black police chief in the city's history, to testify. He told the court that Chauvin's actions were "certainly not part of our ethics or our val-ues." Richard Zimmerman, the head of the Minneapolis Police De-partment's homicide unit, testified that Chauvin's actions were "totally unnecessary." Johnny Mercil, a lieutenant who conducts the department's use-of-force training, said that officers, when using body weight to control a suspect, are instructed to "stay away from the neck when possible." When he was asked whether placing a knee on the neck of a suspect who is "under control and hand-cuffed" would be authorized, he replied, "I would say no."

The recruitment of Blackwell, Schleicher, and two other attor-neys, Lola Velazquez-Aguilu and Neal Katyal, all of whom are in private practice, was credited to Keith Ellison, the former congress-man who is the first Muslim attorney general of Minnesota and the first African American elected to statewide office there. Ellison had taken over the case from the Hennepin County attorney, Mike Freeman, at the request of Governor Tim Walz, a Democrat. This arrangement was hailed as tactically brilliant—Ellison had credibil-ity among progressives who were skeptical of the system's ability to handle the case—but it also reflected the fraught circumstances under which the trial took place.

In 2019, Freeman, who is the son of the former governor Orville Freeman and had previously served as a Democratic state senator, oversaw the prosecution in another prominent police shooting. In 2017, Justine Damond, a white Minneapolis resident originally from Australia, called the police to report a possible assault taking place in an alley behind her home. Mohamed Noor, a black officer of Somali descent, arrived and, mistaking Damond for an assailant, shot her dead. He was convicted and sentenced to twelve and a half years in prison. Yet the case caused consternation because, amid a spate of killings in the area committed by white police, Noor was the only officer found guilty. His conviction fueled the perception that in Minnesota there were separate legal systems for blacks and for whites.

A consequence of this belief was that activists, notably Nekima Levy Armstrong, a lawyer and former president of the Minneapolis NAACP, began pushing for the Chauvin prosecution to be handled by outside counsel. "The activists were demanding it," Ellison, who ran as a progressive reformer and was elected in 2018, told me, but Freeman, whom he described as a friend, had also asked him to take on the case. "It was really the county attorney asking the AG to be involved, and the governor appointed us at the same time," he said. Freeman assisted the prosecution team, but Ellison's presence was reassuring in a system whose legitimacy had come into question.

Last year, Samuel Myers, Jr., a professor at the University of Minnesota's Hubert H. Humphrey School of Public Affairs, published a post on the school's website about what he called the Minnesota Paradox. The state, which typically ranks among the best places to live in the country, has a strong economy (3M, U.S. Bancorp, General Mills, and Cargill are all headquartered there), respected institutions of higher education, affordable homes, abundant natural resources, and a landscape (eleven thousand lakes) that feeds a thriving outdoor recreation industry. The Twin Cities, in particular, seem to have been granted an exemption from the postindustrial malaise that has defined other Midwestern cities. Moreover, the area's long liberal political tradition and the presence of resettled Somali and Hmong refugee communities have burnished its reputation as an outpost of progressivism.

But, Myers wrote, "measured by racial gaps in unemployment rates, wage and salary incomes, incarceration rates, arrest rates, home ownership rates, mortgage lending rates, test scores, reported child maltreatment rates, school disciplinary and suspension rates, and even drowning rates, African Americans are worse off in Minnesota than they are in virtually every other state in the nation." Blacks constitute just 7 percent of the state's population (of 5.5 million), a number that includes both African Americans and recently arrived immigrants, such as the Somali refugees. The median-income gap between black and white Minneapolis families—$47,000, as of 2018—is among the largest in the nation. Floyd's death was one of some eighty homicides in Minneapolis last year; the majority of the victims were black and male. Duchess Harris, a professor of American studies at Macalester College in St. Paul, told me that Minnesota is "everything anybody would ever want, unless you're black." She echoed a sentiment voiced by Leslie Redmond, another former president of the Minneapolis NAACP, that the state is "Wakanda for white people."

"It's not that Minnesota is not a liberal state," Ellison said. "It's just it's not only a liberal state." For most of the twentieth century, a limit of that liberalism could be found at the edge of the Northside, where the historic black community was relegated, owing to restrictive housing covenants and redlining. By the 1930s, St. Paul had a thriving black middle-class neighborhood, called Rondo, but in the sixties it was, as with many such enclaves in American cities, partly demolished to make way for an interstate highway.

The black population of Minneapolis grew significantly during the eighties and nineties as residents of struggling communities in Detroit, Chicago, and Gary, Indiana, sought opportunities there. Ellison, who is fifty-six, grew up in Detroit and attended law school at the University of Minnesota, and he recalls the disdain that some white Minnesotans expressed. "When I first got here, people moving from Gary were being told, 'We'll give you a one-way ticket back.'" Those new arrivals also entered a climate in which relations with the police were becoming increasingly antagonistic—a situation that intensified in recent years with a couple of high-profile cases.

In November 2015, officers responding to a call about a dispute at a party fatally shot Jamar Clark in the head while attempting to arrest him. The officers maintained that Clark, who was twenty-four, had tried to take a gun from one of them. Some witnesses disputed that account, saying that Clark was already in handcuffs when he was shot. (Freeman, the Hennepin County attorney, did not file charges in the case.) The Clark shooting, which occurred a year after the national wave of protests over the killing of Michael Brown in Ferguson, galvanized the Black Lives Matter affiliate in Minneapolis and led to an eighteen-day occupation of the grounds of the Fourth Precinct. A week into the occupation, Allen Scarsella, a twenty-three-year-old white man, fired a gun in the direction of the protesters. It was later discovered that he was friends with a Minnesota police officer who testified during Scarsella's trial that the two had frequently exchanged racist messages.

The following summer, the police officer Jeronimo Yanez fatally shot Philando Castile, a thirty-two-year-old school cafeteria worker, during a traffic stop in a St. Paul suburb as he sat in his car with his girlfriend and her young daughter. Castile, who was a licensed gun owner, had told Yanez, as he complied with the officer's request to retrieve his driver's license, that he had a weapon in his possession. Yanez was charged with second-degree manslaughter and was acquitted in 2017. In the midst of these conflicts, the BLM affiliate disbanded. Under the glare of national attention, and with scant funding, the group "burned out," in the words of Kandace Montgomery, one of its organizers.

That year, which marked the 150th anniversary of the MPD's founding, a coalition of activists calling themselves MPD150 produced a report titled *Enough Is Enough*. It concluded, among other things, that the department's core function is to protect the wealthy and that "racialized violence" has always been part of that imperative. Communities United Against Police Brutality, a grassroots organization that documents and investigates incidents of excessive police force, has compiled data from the city's Office of Police Conduct Review. The group found that, of nearly 2,800 civilian complaints lodged during the eight years before Floyd's death, the department ruled that only thirteen were warranted.

This history helps explain why, locally, people tended to view Floyd's killing not as an anomaly but as part of an enduring narrative. "Police have killed other people," Steve Floyd, a sixty-two-year-old gang-outreach worker in Minneapolis, told me. "Not only Philando and Clark—all the other people who have been killed at the hands of the police." (*The Minneapolis Star Tribune* has recorded 209 such incidents statewide since 2000.) Floyd, who is originally from Chicago and is not related to George Floyd, advises the Agape Movement, a violence-intervention organization created in 2020. The group has enlisted former gang members to defuse community conflicts and has coordinated patrols of the Square. For the past nine months, it has been housed in a building two doors down from Cup Foods.

As Floyd knows from experience, another element of life in the Square that went largely unnoticed in the tumult and debate of the past year was the level of internecine violence. Chicago Avenue between East Thirty-Seventh and East Thirty-Eighth Streets is tattooed with graffiti featuring the names of people of color, most of whom died in interactions with the police. But there is also graffiti identifying the block as a redoubt of the Rolling 30s Bloods gang, which has operated in the area for decades. In the Twin Cities during the mid-1990s, the growth of gangs associated with other cities, such as the Chicago-based Vice Lords and the Los Angeles–born Bloods, gave rise to a police task force. Murder rates in Minneapolis have declined since then, as they have across the nation, but, according to the *Star Tribune,* a significant number of the forty-eight homicides that occurred there in 2019 are thought to be gang-related.

On March 6, as jury selection for the Chauvin trial was about to begin, a thirty-year-old man named Imez Wright was standing near Cup Foods when another man jumped out of an SUV and shot him several times in the chest. Wright, who had two young children, died just feet away from where George Floyd was killed. Prosecutors attributed the homicide to a conflict within the Rolling 30s Bloods. A suspect, identified as a member of the gang, has been arrested; according to court documents, he will argue that he was acting in self-defense.

Wright had joined the gang in his youth, but he sought to leave that life and expressed a desire to help young people avoid the mistakes he'd made. Steve Floyd had helped supervise him at another organization, where Wright mentored schoolchildren. Floyd cited his story as an example of the dangers that continue to plague the neighborhood. "That's what we deal with all the time," he told me.

The community patrols have stepped up in recent months in response to a spike in neighborhood crime. In March, Arradondo, the police chief, reported that in 2019 there were three victims of nonfatal shootings in the vicinity of Thirty-Eighth and Chicago; last year, that number rose to eighteen. The city's ShotSpotter technology, which detects the sound signature of gunfire, logged thirty-three shots fired in the area in 2019 and seven hundred in 2020. But crime has increased throughout Minneapolis and in cities across the country. Steve Floyd added that a common misconception that the police were staying out of the Square had also made it vulnerable to crimes of opportunity. (A spokesperson for the MPD said that it "patrols all areas of the city—bar none.") Three people had committed robbery and assault at a pizzeria just outside the Square, Floyd said, and then had run past the barricades into the area, thinking that they'd be less likely to be caught there. It appears to have worked.

The city first announced last August that it planned to reopen the Square. Some people who had become regulars there set out to draft a response. One of the leaders of the group was Marcia Howard, a former marine in her late forties who teaches English at the nearby Roosevelt High School. (Imez Wright and Darnella Frazier had both been her students.) When I met her one morning in April, she bounded across the Square despite the fact that she had been on guard duty since 3 A.M.—and that it had started to sleet. She called out, "The late, great Prince said, 'Sometimes it snows in April.'" Howard has lived a block away from the spot where George Floyd died since 1998. (The day she moved in, she told me, there was a drug raid at that intersection.) Shocked by the murder, she found herself drawn into the activist network, took a leave from teaching, and spent nearly every day in the Square. Her front porch was crammed with boxes of goggles, hand sanitizer, and Gatorade, which supporters across the country had sent through an Amazon wish list. "Welcome to the quartermaster's office for the movement," she said.

Howard and others canvassed residents, and in August they released "Justice Resolution 001," a list of twenty-four demands that needed to be met before they would agree to a reopening. The list included the immediate recall of County Attorney Freeman, millions of dollars in investment in businesses in and around the Square, and information on or investigations into ten police-related deaths dating back to 2002.

But, over time, there was disagreement about the Square. In March of this year, the city conducted its own survey, asking about four thousand residents and business owners for input on its proposals for the future of the Square. Most of the respondents supported retaining some aspect of the memorial, but in a way that allowed for reopening the streets to traffic. Andrea Jenkins is a city council member whose district includes most of the Square. In 2017, she ran on a progressive platform and became the first openly trans black woman elected to political office in the country. We spoke by phone after Chauvin was convicted, and she told me that most of the community favored the reopening. "We hear from a small number of people who are occupying this space, and those are the people who are saying that the trial wasn't justice and there needs to be more," she said. "It's almost like they're asking the city of Minneapolis to atone for the four hundred years of oppression that America has brought on African Americans." She paused for a moment, then added, "That's not to say that Minneapolis has not contributed mightily to it."

The near unanimity of the law enforcement opposition to Chauvin on the stand heartened people, but it also raised other concerns: if officers' testimony made the difference between acquittal and conviction in this case, it suggested that their reluctance to testify in previous cases may have been a causal factor in failures to convict. More profoundly, it suggested that the police are still the arbiters of good judgment, even in cases that call that presumption into question.

The officers on the stand could not have appeared more unlike the ex-officer on trial—and that, perhaps, was the point. Chauvin was a bad cop, and the rest are not. Yet the distinctions don't entirely hold up. The MPD fired Chauvin a day after Floyd's death, but a police association funded his defense. He worked for the department for nineteen years, including as a field-training officer. That fact weakened the argument that he was fundamentally different from the men who said that his actions were "uncalled for" and contrary to his training. Chauvin was employed, promoted, and rewarded by the same system whose representatives now condemned his actions from the stand. In that sense, the jury—and the public—was being good-copped. And all parties were acutely aware that Minneapolis and many other cities would likely explode if Chauvin went free.

The Reverend Al Sharpton, who since the 1980s has been an activist involved in police use-of-force cases—pushing prosecutors to bring charges and pressuring elected officials to institute reforms—arrived in the city shortly before the end of the trial. He told me that, in the past, "the blue wall of silence is the wall that separated us from justice." Floyd's death was so egregious, though, that "the officers started to see Chauvin the same way I see jackleg preachers—just bad for the profession." Yet the idea that Chauvin's trial might serve as redemption for the police establishment was undercut, just before the third week of the proceedings, by the death of Daunte Wright.

Ten miles north of the courthouse on the afternoon of April 11, three officers from the Brooklyn Center Police Department pulled over Wright, who was twenty years old, for a tag violation. He called his mother and remained on the phone with her during an exchange with the police. That ended when Wright, who had stepped out of his car, tried to get back in. As an officer attempted to stop him,

Kim Potter, a twenty-six-year veteran of the department, drew her gun and, shouting "Taser!," fired a single round into Wright's chest. (The police later said that Potter had mistakenly drawn her gun. She resigned—as did the city's police chief—and was charged with second-degree manslaughter. Her trial is scheduled to begin in December; Ellison will again lead the prosecution.)

About four hours after the shooting, Kieran Knutson, an activist and the president of Communications Workers of America Local 7250, which represents AT&T workers, sent me a link to a live stream of a protest on a street in Brooklyn Center. When I arrived thirty minutes later, the demonstration was breaking up, but about two dozen people lingered and members of Wright's family were speaking quietly with local activists. Some wrote his name on the street in chalk. Much of the crowd reconvened about three miles away in front of the Brooklyn Center Police Department. Scores of officers in riot gear stood outside as the crowd grew to a few hundred. Demonstrators started to throw rocks and garbage toward the police, and the officers responded with flash grenades and tear gas. The crowd scattered but then regrouped nearby. The winds were in the protesters' favor, and most of the tear gas blew back toward the police line. A young man standing next to me reached into his pocket and dropped a large rock onto the grass. This point-and-counterpoint went on for hours that night and on several subsequent nights.

Wright's death was interpreted as a rejoinder to the contention that the current system is redeemable. Calls to defund or abolish the police, which were also being heard in Seattle, San Francisco, and other cities, began to gather momentum among groups including Reclaim the Block, which formed in 2018 and advocates for defunding, and Black Visions, a network of activists that formed after the local Black Lives Matter affiliate dissolved. Last June, the Minneapolis city council voted unanimously to take a first step toward creating a "transformative new model for cultivating community safety." The municipal charter requires the city to have a police department, which reports directly to the mayor's office. But there are multiple routes to amending the charter, including with an ordinance from the city council, calling for a referendum on the amendment in question, or with a citizen petition that garners twelve thousand signatures, which would also trigger a referendum.

This situation has been complicated by a depletion of the MPD ranks. In February, the department reported that it had only 638 officers—roughly 200 fewer than it would normally have—as a result of an exodus after last year's riots. So the same city council that had voted in favor of creating a new model for community safety also voted unanimously to release $6.4 million to hire more officers for the old one. The seeming reversal soured relations with some in the activist community.

Michelle Phelps, a sociologist at the University of Minnesota who has studied the recent rise of police-related activism, told me that the council members were caught in the crosscurrents of public opinion. She noted that Andrea Jenkins has "described herself as an abolitionist and yet is consistently voting with the camp on the city council to keep giving money to the Minneapolis police. Why does she do that? It's not because she's duplicitous. It's because she also hears from her constituents—many of whom are people of color—that they are worried about violent crime in their neighborhood." Abolition, Jenkins told me, "is an aspirational goal," but there are practical realities for which, in her view, it has few answers. "Everybody has got guns," she said, speaking of the country at large. "Help me figure out how you have an unarmed police department when everybody has got guns."

The clash between those in favor of replacing or getting rid of the department and those trying to retain it did not capture the entire spectrum of sentiment. Dave Bicking, a member of the board of Communities United Against Police Brutality, said that serious reform was needed but that, in his assessment, the council's pronouncements last June were "all rhetoric." He told me, "It had no basis in reality from the standpoint that anybody thought that it was possible or desirable, and was merely a way to calm the crowd."

It is unclear what would come after abolition. "The current proposal that we are offering the residents of Minneapolis is a department of public safety to be created and the Minneapolis Police Department to be dissolved," Julia Johnson, a twenty-nine-year-old organizer with Black Visions, told me. The group argues for moving responsibilities such as mental health interventions and traffic enforcement from armed officers to unarmed civil service groups, while maintaining a small number of armed "peace officers" who would respond solely to violent conflict. I pointed out that the proposal resembles those of groups calling to defund police departments, not to abolish them. Johnson corrected me. The ultimate objective is "total abolition," she said. "We want to reach, in the next couple, five, ten years, a place where we no longer need police officers to be part of our community safety system." When I asked how this would work in a nation that has more firearms than people, she said, "There was a time before police, and there will be a time after police."

Ten days after the Chauvin verdict, Yes 4 Minneapolis, a campaign gathering signatures for a referendum, delivered more than twenty thousand of them, and a vote will be held in November. Public opinion is divided. In a poll last August, 61 percent of likely voters in Minneapolis supported a charter change that would give the council the authority to replace the current police department with a new public safety entity. Another poll showed that nearly three-quarters of registered voters supported cutting the police budget to support social services. But, in the same poll, only 35 percent of black respondents (and 41 percent of white respondents) supported even reducing the size of the police force.

Michelle Phelps told me that a backlash is already building against council members who are considered to be too closely aligned with abolition. "There could be a world in which the charter amendment passes but the people who were behind it and have the vision for it get voted out," she said.

The outcome of the Chauvin trial offered the city a temporary re-prieve from these debates. On April 20, outside the Hennepin County courthouse, people crowded around cellphones waiting for word of the verdict. A fifty-four-year-old man named Willie Austin told me that he was trying not to get his hopes up. "I mean, it can get ugly either way it goes," he said. A man in a green T-shirt and a matching ski cap strode past me, holding a large wooden cutout of a hand with a raised middle finger and "ACAB" (All Cops Are Bas-tards) written across the bottom. But when another man with a bullhorn shouted "Guilty!" on all three counts, people broke into cheers, many of them crying as they hugged apparent strangers. A contingent of National Guard troops watched from an elevated plaza. Amid the jubilation, the man with the bullhorn offered a se-date verdict of his own. "Justice," he said, "is living in a world where George Floyd never died." I made my way across town, to George Floyd Square, where an interracial crowd that numbered in the thousands had poured into the intersection. A procession led by two trumpeters and a man playing the tuba chanted, "We got that justice, now we got that peace." A few hours later, I found Willie Austin in the Square. "It feels good to finally win one," he told me.

Two days later, though, a kind of civic whiplash set in as Daunte Wright was laid to rest. The Shiloh Temple International Ministries Church is in a broad, low-slung building at the intersection of West Broadway and North Girard Avenues in a weathered portion of Minneapolis's Northside. A crowd spilled into the street as a few photographers navigated drones overhead. A security team from a black paramilitary group called the Minnesota Freedom Fighters was positioned along the street, bearing rifles. (Minnesota is a licensed-open-carry state.) Inside, Al Sharpton, who delivered the eulogy, sat on a dais near the altar alongside Benjamin Crump, the seemingly ubiquitous trial attorney who, with Antonio Romanucci and others, represented the Floyd family in a civil suit and, in March, secured a $27 million settlement from the city. Tim Walz, Keith El-lison, and Amy Klobuchar, the state's senior U.S. senator, sat nearby. Mike Elliott, the thirty-seven-year-old black mayor of Brooklyn Center, sat in the audience.

As the service began, a trumpeter named Keyon Harrold played "Amazing Grace." Last year, Harrold, who is black, was in the lobby of the Arlo Hotel in New York City with his fourteen-year-old son, Keyon, Jr., when a white woman accosted the boy, accusing him of stealing her cellphone. (It was later found by an Uber driver in whose car the woman had left it.) Crump took on the Harrolds as clients. He also represents the Wright family, and when he stood to deliver his comments he introduced not the dignitaries in attendance but the people who had been inducted into what he called "a fraternity that no family wants to be a part of." Valerie Castile, the mother of Philando Castile, was there, as were members of the families of Emmett Till, Jamar Clark, and Oscar Grant, who was killed in Oakland in 2009, also by a police officer who said that he had been reaching for his Taser. Many of George Floyd's relatives were present as well.

During the invocation, a pastor named Carmen Means said, "We experienced this week the god of justice," and prayed that that god would do for the Wright family what he had done for the Floyds. The prayer, as much as anything else said that day or on any other in the past year, summarized what George Floyd has become in death: an aspirational symbol for justice, offering a plaintive hope that, if people fail to prevent more deaths of this kind, then at least let the extinguished life be mourned and the wrong adjudicated.

The reopening of George Floyd Square came six weeks after Wright's funeral. Steve Floyd and some members of Agape provided security as the workers began dismantling the barricades. He told me that people in the Square were shocked that they were assisting with the reopening. But it was apparent to him that the city would reopen the streets eventually, and so the most practical thing to do was to negotiate with the officials as it happened. The city agreed not to remove the artwork and the memorial, a decision that Floyd credited to such discussions. For weeks, though, Marcia Howard had been decrying "plantation politics"—an assumption that the city would use black people to undermine the Square, a monument to lost black lives. As dawn broke over Chicago Avenue, Howard, streaming updates on her phone, stood in the intersection that was no longer distinct from the city surrounding it.

Jay Webb called Andrea Jenkins's office and the mayor's office to set up meetings to discuss preserving the monument he built and the fist sculpture. Chicago Avenue, he told me, should be remade as a new black Wall Street, the thriving black business hub that was destroyed in the Tulsa massacre a hundred years ago. For Webb, George Floyd's death is an installment in a far longer saga, stretching back to the first Africans enslaved in the North American colonies. He told me, "For the four hundred years we put in, we're gonna get something out."

POSTSCRIPT TO "THE FREE STATE OF GEORGE FLOYD"

Fourteen months after the brutal and public end of George Floyd's life, Derek Chauvin, by then a former Minneapolis police officer, went on trial for murder. I traveled to Minnesota with the intention of covering the legal proceedings—that was the story. The circumstances of Chauvin's trial outlined in the piece presented a complication: the pandemic protocols meant that only a handful of pool reporters would be allowed into the courtroom each day. The majority were exiled to a nearby administrative building where a large television and seating had been arranged. In effect, the journalists were receiving the same information as anyone who watched the proceedings at home. Each evening the pool reporters emailed their observations to the group of reporters stuck in the admin building. Recognizing that there was little insight to be gleaned from group-watching a television screen, I struck out one afternoon for the stretch of South Chicago Avenue where Floyd had died. The barricades, the community patrols, the impromptu art installations that had transformed the landscape—all of it suggested that there was a second sort of trial unfolding in the city, one that was obviously connected to the one happening in the Hennepin County courthouse but also notably independent of it. George Floyd Square owed its origins to the stunned fury and conflagration that followed his death, but its end would not be neatly contingent upon the outcome of the trial. I skipped the remainder of the trial and began spending hours in the Square, talking to the artists, activists, and residents who were collectively responsible for its upkeep. That became the new story.

Later, I began to take note of a third story—the story of the story. My visits to the Square were as notable for who refused to talk to me as they were for who agreed to talk. Most days the spectrum of attitudes there ranged from skeptical to paranoid, and there seemed to be a sense that, having suspended all official bureaucratic authority over this small corner of Minneapolis, they would view any representative of an official institution— media in particular—as deeply suspect. The quotes included in the story were generally the product of repeated interactions with people who eventually came to see me as trustworthy enough to talk to on the record. The feeling of suspicion was, on one level, mutual. Journalists who have worked at the craft for any amount of time learn to become at least slightly suspicious of the person who is *too* eager to talk to you, *too* inclined to offer the linchpin quote that can frame your story. In this case, an activist enthusiastically offered her perspective on the events taking place in parallel to the trial. She gave a detailed origin story of her own activism in the city, hinging upon a dramatic incident of police violence. But in following up on the most basic details she'd supplied, the entire story fell apart. The subtheme in Chauvin's trial was the mendacity of the MPD in the years that preceded Floyd's death, but that interaction reinforced for me the fact that a journalist is required to submit all sides of a story to equal scrutiny. Trust is essential to the work of journalism. Our profession is facilitated by the trust of the public (and that declining trust is at the heart of many of our current difficulties).

But it is also a trust that is hemmed in by skepticism both from the people we seek information from and from us toward them. On some level, the public's trust may actually be strengthened by these mutual suspicions.

The story I wrote was not the one I'd intended to cover. And the story I covered is not the one I talk about most often. The third story—the one about what I picked up along the way—is the one that has endured.

THE MAN BEHIND CRITICAL RACE THEORY

September 20, 2021

The town of Harmony, Mississippi, which owes its origins to a small number of formerly enslaved black people who bought land from former slaveholders after the Civil War, is nestled in Leake County, a perfectly square allotment in the center of the state. According to local lore, Harmony, which was previously called Galilee, was renamed in the early 1920s after a black resident who had contributed money to help build the town's school said, upon its completion, "Now let us live and work in harmony." This story perhaps explains why, nearly four decades later, when a white school board closed the school, it was interpreted as an attack on the heart of the black community. The school was one of five thousand public schools for black children in the South that the philanthropist Julius Rosenwald funded beginning in 1912. Rosenwald's foundation provided the seed money, and community members constructed the building themselves by hand. By the sixties, many of the structures were decrepit, a reflection of the South's ongoing disregard for black education. Nonetheless, the Harmony school provided its students a good education and was a point of pride in the community, which wanted it to remain open. In 1961, the battle sparked the founding of the local chapter of the NAACP.

That year, Winson Hudson, the chapter's vice president, working with local black families, contacted various people in the civil rights movement and eventually spoke to Derrick Bell, a young attorney with the NAACP Legal Defense and Educational Fund, or LDF, in New York City. Bell later wrote, in the foreword to Hudson's memoir *Mississippi Harmony,* that his colleagues had been astonished to learn that her purpose was to reopen the Rosenwald school. He said he told her, "Our crusade was not to save segregated schools, but to eliminate them." He added that, if people in Harmony were interested in enforcing integration, the LDF could help.

Hudson eventually accepted Bell's offer, and in 1964 the LDF won *Hudson v. Leake County School Board* (Winson Hudson's school-age niece Diane was the plaintiff), which mandated that the board comply with desegregation. Harmony's students were enrolled in a white school in the county. Afterward, though, Bell began to question the efficacy of both the case and the drive for integration. Throughout the South, such rulings sparked white flight from the public schools and the creation of private "segregation academies," which meant that black students still attended institutions that were effectively separate. Years later, after Hudson's victory had become part of civil rights history, she and Bell met at a conference, where he told her, "I wonder whether I gave you the right advice." Hudson replied that she did, too.

Bell spent the second half of his career as an academic, and over time he came to recognize that other decisions in landmark civil rights cases were of limited practical impact. He drew an unsettling conclusion: racism is so deeply rooted in the makeup of American society that it has been able to reassert itself after each successive wave of reform aimed at eliminating it. Racism, he began to argue, is permanent. His ideas proved foundational to a body of thought that, in the 1980s, came to be known as critical race theory, or CRT. After more than a quarter of a century, there is an extensive academic field of literature cataloging CRT's insights into the contradictions of anti-discrimination law and the complexities of legal advocacy for social justice.

For the past several months, conservatives have been waging war on a wide-ranging set of claims that they wrongly ascribe to critical race theory while barely mentioning the body of scholarship behind it or even Bell's name. As Christopher F. Rufo, an activist who launched the recent crusade, said on Twitter, the goal from the start was to distort the idea into an absurdist touchstone. "We have successfully frozen their brand—'critical race theory'—into the public conversation and are steadily driving up negative perceptions. We will eventually turn it toxic, as we put all of the various cultural insanities under that brand category," he wrote. Accordingly, CRT has been defined as black supremacist racism, false history, and the terrible apotheosis of "wokeness." Patricia Williams, one of the key scholars of the CRT canon, refers to the ongoing mischaracterization as "definitional theft."

Vinay Harpalani, a law professor at the University of New Mexico who took a constitutional law class that Bell taught at New York University in 2008, remembers his creating a climate of intellectual tolerance. "There were conservative white male students who got along very well with Professor Bell, because he respected their opinion," Harpalani told me. "The irony of the conservative attack is that he was more respectful of conservative students and giving conservatives a voice than anyone." Sarah Lustbader, a public defender based in New York City who was a teaching assistant for Bell's constitutional law class in 2010, has a similar recollection. "When people fear critical race theory, it stems from this idea that their children will be indoctrinated somehow. But Bell's class was the least indoctrinated class I took in law school," she said. "We got the most freedom in that class to reach our own conclusions without judgment, as long as they were good-faith arguments and well argued and reasonable."

Republican lawmakers have been swift to take advantage of the controversy. In June, Governor Greg Abbott of Texas signed a bill that restricts teaching about race in the state's public schools. Oklahoma, Tennessee, Idaho, Iowa, New Hampshire, South Carolina, and Arizona have introduced similar legislation. But in all the outrage and reaction is an unwitting validation of the very arguments that Bell made. Last year, after the murder of George Floyd, Americans started confronting the genealogy of racism in this country in such large numbers that the moment was referred to as a reckoning. Bell, who died in 2011 at the age of eighty, would have been less focused on the fact that white politicians responded to that reckoning by curtailing discussions of race in public schools than that they did so in conjunction with a larger effort to shore up the political structures that disadvantage African Americans. Another irony is that CRT has become a fixation of conservatives despite the fact that some of its sharpest critiques were directed at the ultimate failings of liberalism, beginning with Bell's own early involvement with one of its most heralded achievements.

In May 1954, when the Supreme Court struck down legally mandated racial segregation in public schools in *Brown v. Board of Education,* the decision was instantly recognized as a watershed in the nation's history. A legal team from the NAACP Legal Defense and Educational Fund, led by Thurgood Marshall, argued that segregation violated the equal protection clause of the Fourteenth Amendment by inflicting psychological harm on black children. Chief Justice Earl Warren took the unusual step of persuading the other justices to reach a consensus so that their ruling would carry the weight of unanimity. In time, many came to see the decision as an opening salvo of the modern civil rights movement, and it made Marshall one of the most recognizable lawyers in the country. His stewardship of the case was particularly inspiring to Derrick Bell, who was then a twenty-four-year-old Air Force officer and who had developed a keen interest in matters of equality.

Bell was born in 1930 in Pittsburgh's Hill District, the community immortalized in August Wilson's plays, and he attended Duquesne University before enlisting. After serving two years, he entered the University of Pittsburgh's law school and, in 1957, was the only black graduate in his class. He landed a job in the newly formed civil rights division of the Department of Justice, but when his superiors became aware that he was a member of the NAACP they told him that the membership constituted a conflict of interest and that he had to resign from the organization. In a move that would become a theme in his career, Bell quit his job rather than compromise a principle. He began working, instead, at the Pittsburgh NAACP, where he met Marshall, who hired him in 1960 as a staff attorney at the Legal Defense Fund. The LDF was the legal arm of the NAACP until 1957, when it spun off as a separate organization.

Bell arrived at a crucial moment in the LDF's history. In 1956, two years after *Brown,* it successfully litigated *Browder v. Gayle,* the case that struck down segregation on city buses in Alabama—and handed Martin Luther King, Jr., and the Montgomery Improvement Association a victory in the yearlong boycott they had organized. The LDF launched desegregation lawsuits across the South, and Bell supervised or handled many of them. But, when Winson Hudson contacted him, she opened a window onto the distance between the agenda of the national civil rights organizations and the priorities of the local communities they were charged with serving. In her memoir, she recalled a contentious exchange she had, before she contacted Bell, with a white representative of the school board. She told him, "If you don't bring the school back to Harmony, we will be going to your school." Where the LDF saw integration as the objective, Hudson saw it as leverage to be used in the fight to maintain a quality black school in her community.

The Harmony school had already become a flash point. Medgar Evers, the Mississippi field secretary for the NAACP, visited the town and assisted in organizing the local chapter. He told members that the work they were embarking on could get them killed. Bell, during his trips to the state, made a point of not driving himself; he knew that a wrong turn on unfamiliar roads could have fatal consequences. He was arrested for using a whites-only phone booth in Jackson, and, upon his safe return to New York, Marshall mordantly joked that, if he got himself killed in Mississippi, the LDF would use his funeral as a fundraiser. The dangers, however, were very real. In June 1963, a white supremacist shot and killed Evers in his driveway in Jackson; he was thirty-seven years old. In subsequent years, there was an attempted firebombing of Hudson's home and two bombings at the home of her sister, Dovie, who was Diane

Hudson's mother and was involved in the movement. That suffering and loss could not have eased Bell's growing sense that his efforts had only helped create a more durable system of segregation.

Bell left the LDF in 1966 for an academic career that took him first to the University of Southern California's law school, where he directed the public interest legal center, and then, in 1969, in the aftermath of King's assassination, to Harvard Law School as a lecturer. Derek Bok, the dean of the school, promised Bell that he would be "the first but not the last" of his black hires. In 1971, Bok was made the president of the university, and Bell became Harvard Law's first black tenured professor. He began creating courses that explored the nexus of civil rights and the law—a departure from traditional pedagogy.

In 1970, he had published a casebook titled *Race, Racism and American Law,* a pioneering examination of the unifying themes in civil rights litigation throughout American history. The book also contained the seeds of an idea that became a prominent element in his work: that racial progress had occurred mainly when it aligned with white interests—beginning with emancipation, which, he noted, came about as a prerequisite for saving the Union. Between 1954 and 1968, the civil rights movement brought about changes that were thought of as a second Reconstruction. King's death was a devastating loss, but hope persisted that a broader vista of possibilities for black people and for the nation lay ahead. Yet, within a few years, as volatile conflicts over affirmative action and school busing arose, those victories began to look less like an antidote than like a treatment for an ailment whose worst symptoms can be temporarily alleviated but which cannot be cured. Bell was ahead of many others in reaching this conclusion. If the civil rights movement had been a second Reconstruction, it was worth remembering that the first one had ended in the fiery purges of the so-called Redemption era, in which slavery, though abolished by the Thirteenth Amendment, was resurrected in new forms, such as sharecropping and convict leasing. Bell seemed to have found himself in a position akin to Thomas Paine's: he'd been both a participant in a revolution and a witness to the events that revealed the limitations of its achievements.

Bell's skepticism was deepened by the Supreme Court's 1978 decision in *Regents of the University of California v. Bakke*, which challenged affirmative action in higher education. Allan Bakke, a white prospective medical student, was twice rejected by U.C. Davis. He sued the Regents of the University of California, arguing that he had been denied admission because of the school's minority set-aside admissions, or quotas—and that affirmative action amounted to "reverse discrimination." Upon the appeal of the university, the Supreme Court ruled that race could be considered, among other factors, for admission and that diversifying admissions was both a compelling interest and permissible under the Constitution, but that the University of California's explicit quota system was not. Bakke was admitted to the school.

Bell saw in the decision the beginning of a new phase of challenges. Diversity is not the same as redress, he argued; it could provide the appearance of equality while leaving the underlying machinery of inequality untouched. He criticized the decision as evidence that the court valorized a kind of default color blindness, as opposed to an intentional awareness of race and of the need to address historical wrongs. He likely would have seen the same principle at work in the 2013 Supreme Court ruling in *Shelby County v. Holder*, which gutted the Voting Rights Act.

In the years surrounding the *Bakke* case, Bell published two articles that were considered both brilliant and heretical. The first, "Serving Two Masters," which appeared in March 1976 in *The Yale Law Journal*, cited his own role in the Harmony case. He wrote that the mission of groups engaged in civil rights litigation, such as the NAACP, represented an inherent conflict of interest. The two masters of the title were the groups' interests and those of their clients; what the groups wanted to achieve may not have aligned with what their clients wanted—or even needed. The concept of an inherent conflict was crucial to Bell's understanding of how and why the movement had played out as it did: the heights it had attained had paradoxically shown how far there still was to go and how difficult it would be to get there. Imani Perry, a legal scholar and professor of African American studies at Princeton, who knew Bell, told me how audacious it was at the time for Bell to "raise questions about his own role as an advocate and, perhaps, the way in which we structured civil rights advocacy."

Jack Greenberg, who served as the director-counsel of the LDF from 1961 to 1984, depicted Bell in his memoir *Crusaders in the Courts* as a complex, frustrating figure whose stringent criticism of the organization's history and philosophy led to tensions in their own relationship. Yet Sherrilyn Ifill, the current president and director-counsel, told me that, despite some initial consternation in civil rights circles, Bell's perspective eventually found purchase even among those he had criticized. "I think most of us—especially those who long admired and were mentored by Bell—read his work as a cautionary tale for us as lawyers," Ifill told me. Today, she said, LDF attorneys teach Bell's work to students in New York University's Racial Equity Strategies Clinic.

Bell eventually formulated a broader criticism of the objectives of both the movement and its lawyers. The issue of busing was particularly complicated. *Brown v. Board of Education* centered on the circumstances of Linda Brown, an eight-year-old girl who lived in a mixed neighborhood in Topeka, Kansas, but was forced to travel nearly an hour to a black school rather than attend one closer to her home, which, under the law, was reserved for white children. During the seventies, in an attempt to put integration into practice, school districts sent black students to better-financed white schools. The presumption was that white parents and administrators would not underfund schools that black children attended if white children were also students there. In effect, it was hoped that the valuation of whiteness would be turned against itself. But, in a reversal of Linda Brown's situation, the white schools were generally farther away than the local schools the students would otherwise have gone to. So the remedy effectively imposed the same burden as had been imposed on Brown, albeit with the opposite intentions. Bell "was pessimistic about the effectiveness of busing, and at a time when a lot of people weren't," the scholar Patricia Williams told me.

More significant, Bell was growing doubtful about the prospect of ever achieving racial equality in the United States. The civil rights movement had been based on the idea that the American system could be made to live up to the democratic creed prescribed in its founding documents. But Bell had begun to think that the system was working exactly as it was intended to—that that was why progress was invariably met with reversal. Indeed, by the eighties, it was increasingly clear that the momentum to desegregate schools had stalled; a 2006 study by the Civil Rights Project at UCLA found that many of the advances made in the first years had been erased during the nineties, and that 73 percent of black students around that time attended schools in which most students were minorities.

In Bell's second major article of this period, "*Brown v. Board of Education* and the Interest-Convergence Dilemma," published in January 1980 in the *Harvard Law Review,* he lanced the perception that the societal changes of the mid-twentieth century were the result of a moral awakening among whites. Instead, he wrote, they were a product of "interest convergence" and Cold War pragmatism. Armed with images of American racial hypocrisy, the Soviet Union had a damning counter to American criticism of its behavior in Eastern Europe. (As early as the 1931 Scottsboro trial, in which nine African American teenagers were wrongfully convicted of raping two white women, the Soviets publicized examples of American racism internationally; the tactic became more common after the start of the Cold War.)

The historians Mary L. Dudziak, Carol Anderson, and Penny Von Eschen, among others, later substantiated Bell's point, arguing that America's racial problems were particularly disruptive to diplomatic relations with India and the African states emerging from colonialism, which were subject to pitched competition for their allegiance from the superpowers. The civil rights movement's victories, Bell argued, were not a sign of moral maturation in white America but a reflection of its geopolitical pragmatism. For people who'd been inspired by the idea of the movement as a triumph of conscience, these arguments were deeply unsettling.

In 1980, Bell left Harvard to become the dean of the University of Oregon law school, but he resigned five years later after a search committee declined to extend the offer of a faculty position to an Asian American woman when its first two choices, who were both white men, turned it down. Harvard Law rehired Bell as a professor. His influence had grown measurably since he began teaching; *Race, Racism and American Law,* which was largely overlooked at the time of its publication, had come to be viewed as a foundational text. Yet during his absence from Harvard no one was assigned to teach his key class, which was based on the book. Some students interpreted this omission as disregard for issues of race, and it gave rise to the first of two events that, in particular, led to the creation of CRT. The legal scholar Kimberlé Crenshaw, who was a student at the law school at the time, told me, "We initially coalesced as students and young law professors around this course that the law school refused to teach." In 1982, the group organized a series of guest speakers and conducted a version of the class themselves.

At the same time, the legal academy was roiled by debates generated by a movement called critical legal studies, or CLS; beginning in the seventies, a group of progressive scholars, most of them white, had advanced the then contentious idea that the law, rather than being a neutral system based on objective principles, operated to reinforce established social hierarchies. Another group of scholars found CLS both intriguing and unsatisfying: here was a tool that allowed them to articulate the methods by which the legal system shored up inequality, but in a way that was more insightful about class than it was about race. (The "crits," as the CLS adherents were known, had not "come to terms with the particularity of race," Crenshaw and her co-editors Neil Gotanda, Gary Peller, and Kendall Thomas later noted in the introduction to their 1995 anthology *Critical Race Theory: The Key Writings That Formed the Movement.*)

The next defining moment in CRT's creation came in 1989, when a group that developed out of the Harvard seminars decided to hold a retreat at the University of Wisconsin, where David Trubek, a central figure in the CLS movement, taught. Casting about for a way to describe what the retreat would address, Crenshaw referred to "new developments in critical race theory." The name was meant to situate the group at the intersection of CLS and the intractable questions of race. Legal scholars such as Richard Delgado, Patricia Williams, Mari Matsuda, and Alan Freeman (attacks on CRT have conveniently overlooked the fact that not all its founding scholars were black) began publishing work in legal journals that furthered the discourse around race, power, and law.

Crenshaw contributed what became one of the best-known elements of CRT in 1989, when she published an article in *The University of Chicago Legal Forum* titled "Demarginalizing the Intersection of Race and Sex: A Black Feminist Critique of Antidiscrimination Doctrine, Feminist Theory and Antiracist Politics." Her central argument, about "intersectionality"—the way in which people who belong to more than one marginalized community can be overlooked by anti-discrimination law—was a distillation of the kinds of problems that CRT addressed. These were problems that could not have been seen clearly unless there had been a civil rights movement, but for which liberalism had no ready answer because, in large part, it had never really considered them. Her ideas about intersectionality as a legal blind spot now regularly feature in analyses not only of public policy but of literature, sociology, and history.

As CRT began to take shape, Bell became more deeply involved in an ongoing push to diversify the Harvard Law School faculty. In 1990, he announced that he would take an unpaid leave to protest the fact that Harvard Law had never granted tenure to a black woman. Since Bell's hiring almost twenty years earlier, a few other black men had joined the faculty, including Randall Kennedy in 1984 and Charles Ogletree in 1989. But Bell, cajoled by younger feminist legal scholars, Crenshaw among them, came to recognize the unique burdens that went with being both black and female.

That April, Bell spoke at a rally on campus where he was introduced by the twenty-eight-year-old president of the *Harvard Law Review,* Barack Obama. In his comments, Obama said that Bell's "scholarship has opened up new vistas and new horizons and changed the standards of what legal writing is about." Bell told the crowd, "To be candid, I cannot afford a year or more without my law school salary. But I cannot continue to urge students to take risks for what they believe if I do not practice my own precepts."

In 1991, Bell accepted a visiting professorship at the NYU law school, extended by John Sexton, the dean and a former student of Bell's. Harvard did not hire a black woman and, in the third year of his protest, Bell refused to return, ending his tenure at the university. In 1998, Lani Guinier became the first woman of color to be given tenure at the law school.

Bell remained a visiting professor at NYU for the rest of his life, declining offers to become a tenured member of the faculty. He continued to speak and write on subjects relating to law and race, and some of his most important work during this period came in an unorthodox form. In the eighties, he had begun to write fiction, and in 1992 he published a collection of short stories, *Faces at the Bottom of the Well.* A black female lawyer named Geneva Crenshaw, the protagonist of many of the stories, serves as Bell's alter ego. (Bell later told Kimberlé Crenshaw that he had "borrowed" her surname for the character, who was a composite of black women lawyers who had influenced his thinking.) *Kirkus Reviews* noted that, despite some "lackluster writing," the stories offered "insight into the rage, frustration, and yearning of being black in America." *The New York Times* described the collection as "Jonathan Swift come to law school." But the book's subtitle, *The Permanence of Racism,* garnered nearly as much attention as its literary merits.

The collection includes "The Space Traders," Bell's best-known piece of fiction. In the story, extraterrestrials land in the United States and make an offer: they will reverse the severe damage the nation has done to the environment, provide it with a clean energy source, and give it enough gold to resurrect the economy, which has been ruined by policies favoring the rich. In exchange, the aliens want the government to turn every black person in the country over to them. A consensus emerges that the administration should take the deal, on the ground that mandating that black people leave is not all that different from drafting them to go to war. Whites largely support the measure. Jewish groups oppose it, as an echo of Nazism, but they are silenced when a tide of anti-Semitism sweeps the nation. A corporate coalition opposes the trade, because black people make up so much of the consumer market. Businesses that supply law enforcement and the prison industry oppose it, too, recognizing the impact that the disappearance would have on their bottom line.

A black member of the administration decides that the only way to get white people to veto the proposal is to convince them that leaving with the aliens would be an entitlement that undeserving blacks would achieve at their expense; his plan fails. The story ends with twenty million African Americans, arms linked by chains, preparing to leave "the New World as their forebears had arrived." The narrative is bleak, but it offers a trenchant commentary on the frailty of black citizenship and the tentative nature of inclusion, and it echoes a theme of Bell's earlier work—that black rights have been held hostage to white self-interest.

The late critic and essayist Stanley Crouch told me in 1997 about a panel he appeared on with Bell in which he'd criticized Bell's dire forecasts. "He was *clean*. I'm looking at this beautiful chalk-gray suit he had on that cost about twelve hundred dollars," Crouch told me. "I said to myself, 'There's something wrong with this.' For me having been involved with Friends of SNCC and CORE thirty-five years ago, we'd be talking with guys from Mississippi back then who weren't as pessimistic." He added, "To hear that from him was the height of irresponsibility." In an essay titled "Dumb Bell Blues," Crouch wrote that Bell's theory of interest convergence undermined the importance of black achievements in transforming American society. Whereas he regarded Bell's view as pessimism, to Bell it was hard-won realism. Imani Perry told me, "Even as he had a kind of skepticism about the prospect that racism would end, or that you'd get a just judicial order, he was still thinking about how you move the society, what will move, and what will be much harder to move."

Part of Bell's intent was simply to establish expectations. Crenshaw mentioned to me *Silent Covenants,* a book on the legacy of *Brown,* which Bell published in 2004. In it, he describes a 2002 ceremony at Yale, at which Robert L. Carter was awarded an honorary degree. When the university's president noted that Carter had been one of the attorneys who argued *Brown,* the crowd leaped to its feet in an ovation, which prompted Bell to wonder, "How could a decision that promised so much and, by its terms, accomplished so little, have gained so hallowed a place among some of the nation's better-educated and most-successful individuals?"

Silent Covenants also features an alternative ruling in *Brown.* In this version, which was clearly informed by Bell's reconsideration of *Hudson v. Leake County School Board,* the court holds that enforcing integration would spark such discord that it would likely fail, so the justices issue a mandate to make black and white schools equal and to create a board of oversight to ensure that school districts comply. Bell says in the book that he wrote the ruling when a friend asked him whether the court could have framed its decision "differently from, and better than," the one it chose to hand down. His response is a rebuke to the Warren court's ruling and also, implicitly, to the position taken by the man who gave Bell his job as an LDF attorney—Thurgood Marshall, who had overseen the plaintiff's suit and sought integration as a remedy. Yet, Crenshaw said, "at the end of the day, if Bell had been on the court, would he have written that opinion? Well, I highly doubt it." As she told me, "A lot of what Derrick would do would be intentionally provocative."

The 2008 election of Barack Obama to the presidency, which inherently represented a validation of the civil rights movement, seemed like a refutation of Bell's arguments. I knew Bell casually by that point—in 2001, I had interviewed him for an article on the LDF's legacy, and we had kept in touch. In August 2008, during an email exchange about James Baldwin's birthday, our discussion turned to Obama's campaign. He suggested that Baldwin might have found the senator too reticent and too moderate on matters of race. Bell himself was not much more encouraged. He wrote to me, "We can recognize this campaign as a significant moment like the civil rights protests, the 1963 March for Jobs and Justice in D.C., the Brown decision, so many more great moments that in retrospect promised much and, in the end, signified nothing except that the hostility and alienation toward black people continues in forms that frustrate thoughtful blacks and place the country ever closer to its premature demise."

I was struck by his ominous outlook, especially since someone Bell knew personally, and who had taught his work at the University of Chicago, stood to become the first black president. I thought that his skepticism had turned into fatalism. But, a decade later, during the most reactionary moments of the Trump era, Bell's words seemed clarifying. On January 6, 2021, as a mob stormed the Capitol in an attempt to overturn a presidential election, the words seemed nearly prophetic. It would not have surprised Bell that Obama's election and the strength of the black electorate that had helped him win are central factors in the current tide of white nationalism and voter suppression.

Bell did not live to see the election of Donald Trump, but, as his mention of the nation's "premature demise" suggests, he clearly understood that someone like him could come to power. Still, the current attacks on critical race theory have arrived decades too late to prevent its core tenets from entering the legal canon. The cohort of young legal scholars that Bell influenced went on to important positions in the academy, and many of them, including Crenshaw, Williams, Matsuda, and Cheryl Harris, have influenced subsequent generations of thinkers themselves. People who looked at the deaths of George Floyd and Breonna Taylor and others and concluded that they were not anomalies but evidence that the system was functioning as it was designed to were articulating the conclusion that Bell had drawn decades earlier. "The gap between words and reality in the American project—that is what critical race theory is, where it lies," Perry told me. The gap persists and, consequently, Bell's perspective retains its relevance. Even after his death, it has been far easier to disagree with him than to prove him wrong.

Vinay Harpalani told me, "Someone asked him once, 'What do you say about critical race theory?' " Bell first replied, "I don't know what that is," but then offered, "To me, it means telling the truth, even in the face of criticism." Harpalani added, "He was just telling his story. He was telling his truth, and that's what he wanted everyone to do. So, as far as Derrick Bell goes, that's probably what I think is important."

POSTSCRIPT TO "THE MAN BEHIND CRITICAL RACE THEORY"

Derrick Bell was more familiar than most with test cases. A significant portion of his early career involved identifying situations where a single case might advance principles that went far beyond the particulars of the lawsuit. There is a bitter irony to be found in the fact that the public furor over "critical race theory" that was stoked by right-wing media and Republican politicians reached its peak around 2021–2022 has almost completely disappeared. Having served its cynical purpose in inducing a general paranoia that rationalized book bans and restrictions on school curricula, the fabricated fixation on CRT was dropped nearly as abruptly as it began. But the template endured.

The second Trump administration replaced the obsession over critical race theory with that of another acronym—DEI—and, in its earliest days of existence, attempted to exorcise all traces of discussion of diversity, equity, and inclusion from public life. The defiling of Bell's legacy was a test run for the right's subsequent taint-and-paint campaigns. The playbook against both CRT and DEI bears obvious similarities—both ideas emerged in higher education and attempt to address the ongoing social disparities in American life. In both instances, the playbook involved distorting the actual meaning of these ideas with hyperbolic claims of anti-white discrimination and then capitalizing on the ensuing (white) outrage. The classic demagogue's playbook: repetition of a slanderous caricature until it produces violent outrage. An observer with an eye toward history will recognize strains of Cold War domestic politics here. Communism became so amorphous a damnation, so broad a catchall, that it could be applied to virtually any idea, social practice, or movement in the aim of discrediting it. (The reason Southern politicians in the middle of the twentieth century so often referred to the civil rights movement as a "communist plot" had less to do with whether young activists sympathized with Marx's ideas and everything to do with the fact that segregationists sincerely believed that racial equality *was the definition* of communism.)

I approached this piece through the lens of Derrick Bell's thinking and the ways in which his life's work had been a casualty of the effort to whip up white resentment and fear ahead of a pivotal election. In retrospect, that was only one small part of the story. As the early Trump 2.0 efforts reveal, the anti-CRT campaign was simply a beachhead for an effort to uproot the advances of the civil rights movement itself. In his first week back in office, Donald Trump, in the name of eliminating DEI from the federal government, revoked Lyndon B. Johnson's 1965 executive order prohibiting racial discrimination in federal hiring. Other parts of the federal bureaucracy "suspended" their recognition of Martin Luther King, Jr., Day and Juneteenth with the same rationale. The meaning of "DEI" is, like "communism" in the mouths of their ancestral segregationists, anything that the moment requires. The disingenuous attack upon critical race theory was the beginning of this rearguard march into a dark stretch of history, but, as subsequent events have made painfully obvious, it was certainly not the end of it.

THE POWER OF DAVE CHAPPELLE'S COMEDY

October 24, 2021

Dave Chappelle, early in his new, predictably incendiary Netflix special *The Closer,* says, in an understatement of the obvious, "I'm rich and famous." He says it en route to the larger observation that, if the pandemic has been trying for him—he contracted Covid-19 in January but was asymptomatic—it has been far more so for people who fall into neither category. But from there he detours into an extended series of jokes about the LGBTQ community—he refers to being trans as the gender equivalent of wearing blackface—which have mired the special in controversy.

For two weeks after its release on October 5, *The Closer* was among the ten most viewed programs on Netflix—but it was also met with outrage. Jaclyn Moore, the showrunner for the Netflix series *Dear White People,* who is white and trans, denounced *The Closer* and pledged not to work with Netflix in the future. (This led to a social media backlash from people asking why *Dear White People,* a show about black perspectives on white racism, had a white showrunner to begin with.) B. Pagels-Minor, a black trans nonbinary Netflix employee who was helping organize a workplace walkout to protest *The Closer,* was fired for allegedly leaking internal documents about the special to the press. (Pagels-Minor denied leaking the material.) The walkout took place on October 20.

Meanwhile, in response to allegations that Chappelle's comments in *The Closer* might lead to violence against trans people, Netflix co-CEO Ted Sarandos sent employees a memo in which he defended the special and cited other more LGBTQ-positive content on the platform, such as the comedian Hannah Gadsby's two specials. Gadsby responded by denouncing Netflix, with poetic economy, as an "amoral algorithm cult." Sarandos also noted the company's "strong belief that content on screen doesn't directly translate to real-world harm." This was a curious position, and, on Wednesday, Sarandos felt compelled to concede that, in fact, "content on-screen can have an impact in the real world, positive and negative." Comedy is powerful precisely because it riffs on and ridicules mores and habits. And within that arena no one is more successful, relevant, or influential than Chappelle.

And no one is seemingly more aware of the power of his comedy. In 2005, Chappelle walked away from a reported $50 million contract with Comedy Central for two additional seasons of *Chappelle's Show*, his sketch comedy series. Years later, he explained that he'd been conflicted about the effect of his brand of racial humor, which relied heavily on enacting stereotypes in order to ridicule them. He had begun to wonder whether his audience got the second, more subtle layer of his work, or whether it was entertained purely by the stereotypes. Some critics said that the pressure and expectations that came with the contract and the success of the show's previous seasons had been so intense that the comedian just decided that he wanted out. But Chappelle, as he told David Letterman, was attuned to nuances in his work that it would have been more convenient (and more lucrative) to ignore. There was always the risk, in riffing on the racial absurdities of American culture, of reinforcing rather than undermining them.

The absence of concern of this kind about *The Closer* is striking and suggests that Chappelle's line about being rich and famous is more significant to the controversy than has been noted. Onstage, he refers to himself as the man who walked away from $50 million, but the credibility he derived from that act sixteen years ago is now being deployed defensively and cynically, as if to place above suspicion any possible motive for telling denigrating jokes about trans people. He is also the man who walked into a reported $60 million Netflix deal.

The *Closer* controversy is not happenstance; Chappelle notes that this will be his last special "for a while." It may even be seen, along with some of his previous work, as cancel bait. In *The Bird Revelation,* which aired on Netflix in 2017, Chappelle defended Louis C.K., whose own television series had been canceled owing to allegations—which he admitted to—of sexual misconduct, including masturbating in front of female colleagues. In *The Closer,* Chappelle jokes that he hoped to "negotiate the release of DaBaby," the rapper who was criticized for making homophobic comments and insulting people with HIV/AIDS during a performance in July. (DaBaby apologized on Instagram, albeit in a way that only compounded his problems; he later deleted the post.) Chappelle has argued that taking away people's livelihoods via cancellation is tantamount to killing them—a statement that carries weight coming from someone who has spent three decades creating work that critiques racism. Yet the principle at stake here is not equality but impunity.

The Closer marks a new iteration of the ongoing debate about cancel culture, but not necessarily for the reasons that Chappelle intended. In 2005, it meant something for a black man to reject an enormous pile of money in the name of integrity. The past two weeks reiterated a contrasting point: that black men, too, can be invested in the prerogatives that wealth purchases. Earlier this year, Netflix removed old episodes of *Chappelle's Show* from the platform at the comedian's request, forgoing the revenue it would have reaped, after he described as exploitative the contract that allowed Comedy Central, but not Chappelle, to profit from the show more than a decade and a half after its release. Sarandos has dismissed requests from trans employees that *The Closer* be removed.

The most reactionary and dangerous parts of our current politics and culture are driven by powerful people who claim to be the victims of groups that are far more vulnerable than they are. The irony is that these dynamics are increasingly present in matters of racism.

Days after *The Closer* aired, Chappelle performed at a sold-out event at the Hollywood Bowl before an audience that included Nas, Lizzo, Stevie Wonder, Brad Pitt, and Tiffany Haddish. He remains powerful and influential despite the protests from a comparatively small community of activists and their supporters. The turbulence around *The Closer* will, in all likelihood, amount to just another speed bump in Chappelle's path. In gliding through this situation, he has emphasized a fact about power that was never particularly noteworthy. Because the one thing that has not been canceled is the check.

WHY I QUIT ELON MUSK'S TWITTER

November 27, 2022

It has been an interminable month since Elon Musk assumed control of Twitter and showed up in its headquarters while carrying a bathroom sink. (In a leaden pun that foreshadowed what was to come, Musk tweeted, "let that sink in.") The platform has since shed two-thirds of its workforce; lost half of its top hundred advertisers, including Citigroup, Merck pharmaceuticals, and Chevrolet; witnessed the rushed introduction and abrupt cancellation of a laughable subscription payment scheme; reinstated the account of a former president who used the platform to promote a violent attack on the United States Capitol; and lost at least a million users. Last week, after fourteen years on the platform, I became one of them. Former Twitter users, like digital expats, have turned up on new shores—platforms such as Mastodon and (later defunct) Post News—with hopes of re-creating some semblance of their former online community minus the toxicity that sent them into exile. On November 20, the Mastodon handle @LauraMartinez posted, "I'm here because Elon broke Twitter," which was more a summary of what a great many people felt about the old platform than a zealous endorsement of the buggy, complicated new one.

This is a loss because, for all of Twitter's flaws, people stuck with it for a reason. A decade ago, when Tony Wang, Twitter's general manager in the U.K., notably described the platform as the "free speech wing of the free speech party," he was defending users who had violated British law by sharing the details of public figures who had obtained privacy injunctions from U.K. courts. It was easy in those early days, when the heady afterglow of the Arab Spring still cast social media in a favorable light, to think of Twitter as simply the new frontier of digital democracy. Even after the platform's unsavory practices became more broadly known, such as its monetization of users' attention spans and its algorithmic manipulations, Twitter still offered enough trade-offs to potentially redeem itself.

Scroll back to May 26, 2020, the day after the excruciating video of George Floyd's murder went viral on the platform. First, a large crowd gathered on the streets of Minneapolis, then in Oakland, and then in Pensacola, and even in Frisco, Texas, and outside the Iowa statehouse. Online outrage begat outrage in the streets. The flow of communication was lateral, not vertical. People informed their peers about the nature of our government's failings. Were it not for social media, George Floyd—along with Ahmaud Arbery and Breonna Taylor—would likely have joined the long gallery of invisible dead black people, citizens whose bureaucratized deaths were hidden and ignored. This is what was at stake, quietly and loudly, when Musk acquired Twitter.

The singular virtue of the fiasco Musk has presided over is the possibility that the outcome will sever, at least temporarily, the American conflation of wealth with intellect. Market valuation is not proof of genius. Ahead of the $44 billion deal that gave Musk private control of Twitter, he proclaimed that he would "unlock" the site's potential if given the chance. His admirers hailed his interest with glee. Musk has been marketed as a kind of can-do avatar, a magical mix of Marvel Comics and Ayn Rand—despite serial evidence to the contrary, like the allegations of abusive treatment of Tesla workers.

Mike Tyson famously observed that "everyone has a plan until they get punched in the mouth." The facile idea was that, as Kara Swisher pointed out on her podcast, Musk was potentially the one person who could solve Twitter's long-term profitability problem.

Such praise paved the way for the current state of affairs, where many, including Musk himself, believe Twitter's collapse might be imminent. (Swisher, to her credit, later pointed out where Musk went astray, taking particular note of his tweet, which she deemed homophobic, regarding the assault on Paul Pelosi.)

Musk's vision for Twitter, never entirely coherent, cracked at first contact with economic reality. His disdain for advertising meant that the companies purchasing ads would view him warily. Moreover, his lifting of bans on Twitter's most truculent users inspired understandable fear from advertisers that their products would appear next to homophobic, racist, sexist, or generally misanthropic tweets. Musk's desire to replace lost ad revenue with subscriptions—while simultaneously reducing content moderation—made even less sense. He effectively asked people to pay for membership in a community where they were now more likely to be abused.

Participating in Twitter—with its world-spanning reach, its potential to radically democratize our discourse along with its virtue mobs and trolls—always required a cost-benefit analysis. That analysis began to change, at least for me, immediately after Musk took over. His reinstatement of Donald Trump's account made remaining completely untenable. Following an absurd Twitter poll about whether Trump should be allowed to return, Musk reinstated the former president. The implication was clear: if promoting the January 6, 2021, insurrection—which left at least seven people dead and more than a hundred police officers injured—doesn't warrant suspension to Musk, then nothing else on the platform likely could.

Musk's ownership is markedly different from the one that preceded it. He took the company private, and Twitter is no longer a publicly traded entity. In a sense, the users whose tweets drive what remains of its shrinking ad revenue are his most important employees. My sepia-tinted memories of what Twitter was—or could possibly have become—dissolved at the prospect of stuffing money in the pocket of the richest man on the planet. Yet leaving has yielded its own complications, including unwinding connections to sources, colleagues, and roughly four hundred thousand followers. The alternatives that have gained prominence in recent weeks do not offer the same reach, or the rich vein of dissimilarity across social and geographic lines, that were some of the best aspects of Twitter. As *The New York Times* observed of disgruntled conservatives, vowing to leave Twitter is easier than actually doing so.

My decision to leave yielded a tide of farewells but also two other types of responses. The first was low-grade trolling that had the effect of validating my decision to depart. But the second was more nuanced and complicated, an argument that leaving offered a concession to the abusive, reactionary elements whose presence has become increasingly prominent since Musk took over. One person paraphrased the writer Sarah Kendzior, urging users to "never cede ground in an information war." Those arguments are increasingly frail, though. If there is, in fact, an information war raging on Twitter, Musk is a profiteer. Twitter is what it always was: a moneymaking venture—just more nakedly so. And it now subsidizes a billionaire who understands free speech to be synonymous with the right to abuse others. (While claiming to champion free speech, Musk has selectively granted it, suspending accounts that are critical of him and firing employees who dissented from his view of how the company should be run.) The tech industry's gimmick to monetize our attention has been astoundingly successful even if Twitter has habitually struggled to be profitable. In the end, Musk's leadership of the company appears to be a cynical form of trolling— creating a welcoming environment for some of the platform's worst actors while simultaneously hailing his new order for its inclusivity.

To the extent that people remain active on Twitter, they preserve the fragile viability of Musk's gambit. The illusory sense of community that still lingers on the platform is one of Musk's most significant assets. No matter which side prevails, the true victor in any war is the person selling weapons to both sides. It seems likely that this experiment will conclude with bankruptcy and Twitter falling into the hands of creditors who will have their own ideas of what it should be and whom it should serve. But, at least in the interim, it's worth keeping in mind that some battles are simply not worth fighting, some battles must be fought, but none are worth fighting on terms set by those who win by having the conflict drag on endlessly.

POSTSCRIPT TO "WHY I QUIT ELON MUSK'S TWITTER"

In November 2022, at the midpoint of the Biden presidency, Elon Musk's acquisition of the social media platform Twitter, soon to be renamed "X," appeared to hold foreboding implications given Musk's own tormented understanding of the term "free speech." His early moves were troublesome enough that I exited the platform (but retained the account to prevent anyone from assuming my identity). But I didn't yet fully grasp how Musk's moves fit into a bigger trend of tech and other billionaires using media—both legacy and social—to support and encourage Donald Trump's reactionary movement. In line with the November 2022 reactivation of Trump's account, Musk later went on to speak at rallies on Trump's behalf and poured $100 million into the effort to reelect him. Then Musk became one of the most powerful people in the administration as the leader of the Department of Government Efficiency—which is not, in fact, a department of the government and whose true mandate, ostensibly, has little to do with efficiency. (In the exuberant aftermath of inauguration, Musk made a gesture suspiciously similar to the Nazi "Sieg Heil!" salute at one of the celebratory balls. Given the context, the controversy seemed par for the course.)

Ahead of the election, Jeff Bezos, the founder of Amazon and owner of, among many other things, *The Washington Post*, prohibited the paper from endorsing Kamala Harris, as did Patrick Soon-Shiong, the billionaire owner of the *Los Angeles Times*. Following the election, in December, ABC News paid $15 million to Trump's presidential library fund to settle a civil suit regarding anchor George Stephanopoulos's on-air claim that Trump had been found civilly liable for rape. He was, in fact, found civilly liable for sexual abuse in a case brought against him by the writer E. Jean Carroll, even as the judge deemed the rape allegation "substantially true." Legal commentators agreed that ABC could have fought the case and won. In January 2025, Bezos's Amazon Prime streaming platform inked a reportedly $40 million deal with Melania Trump for the rights to produce a documentary on her life. A few days later, Mark Zuckerberg announced that Meta had fired its fact-checking workforce—long a target of MAGA adherents who saw the Facebook and Instagram fact-checking program as biased toward liberals. Collectively, these developments presented a landscape of media capitulation—if not outright collaboration—with Trump and Trumpism, raising serious questions about the will of media outlets to report critically on the incoming administration.

One aspect of the aftermath of this piece warrants mention: the reaction of other journalists. To a striking degree, journalists and journalism organizations have been reluctant to sever ties with Twitter/X, even as the platform grows increasingly hostile toward credible media. With the site awash in half-baked conspiracy theories and MAGA talking points, journalists there frequently see their efforts dismissed or at the least challenged by fact-free critics. We have yet to grapple with the ultimate implications of this close association between the Fourth Estate and Musk's alternative-fact engine. My essay was written at a time when I expected to see a tide of departures for the very reasons I elucidated. Some of that did happen following the 2024 election, but many journalists continue to post daily on X, with no end in sight. If there was a reckoning right around the corner, it was also a long, long way up the block.

HIP-HOP AT FIFTY: AN ELEGY

March 16, 2023

Three things of note to a particular slice of American culture occurred in recent weeks: On February 5, the Grammy Awards, which were initially reluctant to embrace the genre of hip-hop, recognized the fiftieth anniversary of its existence. (To the extent that something as complex and sprawling as a musical genre can find a single point of origin, hip-hop was born in the summer of 1973 at a fabled party thrown by DJ Kool Herc at 1520 Sedgwick Avenue in the Bronx.) Then, on March 3, the catalog of De La Soul, a cornerstone group whose work helped define the music's golden era but has long been trapped in a skein of legal complications, finally became available on streaming services. The celebration of that development was bittersweet, though, because just a couple of weeks earlier Dave Jolicoeur, one of the group's three founding members, who rapped under the name Trugoy the Dove, had died of congestive heart failure at the age of fifty-four.

There is, in this world, an ambivalent space reserved for revolutionaries who die in their beds and rappers who die of natural causes. From hip-hop's inception, what has distinguished it from other forms of youth culture was its certain awareness of mortality. Rock music, for instance, mourns a group of heroes who died at twenty-seven: Brian Jones, Jimi Hendrix, Janis Joplin, Jim Morrison, Kurt Cobain. But part of the resonance of those deaths is that they came as a shock, and even acquired an aura of romance that hip-hop could never indulge. Their deaths reflected inner turmoil, most during a time of war and social violence, but the violence was not primarily directed at them. That's not the case with hip-hop, an art form crafted in places where it was not unheard of for twenty-seven-year-olds to perish. Here was an art form largely pioneered and dominated by the demographic that is most likely to die as a result of violence in this country: young black men.

The year of Kool Herc's party, there were nearly 1,600 homicides in New York City; a disproportionate number of those killed were black and brown, and a disproportionate number of them died in neighborhoods like the one where hip-hop drew its first breaths. This was the New York of *Taxi Driver* and *Death Wish,* the New York of the untouchable drug hustler Nicky Barnes and the morose slouch of a metropolis sliding into decay. In the beginning, hip-hop mostly featured lighthearted party fare and braggadocio, but, in a comparatively short period of time, it began focusing on weightier social themes. In 1982, just a few years into the history of commercially produced and recorded hip-hop, Grandmaster Flash and the Furious Five released "The Message," a parable of ghetto life that concludes with the preordained death of its subject and the haunting final line "Now your eyes sing the sad, sad song / of how you live so fast and die so young."

That theme only grew as hip-hop increased in popularity—and as the lives of its practitioners began to increasingly mirror the stories they told. A partial list of the deceased would include Scott La Rock, fatally shot in 1987 when he was twenty-five; Big L and Freaky Tah, both murdered in 1999, at twenty-four and twenty-seven, respectively; Jam Master Jay, shot in his studio at age thirty-seven in 2002; Soulja Slim, who was twenty-six when he died the following year; XXXTentacion, who was fatally shot at age twenty in 2018 during an attempted robbery; Nipsey Hussle, killed in 2019 at age thirty-three; Pop Smoke, also killed during an attempted robbery, in 2020, when he was twenty; and Takeoff, killed last November in a gambling dispute at age twenty-eight. In the 1990s, the violent deaths of Tupac Shakur (at twenty-five) and the Notorious B.I.G. (at twenty-four) cemented a pantheon that endures to this day, their images adorning murals, websites, and T-shirts in a kind of Che Guevara–esque cult of the iconically dead.

It now seems quaint that the perspectives of people—particularly people of color born between 1965 and 1980—were once so bound up with the music, ideas, and attitudes that derived from that culture that they were referred to as the "hip-hop generation," but at the time it made a certain sense. More than any other platform or outlet, hip-hop conveyed the frustrations, hopes, ambitions, and fears of a set of people who came of age amid the scourges of crack and AIDS and the generally barren social landscape of the 1980s. And, as with any generation of young people, their growing understanding of the world around them inevitably highlighted the failures of the generation that preceded them, some of which were more vividly revealed than others.

On a summer night when I was eight or nine, a man was shot dead on the street where my family lived in Hollis, Queens. He staggered for a few feet and collapsed in front of our house. My parents admonished me and my siblings to stay away from the windows. They recognized immediately that their attempt to insulate the family from that level of violence by moving from Harlem to Queens a decade earlier had failed. By the time I managed to peek through the curtains, someone had covered the body with a sheet. The police ran tape from the tree in front of our house to a nearby telephone pole, signaling that what moments earlier had been our front yard was now a crime scene. My father, worried about my teenage brother, who had left the house not long before, ventured out to the street. A cop lifted the sheet, and my father stared at the dead man for a minute before shaking his head and walking back inside. "Sideburns," he said to my mother. The dead man had long sideburns; my brother did not. That was the first time I had seen a victim of a fatal shooting, but it was not the last. And I came to recognize that my experience was not unique; a wide swath of my generation was witnessing similar scenes in violence-racked communities across the nation. In college, a classmate from the Bronx told me about a time in high school when he saw a man shot on the street and how the victim insisted on taking his shirt off, tormented by the heat of the bullets in his torso. Another friend said that, when he was seven, he'd seen a man shot dead on Eighty-Fourth Street, between Hoover and Vermont, in Los Angeles. The reality of those memories was reflected most indelibly in the 1991 film *Boyz n the Hood,* which opens with a group of boys happening upon a (young, black) murder victim on their way to school, an event that terribly foreshadows their own futures in South Central Los Angeles.

Hip-hop came of age as the voice of people living through the most violent stretch of the twentieth century in American cities, and the scar tissue was easily discerned. By 1990, the point at which hip-hop had fully emerged as a cultural force across the nation—the pinnacle of what became known as its golden era—New York City had reached a record number of homicides: more than 2,200 that year alone. Los Angeles witnessed a peak of more than 2,500 killings in 1992, and there were staggering per capita homicide rates in Washington, D.C., Chicago, Detroit, and other cities. In 1990, Ice Cube released "Dead Homiez," a haunting tribute to the fallen, which includes the line "I still hear the screams from his mother / as my nigga lay dead in the gutter." He closes the song urging his listeners to take a moment to reflect on their own slain friends— a request that implicitly conveyed how many could relate to the experience. Two years later, A Tribe Called Quest released a remix for the song "Scenario" that featured four guest rappers. Busta Rhymes opened the track by explaining that, of the seven collaborators, there were six rappers "in physical form, one which is in spiritual essence." In the time between first recording the remix and its release, MC Hood had been shot in the head outside the Harlem group home where he had lived. The critic Rob Marriott pointed out in those years that the roots of the hypermasculinity that dominated hip-hop culture lay in the astounding physical vulnerability of the people creating it. The bravado, the contempt, and the veneer of stoicism were all strategically worn masks meant to camouflage their fears and their ultimate powerlessness to change the circumstances that reliably produced such a vast toll of needless deaths—including, quite likely, their own.

Yet the very prominence of this theme makes the confluence of hip-hop's midcentury mark and Dave Jolicoeur's death all the more unsettling. De La Soul's work is defined by its subversive wit and creativity; Jolicoeur chose the name Trugoy the Dove in an attempt to set himself apart from the superficial aggression that had defined so much of the genre even by the time De La Soul emerged in 1989. But the music that so profoundly articulated the tragedy of premature death at twenty is far less vocal on the subject of premature death at fifty. It was easy to draw the parallels between the artists gunned down in the streets and the indexes of violence affecting black and brown communities. Tupac's death resonated precisely because the circumstances under which it occurred, in 1996, were so familiar. It's less common, though, to sketch the connections between Sean Price, the Brooklyn-bred rapper who died in his sleep at age forty-three, and the disparities of health, healthcare, and longevity that impact those same communities.

There's a sense that we have reached the far side of some cruel distribution curve. The memories of those who were culled are increasingly paired with those who have simply succumbed. Homicide remains the leading cause of death for black men aged forty-four and younger in this country. But middle age is dominated by a statistical minefield of health hazards; black people have significantly higher incidences of high blood pressure than whites or Hispanics and are less likely to have their blood pressure under control, a situation compounded by unequal access to healthcare along racial lines. Similar disparities exist in heart disease and diabetes. Black women have a lower incidence rate of breast cancer than white women, but are much more likely to die of it. Racial life expectancy gaps have narrowed dramatically, driven mostly by the way that Covid-19 and the opioid crisis have reduced white life expectancy.

But life expectancy is still lower for black men than for any other demographic group.

In 2018, the year the rapper Phonte turned forty, he released a song titled "Expensive Genes," which includes a line that could be the bookend to the concluding lines of "The Message": "Our biggest fears were shots and armed robberies / Now the biggest fears are clocks and oncology." The hip-hop generation, in the places where it was born, is still dying younger than it should, just more subtly, more quietly, and in ways that are less likely to inspire public vigils and memorial T-shirts.

In January, the Fotografiska museum in Manhattan launched *Hip Hop: Conscious, Unconscious,* a photographic survey of how hip-hop has evolved since the days of Kool Herc and Grandmaster Flash. It features many of the artists who perished at the hands of violent antagonists, but also a not-insignificant number who succumbed in more recent years to the elastic category of "natural causes." That's another growing canon, which includes Phife Dawg, a founding member of A Tribe Called Quest, who died in 2016 at forty-five from complications of diabetes; Bushwick Bill, who succumbed to pancreatic cancer at age fifty-two in 2019; Biz Markie, who died at fifty-seven from complications of type 2 diabetes; and the Kangol Kid, who died of colon cancer at age fifty-five in 2021. On that list, too, are Hurricane G, who was fifty-two when she died of lung cancer in 2022, and Coolio, who suffered a fatal heart attack the same year at age fifty-nine. Also last year, DJ Kay Slay, whose roots in the culture go all the way back to its early years in the Bronx, died of Covid-19. (If the Covid-19 pandemic taught us anything, it is that "natural causes" is a euphemism, and that environmental risks cluster in the same places where other societal shortcomings do.) John Singleton, who wrote and directed *Boyz n the Hood,* died in 2019 from complications stemming from a stroke. He was fifty-one.

Fifty years is scarcely a blink in the life of a culture, but it can be an actual lifetime for human beings. Half a century in the unlikely, inspiring, and unpredictable story of how invisible kids from forgotten precincts crafted art that defined an era remains worth telling. But fifty years is also just long enough to recognize the failures that we will bequeath to the generation that is now just finding its voice. People are born and they die. The fervently whispered hope, the ambient prayer inside everything hip-hop has ever been or said or left unsaid, is that, maybe, in some distant and better world, those two things can happen just a little further apart.

UNPARDONABLE

September 3, 2023

I n early August 1975, President Gerald Ford granted amnesty to a polarizing figure whose actions had posed a grave threat to American democracy. The man in question was not Richard Nixon, whom Ford had pardoned eleven months earlier, but General Robert E. Lee. After the Civil War, the prospect of prosecution had loomed over former members of the Confederacy. In 1865, President Andrew Johnson issued a proclamation that absolved most of them but excluded, among others, Confederate leaders and those who held property worth more than $20,000. Three years later, Johnson, who felt that it was simply time to move on, issued another proclamation, which expanded the pardon to include the men, such as Lee, who had organized and led the rebellion. Still, having renounced their U.S. citizenship and taken up arms against the government, they were required to swear an oath of allegiance and make a formal request to regain their rights. Lee's application was lost—one theory holds that Secretary of State William H. Seward gave Lee's paperwork to a friend as a souvenir—and he died, in 1870, a man without a country.

When Ford reinstated Lee as an American citizen, albeit a dead one, he stretched the truth to the point of prevarication. Lee's character, Ford remarked, had been "an example to succeeding generations" and the reinstatement was therefore "an event in which every American can take pride." Nixon's pardon was far more controversial, but it followed a similar logic. Speaking to Bob Woodward in the late nineties, Ford explained that Watergate had become such a debacle that there was no hope of making progress on any domestic or foreign policy issue until it was resolved. He was, in his telling, motivated by concern for the nation's fate, not Nixon's. Despite the scale and destructiveness of his predecessor's actions, he argued, it was time for the nation to move on.

Late last month, Donald Trump, the twice-impeached, serially indicted former president of the United States, arrived at a courthouse in Atlanta to face charges stemming from his alleged attempt to overturn the results of the 2020 election. By then, the spectacle of a former president being indicted had gone from unprecedented to old hat. In addition to the sprawling Georgia case, grand juries have returned indictments against Trump in a business fraud case brought by District Attorney Alvin Bragg in New York and in two federal cases brought by Jack Smith, a special counsel for the Department of Justice: the first, in Florida, relates to the mishandling of classified materials, and the second, in Washington, D.C., to election interference. (Trump has pleaded not guilty in all of them.) The most damning charges appear in the election cases, which concern Trump's attempts to retain the presidency after being voted out of office. Those attempts, of course, culminated in the January 6 assault on the U.S. Capitol—the most significant threat to the peaceful transition of power since the conflict at the center of Robert E. Lee's forfeited citizenship.

It is not entirely surprising that Trump's federal indictments have inspired murmured appeals for President Biden to issue a preemptive pardon. (On the state level, it's difficult to imagine New York's governor issuing a pardon. In Georgia, the governor has no such authority.) After the first federal indictment in June, Marc Thiessen and Danielle Pletka wrote in *The Washington Post* that "millions will see Trump's prosecution as illegitimate, and any conviction as unjust. That will further erode public confidence in our judicial system and the principle of equal justice under law." After the second, in

August, an op-ed in *The Miami Herald* held that Trump should be pardoned "because the impact an extended trial and sentencing might have on our democracy is just too terrifying." The senseless sloganeering that produced the phrase "too big to fail" during the Great Recession has a contemporary corollary: too big to convict.

The common theme underlying these arguments is the sentiment that the Trump era was rancorous and difficult enough, and the work of upholding the rule of law is slow and protracted and will only deepen national divisions. It is time—let's say it in unison—*for the nation to move on.*

Of all the rationales for pardoning Trump, the most substantial is the contention that prosecuting political rivals is almost always the hallmark of an autocracy. Under most circumstances, this would be true. Yet the proponents of this argument seldom acknowledge the inverse—that the refusal to prosecute someone, or reflexively pardoning that person precisely *because* he's a political rival, is at least equally corrupting to a democracy. It's not unimaginable that thoughts of the Nixon pardon assuaged the members of Trump's inner circle as they rampaged over norms, policies, and laws. Abiding lawlessness among the powerful has a way of breeding more of the same. The relatively lenient terms of the Confederate amnesty, for instance, almost certainly facilitated the rise of violent white militias that nullified the voting and citizenship rights of black people throughout the South in the Civil War's long aftermath.

It's also worth recalling that Trump glided into the White House buoyed by an understandable sense of his own impunity. Despite the years-long tax schemes, chronicled by *The New York Times,* and the claims of sexual assault made by more than two dozen women, there has always somehow been a reason not to prosecute Donald Trump. He has enjoyed the amnesty of wealth his entire life—a troubling exemption, though one that, unlike the current calls for amnesty, was never passed off as something in our collective best interest.

The key problem with "moving on" is the indeterminate direction. Where to? There are times when it is in the best interest of a nation not to seek justice despite egregious wrongs. South Africa's

Truth and Reconciliation Commission, which was premised upon remorse and transparency, is one such example. Trump, whose campaign claimed to have raised $7 million in less than three days after his mug shot was released, adheres to opposite principles: belligerence and deception. At seventy-seven, for the first time in his life, he may suffer real consequences for his actions. In the short run, this will stoke deeper divisions and heighten animosities. In the long term, this is the safest course for a democracy to take. A pardon would embolden Trump and others like him. It would allow the nation to move on, but toward an even more dangerous future.

BLACK LIVES COST

2023

The Bolero Flats apartment complex consists of an imposing tower that looms over a stretch of South Marquette Avenue in the Downtown West section of Minneapolis. Residents who participated in an online survey gave the development a grade of D-minus and one out of five stars for safety. A rental ratings website noted that "the complex is very unsafe and poses serious risks to residents." That was the context in which a stream of Minneapolis police officers in tactical gear filed into the building in the predawn hours of February 2, 2022, with a search warrant for Mekhi Speed, a suspect in a homicide that occurred a month earlier in neighboring St. Paul. Bodycam footage from that morning shows at least nine officers in the hallway as one of them quietly slips a key into the front door of a corner unit. A moment later the officers rush through the door, shouting, "Police! Search warrant!" Twenty-two-year-old Amir Locke, an aspiring musician who was visiting from Dallas and staying with relatives at the complex, was asleep on the couch. He rose, still cloaked in his blanket, with a gun in his hand. Officer Mark Hanneman fired three shots that struck Locke in the chest and wrist, killing him. Locke, who had no criminal record, had a license for the firearm. Andre Locke, Amir's father, later told reporters that his son, who was a delivery driver for DoorDash, had purchased the gun after being robbed while making deliveries.

Amir Locke's death occurred in a particular and racially fraught context: he, a young black man, died at the hands of a white Minneapolis police officer nineteen months after Officer Derek Chauvin killed George Floyd by kneeling on his neck for nearly ten minutes, resulting in an international wave of outrage. Local activists began the now familiar rites of organizing protests and demanding justice for the deceased. But Keith Ellison, the district attorney who brought charges against Chauvin, declined to charge Hanneman, stating that a conviction was unlikely. Months later, Mekhi Speed, Locke's eighteen-year-old cousin, pled guilty to fatally shooting thirty-eight-year-old Otis Elder in the back. For Locke's family, it was confounding that there had been two homicides but only one person brought up on charges.

One evening last spring, Andre Locke told me about the moment he discovered that his son had been killed. Locke, who works as a medical transportation driver, was listening to the radio during morning traffic and heard about a police shooting in downtown Minneapolis. After hearing that the shooting had occurred in Bolero Flats, he called a few relatives, but, failing to get in touch with anyone, he continued working. Roughly an hour later his sister called to tell him that Amir, the second oldest of his five sons, was dead. The information had, in the course of that hour, moved from general news to specific worry to personal tragedy. The weight of the loss left Locke confused. As he tried to process the idea of Amir's death, he told me, he inadvertently drove around the same traffic circle three times—a metaphor for the looping thoughts running through his mind. Not long afterward, he called his ex-wife to tell her about their son's death. And not long after that, the family made another phone call: to the attorney Benjamin Crump. "Mr. Crump came to mind right away," he told me.

"When bad things happen, he's the first person people call," Damon Hewitt, the president of the Lawyers' Committee for Civil Rights Under Law, told me recently. In the past decade, attorney Benjamin Crump has notably represented, among many others,

Jacob Blake, a black man beaten and shot by police in Kenosha, Wisconsin, and Ralph Yarl, a black sixteen-year-old who was shot after mistakenly ringing the wrong doorbell in Kansas City, Missouri. He has represented the families of George Floyd, the black man murdered by an on-duty police officer in Minneapolis; Daunte Wright, a black twenty-year-old killed by a police officer who reportedly mistook her gun for a Taser in a nearby suburb; Breonna Taylor, a twenty-six-year-old black ER technician fatally shot in her home by police in Louisville, Kentucky; Tamir Rice, a black twelve-year-old who was killed by police in Cleveland, Ohio; and Michael Brown, an eighteen-year-old whose shooting death at the hands of police in Ferguson, Missouri, sparked months of unrest and helped launch the Black Lives Matter movement. The sheer preponderance of these cases—high-profile incidents involving inflammatory elements of race, law enforcement, and violence—has made Crump a consistent media presence.

A search for the words "Ben Crump press conference" yields a catalog of racial woe—dozens of videos of Crump, tall, bald, and clean-shaven, typically standing at a podium in a church or outside a police station, next to a bereaved black person as he explains why their loved one should not be dead. He maintains a brutal travel schedule, spending as much as three-quarters of any given month on the road, a pace on which he has built his practice and reputation but which has also diminished the time he is able to spend with his wife and their ten-year-old daughter, Brooklyn. In public, Crump typically betrays a kind of muted outrage and disbelief, especially when speaking about his clients' cases. In private, he projects a kind of pastoral earnestness and conveys a level of sincerity found only in people with a total absence of guile (or, conversely, in those who possess it in great abundance). He is the opposite of a fast-talking operator: he speaks deliberately, his words so inflected with the cadences of his North Carolina roots that he presents as a black version of the old archetype of the country lawyer.

When we spoke following a memorial event for ten African Americans murdered by a white supremacist in Buffalo in 2022, Crump told me that his law offices field roughly five hundred calls per day. Comparatively few of them yield actionable claims, and among those that do he looks for cases that will "shock the conscience" as a way of highlighting the bigger issue. The volume of calls in itself speaks to the extent to which Crump's name, as Andre Locke recalled, tends to "come to mind right away" in these circumstances. A few years ago, Al Sharpton began referring to Crump as "black America's Attorney General." The name stuck and it is not uncommon now for this honorific to be cited as Crump is introduced to speak to predominantly black audiences at memorials, commemorations, and civil rights rallies. At the same time, the velocity at which Crump tends to become associated with these cases has sometimes led, as Damon Hewitt pointed out, to him getting "a negative label of ambulance chaser. Personal injury lawyers show up after the fact."

In 2021, a suit filed by Crump on behalf of George Floyd's family yielded a $27 million settlement from the city of Minneapolis, at the time the largest civil settlement in the nation's history for a case involving a black person killed by the police. The sum had multiple implications. For the city, agreeing to a settlement of that size was a notable gesture of contrition for its part in Floyd's death and the national strife that followed it. For Crump, it represented the success of a strategy he has pursued since the early days of his first legal practice. "I want," he is prone to say, "to make killing black people very expensive."

The idea is counterintuitive, cynical, and, on its surface, confounding. Decades of civil rights legal strategy have sought to affirm the humanity and equality of black people by using the law to create a landscape of social equality. Crump's principle operates on a different set of assumptions: that, as long as racial inequality exists, practical monetary considerations can inhibit the most egregious manifestations of it. "That strategy is reactionary, not prophylactic," Hewitt said to me in the fall, a few weeks after Crump had settled a landmark suit against the biotech giant Thermo Fisher for using, without permission, the cancer cells of a black woman named

Henrietta Lacks for a profitable cancer research program dating back to the 1950s. The fact that Crump's approach could be deemed reactionary, Hewitt later pointed out, didn't necessarily mean it would not work. Crump's strategy, and its resonance with victims, poses questions about his own ideas and motivations but, more fundamentally, about what "civil rights" actually means in this moment and whether the older, loftier strategies associated with that term have reached a permanent impasse. Crump's rise paralleled that of the Black Lives Matter movement, but his underlying ethic is not exactly the same as theirs. Whereas his predecessors both in law and activism anchored themselves in a particular brand of idealism, Crump has pursued something intensely, almost pessimistically practical that might be best summarized as *black lives cost*.

The video of Amir Locke's final moments, which was released on February 3, 2022, and posted online by multiple local news organizations, is conspicuous in one regard: the police do not knock before entering. In some angles of the video, you can see Locke's shrouded form rise somnolently from the couch just seconds before he is shot. The police entered the apartment without announcing themselves beforehand—they'd received a "no knock" warrant prior to the raid. In the wake of Locke's death—following, too, on the 2020 murder of Breonna Taylor under similar circumstances—these warrants became a point of sustained public contention. Amir Locke died amid the ethical haziness of a society in which people are permitted to own firearms but police are also allowed to enter their homes unannounced in the middle of the night.

Keith Ellison, the Minnesota attorney general who oversaw the prosecution of Derek Chauvin, declined to bring charges against the officers involved in Locke's death. Ellison, who is African American, was widely hailed in black political circles following Chauvin's conviction. This highlighted that there were circumstances in which even the figures most sympathetic to civil rights concerns could not deliver the justice that Locke's family was seeking. There have been many other cases where either district attorneys have declined to press charges or juries have declined to convict officers who have been charged. Grand juries, which, according to legal lore, are typically willing to indict a ham sandwich, are notoriously reluctant to bring charges against law enforcement. This has meant that the epilogue to even egregious police shootings has tended to feature a family, not unlike Amir Locke's, that is resigned to the fact that, if they cannot attain justice through the criminal court system, they will have to pursue it by alternate means. This is where Ben Crump typically enters the picture.

There is a long-standing suspicion of plaintiffs' attorneys in American culture. The stereotype is that of a character who is in equal measures unctuous and avaricious. There is an equally long tradition of skepticism, if not contempt, for figures publicly associated with the cause of racial justice—the derisive term "race hustlers" comes to mind. Crump operates in the precise Venn overlap between the two categories, which is why his rise to prominence, particularly early on, inspired murmurs of racial "ambulance chasing," his ubiquity seemingly evidence of unbridled ambition, a penchant for self-promotion, or both. Yet there is another, equally plausible explanation for Crump's saturation-level presence: the types of cases he's best known for representing are so commonplace, so routine a feature of our social landscape, that a high-profile legal advocate is exactly what is needed. There are currently five black attorney generals in the United States. Yet people mean something qualitatively different when they speak of the "attorney general of Black America."

It is significant that Breonna Taylor, fatally shot by police in 2020 as she lay in her bed, died in a state, Kentucky, that at the time had a black attorney general, Daniel Cameron. Five months after her death, Cameron decided not to bring charges against the officers who fired into her apartment that night. (One officer was charged—and acquitted—for endangering Taylor's neighbors.) Cameron's decision outraged and galvanized a wide swath of African Americans in Louisville and beyond. It is perhaps even more significant that Crump represented Taylor's family and, within eight months, was able to achieve a $12 million settlement—the largest payout in Louisville's history for a police brutality case. The contrast between the criminal and civil systems' responses to Taylor's death underscores the distinction that Crump's unofficial title alludes to. Notably, Eric Holder, the first black attorney general of the United States, described Crump's impact as "extremely beneficial" in ways that don't neatly align with the roles we associate with a civil attorney. Crump's presence "makes those who are in official positions understand that they have to deal with this lawyer with a national reputation and with lots of followers and supporters. And they've got to deal with him in a substantial way."

Holder's point was exemplified by an exchange that took place in the immediate aftermath of the 2021 Daunte Wright shooting. Wright was shot in Brooklyn Center, Minnesota, a suburb about ten miles north of Minneapolis. The shooting took place against the already tense backdrop of the Derek Chauvin trial. When I spoke to Crump on the evening of April 11, a few hours after Wright's death, he had not yet heard about the shooting. When I turned on my television the next morning, he and Antonio Romanucci, the local Minnesota attorney with whom Crump had partnered in the Floyd case, were representing Wright's family and outlining the case at a press conference. When, the following day, I met Crump at a conference room in his hotel, he was surrounded by attorneys and investigators from his law firm and holding a conference call with Jim Thomson, the prosecutor responsible for Brooklyn Center. Over the course of the conversation, Thomson criticized Minneapolis prosecutors for taking too long to charge Derek Chauvin; assured Crump that he intended to quickly charge Kim Potter, the officer who shot Wright; and, unbidden, announced that he had no problem sending a white officer to prison. At another point in the conversation, he mentioned his close friendship with a black neighbor during his childhood—a disclosure that prompted eye-rolling among Crump's staffers. The lines of authority seemed to have switched places during the exchange, and Thomson was interacting not only with Benjamin Crump, trial lawyer for justice (as his website identifies him), but with an entire movement that Crump implicitly brought into the room with him.

Ten days later, at Wright's funeral, Crump addressed the mourners alongside Al Sharpton. Crump told the audience and dozens of reporters that "Daunte Wright's life mattered." George Floyd's family members sat near the front of the sanctuary wearing masks with "8:46" printed on the front, a reference to the length of the video depicting Chauvin kneeling on their deceased relative's neck. This was not a coincidence. Philonise Floyd, George's brother, had, at Crump's behest, spoken to Wright's family about what they should anticipate in the coming weeks and months. The sanctuary, quite deliberately, included representatives of similarly traumatized black families, spanning from painfully recent traumas like those of Floyd and Breonna Taylor, whose boyfriend Kenneth Walker was present, all the way back to the 1955 lynching of Emmett Till, whose relatives stood in the back of the church. Crump pointed out to me that this part of the work does not strictly qualify as legal services. But it occurred to me that the funeral was, in fact, part of the legal representation. By merely associating Wright with this lineage of the wrongfully dead—including Till, whose death helped launch the civil rights movement—Crump was laying out his case. The city eventually settled with Wright's family for just over $3 million.

Ben Crump was born in Lumberton, North Carolina, a small city in Robeson County located just east of Interstate 95 in the state's Inner Banks region. He is fifty-four years old and came of age at a time when the contentious battles over civil rights were hardly distant memories. A quarter century after the *Brown v. Board of Education* decision, his home county, as he frames it, was "just getting around to that 'all deliberate speed' stuff," a reference to the Supreme Court's language about how quickly integration should occur. He describes the Lumberton of his youth as a "little, conservative, discriminatory town in eastern North Carolina," but which had integrated its schools, albeit reluctantly. "Little black kids got on the bus, went to the little white kids' new school—new technology, new everything, new books," he told me. (He cites as a formative moment the conversation in which his mother explained to him

that he was able to attend the new, mostly white school only because of a lawsuit Thurgood Marshall had filed.)

Crump did not meet his biological father until his second year of
college, but he'd developed a close bond with his stepfather, Bennie
Heywood, who was a high school math teacher. His mother, Helen,
worked as a hotel maid, then took a job working on the assembly
line at the nearby Converse sneaker factory. The couple split when
Crump was four years old, but his relationship with Bennie endured. His maternal grandmother, Mittie Cordell, took on an outsized role during his childhood. When he was seven or eight, his
grandmother told him that the family's future fortunes would rest
on his shoulders. He recalls her warning him away from vice, saying, "I've watched alcohol and drugs destroy the men of this
family"—an assertion he cites as the reason he neither drinks nor
smokes to this day. When he reached adolescence, his mother did
what he describes as "the most unselfish thing a mother could do"
by sending him to live with his stepfather, who had relocated to
Miami. "She said I would get better opportunities in a big city versus this small, segregated town," he told me. "She watched a lot of
people in our community end up in jail or dead or on drugs, and
she wanted a different future for me. She still says it was one of the
hardest things she ever did."

The transition to big-city life was a shock. Whereas Lumberton
had a population of roughly twenty thousand people, metro Miami
at the time was home to more than three million. He credits Heywood with teaching him self-reliance. When he got his first job in
high school, Heywood began charging him rent, telling him that
no one would give him anything for free in life. "I challenged myself to do well in the big city where I'm now going to school with
all these diverse people, all these Hispanic, Jewish, Haitian, Jamaican, Bahamian classmates of mine," he said. Crump did well in high
school and earned a scholarship from *The Miami Herald*, which
stipulated that the recipient attend a school in the state. He chose
Florida State University. When he left for college, his stepfather,
who had saved all those rent payments, gave the money back to

help him cover his school expenses. Crump majored in criminal justice, became president of the Black Student Union, and pledged Omega Psi Phi, a historically black fraternity known for its clamorous nonconformity and whose ranks include Langston Hughes, Jesse Jackson, and Vernon Jordan. In his sophomore year, he befriended Daryl Parks, who was the student government president at Florida A&M University, a nearby HBCU. The two shared an aspiration to pursue careers in the law, and, after graduating from Florida State's law school, they opened a practice together in Tallahassee.

From the outset, Crump was oriented toward civil rights work, while Parks, the more pragmatic of the two, was interested in whatever would pay the bills. "We did a little bit of probate, a little family law, though I can count on one hand the number of family cases we did," Parks told me. In the early years, claims arising from car accidents provided a steady stream of income, alongside a growing caseload of criminal defense work. "Criminal law is the entrée if you want to get the experience to be a litigator," Parks continued. During law school, Parks had interned with Willie Gary, the famed black litigator whose successful—and lucrative—civil suits against large companies had earned him the nickname "the Giant Killer." Early on, Crump and Parks had in Gary a reference point for litigation that could be both socially impactful and lucrative.

The firm's orientation shifted, though, in 2006. Martin Lee Anderson, a fourteen-year-old African American who'd been sent to a Florida boot camp reform program for joyriding in his grandmother's car, died at the facility under questionable circumstances. An official autopsy listed the cause of death as complications from sickle cell trait, but a subsequent investigation revealed video of Anderson being kicked and beaten by guards at the Panama City facility before his death. A subsequent autopsy revealed the cause of death to be suffocation. A classmate from Florida State connected Anderson's family with Crump and Parks. Early on, they realized that media would be key to the case. "We had the wherewithal—and I credit Ben with this—to move the news activities from Panama City to Tallahassee, where the legislature was meeting." The two lawyers pushed information about the case to the Black Caucus in particular. Despite the video and the second autopsy report, a jury acquitted seven guards and one nurse of manslaughter charges the following year. Parks and Crump, however, secured a combined $7.4 million settlement from state and county authorities. When I asked Crump if he felt those substantial civil payouts functioned as a kind of trade-off for miscarriages in the criminal system, he replied, "Back then it was. You have to remember, twenty-five or thirty years ago, you didn't get *nothing* when the police killed you. You didn't get any civil justice or criminal justice."

The Anderson case was high-profile enough that, five years after the settlement, when seventeen-year-old Trayvon Martin was shot by the volunteer neighborhood watchman George Zimmerman in Sanford, also in Florida, Martin's family knew to seek out Crump and Parks. Sybrina Fulton, Martin's mother, wrote about their first encounter in *Rest in Power,* the memoir she co-wrote with Tracy Martin, Trayvon's father. "He was clearly well educated and wore a sharp business suit," she wrote in a description of Crump, "but he also had the kind of deep Southern accent some people associate with uneducated individuals. . . . He wasn't aggressive or edgy or slick—he was polite but efficient, clearly a dogged, hard worker." When I asked her about that passage, Fulton said, "People think attorneys are just one cookie-cutter way, and he's different. He does everything different. People underestimate him." That last point was significant.

The Martin case brought national attention but also put Crump into sustained contact with Al Sharpton, whom he now refers to as his mentor. In the midst of the campaign to pressure police into arresting and charging Zimmerman, Sharpton encouraged Crump to cultivate a more visible presence, seeing a national need for the kind of legal work that was becoming his specialty. Crump was initially reluctant. Sharpton recalled Crump telling him, "I ain't good with soundbites like you. I'm not good with oratory like you." Sharpton replied that this was exactly why he was needed. He told Crump, "You didn't know me when I wore a tracksuit and was three hundred pounds. You *want* them to underestimate you, because you'll get there before they ever see you coming." The two forged a symbiotic strategy that has been replayed in numerous theaters of their social justice crusade. Sharpton distilled their complementary roles succinctly, saying, "The public rallying is to keep attention on a case until you can get it into court. The legal work is, make sure they get into court."

As he had with the Anderson case, Crump relied on media coverage of Martin's death to elevate the civil case he was building. But in the six years between Anderson's and Martin's deaths, social media had exploded as a means of communication. Rather than pursue the attention of the legislature by holding press conferences in their vicinity, you could now create a digital press conference and rely upon millions of voices in Florida and far beyond to pressure the elected officials on your behalf. The result was that Martin became the rallying cry for an emerging generation of activists, and Crump was catapulted into national recognition. He and Parks dissolved their firm over differences regarding the direction they wanted to pursue in their careers, but Parks emphasized to me that the two remain close friends. Crump emerged at a moment when the limits of earlier civil rights achievements were becoming most apparent. A black president had been elected, yet the old deprivations persisted. The moment seemed to call for a new or at least broader definition of what social justice could look like.

Efforts to use the Constitution to seek redress for racial discrimination are nearly as old, in this country, as racial discrimination itself. The modern conception of civil rights lawyering, however, owes its origins to the aftermath of Reconstruction and the campaigns to use the Fourteenth Amendment to defend the fragile freedoms African Americans attained after the Civil War. Though the case is now notorious for codifying segregation in the United States, it's worth noting that *Plessy v. Ferguson* started out as an attempt to overturn the Jim Crow accommodations policy of Louisiana railcars. Albion Tourgée, the attorney who represented Homer Adolph Plessy, was hoping to establish precedent that could anchor a legal crusade for civil rights, though his effort inadvertently had the opposite effect. The body of case law associated with this cause, so familiar to civil rights lawyers and historians, includes: *Buchanan v. Warley,* the 1917 ruling that outlawed discriminatory housing covenants (and *Corrigan v. Buckley,* the 1926 ruling that restored them); *Smith v. Allwright,* the 1944 case that dismantled the Texas laws prohibiting black and Mexican voters from participating in primary elections; *Sweatt v. Painter,* which in 1950 forbade the exclusion of black students from the University of Texas law school; and *Brown v. Board of Education,* the most singularly recognizable civil rights ruling in the nation's history, which struck down school segregation in 1954. Laid out in sequence, the cases suggest a deliberate but steady accretion of progress across the years, but a closer look yields entire decades that were defined more by inertia than momentum. The lawyers associated with this tradition include names like Charles Hamilton Houston, the architect of the legal strategy that eventually culminated in *Brown v. Board of Education;* Thurgood Marshall, the nation's first black justice of the Supreme Court; Jack Greenberg, who led the NAACP Legal Defense Fund during some of its most crucial years; the brilliant legal strategist Pauli Murray; Constance Baker Motley, who argued key cases in the sixties; and Derrick Bell, who fought desegregation cases before becoming the pivotal figure in the critical race theory movement.

Marshall in particular looms large in Crump's thinking for reasons that are not difficult to discern. Though Marshall is best known as the first black justice of the Supreme Court, his early career was not dissimilar to the niche Crump currently occupies. Marshall graduated from Howard University Law School and was immediately recruited by his law professor Charles Hamilton Houston, who was simultaneously leading the NAACP's assault upon the legal edifice of segregation. The two barnstormed the country, arguing voting rights and segregation cases as well as egregious cases involving racism in the criminal justice system. By the time Marshall oversaw the team of lawyers who won *Brown v. Board of Education* in 1954, he had nearly two decades of experience handling these cases, many of which resemble those that Crump has taken on in the past ten years. In 1943, Marshall conducted an investigation

into the actions of Detroit's overwhelmingly white police department amid a race riot that erupted in the community. He concluded
that the police had effectively taken the side of the white mob that
pursued black residents through the city's streets.

Yet, at the same time, Marshall and Crump occupy distinct niches
even in their pursuit of broadly similar aims. Marshall was notably
impecunious during his years with the NAACP Legal Defense
Fund, an idealist in a common man's suit. Crump, by contrast, is an
avatar of black success. He advises young African American lawyers
that there need not be any conflict between doing good and doing
well. Civil rights work, he told me two years ago during a commemoration for the infamous 1921 race massacre in Tulsa, is the
least profitable portion of his practice. He is currently involved in
litigation against Johnson & Johnson over the contention that the
company specifically promoted its baby powder to black women
despite knowing the product's association with uterine cancer. "The
history of America," he told me, is the history of powerful interests
asking who are "the cheapest people we can harm without stopping
our profits." Eric Holder, whose Department of Justice oversaw the
investigation in Ferguson following Michael Brown's death, saw no
contradiction in Crump's approach. He said, "If you want to stop
Ben Crump from earning money in that way, stop killing unarmed
black guys."

That perspective is, however, notably contrasted by the sharp
criticism publicly made in 2021 by Samaria Rice, the mother of
Tamir Rice. In a series of social media posts, Rice referred to Crump
and Lee Merritt, another attorney who frequently handles cases
with social justice implications, as "ambulance chasers" and included them in a broader critique that the Black Lives Matter movement was led by self-interested cynics who were, in her words,
"hustling black death" in exchange for media attention, book deals,
and financial rewards. In 2019, Crump published the book *Open
Season: Legalized Genocide of Colored People,* in which he walks
through the legal and social implications of issues like voter suppression, environmental racism, "Stand Your Ground" gun laws,
and discrimination in the criminal justice system. In 2017, he hosted

a show on A&E called *Who Killed Tupac?* (Crump and Shakur's mothers grew up together in Lumberton, North Carolina.) In June 2022, Netflix debuted *Civil*, a documentary about Crump's legal work. When we spoke in November 2022, Rice reiterated her skepticism. "Ben is good for publicity," she told me dismissively. She questioned his helpfulness in the aftermath of her son's death; she had parted ways with Crump after working with him briefly. (When asked about Rice's comments, Crump replied, "I pray for her and wish her well.") Rice's view of Crump, however, was not shared by the clients, past and present, that I spoke to.

Sybrina Fulton, Trayvon Martin's mother, told me that Crump was a crucial source of both legal and emotional support for the traumatized families he works with. Alfred Lacks-Carter, whose grandmother Henrietta Lacks died of cervical cancer in 1951 at Johns Hopkins Hospital, where her cells were nonconsensually harvested and later sold, told me that Crump was key to his family's settlement with Thermo Fisher. "If Ben wasn't involved in this case," he told me, "I don't even think that we would have made the progress that we made." The idea that black life can be made to matter simply by making it cost prohibitive to take one is linked to the idea that these lives can be profitable posthumously. Imani Perry, a legal scholar and professor of African American studies at Princeton, pointed out that the departure Crump represents from the traditional idea of civil rights says more about the current legal landscape—where a conservative Supreme Court in particular seems intent now on reversing civil rights gains in the name of "race blindness"—than it does about his strategy. "The major anti-discrimination cases that actually come up and are successful are those filed by white people," she said to me. "They've targeted efforts to remedy discrimination like affirmative action."

Against this backdrop, it seems to make sense that Crump's strategy has caught on among victims of anti-black violence. "In some ways, it's an effort to look for whatever remedy is possible, but also because in civil law you can get these extensive punitive damages," Perry told me. Unlike the transformational impact a Supreme Court decision can have, the metrics for success with this strategy are more ambiguous. A multimillion-dollar settlement might, as Perry asserted, have a deterrent effect upon a rogue police department. But another influential civil rights attorney was skeptical, pointing out that most of these settlements are paid by municipal insurance and the weight of their impact is felt only obliquely by the institutions in question. It's a riddle that Thurgood Marshall, Constance Baker Motley, or Charles Hamilton Houston would never have been called upon to resolve.

As with any strategy, there are limitations. In the spring of 2023, I watched Crump in a courtroom in lower Manhattan as he pursued a copyright infringement case against the musician Ed Sheeran. The case, brought by the estate of Ed Townsend, the songwriter who wrote the Marvin Gaye classic "Let's Get It On," alleged that Sheeran had lifted the chord progression from that song in his 2014 hit "Thinking Out Loud." The lawsuit generated its own wave of media attention. Ahead of the trial, Crump spoke to me about his strategy of tying Sheeran's song to the long history of artistic theft that has victimized black musicians. (During proceedings, Sheeran's defense sent a letter to the judge complaining that the plaintiff and Crump had "held at least two press events in which they made claims of racism in the music industry and cultural appropriation," which they felt might taint the jury pool.) Later in the trial Crump twice attempted to introduce emails that the judge had previously prohibited, leading the judge to threaten to disqualify him from the case. In turn, the defense put Sheeran on the witness stand—with his guitar—for several days during which he strummed and sang while pointing out musical technicalities and key differences between the two songs. Sheeran, whose singing voice sounded exceptionally clear and evocative even on a courthouse microphone, effectively serenaded the jury for half the week. The next week, following a cursory deliberation, they ruled in Sheeran's favor.

Crump seemed uncharacteristically weary at the end of the trial. This was not a typical Crump case—or at least not typical of the cases he has come to be known for. Unlike the Amir Locke civil suit that was still winding its way through the Minnesota courts, no one had died as a result of potential copyright infringement. The alleged perpetrator was not the agent of a rogue bureaucracy but rather a beloved entertainer. The racial history Crump had highlighted was real but only tangentially connected to the legal issue at hand. Afterward, he complained of being hamstrung by the judge's rulings during the trial. But the case also highlighted the extent to which the protocols he has developed apply to a specific set of problems that occur within a particular social context. His weariness brought me back to a discussion we'd had in a seafood restaurant in Buffalo after the commemoration for the victims of the mass shooting there. While talking about the long trajectory of the racial justice work that had been his mainstay for the past decade, he disclosed, in a similarly weary tone, that he would prefer not to fight these cases. He conveyed a sense that this cause had found him, not the other way around. "I want to stop," he told me. "But they just won't stop killing black people."

2016 AND 2024

November 7, 2024

Eight years ago on Election Night, as the returns came in from North Carolina, where I was reporting, I made a panicked phone call to a friend. I told him that I feared the country was sliding into the hands of a demi-fascist, and that it might even be time to start considering an exit plan. My life, like those of many black people of my generation, was shaped not by the brutality of segregation, as my parents' lives had been, but by the success of the battles of the 1950s and 1960s to uproot it. The prospect that a presidential candidate could be embraced not only by white supremacists but also by one of the two major political parties and almost half the electorate triggered an enduring dread that the progress we had made was fragile and impermanent—and that, with the right incentives, the old order could resurrect itself in the present.

By the end of that late-night phone call, though, we had sorted through the "guardrails" theory of the various checks and precedents that would constrain Donald Trump. The advantage of the sprawling bureaucracy of the federal government is that it takes a brilliant level of orchestra conducting to achieve anything significant—a skill set that a mercurial, chronically uninformed career real estate developer did not likely possess. It was to be presumed that the Republican establishment, craven and increasingly reactionary but on the whole more sound than its presumptive leader, would curb Trump's impulses, or at least dangle enough distractions in front of him to keep him from focusing for too long on any truly destructive goal. The press and the courts would be the redoubt of democracy; they were designed precisely for such a moment.

Conversations like ours took place across the country in the shocked first days and weeks after the 2016 election. The difference between those conversations and the ones that began on Tuesday night is that we can no longer rely on the guardrails theory. Unlike Trump's first election, this one cannot be rationalized as the product of an overconfident Democratic campaign and the nihilistic pivot of around a hundred thousand voters in a handful of swing states. This time, voters in state after state decisively chose Trump, who has become more autocratic and belligerent, building a popular vote advantage for a man now wholly unfit to hold office. He has grown more maniacal over the years, and now he is a maniac with a mandate. It is chilling to observe the landscape of possibilities before him—and us.

Journalism is as eager as it ever was to perform its essential accountability function, but it is also impaired by financial struggles, declining trust, and disruptive new technologies. More ominously, the decisions of the billionaire owners of *The Washington Post* and the *Los Angeles Times* to cancel their papers' planned presidential endorsements suggest that journalists may face complicated impediments even within these news organizations. The courts represent a more consequential and compromised situation: unlike in 2016, the federal judiciary is now stocked with more than two hundred Trump appointees, whom he selected in overtly politicized ways. And any semblance of restraint within the ranks of the GOP establishment vanished long ago. In the coming administration, the executive branch will likely be staffed by acolytes who will co-sign Trump's worst and most random pursuits. The decision of Kamala Harris's campaign to invest heavily in appealing to anti-Trump Republicans and to showcase Liz Cheney's support was a product of bright-side thinking—of an optimistic belief that the ranks of the GOP were not entirely lost and that at least a meaningful minority of the party sees and understands the danger that Trump represents. That thinking was wrong.

There are other equally challenging concerns. In the years since Trump lost the last election, he launched a coup attempt, became a defendant in four criminal cases, and was convicted (so far) of thirty-four felonies. In the past few months, he has spread increasingly unhinged misinformation and racist lies, made lewd comments and gestures, and spewed offensive and obscene language. None of these actions prevented his popularity from expanding in multiple electorates across the country; they may even have facilitated it. Stunningly, Trump fared better in New York City this year than he did in 2020. The questions that confront the Democratic Party are gigantic and existential. Following the election of Barack Obama in 2008, strategists hypothesized that a new electorate was emerging, one that was forward-looking and egalitarian, comfortable with people from backgrounds different than their own. The catastrophic losses in 2016 and 2024 call this idealism into question and also highlight how wildly unlikely Obama's success actually was. Both Hillary Clinton and Harris were eminently qualified for the presidency, and neither ran flawless campaigns—no one does. But it is also inescapable that some portion of the blame for those losses is tied to the identities of the candidates.

The outcome of the election has also turned a new spotlight on crucial moments in the past. At the conclusion of the last election, Trump incited an attack on Congress to prevent the certification of the results, which led to his being impeached for the second time. The cowardice of Senate Republicans—who, having been evacuated from the Capitol building as a Trumpist mob advanced, nonetheless refused to convict Trump—was a catastrophic abdication that directly enabled this moment. It never should have come to this.

We will be a fundamentally different country by the end of the next administration; indeed, we already are. Vice President Harris, in her concession speech at Howard University on Wednesday, said, "I know many people feel like we are entering a dark time, but, for the benefit of us all, I hope that is not the case." Given what we already know about Donald Trump, it is all but certain that it will be. I awoke the morning after the election thinking not of the battles that supplanted segregation but of what people must have felt at the time of *Plessy v. Ferguson,* the 1896 Supreme Court decision that enshrined it. The difficult lesson in that history is that, although further progress is possible, we should not underestimate how arduous it will be to achieve, or how long it will take. We believed that we had broken with history, but it is apparent that history has, in fact, broken some part of us.

EPILOGUE

The clouds rolled in from the west. Standing at the window I could see darkness unfolding across the horizon. Then I noticed the heavy drops of rain that had begun to fall on the Hudson River while the streets below remained dry, their inhabitants largely unaware of the nearby torrent. I called to my sons. They're astute observers of natural phenomena in the way that five-year-olds often are. I pointed to the raindrops that we could see splashing in the river and the dry streets just a few hundred feet away. Almost as if on cue the downpour began on the streets and then a single drop splashed against the window, followed by more until they made a steady percussion against the glass. "What does this tell you?" I asked them. August, who is older than his brother, Hollis, by nine minutes, volunteered an answer. "Storms don't stand still!" he shouted. That's right, I told him. Storms don't stand still so it's important to understand what direction they're headed in.

It strikes me that the work included here could be thought of as a particular type of storm-chasing. What began as a few scattered, angry clouds on the distant horizon at the beginning of this collection coalesced into what looked to be a shower a few years in, a passing storm after that and ultimately the maelstrom of volatile white nationalism that defines the moment at which this book finds its way to publication. We have, in recent years, witnessed the pro-liferation of book bans targeting volumes that explore questions of race, gender, sexuality, and any avenue of history that is not explic-itly complimentary to those who hold power. We have seen the enactment of a federal travel ban that skews heavily toward the Af-rican continent in its restrictions (while encouraging white South Africans to migrate into the United States). Under the banner of eliminating diversity initiatives, a putsch has removed high-ranking people of color from leadership positions of major American insti-tutions. And more of the same is in the offing. These develop-ments were not unpredictable. (History itself often reminds me of meteorology—two undertakings devoted to understanding the conditions that produce storms of various sorts.) These pieces con-stitute a small effort to understand the direction of the winds and therefore where the storm may land next.

Reading this work inspired a reckoning not simply with what I wrote, but with who I was when I wrote it. I would like to believe that I've served as the stoic chronicler of these events, but in fact I did not stand still, either. Times change and times change us. In retrospect the work included here is unintentionally autobiographi-cal. The person who pondered the meaning of Trayvon Martin's death was fundamentally more optimistic than the one who wrote about George Floyd's nearly a decade later. Also, I left out a few things. A cardinal ethic of journalism is the recognition that the story is not about us, the journalists. This is a good and fine prin-ciple that encourages reporters to fulfill our primary mission: to tell the stories of others who might not otherwise be heard. Yet, it is also true that, as with all humans, we exist in dynamic dialogue with our circumstances. When a grand jury in St. Louis declined to in-dict officer Darren Wilson for the death of Michael Brown in 2015, the streets of Ferguson, Missouri, exploded in riotous dissent. I wrote about the events that transpired, but I did not include the fear I felt as bullets whizzed by while I walked down the darkened nearby streets. When I wrote about the closure of Jamaica High School, I was taken by the ways in which a single school in central Queens seemed to reflect so many of the national currents of educational reform (and failure). I also felt a great deal of anger that an institution that factored so grandly in my own history had been allowed to falter, that subsequent generations of black and brown kids would inherit one less avenue for quality education. Other work inspired more humbling sentiments. Amid the absurdist battles over "critical race theory," I was grateful to write about the legal scholar Derrick Bell and the intellectual path he charted as he fought for a more racially equitable society.

One other thing: in the spring semester of 1988 at Howard University, I took a class called Black Diaspora, taught by Professor Adell Patton. The course satisfied a prerequisite that all students take at least one course related to the histories and cultures of people of African descent. I showed up without any sense of what to expect, but over the course of those fifteen weeks my understanding of the world was fundamentally rewired. We covered the transatlantic slave trade and the comparative slaveries of North America, South America, and the Caribbean. We learned about what it had taken to extract black emancipation from those same slaveholding societies and the mechanisms of African colonization that came in its wake. We concluded with a survey of decolonization in Africa and the Caribbean. Dr. Patton did not teach history in the way that I'd experienced previously, as an inert set of facts to be memorized. I took subsequent classes with Dr. Elizabeth Clark-Lewis and Dr. Joseph Harris that built on that foundation. History was being rendered as a dynamic set of relationships between past and present. We were not being taught simply to fulfill a civic obligation but rather to better our odds of survival in the world around us. We were being taught to recognize patterns that might reassert themselves in the present. Storms, they were trying to tell us, don't stand still. This is a collection of journalism that leans heavily upon the understanding that germinated in those early days on the third floor of Douglass Hall at Howard. My hope is that it contributes just a little to our ability to recognize patterns that are reasserting themselves—and maybe even helps discern where the storms are heading next.

ACKNOWLEDGMENTS

Early in my magazine-writing career I drew the conclusion that the caliber of a publication is, more than anything else, a reflection of the caliber of its editors. These pieces are as much a reflection of their meticulous, diligent efforts to achieve maximum clarity of thought and cleanliness of prose as they are any ideas or arguments that occurred to me when I sat down to write. I'm deeply indebted to the editors I've had the pleasure of working with at *The New Yorker*. David Remnick has given wise counsel, thoughtful interrogation, and deep engagement to all this work at some stage of its development, and I'm greatly appreciative of his support as an editor. I'm particularly indebted to Virginia Cannon, who has been my primary editor since 2015. I'm also grateful for others who have edited my work along the way, a list that includes Amy Davidson Sorkin, David Rohde, Alex Koppelman, and Daniel Zalewski. I have benefited from the efforts of too many of *The New Yorker*'s fact-checkers to count, but I'll take a moment to thank Kelvin Williams and Brianna Milord, the latter of whom I had the good fortune to teach when she was a student at the Columbia Journalism School. Among the things I love most about *The New Yorker* is the conversations with my colleagues whose wit, intelligence, and talent have been consistent sources of inspiration.

I appreciate Chris Jackson for his perspective in shaping this collection into the book you hold in your hands. I should also convey my thanks to the readers who have engaged with my work over the past thirteen years at *The New Yorker*. I've had the good fortune of having a smart, thoughtful (and extremely grammatically oriented) audience, who invariably sharpened my own thinking and offered me insights I might not have considered otherwise. On the subject of insights, I also appreciate my colleagues, staff, and students at the Columbia Journalism School, where I've taught and served as Dean during the bulk of the time in which these pieces were written. In no particular order, I'd like to shout-out Valerie and Natasha Foster & the extended clan, Christine and Kwinze Ogbue, Clive Powell (Sr. and Jr.), Deborah Powell, Delorian Bennett, Mark Mason, Sherman Brown, Joshua Nehemiah Bester, Don Sinkfield, Thomas Breeze, Sharon Sanders, Ta-Nehisi Coates, Thomas Fisher, Adam Serwer, Mali Fleming, Devon Sanders, Eric Easter, Mikael Moore, Khalil Muhammad, and Matt Guterl. Finally, I'd like to thank my family—Danielle, Nandi, Lenox, August, and Hollis—for being the reason I do this work in the first place.

INDEX

ABOUT THE AUTHOR

JELANI COBB is the Dean of Columbia's Graduate School of Journalism. He is a staff writer at *The New Yorker* and the author of several books, including *The Substance of Hope: Barack Obama and the Paradox of Progress* and *To the Break of Dawn: A Freestyle on the Hip Hop Aesthetic.* He is the editor/co-editor of multiple volumes, including *The Matter of Black Lives* and *The Essential Kerner Commission Report.* Dr. Cobb is the producer/co-producer of such documentaries as *The Riot Report.* He is the recipient of a Peabody Award and was a finalist for the Pulitzer Prize in Commentary. Dr. Cobb currently serves on the board of directors of the American Journalism Project and the board of trustees of the New York Public Library.

ABOUT THE TYPE

This book was set in Galliard, a typeface designed in 1978 by Matthew Carter (b. 1937) for the Mergenthaler Linotype Company. Galliard is based on the sixteenth-century typefaces of Robert Granjon (1513–89).